Dr Barbara Thiering  University of Sydney's years and is now a full scholarly articles and bo earned her a world rep the author of the bes *Interpretation from the Dead Sea Scrolls*, also published by Corgi Books. She lives in Sydney and has a grown family.

Praise for *Jesus the Man*:

'[The] sensational nature [of the book's findings] may disguise the strength of the research and scholarship which Thiering has deployed in the course of her narrative'
Peter Ackroyd, *The Times*

'The impact of *Jesus the Man* by Barbara Thiering may turn out to be as profound as that of Darwin's *Origin of the Species* on theories of human evolution'
Focus Magazine

'Some will see her as an anti-Christ, a mischievous scholar determined to destroy Christianity. To others she will be a source of comfort and peace enabling them to live Christian lives without having to accept as fact Jesus's divinity, his miracles, the virgin birth and resurrection'
The Australian Magazine

'This massive work of courage and conviction throws much of what the Church teaches out the stained glass window'
Sunday Age, Melbourne

'This work of courage by Barbara Thiering has left critics applauding her ability to bring to light such a controversial topic'
Gisborne Herald

Also by Barbara Thiering

JESUS THE MAN

and published by Corgi Books

JESUS OF THE APOCALYPSE

The Life of Jesus after the Crucifixion

Barbara Thiering

CORGI BOOKS

JESUS OF THE APOCALYPSE
A CORGI BOOK : 0 552 14238 7

Originally published in Great Britain by Doubleday,
a division of Transworld Publishers Ltd

PRINTING HISTORY
Doubleday edition published 1996
Corgi edition published 1997

Set in 10/11½ Monotype Plantin by
Phoenix Typesetting, Ilkley, West Yorkshire.

Corgi Books are published by Transworld Publishers Ltd,
61–63 Uxbridge Road, London W5 5SA,
in Australia by Transworld Publishers (Australia) Pty Ltd,
15–25 Helles Avenue, Moorebank, NSW 2170,
and in New Zealand by Transworld Publishers (NZ) Ltd,
3 William Pickering Drive, Albany, Auckland.

Reproduced, printed and bound in Great Britain by
Cox & Wyman Ltd, Reading, Berks.

Contents

Introduction

The Book of Revelation, the last book in the New Testament, is a mysterious document. The writer, it appears, saw a vision, in which a heavenly figure on a throne was surrounded by twenty-four elders with golden crowns on their heads. Near to the throne were four living creatures, one like a lion, another like a calf, another like a man, another like a flying eagle. Soon the Lamb appeared, obviously enough Jesus; he opened seven seals. Four horses were then seen: a white one, a red one, a black one, and – in the Greek text – a green one, although it has been translated as 'pale'.

The pale horse, whose rider's name was Death, with Hades following after, has caused many a reader to shudder. It was a central image in the thought of a religious fanatic of recent times whose catastrophic end, with his followers, aroused worldwide horror. The Book of Revelation, long set aside as simply an embarrassment by rational Christians, was again perceived, following this episode, as the product of an unbalanced mind, one of the less healthy expressions of Christian thought.

But it remains intriguing, full of themes that have become mythic: Armageddon, the Beast whose number is 666, the Great Harlot clothed in purple and scarlet. They are used only as metaphors now, and it is taken for granted that they had no other purpose in their own time.

This may no longer be assumed. New information has

become available which is capable of giving a quite different understanding. The Dead Sea Scrolls, discovered in the late nineteen forties, were seen at once to have a particular affinity with the Book of Revelation. But they give us more than that: they give us a key which was always intended to be used on this book, and on other books of the New Testament.

It is now possible to show that Revelation is not the product of irrational minds. It is the product of very clever minds, and its writers had an honest historical intention. The bizarre images of the book were quite deliberately constructed; they were not intended as a record of revelations received in a visionary state. They were written in a double way, to read like fantastic images, but to convey through this form actual historical information.[1]

The rider on the white horse was a real person. His identity would be known to a special kind of reader. So also were the four 'living creatures', the Great Harlot, the Beast 666; and, in fact, every 'vision' of the book was describing a real person or event. These were down-to-earth people and actual events that were happening in the cathedral in Ephesus in the first century AD. Some of the events took place in Judea, and Armageddon was to be found at Qumran, near the Dead Sea, the place to which some Jewish troops were summoned before the fall of Jerusalem in AD 70.

Above all, the Book of Revelation contains evidence, supplied by the early Christians themselves, that Jesus survived the crucifixion and remained active for many years afterwards. To trace this part of his history is the primary purpose of the book.

The 'Lamb' who appeared in the 'vision' of Chapter 5 was, indeed, Jesus, and the year was AD 49. He was in Ephesus in that year and again in subsequent years, and at other times in Rome. His 'resurrection' had been a revival, as the gospels themselves show when the same key is applied to them. Belief in it was spread for political reasons, and it became a powerful symbol for the great number of ordinary believers. But it was also necessary to preserve the record of what really happened, and this purpose was achieved through the gospels, which are constructed in the same double form as the Book of Revelation. The technique to which they yield, and its results, are set out in *Jesus the Man* (Doubleday, 1992).

Revelation complements the Book of Acts in describing the movements of Jesus during the years following AD 33. In Acts also he continues to appear in 'visions'; that is, he was having secret meetings with the leaders of his party, Peter and Paul. Revelation shows him with the more eastern branch of his party, led by James and John, meeting in Ephesus on the coast of Asia Minor (present-day Turkey).

Jesus had risen from an apparent death. He had been crucified in Judea in March AD 33, because he was believed to be an associate of anti-Roman zealots. Crucifixion, the Roman method of capital punishment, was a particularly cruel method of execution because it took days or even weeks for the victim to die. It would be very surprising, as Pilate pointed out, if anyone died after only six hours on the cross. At 3 p.m. on Good Friday, when Jesus cried 'I thirst', he had, as arranged, been given a drink of poison as a way of committing suicide. But the poison would take some hours to act, and when the two 'thieves' (zealots) were placed in the burial cave with him, one of them, sitting beside his head, administered the medicine that his friends had brought to the cave: a huge quantity of aloes, the juice of which acts as a purgative. The poison was expelled, and when he had recovered sufficiently he was brought out of the cave. But one of his associates, the man who had revived him, had strong political reasons for proclaiming that a resurrection had taken place.

Jesus was no solitary preacher appearing suddenly on the shores of Lake Galilee. He was a central figure in a major political movement which was working at over-throwing the pagan Roman empire. The enormous numbers of followers of the new, still underground religion – introduced from Judea well before the time of Jesus – were ready to believe in divine figures who were the subjects of visions and miracles. It was the world of Hellenism, where pagan religions had encouraged the idea of human beings as incarnations of gods. Religious leaders invested with such significance could count on popular acceptance, and the associations were cultivated in order to bring to the Greco-Roman world the new religion, an adapted form of Judaism which in the hands of Jesus and his party would evolve into Christianity.

The writers of Revelation and of the gospels were religious leaders, and they did what religious leaders, and political leaders, have always had to do. They gave the people the images they wanted, images that comforted and inspired. To them, the recipients of the miracles and visions were 'babes in Christ', that is to say, like children, who must be given easy teaching that was like 'milk'. Others were more mature, and could be given 'meat'.[2]

The 'meat' in the Book of Revelation is a real history, of actual events. The events include the history of the Herods, the Jewish kings who had actually founded the new religion, and whose friendship with Roman emperors was the channel through which it came to Rome. The figure sitting on the 'heavenly throne' in the scene where the Lamb appeared was Agrippa II, the young Herod who, according to the Book of Acts, was sympathetic to Christians, a party within his following who were intent on dropping Jewish identity.

The period of the forties and fifties AD was one of intense struggle with the original Jewish framework of the mission, leading to the final emergence of Christians, who had taken up the Gentile membership. The Beast with the number 666 was the head of the Jewish party, who was hated for his zealotry and harsh monastic system. All of this is recorded through 'visions' of angels, trumpets, seals and similar devices.

The history, written in several stages by different hands, then moves on to the sixties and seventies AD. The fall of Jerusalem is vividly described. In AD 73 the 'marriage of the Lamb' is, in fact, the marriage of Jesus Justus, the son of Jesus, who inherited his father's titles. An account of his 'coronation' is given, implying the death of Jesus, whose last recorded appearance in Revelation was at a council in AD 70.

The year AD 100 – a number produced by the chronological theory behind the history – was a crucial one, because it was believed that a thousand year empire would be inaugurated with a dramatic intervention from heaven; when it did not happen, the leaders were discredited. The book ends after another fourteen years, with the mission in Ephesus developing as the monastic form of Christianity.

The fact that this history lies behind the bizarre visions of Revelation is able to be proved. The explanation of the method used is set out in the following pages. It will be shown that the history was deliberately placed in the text; it is not a matter of personal interpretation, but would be found by anyone using the same technique and information.

A further matter of the greatest interest at the present time is that the Book of Revelation contains calendar material which shows why the year AD 1 was chosen as the first of the Christian era. It was not the year of the birth of Jesus; the gospels themselves make that quite plain. But it was not randomly chosen, and it was not chosen at a very much later time, as has usually been believed. It came into use in Christian circles early, and depended on a longstanding chronological scheme that went back to apocryphal works such as the Book of Enoch and the Book of Jubilees. The discovery of the Dead Sea Scrolls has also given the key to understanding this material, and it can only be considered fortuitous that it has become available just as the year 2000 of the era that was set so long ago is coming into view.

THE PESHER TECHNIQUE

The historical information about Jesus that is set out in this book and in its predecessor *Jesus the Man* is the result of the application of a newly discovered technique, suggested by the Dead Sea Scrolls, that may be called the pesher technique.

The gospels of the New Testament, and the Book of Revelation, are written in a special language. They make not just an occasional use of symbolism, as most people would concede, but a thoroughgoing, systematic use of sequences of symbols and images, to the extent that a whole new language has been created, and one that needs special information to understand. In that sense, it is a code, although the purpose is not a trivial one.

The purpose was to record a complete and exact history of Jesus and of the events that led to the formation of the Christian Church. But to most of the audience for which it was intended – both then and now – Christianity, with Jesus as a divine human being, was a revelation from heaven, supported by miracles and supernatural events to prove its truth. What they believed they needed was scripture, not a history book.

To those who had lived through the events, however, there was a dilemma. They knew that belief in revelation and miracles was a product of a less mature kind of faith, the faith of a child. It was a necessary step in faith, but it could not be left as the whole content of religion. There was an urgent need to give a means of growing out of fantasy into an adult religion.

The solution came from a definition of scripture that they had developed when they tried to wrestle with the unbelievable parts of the Old Testament. Living at a time of historical crisis for Judaism, they had come to think that

12

their own history was contained within the pages of the Old Testament, but could be seen only because of their special knowledge. When it said, for instance, that 'the righteous will live by faith' and 'the wicked will prosper', it was not simply making general ethical statements, but was giving facts about the Teacher of Righteousness and the Wicked Priest or Man of a Lie, their two leaders. Details of what had happened to these two were read into the words of the prophets.

For example, when the prophet Habakkuk wrote:

O traitors, why do you look and stay silent when the wicked one swallows up one who is more righteous than he? (Hab 1:13),

its meaning to those who knew how to read it was:

'Its pesher (interpretation) concerns the House of Absalom and the men of its council, who were silent at the chastisement of the Teacher of Righteousness, and they did not help him against the Man of a Lie, who flouted the Law in the midst of their whole congregation.'[3]

Scripture, then, in their view, contained hidden historical facts. In the case of the Old Testament, they had read the facts into it; they were not really there. But the definition gave them an ideal way of solving their problems. A new scripture was needed; and, moreover, they needed to record in full detail their history, a history that must, by religious necessity, remain partly secret. This time, the history would be objectively present in their scripture, because they had placed it there.

In the gospels and Acts of the New Testament, they produced a masterpiece. The outline of the real history of Jesus was given on the surface, but dressed in so much apparent miracle that he was presented as the kind of divine human being needed by simple faith. But they set up within it, by symbols, images, double meanings, special meanings, the complete history. It was placed within the stories in a way that was subject to decipherment by those in possession of the special knowledge required. Everyone who worked on it with the special knowledge would arrive at the same result. It was like a puzzle with a solution, and there could only be one solution.

One of the methods was to present human beings, religious leaders, in the form of supernatural beings, and real places in the form of heavenly places. Stories such as parables and miracles, apparently dealing with a metaphorical reality or another world, actually record normal human history. These are some examples from the gospels and Acts:

- When Jesus was 'tempted by Satan', he was in fact having political discussions with Judas Iscariot, called 'Satan' as a leader of political revolutionaries. When Jesus 'ascended into heaven', he actually went to a monastery, called 'heaven' because it was the place where priests and levites, called 'gods' and 'angels', conducted a perpetual liturgy.
- When 'a star guided the wise men' to the birthplace of Jesus, there was no real star. It was Joseph, his father, who was the Star of David, leading the Magians, his political associates, to witness the fact that an heir to his dynasty had been born.
- The 'raising of Lazarus' was a lifting of the excommunication of an expelled monk, who had 'died', because excommunication was treated as a spiritual death.
- The Prodigal Son was a real person who, when he divided his father's property with the Elder Brother, brought about a schism in the community that was of lasting political significance.

The gospels themselves suggest the method of approach to such stories when Jesus says, in Mark 4:11, 'for those outside, everything is in parables', but says to his inner circle: 'To you has been given the secret (Greek *mystērion*) of the Kingdom of God'. Hellenistic literature, especially Jewish Hellenistic literature, has many examples of such a theory of scripture.[4]

Even at first sight, the Book of Revelation looks as if it might lend itself to such an approach. It speaks frequently of a mystery, and even illustrates the form of its solution: 'I will tell you the mystery of the woman, and of the beast with seven heads . . . the seven heads are seven mountains on which the woman sits . . . ' (Rev 17:7-9); obviously enough, Rome. In another passage (1:20), Jesus says: 'The mystery of the seven stars . . . the seven stars are angels of the seven churches'.

The term used in the Dead Sea Scrolls for Old Testament scripture was 'mystery', with an 'interpretation'. The Hebrew words were *raz* (mystery) and *pesher* (interpretation, but in the sense of solution, not subjective). The word pesher may usefully be retained to refer to a hidden layer of history in scripture.

One of the most striking passages in Revelation, in Chapter 12, reads:

And a great sign appeared in heaven, a woman clothed with the sun, with the moon under her feet, and on her head a crown of twelve stars; she was with child and she cried out in her birthpangs, in torment to give birth. And another sign appeared in heaven; behold, a great red dragon, with seven heads and ten horns, and seven diadems upon his heads. His tail swept down a third of the stars of heaven, and cast them to the earth. And the dragon stood before the woman who was about to bear a child, that he might devour her child when she brought it forth; she brought forth a male child, one who is to rule all the nations with a rod of iron, but her child was caught up to God and to his throne, and the woman fled into the wilderness, where she has a place prepared by God, in which

15

to be fed for one thousand two hundred and sixty days.

Is this simply rich mythology? Fantasy outside the normal range of reason, using images drawn from the writer's culture in a way that is not intended for rational analysis? That is the normal understanding of apocalyptic.

Yet there are details that do not fit this understanding. Why is such an exact figure given, 1260 days? It sounds like an exact date, which hardly seems to be relevant to the cosmic scale of events. Moreover, new knowledge about calendars shows that it is a very exact date. In terms of the solar calendar now known from the Dead Sea Scrolls, it must mean that it was one of a series of years occurring every fourteen years, and that the day in question can be exactly identified once the year is known, as the 31st of the solar calendar month, falling near the March equinox. For the explanation of this, see pp.234–238.

In the Dead Sea Scrolls, which are certainly to be linked with Revelation, there is a passage very similar to this one, using an image of a woman in labour giving birth to a Messiah.[5] The Messiah in that passage is identified through a quotation from an Old Testament messianic verse, and the same method is used in this passage: he is to 'rule the nations with a rod of iron', a quotation from Psalm 2. This passage says, then, to those who knew their Old Testament, that at an identifiable date a woman gave birth to a Messiah. If that was all it said, it would have the form of a statement about an actual birth of a man who would be called the Messiah, as a figure in the religio-political history of the first century.

The other main figure in the passage is a great red dragon with seven heads and ten horns. This feature appears twice more in Revelation, two beasts also having seven heads and ten horns. Why are such exact figures given? For mythological creatures, why not say they were multiheaded and multihorned? The figures introduce an

16

absurdity: how could the ten horns fit on the seven heads? Why such exactitude in a form of writing that is entirely the opposite of the measurably exact?

The dragon of this passage and the one that follows it was at one moment engaged with the powers of heaven, but then became part of the human scene again. He pursued the woman who had borne the male child, then later was 'angry with the woman, and went off to make war with the rest of her offspring, on those who keep the commandments of God and bear testimony to Jesus'. Perhaps this is just a mythological way of talking about the difficulties Christians have. But, given that there is a hint, in the exact figures, that real events were happening, is it possible that it was a way of talking about difficulties that Christians *did* have? That it is a way of recording history? That the 'Dragon' was a pseudonym for a person, a real political figure, who attacked Mary and Jesus and Christians?

Such ways of talking about powerful people were well known in the biblical world, and are still understood today. When the Roman emperor Tiberius died, the message was given in code to the Jewish king; 'The Lion is dead'.[6] Most people would accept that the Beast of the Book of Revelation, with the number 666, was a political figure, usually conjectured to be the emperor. Why not carry this understanding further? Were the Dragon, and the Beasts, and all other such figures, real persons?

The rest of this book shows that the answer to this question is in the affirmative, and that the whole of Revelation contains the missing political history of the first century AD.

It will be apparent that if such meanings are objectively present behind the text of Revelation, then there are multiple tests of consistency to be applied. Terms are given special or technical meanings, and universals are treated as particulars. The same terms must always have the same special meanings, in all the books concerned.

17

When they appear in a new context, that context must make sense in itself, and it must be consistent with other contexts. The whole history must be consistent with what is known from other sources. An exact chronology is discovered, and this poses a very rigorous test of consistency, needing mathematical exactitude. The same rules about time, which are said to depend on a common calendar, must be applied in exactly the same way in every part of the book, and in other books which are said to rely on the same special knowledge, that is, the gospels and Acts.

A formidable amount of evidence is needed in order to prove that the special meaning is really in the text, and not simply wilfully imposed. This book sets out the evidence in three Parts: I, where the overall history is given in a simpler form, not only to make easier reading but also to give the general map against which the detailed study is done; II, where the special knowledge to be used by the pesharist is set out in a systematic way, with an account of the organisation of the community and detail of the calendar and chronology; and III, a lexicon giving the special meaning of terms, and finally the word for word pesher of Revelation, set out side by side with the text so that the tests of consistency may be made.

THE DEAD SEA SCROLLS
Some information about the Dead Sea Scrolls may be given before going on to the main subject. The reader is referred to the Bibliography for further detail.

The Dead Sea Scrolls, discovered from 1947 onwards in caves near Qumran at the north-western corner of the Dead Sea, include writings of a Jewish sect from the time of Christian origins who were in many ways similar to the early Christians. The question of their exact relationship to the early Christians was a subject of fierce controversy from the start, and has been revived again in recent years.

Apart from copies of the Old Testament, there were a

dozen or so complete or nearly complete scrolls containing quite new writings, together with thousands of fragments, some of considerable size, others very small. All complete scrolls and those of a reasonable size were fully published from the start, although the smaller fragments tended to be left and have only recently been made available. There was not, however, any 'suppression' of useful written material, as has come to be widely believed.

The major new writings include the Temple Scroll, 67 columns long. It is a plan for a new temple, said to have been dictated by God, and includes laws about how to keep the temple and its precincts holy, including the notorious one that no blind man is allowed in for the whole of his life; nor is any man allowed in who has recently had sexual intercourse.[7]

The Manual of Discipline gives rules for living of a strictly ascetic community, calling themselves the Sons of Light. The rules include having a daily sacred meal of bread and wine; community of property; and being subject to penances such as exclusion from the sacred meal for periods of ten days up to two years for offences such as laughing loudly, misappropriating property, allowing one's nakedness to be seen, or disobeying the authority of the community.[8] The War Scroll sets out the battle plan for a great final battle between the Sons of Light and the Sons of Darkness, one which would result in the elimination of the Kittim, a name that was soon seen to mean the Romans. In the Hymns of Thanksgiving, prayers are recorded, supplying much of the theology. One group of them has been attributed to the Teacher of Righteousness.[9]

Of interest for the history is the Damascus Document, a work that had already been discovered in Cairo early in the twentieth century, and which now turned up in numerous copies in the Dead Sea Scrolls, and clearly came from the same writers. It and another group, the pesharim (plural of pesher; writings giving the 'hidden meanings' of the Old Testament in the way that has been described above) are very much concerned with the conflict between the two leaders, the Teacher of Righteousness and the Wicked Priest or Man of a Lie.

Given the constant evidences of close organisational and doctrinal links between the community of the Dead Sea Scrolls and the early Christians, the question of the identity of these two persons is a pressing one. An early view, formed before some important scrolls were found and published, was that they were figures of Jewish history who lived before 100 BC. But the treatment of evidence on which this conclusion was based is subject to challenge. There is better evidence, I believe, that the Teacher of Righteousness was John the Baptist, and the rival teacher, called by a number of opprobrious names, was Jesus. The scrolls are, in that case, writings of enemies of Jesus, enemies such as those who were quoted in the gospels. From them and from the method they teach us we are able to rediscover him as a historical person.

For help in the production of the present work, and for support during the intense controversies that the publication of *Jesus the Man* evoked, I would like to thank my publishers, Transworld, especially Judith Curr, Julie Stanton, and Maggie Hamilton; as well as Dr Leonie Star, Phillip Adams (broadcaster), Rowan Ayers; academic friends who have been personally supportive; and the writers of thousands of letters from all over the world. There is, naturally, widespread excitement at the possibility that the Dead Sea Scrolls have given us the historical Jesus. In the following pages, further evidence will be offered that this is what they and the New Testament, when read by their method, do give to the modern world.

Part I

The History

CHAPTER 1

From Herod to Ephesus

THE CHURCH BEFORE THE CHURCH AND THE BOOK OF REVELATION

The real founder of the Church – or, at least, its sponsor – was Herod the Great, the king who ruled the Jews from 37 to 4 BC. But no individual was really responsible for its foundation. It was the product of social and historical forces. The world of Greece and Rome had its science, technology and philosophy; human reason had been brought to the highest level of development so far known in the west. But it did not have religion. The Jews had religion, one of the purest forms of theology that had so far been developed outside eastern countries: one God, who could not be objectified by images or even by a name, and a strong interest in ethics. But on their side, they longed for Greek learning. Two equal needs drew each other together, and the Church was born.

It began among the hundreds of thousands of Jews who were living in countries outside Palestine, in what was known collectively as the Diaspora. The situation for Jews in the first centuries BC and AD was very much as it is now, with far more living outside the homeland than in it. They were actively involved in the social, intellectual and

23

commercial life of the great cities of the world, of Alexandria, Ephesus, Babylon, and as far away as Rome.

It was an exciting and creative time in which to be living. Hellenism meant that everyone knew something of philosophy, of science, of other cultures. The world, from Babylon to Rome, was reasonably peaceful, and unified. The Roman empire was rising, and stood for strong government. There was a feeling of confidence in human possibilities, of liberation of the intellect.

Jews living in the Diaspora both benefited from the intellectual achievements of Hellenism, and gave something to it. With their traditional love of wisdom, they absorbed Greek learning in every field, and at the same time found themselves objects of interest, as they lived by their ideal of purity and devotion.

But the problem of identity was a pressing one. The attractions of Hellenism were so great that many Jews were beginning to lose their sense of distinctiveness. There seemed little point in emphasising the practices that made them different from Greeks: attendance at the synagogue, circumcision, observing rituals and food laws that had ceased to be relevant to their contemporary life. Gentiles, while attracted to their theology and ethics, were not prepared to commit themselves to a culture that for them was quite alien.

During the first century BC, under the energetic kingship of Herod the Great, a solution to this and many other problems suggested itself. There would be a mission, from Palestinian Jews to Diaspora Jews. Missionaries would go out to the great cities of the Diaspora, find Jews who were in danger of lapsing from their faith, and persuade them to 'return to the Law of Moses with a whole heart and soul' (a phrase that is found in the Dead Sea Scrolls).[1] As a sign of their renewed commitment to Judaism, they would be baptised in water, a practice that had been introduced in Judea by the sage Hillel. The baptism would purify them, and they would now be true Jews, members not simply of the Old Covenant of Abraham but of a New Covenant.

The Judaism they would be taught was a greatly modified version, with many of its more primitive practices, such as animal sacrifice in the temple, discarded. It was an updated, Hellenised kind of Judaism, a New Israel that was an improvement on the old.

For this New Israel, there would be a new Abraham, Isaac and Jacob. The men who founded the mission, in the first century BC, used these names as pseudonyms, and the practice continued of using biblical pseudonyms. One group of Diaspora Jews, who used a liturgy based on Exodus symbolism, called their leader 'Moses', and a female leader who acted with him was called 'Miriam', the name of the sister of Moses.

The missionaries who began this project were men of an even greater religious dedication than was usual. They were ascetics, who had learned their way of life from the Essenes, a party of Jews who ranked with Pharisees and Sadducees, but who kept themselves apart from the mainstream and valued a kind of life that would have to be called monastic. Their centre was at Qumran, on the north-west corner of the Dead Sea, where the Dead Sea Scrolls were discovered. The scrolls were their writings, and one group of them reflects the history of the mission from the time of Herod the Great up to the mid first century AD.

There were Essenes also in the Diaspora, and, in the first century BC, men who held the views of Pharisees and Sadducees also adopted an ascetic way of life, practising prayers and fasting, initiations, some forms of renunciation of marriage, and concentration on personal holiness. These did not live in monasteries but in the world, but met together for sacred meals of initiates as the Essenes did, and were rewarded for their ascetic achievements by promotions in the system of grades that expressed their highly developed hierarchy.

The motive of the missionaries themselves was purely spiritual. Their main inspiration came from Hillel, called the Great, who is still revered in Jewish tradition, and who was the 'Abraham' of the New Israel. It was Hillel who taught the Golden Rule, and much of the content of the Sermon on the Mount is similar to his teaching.[2] But the mission gained the enthusiastic support of Herod the Great when it became also a very successful means of generating money.

Diaspora Judaism was wealthy, but Palestinian Judaism poor. Herod had grand ambitions, to rebuild Jerusalem, to build a new temple, to fortify the harbour of Caesarea, to build himself a palace on the rocky cliff of Masada. Remains of all of these projects have been discovered, and the ancient Jewish historian Josephus – who is our primary source for the history of the Herods – gives a full account of the rebuilding of the temple. Josephus also tells us that Herod made a point of favouring the Essenes.[3] They had previously been exiles from Jerusalem, having lost the power they once held as priests and kings, but they now began to enjoy royal patronage and new influence.

When Jews in the Diaspora joined the New Covenant, or the New Israel – it used a variety of names – they went through an initiation rite that was understood to give them salvation, in this world or the next. They were declared to have been purified from sin, and their souls ransomed. For this privilege, they paid a half shekel, which was about a day's income. In practice, it was a membership fee of the society they were now joining, which had regular meetings of initiates to partake of the sacred meal and to receive instruction. One of the Dead Sea Scrolls speaks of the half shekel as a 'ransom for one's soul'.[4] Moreover, every year they would present themselves for promotion, give proof of virtue, receive a declaration of freedom from sin, and pay another half shekel, as a 'peace offering'.[5] This money was understood as a more modern and practical version of the old practice of offering an animal in sacrifice to gain removal of sin. Much later on in the history, these declarations of forgiveness, received in return for money, were called indulgences.

The mission was just what was needed to bring Diaspora Jews together, give them a great society with branches all over the world, and give them a link with the homeland. Very large numbers joined, and this meant a huge income, which was brought back to Palestine by the missionaries to be used for Herod's building projects. As the city of Jerusalem was so much part of Jewish religion, the money was seen as being given to religion. But there was another point of view, maintaining that the mission was selling salvation for money. It was, in the words of Jesus, when he came to it later, to make the house of God a 'shop', and the missionaries into 'salesmen'.

Gentiles, particularly in the west, had always taken an interest in the Jewish religion, and now that it was in a version that was much more acceptable to them, they began to convert to it in numbers. Jews themselves had to undergo a rite of baptism and initiation in order to become truly Jews, so that Gentiles had only to take the same steps and they would also become Jews. Many became full converts, receiving circumcision, and acting in every respect like Jews. Others drew the line at the cultural practices, refused circumcision and even synagogue attendance, but studied a non-ritual kind of Judaism at the meetings and sacred meals of the great society they had joined.

So great was the success of the mission during its first forty years that the idea began to be cherished that Judaism was on its way to becoming the religion of the Roman empire. Jews and Gentile converts, at least, thought that this might be the case. Paganism was in decline; no educated Hellene believed any longer in the myths of the ancient gods. The Roman empire needed a religion, and needed also an ethical system, for in Rome, power had gone to the heads of many members of the newly rich governing class, and sexual licence was the order of the day.

The concept of a Kingdom of God began to develop; a spiritual form of the Roman empire. Judaism had always been a theocracy, with no distinction between religion and state. If the empire was won for God, Judaism would have both material and religious power. A longstanding dream might be thus fulfilled.

The Essenes, catching the dream, gave it a time dimension. They were on the verge of a thousand year empire of the Jews. This could be said because, as experts in study of the calendar and prophecies based on it, they believed that the year of Herod's rise to power was the beginning of the last thousand years of world history. Their chronological calculations were a part of the history, and gave reason for the confidence felt by many that their political time had come. The series of crises in the first century BC and AD were connected with prophecies based on the calendar, and the Book of Revelation has a particular interest in the subject. The thousand years of which its final chapters speak were part of the same system.

King Herod would inaugurate the thousand year Kingdom of God, and be its central power, although religious control would be exercised by priests. But there was room also for another royal dynasty, that was prepared to accept a purely spiritual role. This was the dynasty of King David, the great king of the past who had set the ideal of the Messiah. The word 'Messiah' meant 'the anointed one', and in the minds of most it meant simply a descendant of King David who would be part of their religious hierarchy.

The dynasty of the Davids had been preserved, long after they had ceased to occupy the throne of Israel. From the time of the abolition of the Zadokite high priests and the Davids in the sixth and fifth centuries BC, the party of Essenes had formed, one of their main purposes being to preserve and protect the men whom they believed to be the rightful rulers of Israel. From the start the Essenes had been the expelled aristocrats, studying their calendar for the signs of a time when they would be restored. The Restoration was their hope, and when Herod began to favour them, they saw it as God's plan for them, coming at the appointed time of prophecy.

At the time of the foundation of the mission, there emerged a man who was a direct descendant of Nathan, one of the younger sons of King David. His name was Heli. He was prepared to co-operate in the mission, and to take particular responsibility for work in the western side of the world, including responsibility for the baptism and initiation of Gentiles. This was a sign of the humble role he was prepared to play, for contact with Gentiles, if they were uncircumcised, was to touch what was ritually unclean.

Heli was appointed the 'patriarch Jacob' of the new triarchy of leaders, 'Abraham, Isaac and Jacob'. 'Abraham' used the traditional title of 'Father', a word which became 'Pope', while 'Isaac' and 'Jacob' were the eastern and western patriarchs respectively. When, in the words of the gospel, 'many will come from east and west and sit down at table with Abraham, Isaac and Jacob',[6] the meaning was not about a supernatural future, but about the council meetings of the society, when the three leaders would take the central positions and delegates from the distant parts of the Kingdom would come to discuss questions of policy. The Pope and patriarchs of the original Herodian movement established the positions of Pope and patriarchs of the Christian Church.

As Heli was a 'Jacob', his son had the title of Jacob's favourite son, Joseph. In 44 BC (as the concealed chronology shows), Jacob-Heli had a son, Joseph. In March 7 BC, Joseph had a son, whose name and title was Jesus. Each of the three men, like their ancestors before them, bore the title 'the Christ', meaning that they were the heirs of David, the Anointed One. It was quite an accepted title: Josephus wrote about Jesus' brother James as 'the brother of Jesus called Christ'.[7] Jesus the Christ, when he came of age, would inherit the lowly position in the ruling hierarchy that Heli had accepted. Superior to him were the priests and the ruling Herod. But he was permitted to teach Gentile converts, and had a particular responsibility for them.

But Jesus was born to an uncertain legitimacy as the heir of David. His father lived, as all the Davids did, under the Essene marriage rules. Through Greek influence they had come to prize virginity as the highest way of life, believing that sexual intercourse was a form of defilement. But the ancient dynastic lines had to be preserved, and the descendants of these lines were required to marry, but live as far as possible like the holy celibates. They met with their wives only for the purpose of conception, and between births both husband and wife lived in celibate communities.[8]

The woman in these marriages lived like a dedicated nun. Before her marriage, as physically a virgin, she took a vow which made her also legally a Virgin, a woman in a religious order like the Vestal Virgins of the Greek world. The couple were betrothed to each other, and had to go through a long betrothal period as an exercise in discipline. If, by a breach of the discipline, a child was conceived during the betrothal period before the wedding, then it was the case that a Virgin (a nun) had conceived.

This had been the story of Mary and Joseph. Joseph, in 8 BC, had become involved in nationalist politics, as even some peace loving Essenes were obliged to do during the final tumultuous years of Herod the Great. Fighting in the world for Jewish identity, there seemed less reason for renunciation of the world and the flesh. Jesus was conceived after their final betrothal ceremony – one that was considered binding – but before their wedding.

The fact that he was conceived after the binding

betrothal meant that his status was ambiguous. For a more liberal point of view, that of the upper class Sadducees, he was legitimate, and could inherit the titles of King David when the Kingdom came. But for a stricter view, held by the Pharisees, who were closer to the ordinary people, he must be considered an extranuptial child of Joseph, whereas his younger brother James, who had been conceived during the marriage in accordance with all the rules, was the true heir.

The question of Jesus' right to inherit was one of the many that tore the mission apart during the first century. A schism between east and west was opening up, for far bigger reasons, but when it could be said that Jesus, who went as far as it was possible to go with the west, was in any case a bastard (a Man of a Lie, as the Dead Sea Scrolls call him) it gave moral authority to the eastern traditionalists.

His personal situation may have been part of the reason why Jesus from the start threw in his lot with the 'unclean'. In the Jewish mission, the 'unclean' were Gentiles; any man not of Jewish race who was not circumcised and did not keep Jewish ritual law. They were, legally, the equivalent of women, and of the mentally deficient. An orthodox Jew thanked God every day that he had not been born a woman, a pagan, or a fool.

The history that is concealed in the gospels and Acts and in the Book of Revelation is the record of the transformation of the original mission. Jesus did not found a religion and a church; he simply reformed it. By the time he took his place at the council table, the Gentile membership had become so numerous and influential that it was no longer possible to treat them as an unclean minority. They, for their part, no longer wanted any form of Jewish identity. Jesus was the one who gave the Gentiles new dignity, treated them as equal with Jews, and eventually led them into an independent structure that became a separate religion. Under the name of Christianity it

31

fulfilled the original dream of a Kingdom of God, the religion of the Roman empire.

Between the years AD 29 and 33, Jesus was drawn into the conflicts that by now were besetting the great society. The major one was its relationship with Rome: since the Romans had removed Herod and made Judea an occupied country under the direct rule of procurators, there was a continuing threat to the Jewish state that aroused the fervour of zealots, men who were prepared to use military methods and lay down their lives in defence of Judaism. To oppose these and to show friendship to Rome was, in their eyes, to be a traitor to the nationalist cause. But Jesus said: 'Love your enemies', and this meant the Romans.

Another issue existed between priests and the laity, especially Sadducee priests. Men who had been born into the tribe of Levi were priests from birth, and had many privileges, including the right to be financially supported. Sadducee priests had a particularly high view of their role, accepting a view influenced by Greek thought that the high priest was more than human, somewhere between God and man, and God was incarnate in him, so that prayers addressed to him were prayers to God.[9] He could even be called 'God', on this understanding.

Jesus held a view of the priesthood of all believers. No one, he believed, had greater privileges than others in the sight of God; all were equal. He fought for his view, even to the extent of usurping the ritual role of the man who was intended by the ascetics to be high priest. Jesus, by putting on the priestly vestments on the Day of Atonement, wrested from him the role of making the atonement. This was close to being blasphemy, for those to whom the high priest was 'God'.

By March 33, Jesus had alienated all sides in the different factions with which the mission was beset. An opportunity came to betray him to Pontius Pilate, and he was crucified, on the technically correct charge of being in an organisation of zealots.

Jesus did not die on the cross. This central fact, and the account of what did happen, is given in the pesher of the gospels and Acts. The Book of Revelation is another of the sources, and when treated by the same technique, not only confirms the fact but gives a detailed account of the movements of Jesus after the crucifixion that fits in exactly with the account of the Book of Acts.

For nearly forty years after the crucifixion Jesus remained the leader of his party, directing their movements until they finally reached Rome. He remained in deep seclusion, partly because he was observing the celibate rule of the ascetics, partly for political reasons. In the first few years he may well have been under constraint from Simon Magus, the zealot who had been crucified beside him, and who had been rescued himself and risen to power as a result of his claim that he had brought about a supernatural resurrection of Jesus. He had meetings with his lieutenants Peter and Paul, described in the form of 'visions', in which he guided them in the changes of doctrine and policy that finally led to the separation of Christians.

In AD 44 a major change took place. Following the death of Agrippa I, an event desired by all because of his increasing imbalance of mind, but brought about (as the Book of Acts shows) by a poisoning directed by Simon Magus, the mission leaders were expelled from Palestine. The zealots had already set up a new centre in Damascus, from which they continued to work for the triumph of their version of Judaism in the Roman empire. In Damascus they wrote the Damascus Document, found among the Dead Sea Scrolls, in which they condemned the western party (Herodians and Christians) for what they claimed to be heresy and immorality.[10]

Those with more westernised views moved to Antioch.

33

When, under Peter's influence, the Antioch members began to call themselves Christians, it meant that the inevitable schism had taken place. The mission had split into two, the eastern half continuing to preach Judaism, the western half so adapting their doctrine that it was ceasing to be Jewish.

At a grand council in 46, the new identity was recognised, and negotiations began between those who wanted to be fully Christian, and those, led by James the brother of Jesus, who preferred to think of themselves as Jewish Christian, and could still associate with nationalists. Within the Christians themselves, there were also differences. Peter believed that there should still be a Sadducee priest to perform priestly duties. For him, Jesus was the Christ, only, that is, a king but not a priest; hence his use of the name Christian. When Peter had said to Jesus during the gospel period, 'You are the Christ', he was agreeing that he was legitimate, but at the same time rebuking him for trying to act like a priest, and Jesus' attack on him was partly caused by their difference on this question. But for Paul, Jesus was both a priest and a king, and the Jewish priesthood was unnecessary. It was Paul who took the final step that separated their party altogether from Judaism.

From Antioch, the Christians turned west, their final goal an independent centre in Rome, where they should not have met opposition as they were not political enemies of Rome. An attempt was made, from 46 to 49, to bring their doctrine to the existing Rome mission. But Jewish interests in Rome were strong enough, at that time, to have them expelled as renegade Jews. The emperor Claudius issued an edict against Jews who were 'rioting in the name of Chrestus'.[11] Jesus, the Christ, was in the group who had gone to Rome, and so also was Peter.

When they were expelled, they came back to Ephesus, for it was a natural halfway house for them.

Ephesus remained their base between 49 and 57. From Ephesus, they made forays into Greece, and planned for another attempt on Rome. After a frustrating two years back in Judea, that attempt succeeded, and from 61 onwards Peter, Paul, and those who succeeded them in their offices conducted their mission from Rome.

In the original plan of the mission, Ephesus had been the main centre for the west,[12] with Rome being considered too far away to be an effective base. Half of the Jewish membership came from Asia Minor, which was an extension of Judea offering room for settlement. It was sufficiently close to the homeland to encourage a moderate nationalism, and it eventually became the boundary for Jewish Christians. At the mid century, with the Christians driven back there also, it was the council centre for the Church, where its future directions were debated.

Each of the phases of those years is recorded in the Book of Revelation, which came from Ephesus. The device is used of a 'seer' who saw 'visions', apparently of heavenly events. Under the influence of popular platonism, it was believed that what was happening on earth was a reproduction of what happened in heaven. An earthly worship service was a reflection of the continuous worship of God in heaven. Conversely, when a heavenly service was described, it was a way of describing an earthly service. The belief in a dual order supplied the device which enabled a real history – of Agrippa, of Jesus, of Peter and their fellow ministers – to be recorded in the disguise of a vision.

The 'seer' was actually a bishop, sitting at the front of the congregation in the cathedral at Ephesus. Cathedrals had already been established, the buildings where the *kathedra*, the seat of the priest, was to be found. They were in the capital cities, and at the festival seasons of the calendar, such as Pentecost, bishops and members from outlying villages came to the cathedral for councils and special services, as had long been done in Judea, when Qumran had been the centre for Essenes.

The seer, coming from one of the attached communities and sitting in the place of a Gentile bishop, was able to see what was happening on the tiered platform before him. It had three tiers, of considerable height in Herodian buildings. The highest tier was where King Herod sat, the descendants of Herod the Great who were still the official heads of the mission. From AD 49, 'he who sat on the throne' was Agrippa II, who was given a coronation in Ephesus on the day of Pentecost in that year. The 'seer' in the front row could only just see him; the height serving to enhance his mystique. On the middle tier were the ministers whom he could see, the subordinates of Herod. On the ground floor, just before him, were ministers of lower status. One of them, on the day of Pentecost in 49, was the Lamb, Jesus. He was present for that part of the service in which the 'seven seals were opened', when the first stage of the canonisation of the New Testament took place.

The last recorded appearance of Jesus in Ephesus was in the year AD 70, at the age of seventy-six. In that year he took part in a council of the greatest political importance, concerned with the consequences of the imminent fall of Jerusalem.

The accession of his son to the position and titles of the heir of David is described, in June AD 73. No exact date of Jesus' death is given.

There could be no open record of his death, for by ordinary believers he was thought to have died forty years before. Perhaps his bones were preserved in place of the bones of his representative, Peter, in the silver casket that is now under the high altar in St Peter's Basilica in Rome. But in the intense politics through which his religion of peace came to be that of the Roman empire, much happened that was never recorded, even in the concealed layer of the New Testament. At least, now, with the discovery of the diatribes of his enemies against him, hidden for two thousand years in caves near the Dead Sea, far more may be known about him, and he may be understood for what he was, one of the greatest human figures in western history.

CHAPTER 2

'He who was seated on the throne'

KING HEROD IN THE PLACE OF GOD

The Herod family, who took over the kingship of the Jewish people in the first century BC, were from many points of view sheer upstarts. They were not even Jewish, but came from an Idumean family who were closer to being Arab.[1] Antipater, the founder, had seen his opportunity when Queen Salome, the widow of the cruel and irresponsible Alexander Jannaeus, became queen regnant in 79 BC. She found herself with two sons of very different character. The elder, Hyrcanus, was so weak that he was widely considered not fit to reign after his mother, while the younger, Aristobulus, was much more capable. A long feud about the succession broke out between the two brothers, and it had to be resolved when Pompey arrived in 63 BC to take over control of the country on behalf of the Romans. Antipater had befriended the elder brother, and as Pompey decided to follow law and appoint him (although as high priest, not as king), Antipater was on the winning side, and came to be looked on by Rome as the man they could deal with.[2]

His son Herod the Great learned the same lesson. Pompey had left the country in the care of its high priests, who had limited power. The way was therefore open for a strong ruler who belonged to the country, even though distant Rome was officially the overlord. Herod had earned admiration for his early exploits, such as the destruction of a horde of Galilean brigands who lived in caves,[3] and was readily accepted by all sides as king. For the first twenty years of his reign he was popular and progressive, and it was in this creative phase that he was hailed by the missionaries to the Diaspora as the inaugurator of the thousand year Kingdom of the Jews.

Before his rise to power he had married Doris, a woman of ordinary birth, with whom he had a son, also called Antipater. But as his grandeur increased he looked higher, and began the polygamous habits which led to his having nine wives in all,[4] and numerous offspring. Inevitably, quarrels about the succession raged all through the following century.

His second wife was Mariamme, called the first because later there was another by the same name. She was an aristocrat, a descendant of the Hasmoneans, the family who had been the Jewish nobility since the previous century. She was undoubtedly his favourite wife, and bore him two sons who were popular with the people. But he suspected her of being unfaithful to him, and had her put to death. Years later her two sons suffered the same fate. It was from about this time that Herod began to degenerate into a period of rage and physical disease that persisted through his later years.[5]

Herod had to appoint high priests to perform the rites of religion, and he soon dispensed with ideas about traditional lines. He took it upon himself to dismiss high priests; it was no longer a lifetime office. The custom continued under the Romans, high priests being appointed and dismissed for political reasons, often through bribery. Sometimes they lasted only as long as six months.

The Pharisee high priest Boethus was appointed because Herod wanted to marry his daughter, the second Mariamme. But, nearing the end of his life, his insanity was increasing to such a point that a plot was formed to poison him. Mariamme and her father were found to be involved in it. Boethus was dismissed, she was divorced, and her son was disinherited.[6]

Herod also married a Samaritan woman, Malthace, of whom were born Archelaus and Antipas. But the sons of the earlier wives were the prior heirs. In the two years before his death, after the sons of Mariamme I were executed and the son of the second Mariamme disinherited, it finally appeared that his first son Antipater, the son of Doris, would receive the succession. But five days before Herod's own death, in 4 BC, the order went out to kill him also. Archelaus and Antipas were left to fight out the succession, going to Rome to continue their dispute. [7] The result was that in AD 6 the Romans tired of the Herods and dismissed Archelaus.[8] For some time it appeared as if the Herod dynasty was finished, and the way was made open, at the beginning of the first century AD, for the Annas priests to declare that they were the true rulers of the Jewish people, in co- operation with Rome, and (as the gospels show) to keep the Davids as a kind of spiritual king without temporal power.

When Herod the Great allied himself with the ascetic community in what was to him a revenue raising project, he made sure that he held all positions in the hierarchy, with the traditional holders of the offices, including priests, simply acting in his place.

Following the example of the high priest, he said prayers on the roof of a house, and sat on a throne on the highest tier of the structures used in worship, the level that stood for 'heaven'. On most occasions Herod was not present, and the priest representing him was the active leader, but when he did appear, on great occasions, it was as if he were a higher God. In the east the doctrine of a divine king was common, and Herod encouraged the belief.

The Herodian monarchy proved to be too resilient to die out so easily. After a generation's gap, Agrippa I, a grandson of Herod the Great and son of one of the two murdered princes, succeeded in gaining Rome's approval to wear the crown.

Agrippa, as a young man being educated in Rome, had used his house to give lavish banquets to entertain the highest ranks of Roman society, with the result that he came close to bankruptcy. He had to leave Rome and go back to his own country, where he was under such emotional pressure that he attempted suicide, but was rescued by help from his wife and sister.[9] He was in Judea during the gospel period, and was involved in the sequence of political events that led to the crucifixion. Shortly afterwards he returned to Rome, where he plotted with Gaius Caligula to help him become emperor following Tiberius. Gaius at his accession gave him the kingship.[10]

Agrippa, like his grandfather, was popular at the outset of his career, but by the end of it he had descended into the same megalomania. In his case, he had before him the example of Gaius Caligula, the crazed emperor. Taking seriously his role of messianic priest and messianic king who would come at the appointed time, Agrippa chose one of the significant dates of the calendar, in AD 44, to stage a dramatic demonstration on his rooftop in Caesarea. He appeared at sunrise, clad in a glittering silver garment, and the congregation below shouted in adulation 'a voice of a God and not of a man!'[11] They were not expressing this as a quite new idea, but drawing on known claims of the Herods. In Agrippa's mind it was not simply a claim to personal admiration, but was the basis of a claim to be an emperor; if not in Rome, at least in the east as a delegate of the emperor, who was already hailed as divine in eastern countries.

Agrippa was promptly 'smitten by an angel of the Lord', and was 'eaten by worms'. The pesher of Acts gives what Josephus does not say openly, that the sudden illness which then struck Agrippa, of which he died some days later, was the result of poisoning. Poisoning was a very common method of getting rid of political rivals in the Roman empire. Simon Magus was the 'angel of the Lord', the leader of the Samaritan party who had turned against the Herodian monarchy. The enemies had 'persuaded' Blastus, who was 'over the king's bedroom', to administer the poison.[12]

The consequence of Agrippa's excess, deeply offensive to Palestinian Jewish religion, was that the reigning Herods could no longer act in the place of God. Their legal position was changed, and they lost the right to appoint high priests. The right was given to Herod of Chalcis, a brother of Agrippa, who had probably been involved in the murder plot. He became an acting king until Agrippa II came of age, and was allied with the eastern ascetics who in this decisive year, 44, separated from the westerners, including the Christians.

The Herod who apppears at the centre of events in the book of Revelation was Agrippa II, also called Agrippa the Younger. He was born in AD 27, and was sixteen and a half at his father's death in March 44. He remained unmarried throughout his life, and his female consort was his twin sister Bernice.

Agrippa II, as Acts shows quite openly, was sympathetic with Christians. He is shown as saying to Paul 'You almost persuade me to be a Christian!'. He had, as the underlying history shows, been involved with the ascetic party all his life, as every Herod was, for it was one of their main sources of income.

As is seen from Acts, Agrippa's tutor had been the apostle Paul, who belonged to the order of Pharisees which had been set up as tutors in Greek learning to Jewish kings from the time of Queen Salome. Agrippa appears in Acts under the name of Sergius Paulus on the island of Cyprus, at the age of seventeen, at the time he was visiting the island and acting as the representative of Rome in the place of the proconsul. A contest for influence over him was being waged between Simon Magus (Bar-Jesus the Magus), whose order also taught kings, and Paul (whose name he used, as a pupil was a kind of servant to a master, and servants used the names of masters). Paul won the contest, for Simon Magus had been leader of the poison plot.[13]

Agrippa, educated in Rome, had westernised views, and little sentiment for his native country. He spent most of his time out of it, and at the crisis of the fall of Jerusalem told his people that God was on the side of the Romans.[14] His views made it easy for him to ally with the Christians, although he maintained the necessity for Jewish identity. Two western parties in the mission developed, able to co-operate with each other: Herodians and Christians. Both were equally opposed to the zealots, based in the east but often working in the west, for whom the whole aim of the mission was the promotion of Jewish nationality and its supremacy in the Roman empire.

Agrippa continued to occupy the throne on the upper tier in Herodian places of worship, preserving the imagery, drawn from the Old Testament, that enhanced the mystique of the king. At his second coronation, in Ephesus in June AD 49, described in Revelation 4 and 5, Agrippa, then aged twenty-one, was 'he who sits on the throne'. But the term 'God' was carefully avoided. His position was the one that later came to be called Pontifex Maximus, for he preserved the role of Michael, the Zadokite who claimed the high priesthood. The active religious leader was the Annas priest, who was technically second in rank to Agrippa. Preserving the position of Father that had been used at the foundation of the mission, he was the Priest- Pope. Matthew Annas, who held this position up to AD 51, was at times the mere representative of Herod, and at other times acted independently. The issue of their respective roles was central to the leadership. Ultimately, both the roles of Annas priest and Herod king were lost, and the positions of Pontifex Maximus and Priest-Pope were combined in the Christian papacy.

Other members of the Herod family were also involved in the history, and appear in the Book of Revelation.

The ruling Herods, using Herod's house in Rome, continued after Archelaus, and were more inclined to co-operate with Rome. The loser in the contest for succession, the tetrarch Antipas – the one who in the gospel period was responsible for the death of John the Baptist – was involved with the Magians.

Antipas' marriages were a significant factor in the history of the thirties AD. He had first married the daughter of Aretas king of Arabia, and when he divorced her the dishonour was so great that Aretas made war on the Jews, and was only deterred when Vitellius the Roman procurator marched against him in AD 37 in support of Antipas.[15] Aretas governed the city of Damascus,[16] and gave shelter in it to ascetics who were escaping from the Herods; it was there that the Damascus Document of the Dead Sea Scrolls was written. Damascus was from this time on the centre of mission for the anti- Herodian party.

The reason for Antipas' divorce was that he wanted to marry Herodias, a near relative who was a sister of Agrippa I. She had been promised in childhood to another of Herod's sons, the luckless son of the second Mariamme whom he subsequently disinherited. The marriage went ahead, and they had a daughter, but Herodias then left her husband to marry a more attractive relative, Antipas. Such a marriage was contrary to strict Jewish law, and it incurred the wrath of John the Baptist, who was priestly leader of the ascetics in the early gospel period. His attack on Antipas was the personal reason why he was put to

44

death, but there were also much stronger political reasons, as Josephus shows.[17]

Antipas and Herodias (who constantly urged him to try to get the succession for himself) were driven into exile, to the south of France, at the accession of Agrippa I.

Agrippa II had to appoint an heir from among his relatives, as he himself was childless. It appears that the man named Timothy in the New Testament was actually Timothy Herod, who was made crown prince to Agrippa II. This may be argued from several different sources. Agrippa's nearest male relatives were the line from his uncle Herod of Chalcis: Aristobulus the Younger, and his eldest son, who is simply called Herod by Josephus,[18] and who may be identified with Timothy.

Aristobulus the Younger had taken as his wife Salome, the daughter of the famous Herodias. Salome had first married another Herod relative, the tetrarch Philip, but after his death in AD 34 married Aristobulus. Thus Aristobulus' eldest son had both a mother (Salome) and grandmother (Herodias) who were initiates in Herodian orders. This agrees with the fact that Paul, in writing to Timothy, spoke of the faith that had dwelt in his mother and grandmother (who were called by different names, as new names were given at initiation).[19]

Paul, who as seen above was a tutor to Herod princes, called Timothy his 'son', and had a long relationship with him as adviser. In AD 48 Paul 'circumcised' Timothy, meaning that he gave him the form of early initiation given to a twelve-year-old boy; Jesus also was 'circumcised' at the age of twelve.[20] This would mean that Timothy was born in 36; this fits the fact that Salome married Aristobulus the Younger after 34.

Timothy was an important figure in Paul's strategy, and was in charge of the mission in Ephesus when Paul left. In his first letter to him, Paul spoke of 'the sayings of the prophecy leading towards you',[21] an expression putting him on a level with the David, who was believed to be the subject of Old Testament prophecy. The David and the Herod crown prince were equal with one another, both being a grade below King Herod. In the organisation these two were in charge of the lower division of the membership, Gentiles.

Timothy became fully a Christian under Paul's guidance, and this was a major coup for the Christians. He was so allied with them that he suffered imprisonment under Nero, as a New Testament epistle shows,[22] and the pesher of Revelation shows that he died in the persecution of AD 64, with Paul and Peter.

In the later parts of Revelation, further figures appear, usually called by titles or pseudonyms, who are to be identified with three further members of the Herod family prominent in the years before the fall of the city. According to Josephus, they 'collected gangs of villains', but at the same time he shows that one of them was the treasurer of the city, and that another tried to negotiate with Nero to prevent further war.[23]

They were called Antipas, Costobar and Saul, and it is not stated from which of the Herod lines they came. Antipas the treasurer of Jerusalem was killed by the unruly mobs in AD 67. He is to be identified with the Antipas who is named in the letter to Pergamum, written in AD 49, for all three figures appear in Ephesus, the external court of Agrippa II at the time of his coronation in AD 49.

The Herod called Saul is said to have gone to Achaia to negotiate with Nero. From the detail of the pesher, it is seen that this is the man called Erastus, an associate of Paul and of Timothy. Paul calls him the 'treasurer of the city (Gentile monastery)', and in Paul's last letter, he notes that 'Erastus remained in Corinth (in Achaia)'.[24] From detail of the pesher, it is seen that Erastus, the least in rank of the three, was the treasurer of the property of Gentiles who were under Agrippa. The property had been transferred from Caesarea at the time of the schism, and stored in one of the provinces that were given over to

Gentiles. Erastus was Herodian rather than Christian, upholding the system of receiving membership fees from Gentiles.

The third member of the group, Costobar Herod, may be identified with the Gaius whom Paul calls 'host', with Gaius of Derbe who was linked with Timothy in Acts, and with the Gaius to whom one of the epistles of John was written.[25] He was a leader of Herodian celibates, and after the death of Antipas the treasurer of Jerusalem, he became custodian of Herodian Jewish property, using it for the defence of Jerusalem and of Masada. Having left the country in 68 with other leaders, 'as swimmers desert a sinking ship' (in Josephus' phrase), he sent money back from abroad. This is seen from the part of Revelation dealing with this period, when a treasurer was 'pouring down talents like hail', on 'the Men', a title that was then being used for the tyrant of Masada, Eleazar Ben Jair.[26]

There were yet further descendants of Herod the Great, again appearing under pseudonyms in Revelation. It appears, although Josephus does not record it, that during the interim period before Agrippa II was crowned, another descendant challenged his right, and was supported throughout his reign by the Damascus party. He is called the False One, *pseudos*. He must have been a descendant of the other murdered son of Mariamme I, who at one time had been named by Herod the Great as his successor. He may be seen as Tigranes, the grandson, king of Armenia, a contemporary of Nero, who was supported by the eastern party in Damascus, and subsequently his son Alexander, a contemporary of Vespasian.[27]

In the final section of Revelation terms meaning a Herod are used in a way that shows that the seer is friendly to him. This Herod is said to be 'written in the book of life of the Lamb'.[28] But at the same time there is condemnation of another 'False One'. The final paragraph of Revelation is a warning to the approved Herod that if he follows the New Testament he is acceptable, but if he turns back to the Septuagint (the Greek translation of the Old Testament) he will be excluded. The placing of the warning shows that it is a matter of some importance.

This Herod may very well be identified with 'the offspring of Alexander (son of Tigranes), (who) abandoned from birth the observance of the ways of the Jewish land and ranged themselves with Greek tradition', as reported by Josephus.[29] To be Christian meant to follow Greek tradition against the Jewish, and it would be politically valuable if a linear descendant of Herod the Great had turned decisively against the east in favour of the Christian version of the mission.

The later years of the long reign of Agrippa II were marked by a loss of power, caused mainly by the destruction of Jerusalem and by the extravagant behaviour of his sister Bernice. As even his nominal authority over the mission declined, that of the Christians rose. By the end of the century the Davids had received the positions and titles that had been claimed by the Herods, except the one that they had claimed and lost, the title of God himself. No human king could claim it, and eventually no Jewish priest. The 'throne of God' on the upper tier in cathedrals remained empty, and God from now on had no incarnation in a living human.

CHAPTER 3

The Marriage of the Lamb

THE JESUS DYNASTY

In June AD 73, the son of Jesus was married in the cathedral at Ephesus. The occasion was described near the end of the Book of Revelation:

Hallelujah! For the Lord our God the Almighty reigns.
Let us rejoice and exult and give him the glory,
For the marriage of the Lamb has come,
And his Bride has made herself ready
And it was given to her to be clothed in fine linen, bright and pure
Blessed are those who are invited to the marriage supper of the Lamb.[1]

The son of Jesus, whose name and title was Jesus Justus, was born in June AD 37, the second child and first son of Jesus and Mary Magdalene.

Jesus himself had been married, according to the rule for his dynasty, at the age of thirty-six, in September AD 30. In matters political and intellectual, he had rebelled against the system into which he had been born, but in his personal sexual discipline had followed the principles that were intended to ensure that sex was used only for the sake of procreation.

Men belonging to the Essene dynastic order lived for most of the time in enclosed communities with other male celibates, following the monastic regime of daily prayer and study. When the time came to continue their line, they left the community and went to live among married people in a town or village.

There was at first a betrothal period, and during it the man acted as a teacher in the village. The heir of David at this time used the title 'the Word of God', meaning that he was a teacher only, not permitted to preside at the sacred meal, and under the authority of the local priest. A series of stages brought the man and his bride closer together, but at the same time delayed the consummation until well within the marriage. Even after the wedding ceremony three further months were allowed before sex could take place. Ideally, the couple came together in December, a less holy season when there were no traditional Jewish feasts. If conception occurred immediately, the couple stayed together but without intercourse until the woman was three months pregnant and the danger of miscarriage was less. They then underwent a second wedding ceremony, which was binding. The man returned to his community through a further series of stages, becoming enclosed again after the birth of the child. If a daughter was born, he returned to his wife after three years; if a son, after six years. It was for this reason that he married at the age of thirty-six, for if the first child was a daughter, he still had time to have a son in his fortieth year, so continuing the forty year generations which were attributed to kings.

If conception did not take place immediately, the couple stayed together for up to three years. This was the case for Jesus and Mary Magdalene. Their trial marriage was taking place during the years covered by the gospel stories. A conception finally occurred in December

AD 32, and the second wedding, when Mary was three months pregnant, took place a few days before the crucifixion. She was the woman with the alabaster jar of ointment, who carried out a wedding ritual dating back to the Song of Solomon, kissing the bridegroom's feet and anointing them with ointment as a symbol of sexual union. The erotic symbolism of this story has always been evident, and the newly discovered Gospel of Philip confirms that Mary Magdalene was the sexual companion of Jesus.[2]

At every point, the wedding symbolism used in the gospels and in the Book of Revelation stood for more than a personal history. Jesus as the heir of David inherited the associations of the king's wedding, long a part of the political theory of the ancient Near East. It was a sacred wedding, standing for the fertility and prosperity of the whole people. By the time of Jesus, new meaning had been added. In the Jewish mission to the world of which Jesus was a part, the bride stood for Gentiles. Jesus' marriage stood also for his 'marriage' with the Church, that is, with Gentiles.

It has always been recognised that the wedding symbolism of the Book of Revelation stood for the mystical unity between Christ and his Church. The fresh point that our new sources offer is that it was derived from real weddings, which were necessary in order to continue the dynasty of King David.

A daughter was born to Mary Magdalene in September 33. This fact is given in an indirect way, for when a son was born it was said 'the Word of God increased', but when a daughter, there was no such statement. But in Acts, in a speech of Peter given in September 33 (as the concealed chronology shows), he is quoted as saying: ' . . . that (God) may send the Christ appointed for you, Jesus, whom Heaven must receive until the times of the Restoration of All Things . . .'.[3] The 'Restoration' was not an abstract concept, but the Restoration of the Herod dynasty. Supporters of Agrippa were relying on the chronological theory to predict a date of AD 36 for his return to the throne, seven years from what they had called 'the Last Jubilee' in September AD 29. This theory is central to the Book of Revelation (See further pp.220–225). A return of Jesus after three years meant that a daughter had been born.

For the conception of the second child, there was no delay after the return. At a date shown by the chronological language to be June 37, the statement is given: 'the Word of God increased'.[4] Then, at the season of the death of Agrippa I, March AD 44, it is again said that the Word of God increased.[5] A second son had been born.

But the marriage, which according to the rule observed by Jesus should have been permanent, ceased after the birth of the third child. Mary Magdalene had refused to accept the reforms that Jesus brought about, and had returned to her zealot associates. She became again the 'woman with the seven demons', that is, committed to zealotry. When, in AD 44, a formal schism between east and west took place, Mary remained with the eastern party, with her friends Simon Magus and his mistress Helena. The term 'Christian' was at this point adopted, but applied only to Gentiles in the western party. Mary was not a Christian, and according to what was now law, as argued by Paul, the marriage could be dissolved, because Mary was not a believer.

Six years after the birth of the second son, in March AD 50, Jesus married again, the timing showing that he was following the dynastic rule.

Jesus was not only required by the system to have further sons, but a second marriage was an expression of both the more liberal views he stood for, against the strict views of the eastern party; and also of his political views. He was at this time close to Paul, who as a former Pharisee permitted divorce. Paul worked out the difficult problems that the marriage set up for the Christian party in his letter to the Corinthians. The Damascus Document of the Dead Sea Scrolls, written at this time, accused Jesus of polygamy. Paul dealt with the fine legal points, quoting both his own opinion and that of 'the Lord': Jesus, who was advising him in private.[6]

Once it is known that Jesus was actually present and not a visionary figure, the statement in Acts that Jesus 'opened the heart' of the woman Lydia, a 'seller of purple from Thyatira', suggests a sexual relationship.[7] If it meant simply a spiritual awakening, a less ambiguous phrase would have been used. Ambiguities are deliberate in a work whose every word was controlled. Lydia, who appears in Philippi in March AD 50, was one of the Virgins, from the women's community at Thyatira in Asia, who under the rules of hierarchy was permitted to advance to be a lay bishop, wearing purple, and giving to other women the same status.

Jesus' second marriage, to Lydia, was being prepared for in June 49, when he spoke to the seer John and dictated to him the seven letters, one of them to Thyatira.[8] He had recently returned from Rome to Ephesus, and was both dealing with problems that had arisen in the Gentile communities of Asia, and making personal arrangements.

Under the system which meant long separations between husbands and wives, a go-between was needed, a man who could represent the husband to the wife and the wife to the husband. One of his functions was to ensure that the wife remained faithful, acting like the eunuch in an eastern royal court, but in this case he was a spiritual 'eunuch' only. He was a celibate, and his title when representing the wife to the husband was 'the Beloved Disciple'. During the marriage with Mary Magdalene John Mark had been the Beloved Disciple, but he had remained with Mary's eastern party, and still accepted 'the woman Jezebel', that is, Helena, who, with Simon Magus, worked to bring proselytes into the zealot party.

53

One of the purposes of the letter to Thyatira was to say to John Mark that although he was still personally accepted, he was being replaced by a new companion for the new marriage, one who did not 'know the deep things of Satan', that is, hold eastern teaching. The new man was Luke, the Beloved Physician. He had been a servant of Agrippa I, under the name Cornelius, and at the move to Antioch had adopted Christian doctrine and a new name.[9] As the physician to Jesus (who still suffered from the effects of the crucifixion), he was very close to him from 50 onwards, and travelled also with Paul, who was Jesus' chief minister.

When Luke, writing Acts, suddenly changed in the course of narrative from 'they' to 'we', he was showing to those who understood that he was present as the close companion of Jesus, and that Jesus himself was also there. The go-between did not speak for himself but for the husband, so used the pronoun 'we'. It was in this way that Luke conveyed that Jesus was with them on the ship journey to Rome. It was Luke who, as the man of Macedonia speaking for Lydia and again saying 'we', said to Jesus with Paul in Troas: 'Come over and be a Helper (husband) to us'.[10]

The title of the eldest son, the heir of Jesus, is given at the end of Paul's letter to the Colossians, when he sent greetings from other Jews, 'the men of the circumcision', and added greetings from Jesus called Justus.[11] Justus, the Latin for 'righteous', was a title for the David crown prince. It was the title by which James the brother of Jesus was best known in contemporary literature, where he is called James the Just.[12] James was the crown prince to Jesus during the gospel period, before the birth of his own son. Joseph, their father, was crown prince at the time of Jesus' conception, and he was called *dikaios*, 'righteous' in Greek.[13] 'Righteous' was the next grade below 'holy', and the David at his highest was 'holy' while the crown prince was 'righteous'.

Some of the history of Jesus Justus is to be traced through Revelation. At the age of twelve, in June 49, he appeared with Jesus at the midnight Pentecost service in Ephesus. He was 'the seven stars in Jesus' right hand', using the title of the Star of David that belonged to the king or prince. The letter to Thyatira, written the same day, also spoke of him at the end, saying that his education was to begin, and was to be the same as that which Jesus had received at twelve. It added 'I will give him the Morning Star'[14].

The twentieth birthday of Jesus Justus, when he 'increased' on reaching sexual manhood, was held in Ephesus, as is shown in Acts at June 57.[15] Jesus was present on that occasion, as seen in both Acts and Revelation.

Jesus Justus appears again in AD 70, at the description of the communion service at the hermitage outside Ephesus at which Bernice Herod, 'the woman clothed in purple and scarlet', presided as a priest.[16] The story contains a hint of his personal views, that, like the seer of Ephesus of that period, he was prepared to join with Herodian nationalists in sympathy with the plight of Jerusalem.

The 'marriage of the Lamb' described in Revelation 19 was the wedding of Jesus Justus, aged thirty-six in June 73. His bride was 'clothed in fine linen, bright and pure', standing both for her virginity and for the purity of Gentiles practising a permanent celibate discipline.

A fortnight after the wedding the 'coronation' of Jesus Justus took place, when he received all the titles that Jesus had held as the heir of David, and in addition, some of the titles of the Sadducee priests, who were being superseded by the Davids in every position except that of 'God'.

In the last chapters of Revelation, the word 'bride' is used several times. The New Jerusalem is likened to a woman, 'coming down from heaven . . . prepared as a bride adorned for her husband'. In these chapters also, shown by the dating to be from AD 110–113, the third Jesus appears, born, as is indicated by the chronological detail, in AD 77. He is shown as saying: 'I am the Alpha and the Omega', using the titles that had been those of the Sadducee priest and originally of Herod himself. There were no more Herods: none had been appointed after the death of Agrippa II in AD 102.[17] Jesus III was receiving what had been prepared by the sufferings of the first Jesus: full priesthood, combining the roles of king and priest, with the Davids as the only kings. But now they were no longer kings of the Jews, but of the Christian form of the Kingdom of Heaven.

At the time of his wedding in June 113, the third Jesus spoke: 'I Jesus have sent my angel to witness these things to you concerning the churches. I am the Root, the Descendant of David, the bright Morning Star'. With him in the same scene were the Spirit (the Sadducee priest still accepted by Jewish Christians), and the Bride.[18]

The very last verse reads: 'The Grace of the Lord Jesus is with the holy ones'. 'Grace' was a title of the David crown prince in his role of minister to lower ranking Gentiles who, in the original Jewish system, were not asked to pay fees as they could not receive initiation. Their salvation was free, 'by grace'. When Jesus himself became the crown prince at the accession of his father, the fact was given by Luke in the form: 'The Grace of God came upon him'.[19] The last verse says, then, that a new crown prince had been born. The year is seen from the chronological structure to be AD 114.

The line would continue; for how long is not known. From the persistent traditions of descendants of Jesus in the south of France, and from the fact that there were Herodian estates in Vienne and Lyons,[20] it is to be suspected that the family sought refuge over the Alps when the political ambitions of their supporters again surfaced. An early Church father reports that during the reign of the emperor Domitian (AD 81–96), the grandsons of Jude the brother of Jesus were informed against 'as belonging to the family of David', and questioned about the nature of Christ's kingdom.[21]

The many evidences that Christianity reached England very early are well known. One writer, Gildas, a sixth century British monk, says that in the reign of Tiberius Caesar (died AD 37) 'the holy precepts of Christ, the true Sun' came to 'these islands, stiff with cold and frost, in a distant region of the world, remote from the visible sun'.[22]

The new information about the purposes of the Kingdom of God would explain why Britain was one of its early goals, as being 'the uttermost parts of the earth'. Josephus, a Jewish writer, was aware of Britain because it had been subdued by Vespasian, who had also led the first stage of the Jewish war. '(Vespasian) had by his military genius added to the empire Britain, till then almost unknown.'[23] It had first been invaded by Julius Caesar in 55 BC, and the emperor Claudius had made the southern part a province, visiting it himself in AD 43.[24] Wherever the Roman empire went, the Jewish mission went, for their aim was spiritual power, and at first also material power within the structure of the empire.

Further light may also be thrown on individuals whose names appear in the reports of early Christian Britain. A man named Aristobulus is said to have been 'bishop of Britain', and 'chosen by St Paul to be the missionary bishop to the land of Britain, inhabited by a very fierce and warlike race'. As has been pointed out by Geoffrey Ashe,[25] there may be a connection with the Aristobulus to whom Paul sends greetings in his letter to Romans. To this observation may be added the evidence that the Herods were the real leaders of the mission, and that Aristobulus is a name that frequently occurs in their family tree.

Even more interestingly, the connection has been

pointed out by Ashe[26] between the Claudia and Pudens who are named as Christians in Rome at the end of Paul's last letter, and the British lady named Claudia ('of azure-painted Britons born') who lived in Rome with her husband named Pudens, according to a Roman writer. Some traditions said that Claudia was the daughter of Caractacus, the British prince who had been brought as a captive to Rome in AD 51. Women in Rome had always shown an interest in the mission, beginning with the early Jewish form presented by Agrippa I to his patroness Antonia, the most influential woman in Rome.[27] One Roman woman of high rank, Fulvia, had early become a convert to the Samaritan form of the mission.[28] Claudia from Britain may well have been drawn into missionary circles in Rome.

A very early mission to Britain accompanying the Roman empire would make a date of before AD 37 quite possible, for it now may be seen that the mission did not begin with Jesus but in the previous century. Once it was known that these islands existed at the limits of the inhabited world, as was thought, there would be a natural attraction to them for the Herodian aim of empire. Moreover, if they were thought of as the most remote place on earth, they would be the best hiding place for refugees from the Roman power, bringing with them objects they considered most sacred.

The cup that was used at communion was the sign of authority of a Herodian sacred meal, for it was the cup used by the Herods when they entertained the emperor. 'The cup' was used by Agrippa II when he fled Jerusalem to Rome in AD 69, as a detail in the pesher of Revelation shows. An original cup,[29] or at least a cup that was a sign of Herodian or Christian authority, may well have been brought to England, and deposited at a place on the far side of the island that had been wrested from the Druids, at Glastonbury. It may have been brought, as the legend of the Holy Grail says, by a Joseph of Arimathea, that is, a servant of a David crown prince, one of whose titles was Joseph.

Every historian treats religious legends with caution, knowing the easy transition from religion to imagination. But if new historical evidence becomes available, it may help to account for the nucleus of the legend. Such new evidence is available, when what is concealed in the New Testament itself becomes known. Even with the limited literary sources, there is reason for seeing that the religion that came to Britain, and from there to much of the rest of the world, began in Judea well before the time of Christ, and had been a Herodian Jewish one before it became fully Christian.

CHAPTER 4

Miriam the Missionary

MARY, BAPTISER OF GENTILES

The woman of Revelation Chapter 12, who had on her head a crown of twelve stars, and who cried out in labour with the Messiah, was, indeed, Mary the mother of Jesus. The Hebrew form of her name was Miriam, and her place in life was determined by the fact that she was married to Joseph, the son of Jacob-Heli, who had volunteered to join Herod the Great in the mission to Diaspora Jews and to Gentiles.

One of the main images used to conceptualise the mission was that it was a New Exodus, leading to a new Promised Land, with Judaism dominant in the world of Greece and Rome. As the original Exodus had lasted forty years, so would the new one, and the careful calculations about the number of members and the income they would bring in were based on the figure of forty years.

The Exodus ideal had long been held by Jews living in Egypt, near the shores of Lake Mareotis. They saw themselves, and all other Diaspora Jews, as exiles from their homeland, longing to return to it as their spiritual centre, yet valuing their life in the Greek cities and thinking of themselves as nomads in a wilderness, ever journeying.

Sharing many of the ideas of the Essenes, they were called the Therapeuts, or Healers, because of their special interest in the medical arts. They had developed an ascetic lifestyle around the image of the wilderness (Greek *erēmos*, giving the word 'hermit').[1]

For most of the time they lived, both men and women, like contemplative hermits; but every seven weeks they came together for a 'banquet', a simple meal of bread and water, but which went on all night and became an occasion of spiritual ecstasy. As the liturgy began, two choirs were formed, the men led by a 'prophet Moses', and the women by a 'prophetess Miriam', the sister of Moses. The book of Exodus has a Song of Moses and a Song of Miriam, said to have been uttered at the crossing of the Red Sea. They enacted the drama of the sea crossing, singing hymns of thanksgiving.[2]

King Herod, as the supreme head of the mission, was the superior of all Jews who entered it and advanced through its grades, paying him fees as they progressed. But down in its lower ranks were the Gentiles, who could never advance beyond the lesser grades. They fell into two broad classes: proselytes, who became circumcised and lived in every respect like Jews; and the uncircumcised, who did not want Jewish nationality but valued the ideas of the mission. For the latter, 'Miriam' was an essential minister, for only a woman, being uncircumcised, could touch uncircumcised Gentiles, and the baptism rite required physical contact. It was a well-known Essene rule, noted by Josephus, that if a man of higher grade even touched one of lower grade within the community, he went and bathed himself, 'as if after contact with an alien'.[3]

Jacob-Heli of the Essenes, when he joined King Herod, had perforce to accept a lesser position than that of king, just as his descendants had to do when they were allied with the Herods. Their status was that of a prince under King Herod, the same as that of his crown prince. Both princes were put in charge of Gentiles. But the Herod crown prince headed the circumcised proselytes, while the David was leader of the uncircumcised.

Some uncircumcised Gentiles, such as John Mark the Beloved Disciple, lived in communities patterned on those of monastic Essenes, and their celibacy and discipline gave them merit counted as equal to that of circumcised proselytes. The David was their direct superior, while the lower grades of the same orders were under the authority of the wife of the David, in the role of Miriam. She it was who joined with her husband in the mission to Gentiles, and when it came to the point of accepting baptism, she performed the actual rite.

Her title was Miriam, a title that was passed on to the wives of the successive Davids. Mary the mother of Jesus held the position, and was followed by Mary Magdalene. Among the four leading women reported by John's gospel to be gathered at the cross,[4] three were called Mary, the other one being Mary of Cleopas, the young woman who was to marry James, who was the David while Caiaphas was high priest.

The fourth woman at the cross was actually the superior of the other three, who as equal to 'Miriam' were 'Sisters'. The other woman was a 'Mother': 'Mother Sarah'. From the start of the mission to Jews led by 'Abraham', a 'Sarah' had been needed for higher Gentiles. The title was given to the woman who assisted the current 'Abraham', the Pope. At the cross, this was Helena.

The newly discovered gospel of Philip confirms that the pre-Christian form of the mission had a woman as Gentile superior. It says: 'When we were Hebrews we were orphans and had only our mother; but when we became Christians we had both father and mother'.[5]

The image of Mother was useful in places like Ephesus, where the Jewish mission had to compete with the mystery cults centred around women, such as that of Cybele, and of Diana or Artemis, whose temple in Ephesus was one of the wonders of the world. Herodians soon discovered the value of claiming that their 'Sarah' was an incarnation of Diana, an acceptable idea to Greeks, who, as Acts shows, were prepared to believe that Barnabas and Paul were incarnations of Zeus and Hermes.[6] On the occasion recorded in the Book of Acts when there was a riot in Ephesus concerning the cult of Diana,[7] the actual history was that the mission was in intense conflict on the question over whether 'Sarah' should be allowed to continue acting as a priestess and oracle. The convent of Thyatira, in the same province, was the place where women following her were educated.

When the Christians finally won, there was a continuing interest in a Mother figure in Ephesus. A 'Sister' could be promoted to 'a Mother', if she had sufficient merit, and this was the case with Mary the mother of Jesus, who at the schism of AD 44 became the chief woman to the Christians. The tomb claimed to be that of Mary is still to be seen outside Ephesus, at just the distance away from the city required by the Essene law for places occupied by females.

In Revelation Chapter 12, a description is given of Mary's method of baptism of Gentiles in the early years of the first century, while the mission centre was still in the Wilderness of Judea. They used the magnificent setting at the place now called Khirbet Mird or Hyrcania, a fortress owned by the Herods. The building itself was set on a prominent height overlooking the Buqeia, the plateau leading down to the Dead Sea. To its west an aqueduct had been built, conducting water along the spine of a ridge to the building.[8]

According to the passage, 'the Serpent threw water like a river out of his mouth after the woman, that she might be made as one carried by a river'.[9] The Israelites had escaped from Pharaoh and the 'fleshpots of Egypt', and the escape was enacted, with a man playing the part of Pharaoh, standing at the beginning of the aqueduct.

The role of 'Miriam' was to begin at the aqueduct, when it was swollen by the winter rains, and to enact a form of baptism on behalf of Gentiles by being 'carried by the river', that is wading through it as a kind of immersion baptism. She would lead Gentiles after her as she sang the Song of Miriam ('Sing to the Lord, for he has triumphed gloriously; the horse and his rider he has thrown into the sea').[10]

Then 'the Earth helped the woman'.[11] She arrived at the building, and was there met by the chief layman, who was her husband and Helper, Joseph. He was 'the Earth' and she was 'the Sea'.[12] Husband and wife worked together as missionaries to Gentiles, he instructing them after she had baptised them.

Mary, the mother of Jesus, continued in her role of minister. In AD 32 she began the three year process of becoming an 'enrolled Widow', a higher form of ministry described in the New Testament as permitted to women of sixty.[13] Her first step in education for the position is described in Luke's gospel, in the guise of the story about the 'crippled woman'. To be 'crippled' simply meant that she was one of the class of the aged, a category in the highly organised community. The story notes that she had been 'bound by Satan for eighteen years'. This means 'in year 18', that is, AD 23 by the dating that was in use at that time (see p.545, Note 15). In that year, she had come under the authority of 'Satan', a name for the Chief Scribe. In other words, Joseph died in AD 23 and Mary became a literal widow.

At the crucifixion, Jesus entrusted his mother to the 'Beloved Disciple', John Mark, who was one of those who looked to a Miriam as their woman missionary. In AD 44, another ceremony took place at Qumran, described in both Acts and Revelation, and the description of Acts includes a reference to 'the house of Mary the mother of John Mark'[14]. It means the Qumran vestry, where Mary and subsequent David queens acted as doorkeepers. Mary was by now in her late sixties.

Her title 'the Virgin' would have been particularly acceptable in Ephesus, where the Christians were following the practice of Jewish missionaries, who had consciously substituted their chief woman for Diana the Virgin.

Such a background for the cult of Mary has often been suggested, but the new information shows much more precisely that it came about, not simply through the general dissemination of Hellenistic ideas, but consciously, as the logical result of a strategy of mission. Mary, in reality, was a missionary and a minister of her religion.

CHAPTER 5

The Beast 666

THE ZEALOT ANTI-POPE

Probably the best known character of the Book of Revelation is the beast whose number is 666.

And I saw a beast rising out of the sea, having ten horns and seven heads, and on its horns ten diadems, and on its heads a name of blasphemy . . . Then I saw another beast rising out of the earth, and it had two horns like a lamb and it spoke like a dragon . . . It causes all, small and great, rich and poor, freemen and slaves, to be given a mark on their right hand or on their forehead, so that no one may buy or sell unless he has the mark, the name of the beast or the number of his name. Here is wisdom. He who has understanding, let him count the number of the beast, for it is a number of a man; its number is six hundred and sixty-six.[1]

It is quite obvious that some kind of code is being drawn upon and that a real enemy is referred to. More orthodox commentators have had to accept the opinion that it refers to a Roman emperor, possibly Nero, without being able to explain the detail or the number.

In a way, it does refer to a Caesar, but only very indirectly. The main subject of the passage was the leader of the Jewish zealots, who aimed to become a Caesar when the party of fervent nationalists had overcome the Roman power. For the writers of Revelation, and the seer of its earliest section in particular, the Beast was the anti-Pope, Simon Magus, who was the powerful leader of the traditional party. It was the Christians who, technically, were the heretics, as the Dead Sea Scrolls declare. The two parties were conducting rival missions, fighting for the souls of Gentiles, one side in order to make them Jews, the other to give them a new form of religion that was not Jewish. Although they had begun together, the tensions between them were now so great that each side called the other evil, deceivers, blasphemous. Paul described Simon Magus as: 'the son of perdition, who opposes and exalts himself against all that is called God or to be revered; he sits in the sanctuary of God, proclaiming himself to be God'.[2] One of the Dead Sea Scrolls called the Christians 'the men of iniquity walking in the way of wickedness . . . They are not counted in his Covenant . . .. Wrath shall rise up for judgment, and they will be avenged with vengeance by the curses of the Covenant.'[3]

The number 666 is indeed the clue, to those who knew the Hebrew alphabet and the way it was used in the gnostic monastic system out of which the zealot movement arose. The letters of the Hebrew alphabet were used also for numbers. The last letter, Taw ('t') was used for 400, the second last, Shin ('s') for 300, and the third last, Resh ('r') for 200. The number 600 was made up of 400 and 200, Taw and Resh. The number 60 was further down the alphabet, at Samekh (another 's'). The number 6 was near the beginning of the alphabet, at Waw ('v'). This letter, Waw, was used with an initial or group of initials; there are further illustrations of the usage in the scrolls.[4] So, the letters representing 666 were: Taw, Resh, Samekh (TRS, 660) with the extra Waw (6) to show that initials were being used.

In the Jewish monastic system letters were used for the

grades attained each year, as in a school system. These are set out fully on pp.179–182. The very highest grade was Taw, the last letter of the alphabet being used to show that promotions could go no higher. It was normally reached at the age of thirty after ten years of study. The year before, Shin was reached, and before that Resh. The special privilege attached to Resh was that the higher students, who were now graduates, could enter the room used as the substitute temple and say prayers there, as if they were temple priests. Previously they had not been allowed to enter it.

Of the ten years of study, the first three, from ages twenty to twenty-three, were used to prepare for initiation. It was only at twenty-three that Samekh, the grade of initiation, was reached. Thus it was the other major milestone. Taw, Resh and Samekh represented the three main steps in the career of a student in a monastery. So, when the eastern monastic system, with its oppressive discipline and covert military purpose, was rejected by the Christians, they spoke of it contemptuously as 'the 666'.

This explanation also helps to account for one of the minor mysteries of Roman history. Graffiti in the form of a word square have been found scratched on walls from Roman times: including two at Pompeii and four at Dura-Europos in Mesopotamia.[5] The square runs:

> R O T A S
> O P E R A
> T E N E T
> A R E P O
> S A T O R

The letters are the same when read across and down. Some of the words are Latin, but not all are known. When the vowels are disregarded – as was habitual for anyone reading Hebrew – the consonants round the sides are R-T-S. These are the three letters indicating the monastic system (TRS), with the T in the middle as it was the highest letter: the most important member of a hierarchy stood in the centre. The graffiti may be accounted for as propaganda for the gnostic monasteries, appearing in both Mesopotamia and Rome, the east and west limits of the 'Kingdom of God'.

The zealots, whose activities were first recorded in AD 6, were either heroic martyrs or murderers, according to one's point of view. They harassed the Romans throughout the first century AD, bringing about the catastrophic destruction of Jerusalem in AD 70; this meant the final loss of the Jewish state, and led to a history of homelessness which for Jews reached a dramatic climax in the twentieth century AD.

Josephus writes of them under their leader in AD 6, Judas the Galilean. 'They have a passion for liberty that is almost unconquerable, since they are convinced that God alone is their leader and master. They think little of submitting to death in unusual forms and permitting vengeance to fall on kinsmen and friends if only they may avoid calling any man master.'[6] Holding the belief of the Pharisees in resurrection from the dead, the remnants of the zealots committed mass suicide on Masada in AD 74, stirred by a speech from their leader Eleazar, who urged that they would rise again gloriously. This, he declared, would be better than submitting to the Romans, who were even now scaling the sides of their mountain fortress.[7]

But from another perspective, often expressed by the historian Josephus, the zealots 'sowed the seed of every kind of misery'. 'These men madly had recourse to butchery of each other and of themselves from a longing not to be outdone by their opponents.'[8]

The new historical fact that comes out of the discovery of the Dead Sea Scrolls, together with the application of the pesher technique to the gospels, is that the Christians arose from within this movement. They had shared with it the hope of a Kingdom of God, which would take up power in and overcome the Roman empire. But where the zealots held that the only way to proceed was by force of arms, in order to gain an empire in this world, the Christians, under the leadership of Jesus, had seen that there was no hope of this worldly empire, nor should a religious Kingdom of God be interpreted as Jewish. It should be a worldwide religion concerned with love of God, transcending national boundaries. All should be equal in it: Jew and Gentile, slave and freeman, male and female, maimed and whole. From the point of view of zealots, the Christians were traitors to the Jewish cause, and had gone over to the hated Romans. The betrayal and crucifixion of Jesus were the result of a conspiracy to rid the party of him.

The beginnings of the movement went back a long way. Inspiration for a fervent Jewish nationalism that could triumph over a pagan enemy came from the Maccabean era of the second century BC, when a family of Jewish priests led by Mattathias had rallied the people with such effect that they had thrown off their Syrian overlord, the fanatical Antiochus Epiphanes, and had gained a political independence that they had not known for many centuries.

All Jews had gathered around the heroic priest Mattathias and his five sons – at first. But after the victory, party squabbles broke out. Conservatives believed that only a priest from one of the traditional families should rule in the temple in Jerusalem. When the sons of the priest Mattathias were swept in to the high priesthood by popular adulation, the conservatives were outraged. They turned to support a rival high priest, who at least had the right descent.[9]

At this stage the conservatives consisted mainly of Essenes, a recognisably separate group who kept a different calendar from the rest of the nation. Theirs was a solar calendar, such as had been used in the first temple and developed during the exile in Babylon. To keep a different calendar meant observing the Jewish feasts on different days, so they were like a sect, worshipping separately.

The protest of Essenes against the popular Maccabeans finally led to their expulsion from Jerusalem. They went into political exile, not far away, but to a place which no one else wanted to inhabit, by the shores of the Dead Sea; the place that is now called Qumran. It had, apparently, belonged to the David family, and was used by them when they had to go into retreat. In their own words, 'they returned to their desolate country'. The date they gave for their exile was about 140 BC.[10]

The Essenes themselves had two branches: those who lived in Palestine, centring all their hopes on recovery of the temple; and those who lived in the Diaspora, chiefly in the great cities of Babylon, Ephesus, Alexandria and Rome. For these, the Palestinian institutions were not really necessary. Diaspora Essenes were marked by 'zeal', a word that meant at first spiritual fervour as a substitute for priestly birth. They themselves, as a result of their ascetic discipline, had become holy enough to do the duties of priests. In the Diaspora, where men born into the tribe of Levi were often in short supply, and where distances were too great to travel to Judea, this was a useful adaptation.

They were often deeply involved in the cultural life of the cities in which they lived, like the Alexandrian Jewish writer Philo, who had considerable sympathy with Essenes.[11] Greatly attracted by Greek learning, they had a reputation for scholarship. But with less loyalty to ritual laws, they were called by Palestinians the 'seekers after smooth things'.[12]

Those who were exiled to Qumran were, at first, Palestinian Essenes. They extended the buildings, added a substitute sanctuary, and built a scriptorium, in which

71

their scribes spent their days making copies of books of the Old Testament. Their leaders were priests, descendants of the old priestly lines, and with them they took laymen who acted as acolytes, doing the physical work. Qumran was so desolate that no food could properly be grown there, but food was supplied by men throughout the country who retained loyalty to the old priestly families and brought to them their tithes of corn, wine and oil instead of to the Jerusalem temple. The meals taken from these food offerings were considered sacred, and the acolytes were allowed access to them only on condition that they had committed no sin;[13] thus they were an effective means of control of the priests over the laymen. Their sacred meal was the first stage of the Christian Eucharist.

In the eighties BC the Palestinian Essenes at Qumran lost their authority as the result of the failure of one of their long held prophecies. It was at about this time that Queen Salome was looking for teachers for her two sons. Diaspora Essenes would bring the benefits of Greek learning and help to break the cultural isolation of Judea. Some of them were invited to come, and to set up schools. Following Pythagorean ideals of the pursuit of learning in places of retreat,[14] they used places in the Wilderness of Judea, physically close to Jerusalem but very desolate. The building at Mird, or Hyrcania, which was Queen Salome's treasury, was used as a more elementary school, and further to the east, on the coast of the Dead Sea, Qumran became the more advanced school, now taken over by the Hellenised party. Antipater, the associate of Salome's elder son, was at Qumran in about 60 BC, according to a detail in the pesher of Acts.[15]

Queen Salome came under the influence of Pharisees, who rose to be the dominant party of Jews during her reign.[16] Some Diaspora Pharisees had linked with the ascetics, practising a higher than normal discipline. Some of these formed an ascetic order of a thousand men who came to be called the 'tribe' of Benjamin. Its best known member, living in the first century BC, was Hillel the Great.[17] The order of Benjamin took on the role of tutors to princes, at first to Salome's sons, and later to the sons of the Herods. They instructed them in Greek philosophy and related subjects. Paul, a later member of the order, demonstrated his knowledge of Greek philosophy while he was in Athens, and when he was instructing the governor Felix. 'He held a dialogue concerning justice and self-control'[18] . . . Paul had sat at the feet of Gamaliel, a descendant of Hillel.[19]

Another order was formed, who used the solar calendar of the Essenes. These were the ones who used the term 'zeal' for their ascetic discipline. Whereas the men of Benjamin stayed in the world, these men, called the 'tribe' or order of Manasseh, lived in celibate communities that were monastic in varying degrees, although not as enclosed as those of the Palestinian Essenes.

It was they who, when political events determined it, were drawn into the project of taking over the Roman empire in order to implement their version of Judaism, at first through mission, then later, when the situation became desperate under the procurators, by force of arms.

There were two branches of the order of Manasseh, west and east, corresponding to the divisions of the ancient tribe of Manasseh, which had occupied both sides of the river Jordan. The men of West Manasseh, coming from Samaria, worked in the western Diaspora, and had no difficulty with aspects of its culture, including use of the Julian calendar.[20] The men of East Manasseh were much more eastern in their orientation, and kept to the old Jewish calendar, which began its year in March.

Both groups made Gentile proselytes in addition to their Jewish initiates, but East Manasseh insisted that they should be circumcised, whereas the missionaries from West Manasseh agreed to allow them to remain uncircumcised as long as they attended synagogue and learned their highly gnostic form of Judaism.[21]

Under Herod the Great, Menahem the Essene was the man who influenced Herod to favour the Essenes again.[22] He was a Diaspora Essene, and he was the prime mover in the mission, becoming its 'patriarch Isaac'. He belonged to the order of West Manasseh.

His successor in the time of Jesus was Simon Magus, called by many different pseudonyms. These included Simon the Zealot, in the list of twelve apostles. The term 'Magus' (magician) was used, not because he was literally one of the priests of the old Iranian religion – the proper meaning of the word – but as a nickname for himself and his order. They had learned their calendar science, medicine and political skills in Babylon, where they had profited from the enforced exile of Samaritans in the eighth century BC; but they were Samaritan Jews, who had a high reputation for learning, and had combined Jewish religion with Hellenistic knowledge in a way that had already become gnosticism, that is, the belief that there was a superior kind of salvation for men of learning. In their celibate communities they lived very much as the Pythagoreans did, devoted to the pursuit of knowledge as a religious way of life.

The Magians were led by Joseph, 'the Star of David', to the place where Jesus was born, because, having Hellenised views on sexual morality, they could accept that he was the legitimate heir of David.[23] His birth in 7 BC was an event of the greatest importance to them, for they had just formalised their recent protest against Herod the Great by reoccupying Qumran and setting up an opposition party to him. All Pharisees had protested when Herod required them to take an oath of loyalty to Caesar.[24] The Magian plan was now to have a Kingdom of God in which their leader would be a high priest, taking the priestly positions that had been claimed by Herod. Under him would be the David, in much the same role that he had had under Herod, responsible for Gentiles. But there would be no other king, so that the David was the only true lay leader.

The first known head of East Manasseh was Judas the Galilean, leader of the militant uprising of AD 6.[25] He was called the Beast of the triumvirate of that time; three leaders who aimed to rival the three who had inaugurated the Roman power. Their pseudonyms were the Dragon (the Pharisee high priest Joazar), the Calf (Archelaus Herod) and the Beast (Judas).[26] Judas was also known for his learning; he was described by Josephus as a 'sophist'.[27] He lost his life in the uprising, and in AD 26 a successor received his titles and functions. This was Judas Iscariot, who was the first Beast of the passage in Revelation, the one 'rising out of the sea'.[28]

Judas' relationship with Jesus was a political one. As 'the Devil', a name for him in the monastic position of Chief Examiner, he offered Jesus rule over all the kingdoms of the earth, if Jesus would bow down and worship him. He was offering to renew the arrangement that the men of Manasseh had had with the Davids: he would be the Priest, and Jesus would be the subordinate king. But Jesus, already forming a party that preferred to teach rather than to destroy the Romans, refused his offer.[29] A few years later, Judas took his opportunity to betray Jesus, believing him to be disloyal to the nationalist cause.

The second Beast, with the number 666, was Simon Magus. In AD 31, after the death of John the Baptist, and after an interim period in which Jonathan Annas was Pope, Simon brought his anti-Herodian party into government, and himself became Pope,[30] teaching a doctrine that revised that of the Baptist. He offered the same position to Jesus, who would be his 'Beloved Son', the leader of Gentiles.

This time Jesus accepted the offer, for Simon stood for more than zealotry. His great learning meant that he had built a bridge to the Greek world, and moreover his attitude to Gentiles was a more liberal one; he did not require them to be circumcised.

There appear to have been personal factors also. Jesus may well have been partly under the domination of a man who was already the subject of legend in his own lifetime, and who came to be accepted by thousands of followers as an incarnation of the divine. Simon was the original of the Faust legend, as the Clementine books show.[31]

When Jesus 'raised Lazarus', he had obtained permission to lift the ban of excommunication on Simon, and by doing this, he was knowingly aiding a zealot leader, now a wanted criminal, in such a way as to give evidence of his own complicity. It was because of such actions as these that Pilate could order the execution of Jesus, as the third in a triumvirate of Priest (Simon), Prophet or Levite (Judas Iscariot) and King (David).[32]

Up to 37, the pressures keeping Jesus together with Simon were strong. Simon had saved Jesus' life in the burial cave, and their party in the mission was the only alternative to Palestinian traditionalism. But when Agrippa I was appointed ruler after the death of Tiberius, their separation began. Simon was and remained a bitter enemy of all reigning Herods, and would be the agent of Agrippa's death. Jesus followed the Annas priests into cooperation with Agrippa.

In 37 Peter attacked Simon for his financial exploitation, and in 44 Paul attacked him for his 'deceit and villainy', and separated Jesus decisively from him.[33] It was from this point that the schism was recognised. In the west were Herodians and Christians, the latter now using the name for the first time; in the east were the men of Manasseh, led by Simon Magus as their Pope. But he was the anti- Pope to the Christians, the author of all blasphemy, 'proclaiming himself to be God'.

There was to be a Chief Monk, a Beast, on the Herodian side, but the only one who can be identified was almost a comic version of Simon. When a figure called

'Balaam' is introduced in one of the seven letters, it is clear that we are dealing with another Magus, for 'Balaam' was the name of a magician in the Old Testament. The context shows that it is the Cyprian Jew named Atomus, a Magus (magician) mentioned by Josephus as a man who became a kind of marriage broker to the Agrippa family. In about AD 55 he was called upon by the procurator Felix to arrange for his marriage with the beautiful Drusilla, the younger sister of Agrippa, and succeeded in persuading her to marry outside her religion.[34]

It becomes apparent that his involvement with the royal family was closer than Josephus records. Cyprus was the place where Paul brought about the final separation between Jesus and Simon Magus, and the young Agrippa was present there.[35] It would follow that the Cyprian Magians had changed their allegiance at this point, Simon being sent to Damascus and Atomus taking over. He practised his 'magical' arts in the matter of another marriage, that of Bernice, Agrippa's twin sister, who in the early fifties married Polemo of Cilicia, also a Gentile;[36] this was the reason for his introduction in one of the letters, written in AD 49.

The position of Chief Monk corresponded to one that had originally been held by 'Gabriel', the archangel for Passover and spring, whose liturgical colour was green (see p.156). Atomus, as Chief Monk in the court of Herod, was 'the rider on the green horse' of the four horsemen of Revelation Chapter 6. 'His name was Death' because he had the power to excommunicate. With him was 'Hades', a name for another member of Herod's court in Ephesus, who held a position like that of the 'Devil'.

During the fifties and early sixties a party of Herodian militants developed under the leadership of Bernice, the sister of Agrippa. Their history is the main subject of the third part of Revelation, as can be seen when it is read together with the detailed account of those years by Josephus. The Herodians made Masada, a Herodian property, their headquarters. It became 'the throne of the Beast', with a Herodian Magus as the Chief Monk.[37] The active leader was Eleazar Ben Jair, the hero of Masada, leader of the Sicarii, who stayed there until its fall.[38]

In AD 70 in Ephesus, Bernice as 'the Great Harlot, clothed in purple and scarlet' 'sat upon a scarlet beast'. While they were still in Jerusalem she had claimed the monarchy from her brother, and she claimed also ownership of the Herodian property at Masada.

The Herodian Chief Monk, the Beast who had fled the country with Bernice, was 'trapped' at the Ephesus council of 74, when the news came of the fall of Masada. But another Beast appeared in AD 100, as the last chapters of Revelation record. Zealotry was rising again, and would have its climax under Simon Ben Kosba thirty years later. Ben Kosba's campaign was waged in the southern part of the Dead Sea coastland, and he used caves at Murabbaat for his archives; they were found at the time of the discovery of the Dead Sea Scrolls.[39]

This final Beast would have been a religious leader of militant celibates with Ben Kosba. His failed uprising was the last; and Jerusalem was closed by the Romans to any Jews and renamed as a Gentile city.[40] The Beast had had his way, and his end, as the Christians had predicted, was destruction.

CHAPTER 6

The Woman Jezebel

A FEMALE PRIEST

In one of his letters to the seven churches, the letter to Thyatira, Jesus condemns in no uncertain terms a woman whom he calls 'Jezebel':

> But I have this against you, that you accept the woman Jezebel, who calls herself a prophetess and is teaching and leading astray my servants to prac- tise fornication and to eat food sacrificed to idols. I gave her time to repent, but she will not repent of her fornication. Behold, I throw her on a bed, and those who commit adultery with her I will throw into great tribulation, if they do not repent of her works, and her children I will strike dead.[1]

The woman he was speaking of was Helena, the mistress of Simon Magus. She and Simon had once been friends and associates of Jesus, and the note of intense anger in his letter was a reflection of what had happened in the years since the crucifixion. Their ways had decisively parted. Simon and Helena had chosen the role of leaders of a gnostic sect, worshipped by their followers as if they were divine, unscrupulous about sexual morality and financial exploitation. They had become notorious in the Roman world, so that Justin, a second century Christian, could write:

> There was a Samaritan, Simon . . . who in the reign of Claudius Caesar . . . did mighty acts of magic, by virtue of the art of the devils operating in him. He was considered a god . . . And almost all the Samaritans, and a few even of other nations, worship him, and acknowledge him as the first god; and a woman, Helena, who went about with him at that time, and had formerly been a prostitute, they say is the first idea generated by him.[2]

According to the Clementine books, a valuable source for the history (see Chapter 7), John the Baptist's disciples had included Helena, also known as Luna (the Moon). Simon Magus had fallen in love with her, and she was one reason why he was ambitious for fame.

He made for himself a reputation as thaumaturge by pretending to perform magical tricks. His political stratagems led to his ousting the Baptist's immediate successor and taking his place as head of the Baptist sect.[3]

Both Simon and Helena appear in the gospels and Acts under a variety of different names. In the Scrolls and the New Testament, the principle is that the more powerful the person, the greater the number of pseudonyms. Helena appears as the Samaritan woman, as the Syrophoenician woman, as Salome, as Martha, as Sapphira.[4] She and Simon were the two most important and influential figures in the early history, apart from Jesus.

Simon Magus and Helena have gone down in western tradition as Dr Faust, the brilliant scholar, master of all arts, who sold his soul to the devil, and his mistress Helena, also called Marguerite, meaning 'pearl'. One of the guises adopted by Simon in the Clementine account, in fact, is that of Faustus, a Roman.[5] Marlowe's treatment of the story in the sixteenth century includes the point that Helena was an incarnation of Helen of Troy ('was this the face that launched a thousand ships?'). In the Hellenistic world it was accepted that political leaders should claim to be incarnations of gods or heroes of the past; this was one of the many beliefs held by Helena's followers.

The reason why she could be called Jezebel by her opponents was that she was the chief instrument in the execution of John the Baptist. John was likened to Elijah, the Old Testament prophet, and Queen Jezebel had been the enemy of Elijah. Queen Jezebel met a gruesome end: she was thrown down from a wall and eaten by dogs.[6] Helena's influence had become so dangerous that many wished such a fate on her.

She could literally be accused of harlotry, but it was a continuation of the sacred prostitution that had been practised in Samaritan religion centuries before. It was part of her role of 'prophetess', that is, a female priest. The ecstatic banquets of the Therapeuts, in which both men and women engaged in all night celebrations, must, in some communities, have led to sexual expression, especially in the Hellenistic world, where mystery cults worshipping female deities permitted sexual licence. 'Harlots' appear several times in the gospels. Jesus is said to have associated with them, meaning that his party, during the gospel period, included Helena.[7]

Her claim to be a female priest was denounced in the Book of Revelation, which describes the office she held in Ephesus at the time it was occupied by her successor, Bernice the Great Harlot:

I saw a woman sitting on a scarlet beast, full of names of blasphemy . . . The woman was clothed in purple and scarlet, and gilded with gold and precious stones and pearls, having a gold cup in her hand, full of abominations and the unclean things of her fornication.[8]

Her clothes were vestments. The purple meant that she claimed to be a lay bishop, a position permitted to women. But the scarlet meant that she claimed to be a cardinal. She was, in fact, taking over the position of Jesus as priest to Gentiles. Helena was a 'Sarah' rather than a 'Miriam', playing the part of Mother.

In Ephesus in particular there was acceptance of the idea of a priestess, as has been seen. One of the roles of a priestess, imitating Diana, was to act as an oracle, giving mysterious utterances from a shrouded chamber, which could be interpreted at will for their philosophy or political advice. Among the newly discovered gnostic writings from Nag Hammadi in Upper Egypt was a poem that was obviously intended to be used for this purpose. The title given to it on the manuscript is 'Thunder, Perfect Mind', and both these terms give a link with Helena, for she was said to be the Divine Thought of God, and 'Thunder' was one of the titles of a priest of Ephesus. A part of it reads:

> For I am the first and the last.
> I am the honoured one and the scorned one.
> I am the whore and the holy one . . .
> I am the silence that is incomprehensible
> And the idea whose remembrance is frequent.
> I am the voice whose sound is manifold
> And the Word whose appearance is multiple.
> I am the utterance of my name.[9]

In the gospels, Jesus is shown as having conversations with the Samaritan woman, with the Syrophoenician woman, and with Martha, all of the conversations raising points of theology or policy, in which the woman spoke as an intellectual equal.[10] All were names for Helena, and it was during this period that Jesus and Mary Magdalene, and Simon and Helena, were associated as comrades in mission. Together they had formed the Twelve Apostles, a new party that upheld more liberal Diaspora views against the narrow Palestinian views of John the Baptist. When the Baptist failed, their party took over, with Simon as Pope and Jesus as subordinate king. Martha and Mary were the wives of the Pope and of the king.

Simon Magus was the adviser of the tetrarch Antipas, siding with him in his feud with the royal Herods. This meant that he was behind the execution of the Baptist, which, as all records say, was ordered by the tetrarch.[11]

But as Mark's gospel appears to say, Herodias and Salome were the immediate instigators. Antipas had resented the Baptist's criticism of his illicit marriage with Herodias, and when, at a feast, Salome danced, Antipas promised to give her anything, and she asked for the head of the Baptist. (The 'head' that was brought in on a platter was not his actual head, but the headband with the letters signifying his rank. This is always the pesher meaning of *kephalē*, 'head'.)

Herodias did have a daughter named Salome, from her first marriage, but the text of Mark calls Salome 'the daughter of him of Herodias'.[12] A 'daughter' was a position in the hierarchy, as was 'son'. The phrase simply means that this Salome was an initiate. She was the same Salome who was present at the crucifixion.[13] This was Helena, who was the leader of the women at the cross, present to attend Simon Magus, who was on the central cross.[14] The name Salome was taken from the great Queen Salome, the founder of her order of women.

Helena was the instrument of Simon Magus in persuading the tetrarch to execute John the Baptist. The real reason was a political one, as Josephus shows when he says that the Baptist was put to death because the tetrarch feared that his political activity might antagonise

Rome. All were, in fact, aiming at overthrowing Rome, in their different ways. But Simon and John the Baptist were heads of different factions, each believing their own method to be the right one.

Mark's gospel had a reason for emphasising Salome's part and for telling the story in considerable detail, for another rumour was current: that it was Jesus who was responsible for the Baptist's death. One of the fragments of the Dead Sea Scrolls, written (as may be seen from the history) between March and September in AD 31 while the Baptist was under arrest, accused the Wicked Priest (one of its names for Jesus, meaning Anti-Priest, as he had illegally claimed the high priesthood) of plotting against the Baptist, the Teacher of Righteousness. The writer was at that time confident that the Teacher would survive, his confidence drawn from the words of an Old Testament psalm predicting the success of the righteous and the defeat of the wicked.[15]

Jesus was simply the subordinate leader; it was Simon who had the reason and authority to act against the Baptist. But one of the causes of the attack was the Baptist's excessive priestliness. The Baptist had the right to the title of Priest, but it was Jesus who had defied him on this point, claiming that priesthood was received by ordination, not by birth, a claim that threatened the whole of the Jewish religious establishment. So Jesus was singled out as the one to be blamed. With him, according to the scroll, were 'the men of Ephraim and Manasseh', that is Simon and the zealots.

By 49, when the letter to Thyatira was written, Jesus had separated from the zealots, turning from the anti-Herodian party of Simon to co-operate with Agrippa II. The benign reign of Claudius had brought about a new setting for Jesus' mission to Gentiles, and they now called themselves Christian. Helena, like Mary Magdalene her companion, was in a different religion. But because of the previous history she could still have influence in the convent at Thyatira. John Mark, to whom the first part of the letter to Thyatira was addressed, was still allowing her to exercise ministry, and Jesus rebuked him sharply for it.

Helena's name came from her association with Queen Helena of Adiabene, who in the late thirties AD began to receive instruction as a Gentile convert to the Jewish religion. Her conversion was a victory for the mission in the east, and was typical of the aims and methods of the party of Simon Magus. He, or his representative, was the merchant Ananias who figured in the history recorded by Josephus[16] (Simon and Helena were the Ananias and Sapphira of a story of financial exploitation in Acts; and Simon was the Ananias who was in Damascus in AD 40).[17] Helena would have had a part as spiritual adviser to the queen, and taken her name according to the custom of servants using the name of the master.

Queen Helena came from Adiabene, a small country on the east border of Mesopotamia. She had two sons, both of them born of incest with her brother. The younger son was named Izates. Mother and son turned to the Jewish religion, being instructed by Eleazar of Galilee and by Ananias. Hers was a wholehearted commitment which resulted in her giving generous financial gifts to the Jewish people. In the case of Izates a dispute arose between the two Jewish missionaries as to whether he should be circumcised or not. Ananias thought it was not necessary, but Izates gave way to the more eastern view, held by Eleazar of Galilee, and was circumcised.

The family of Izates remained involved in Jewish politics, and Queen Helena built a residence in Jerusalem. At the time of the fall of Jerusalem some family members asked for Roman protection, and were brought as hostages to Rome.[18]

The case of Izates illustrated the tensions between the eastern and western versions of the mission. For a Gentile to accept circumcision was the opposite of what the

Christians stood for. But the issue was a live one in Ephesus, where the eastern and western traditions mingled. A man who had received circumcision and lived in every way like a Jew was called a 'proselyte', whereas this term was not used for a man who was sympathetic with many aspects of Jewish thought but was not circumcised. Proselytes were attached to the Herodians in the west, not to the Christians, but in the forties AD they were still organisationally linked.

This was the reason why in two of his letters, written in AD 49, Jesus spoke in the most condemnatory terms of the Nicolaitans, and in the seventh letter made a strong attack on the recipient, who, he said, was 'neither cold nor hot'. He added: 'I will spew you out of my mouth'. Nicolaus was a name for a proselyte of Antioch listed as the last of a group of seven ministers in Acts.[19] He was the active head of the class of proselytes which included Izates, and, based in Antioch, could go between east and west. The influence of his version of the mission was still being felt in Ephesus, and Jesus saw it as a very great danger.

When he said: 'You are neither cold nor hot', his meaning was that Nicolaus had become so Jewish that he observed festivals only in spring and autumn (Passover and Atonement-Tabernacles), and refused to keep the lesser festivals in winter and summer, which were not major Jewish feasts.

Nicolaus the proselyte is accused of other transgressions by the Christian party. He appears also as 'Brimstone', meaning that he was a sodomite, likened to the men of Sodom on whom brimstone rained down.[20] Living as a celibate, in the highest form of life open to proselytes, and permitting sodomy as eastern monastics did, he would have acted as a 'eunuch', going between husband and wife in a dynastic marriage. Agrippa I had a servant named Blastus who was 'over his bedchamber'.[21] The implication of Acts 12 is that Blastus was the one who administered the poison to Agrippa, under the orders of

Simon Magus. Simon was the superior of eastern proselytes who could come to the west, their early teacher being Helena. Nicolaus, as both chief proselyte and chief 'eunuch', may be seen as the same as Blastus, who had acted under Simon's orders until the schism, then had joined western Herodians under Agrippa II, but still retained his acquired Jewish identity.

The strong expressions used against the mission to proselytes by Jesus, and by Paul in his epistles, came from an acute awareness of the great historical significance of the work in which they were engaged. They knew that they were at a turning point of Greco-Roman culture, and that there was no room for personal sentiment. The doctrine and practices of the Jewish form of the mission must be removed from the province of Asia, and it was one of the purposes of the letters to seven churches to bring about a reform with the approval of the newly crowned Agrippa II.

Jesus' messages in the letters continued to express the ideals he had formed years before, ideals which had separated him more and more from his former superior and the woman who helped him. But his feelings about their betrayal must have been deepened by the memory that he had once hung on a cross beside Simon, and that he had once discussed theology and the directions of the mission with 'the woman Jezebel'.

CHAPTER 7

'I, John, your brother'

THE SEERS OF EPHESUS

In the opening chapter of the Book of Revelation, the writer introduces himself: 'I, John, your brother, your fellow in tribulation and kingdom and endurance, was in the island called Patmos on account of the word of God and the testimony of Jesus. I was in the spirit on the Lord's day, and I heard behind me a loud voice like a trumpet'. . .[1] He goes on to record what was, apparently, given to him in a vision, and the whole Book of Revelation has the form of visions seen by someone who calls himself 'I'.

It has always been known that the seer of Revelation was one of the men associated with Jesus who was called 'John', most likely the John who with a James was one of the 'sons of Zebedee', both being called 'Sons of Thunder'. The source called the Clementine literature supplies further information, giving reason for seeing that James and John were the two brothers called Niceta and Aquila who appear in that story, belonging to the highest ranks of Roman society. They were part of the story of Simon Magus and Helena, and all the people in the story had a significant part in the introduction of Christianity into Rome.

John appears under his Roman name, Aquila ('the Eagle') in other parts of the New Testament, working with his wife Priscilla as a missionary, both being close associates of Paul.[2] It becomes apparent, through an understanding of the chronological structure of Revelation, that he was the seer who wrote only one of its parts. Although his section has been placed first in the final compilation of the book, there was an earlier section, written by James Niceta, and two subsequent sections by two later seers. James and John were the seers of the first two thirds of the book, whose work gave the history of the Herodian mission to Gentiles from AD 1–51.

The actual history of James and John is given in two books called the Clementine Recognitions and Homilies.[3] These have long been known to scholars, but dismissed as 'theological romance'. Their own claim to emanate from the forties AD is not taken seriously, and they are thought to be the result of later Jewish Christian tendencies developing in opposition to mainstream Christianity, which was Pauline.

They certainly have the form of a romance of the kind that was popular in the Hellenistic world. Stories which were probably the bestsellers of their day told tales of wandering thaumaturges dealing in a mixture of magic and philosophy. The stories were an easily digestible way of passing on current philosophical thought, and in addition setting up model figures for popular emulation.

According to the two books (one of them a revision of the other), a man named Clement, a Roman, had set out on a philosophical quest which led him eventually to be instructed in the kind of Christianity taught by the apostle Peter in Caesarea in the late thirties and forties AD. He had had an unhappy family history: his father was a relative of the Caesar family (as is frequently emphasised), and his mother was of the Caesar family also. Their marriage had been arranged by Augustus Caesar. Twin brothers, Niceta and Aquila, had been born in the early years of the first century AD. Then Clement was born, about AD 10.[4] When he was five, his mother had a vision which caused her to leave the country with her twin sons, leaving Clement behind. She later said that she had invented the vision, and the real reason was that she was being pursued by her husband's brother, and being a virtuous woman decided to flee. Her husband put her on board a ship to Athens, to take her twin sons to that city to be educated. But the ship was wrecked, and she was cast up on an island, where she was taken in by another woman and lived for many years as a mendicant. Her sons were captured by pirates and taken to Caesarea, where they were sold to a woman named Justa, who was the Syrophoenician woman of the gospels. She had become converted to the new religion and consequently had been divorced by her husband. The two boys were brought up by her, and their education was given them by Simon Magus. But they subsequently changed from his doctrine to that of Zacchaeus, the man who climbed the sycamore tree in Luke's gospel.

When Clement, still in Rome, was twelve, his father left, to search for any news of the mother, and he himself disappeared. In the late thirties AD Clement was attracted by the teaching of the apostle Barnabas, who was preaching in Rome. He followed the new religion to Judea, arriving in Caesarea, where Peter was engaged in debate with Simon Magus. The debates form the substance of the books. They uphold Peter's doctrine, which was not very like that of Paul, against the magical teachings of Simon.

A surprising series of coincidences followed, resulting in the bringing together of all of Clement's family. Niceta and Aquila were already followers of Peter. The mother was discovered on her island during a visit by Peter, and then the father also, in the guise of an old workman. The father recounted the philosophical quest that had led him to this point, making passing remarks about the infidelity of women, who 'are adulteresses, and love their own slaves, and end their days in foreign travel and in waters'. He added that his own wife had fallen in love with a slave.[5] He began to prepare for baptism, but problems arose when he was found to have the face and appearance of Simon Magus, even though the voice was that of the father (whose name was Faustus).

At this point Cornelius, the centurion of Acts 10, was consulted. He had been sent by Caesar to Caesarea on public business, and had authority to destroy sorcerers. Simon was told that he was being sought, and fled. Peter then devised a stratagem, to send the father, Faustus, to Antioch, pretend to be Simon, and renounce the denunciations of Peter that Simon was known to have uttered in Antioch. The father co-operated, and as a reward had his own face restored to him. All ended happily, with Peter, having worked many healing miracles, in control in Antioch.

According to another document in the Clementine collection, Peter, in the early sixties AD, knowing that his time had come near to die, handed over to Clement as his successor. Clement wrote to James the Lord's brother in Jerusalem, where he 'ruled the holy church of the Hebrews'. (James died in AD 62.) Peter spoke of handing over his 'chair of teaching', as if he were primarily a teacher of philosophy.[6]

Given the new information about the background of Christianity, the Clementine books may be seen to have arisen in the following circumstances.

The Jewish ascetic movement organised as a mission in the time of Herod the Great had reached Rome before the turn of the millennium. It was respected as a new religious philosophy, and known to have places of retreat for ascetics leaving the world; those for women and Gentiles being on islands of the Mediterranean.

The father and mother of Clement did indeed belong to the imperial family, and this was of the greatest importance for the subsequent history. The sexual licence of the Roman court was in full sway, and the mother had an affair with a slave (later alluded to by the father), resulting in the birth of Niceta and Aquila. The subsequent child Clement was, however, the father's son. In about AD 15 further trouble in the marriage arose, with an involvement by the mother with her husband's brother.

The father (Faustus or Faustinianus) then sent his wife away to one of the convents on a Mediterranean island. Islands were commonly used as places of exile. The twin boys were sent away also, as they were not the father's sons. The public reason given, for the purpose of saving face, was that she was taking them to Athens to be educated, but then the ship had been wrecked and she and the boys were lost.

Niceta and Aquila were put into one of the schools for orphans run by the ascetic movement in Caesarea. This had been the origin of the Jewish celibate system: priests from the local shrines had taken in unwanted children who had been exposed, using them as acolytes in the shrines, and giving them some of their own education.[7]

As Gentiles they were placed in one of the Gentile orders, in which their superior was a woman. Helena, the mistress of Simon Magus, became the head of the order. One of her many titles was the Syrophoenician woman.[8] 'Justa' was also a title, meaning that she belonged to a high celibate grade; it was the feminine form of Justus.

Helena thus became the 'Mother of James and John', as the two boys were given Jewish names. They also became the 'sons of Zebedee', for 'Zebedee' was one of the many pseudonyms of Simon Magus.[9]

Simon, as head of the gnostics, was in charge of the school system, which was influenced by his doctrine. With changes in the leadership, the doctrine of Sadducees prevailed against him, and the two young men were then under the authority of 'Thunder', a name used by the Sadducee priest, frequently found in Revelation.

They finally modified their Sadducee views to espouse the Christian views of Peter, including a belief in resurrection. With Peter and Andrew, they engaged in mission to other Gentiles, helping them 'catch fish', their occupation at the opening of the gospels.[10]

In about AD 39, in the reign of Gaius Caligula, Barnabas was preaching in Rome. Clement, the survivor of the family, had philosophical leanings which led him to be independently converted to the new religion, now in its Christian form. He brought Barnabas into his house and protected him from the jeering of the pagan philosophers. Then he, too, went to Judea – possibly also to escape the madness of Caligula – and received instruction from Peter, becoming part of his entourage as he travelled to different centres in Palestine.

The reunion with other members of the family was not due to coincidence, but carefully staged by Peter and the leaders, who had become aware that all members of a distinguished Roman family were now converted to their religion. Once the father had been persuaded to give up Magian views (the meaning of his having the 'face' of the Magus) and to denounce Simon with a public renunciation, it was a tremendous coup for the Christians. The Clementine books were written as propaganda, in the form of a typical romance of the times, leaving out the institutional workings behind the simple story of a family brought together. They contain a real history, and were written no later than AD 43, when Antioch had just been gained by the Christians.

When Peter and the Christians resettled in Rome in AD 61, Clement (mentioned briefly by his name in one of Paul's epistles)[11] was still a follower of Peter, and was, in fact, appointed by him as his successor to the lay papacy in 62. (There was still, at this stage, a Priest-Pope.) Clement's social influence would have been a major factor in strengthening the movement in Rome.

The differences in doctrine between the two brothers

make it possible to discern their two different hands at work in the Book of Revelation.

James Niceta was the first seer (here called 'A') who finished his work in 44 at the time of the schism between east and west. He still had loyalty to Jonathan Annas, 'Thunder', and still held to the Jewish priesthood, agreeing with Peter that a Jewish Sadducee priest was necessary. James Niceta imitated Jonathan Annas in his role of 'Elijah', wanting to call down fire from heaven on the Magians, like a latterday Elijah.[12] The Magians were on an opposite side to Annas on the question of Rome, and James Niceta in his Part A of Revelation expressed his own loyalty to Rome and hatred of Jewish zealotry through his attacks on the Beasts, and especially Beast 666.

James Niceta was consequently opposed to Jesus, who in the gospel period had been allied with Simon, not on the issue of Rome but on the issue of the rights of the laity against the priests, and the dropping of the circumcision requirement. Jesus had been on the same political side as Jonathan Annas, but deeply opposed to him in his pompous view of his own importance as a priest.

The most striking aspect of James Niceta's Part A of Revelation (Rev 8:6 to 14:5) is that he ignores Jesus. In his account of the 'week' AD 30–37,[13] he deals with the Baptist ('the locusts'), Jonathan Annas ('the winged horses'), and another prominent figure of this period ('Apollyon'), but he omits altogether the crucifixion or any reference to Jesus. James the brother of Jesus appears, as the 'star fallen from heaven'. James was, it is true, the legitimate David at this time under Caiaphas the high priest. But James Niceta as a follower of Jonathan Annas was a Hellenist, who held Jesus to be legitimate. His opposition was to Jesus' association at this time with zealots, a fact that had given the reason for his crucifixion.

He does record the events of AD 6,[14] when Jesus at the age of twelve became legitimate on the accession of

Ananus the Elder as high priest. But the emphasis in the story is on Mary and the Sadducee's support of her against the Pharisee 'Dragon'.

In 44 James Niceta joined with Jonathan Annas and many others in turning against Agrippa I. According to Acts, Agrippa just before his death became 'angry with those of Tyre and Sidon', and attacked James the brother of John. Agrippa had quarrelled with the Roman governor of Syria, and James' order, which was based in Tyre and Sidon, would have supported Roman interests, as had also the high priest Matthew Annas.[15]

James Niceta was now given a measuring rod, and told to 'rise up and measure the sanctuary of God'. The meaning is that he now adopted the eremitical life, and went to a place outside Ephesus where he established a new hermitage, carefully modelling it on the pattern of the vestry at Qumran, the central place of worship.

After the traumatic events of 44, when Paul's influence in the western party increased, James' place as seer in the cathedral of Ephesus was taken by his brother John Aquila. John Aquila, with Priscilla, was in Rome with Peter's party between 46 and 49, and was driven out of Rome to Patmos and Ephesus early in 49. His Part B of Revelation (1:1 to 8:5, and parts of Chapter 11) gives the history of the years 44 – 51 in Ephesus. Jesus was now given every honour, and called the Christ. There appears for the first time Theophilus Annas, the 'twenty-four elders', who was in sympathy with Paul.[16] Theophilus, the next Annas brother after Matthew, had become high priest in Jerusalem in September AD 37, and had at once led the people in taking an oath of loyalty to Rome.[17] He was strongly in favour of peace with Rome, and it was to him that Luke dedicated his gospel and Acts.

James Niceta's preoccupation with the Beast was replaced in Part B by interest in the new directions Christians were taking, especially the canonisation of their new scripture.

John, after 51, crossed to Corinth, where with his wife Priscilla he worked with Paul.[18] In early 54 he and Priscilla went with Paul back to Ephesus, as is shown in Acts,[19] and by 55 they were in Rome, probably having travelled there with Agrippa II when he went to pay court to the new emperor, Nero. Paul's letter to the Romans sends greetings to them.[20] They returned to Ephesus, and were there when Paul wrote his final letter from Rome.[21]

In AD 54 the place of seer C in Ephesus was taken by a man who may be identified with Tychicus, named in Acts and in Paul's letters from Rome.[22] He was called by a term meaning 'the initiate of Asia', the province of which Ephesus was the capital. He had been included in Paul's party in Troas in early 58, and went to join him in Rome at his imprisonment, in March 61. In a letter written about this time, Paul referred to him, saying to a church in Asia: 'Tychicus will tell you all about my affairs; he is a beloved brother and faithful minister and fellow servant in the Lord; I have sent him to you'. In another letter: 'Tychicus I have sent to Ephesus'.

Tychicus' writing reflects Pauline doctrine about Jesus, but shows that he was above all a servant of Agrippa II. He went back with him to Judea in June 62, and stayed there during the critical years leading up to the war, which he described. He even volunteered for military service for the defence of Jerusalem in 68, joining those who were summoned to 'Armageddon'.[23] But when Agrippa II left the country the following year, he went with him, going first to Rome and then back to Ephesus, where he witnessed Bernice, the Great Harlot, presiding at a communion service, 'sitting on a scarlet beast', and turned decisively against Herodian zealotry.[24] But he felt sufficient grief at the fall of Jerusalem to record the three 'Lamentations', commemoration services that were held when the news of the fall of the city was received, using words with the usual double meanings to convey the inner history. His work finishes with the account of the reaction in Ephesus to the news of the fall of Masada, in 74.

The last writer, seer D, of Chapters 20 to 22, began his work in AD 100, and there is apparently no way of discovering his identity.[25] Later in his career he was given the title of John, as a successor of John Aquila. He wrote with joy about the development of the hermitage outside Ephesus into a true 'New Jerusalem', that is, a fully Christian monastery, using a plan based on the original Temple Scroll. There was still a Sadducee priest, but no reigning Herods, and only Christians in the ministry and congregation.

The four seers wrote a book which complements the gospels and Acts in giving a record of the history, but does it from the more eastern perspective of Ephesus rather than that of Rome. Its tone, style and much of its contents are very close indeed to the Dead Sea Scrolls, and in many ways it acts as a link between the two sets of literature. Its plan of the New Jerusalem is directly dependent on the plan in the Temple Scroll, and shows exact knowledge of its detail in the order of the gates. It uses the calendar of the scrolls, as the gospels do also, and draws on the symmetry of sevens, the weeks and the jubilees, in a way that is characteristic of the scrolls and related literature. The book which was 'revealed' to the seers of Ephesus is a perfect product of the secret ascetic movement that began at Qumran and became so westernised that it ended as the Christian Church.

CHAPTER 8

The Four Horsemen of the Apocalypse and the Four Living Creatures

MATTHEW, MARK, LUKE AND JOHN

Like many other images of the Book of Revelation, the four horsemen of Chapter 6, appearing in the vision of heaven after the Lamb opened the first of seven seals, have always caught the religious imagination. They have become symbols of the uncanny, ghostly steeds riding from the skies, bringing with them omens of coming doom.

> And I saw when the Lamb opened one of the seven seals, and I heard one of the four living creatures say, as with a voice of thunder, 'Come!'
> And I saw, and behold a white horse, and the one sitting on it had a bow; and a crown was given to him, and he went out conquering and to conquer.[1]

The same formula is repeated in successive verses, so that

there are in all four horses – white, red, black and green (the latter *chlōros*; translated 'pale' to avoid the apparent improbability). Each is associated with one of the four living creatures that have been mentioned in Revelation Chapter 4: the first like a lion, the second like a calf, the third a man, the fourth like a flying eagle. The four living creatures are familiar to students of the Old Testament as the emblems on the chariot throne of God described in the Book of Ezekiel.

From an understanding of the system that lies behind the history, the meaning of the horses and the horsemen and the four living creatures, and the events in which they took part, can be discovered.

It was no vision, but it was an event of such significance that the setting of a vision was appropriate and in many ways necessary. What was actually happening took place in the Ephesus cathedral, with the seer sitting in the front row of the congregation, and ministers on the three-tiered structure before him. There were two connected ceremonies; the first, described in Chapter 4, beginning at noon on the Day of Pentecost, which in AD 49 fell on 1 June; and the second, described in Chapter 6, a little over a fortnight later.

At the first of these ceremonies King Agrippa II was present, sitting on the upper tier. The main purpose of the service was to confirm his coronation, for he had acceded to the throne in this year. His primary coronation had been held in Jerusalem, but he was also a king to Jews of the Diaspora, and Ephesus was the centre where the Herodian version of Judaism was the most favoured.

But there was another, more lasting purpose for the ceremony. The time had come for the Christians to declare that they had a new canon of scripture, the New Testament. For them, the Old Testament was all but obsolete, and for the past two decades they had been preparing what was consciously intended as a new scripture. The four gospels and two of the epistles were ready, and the young Agrippa, who had considerable sympathy with the Christianised form of his religion, was willing to allow his second coronation to be marked by the publication and canonisation of the new set of books, giving them the royal seal of approval.

Present at the ceremony were Agrippa, his current Priest-Pope Matthew Annas, the Herod crown prince, and Matthew's deputy. At the time when the canonisation process began, the four evangelists were grouped on the ground floor, just in front of the congregation. And to this same place, a little later in the service, came Jesus. He had recently arrived back from Rome, and was present for what was to him a crowning achievement. Not only had the Christian version of the religion been created through his teaching and his suffering, but he had been, in all likelihood, the inspiration behind the gospels, the deviser of the form which both told the real historical truth, yet was a suitable scripture for simpler believers.

The six books were attached as an appendix to a bound book[2] containing the Septuagint, the Greek translation of the Old Testament. Each one was closed off by a seal, a tie brought up from its back page to its title page and fastened with a wax seal, indicating that it must not be read until the seal was officially removed. A seventh seal connected the back page with the title page of the whole. At the Pentecost ceremony Agrippa unfastened the tie binding the whole collection, showing that he permitted it to be read, and later in that ceremony Jesus was given the privilege of displaying the main title page. The occasion was marked by a hymn of praise to him.

At the following ceremony a fortnight later, the real work began, of instituting the process of teaching the new scripture. At this service, the 'rider on the white horse' appeared, and the first 'living creature' said to him: 'Come!'. The first of the gospels to be studied was opened by Jesus: 'the Lamb opened one of the seven seals'. Now, over six successive seasons, or eighteen months, each book was to be studied at the Christian school in Ephesus.

To introduce a new scripture was no easy task. For more than a thousand years Judaism had centred around its Law, written first on portable tablets, and later developed in the form of scrolls. They were the most holy objects that Israel owned, and in the previous five hundred years had been the centre of all their worship, replacing the temple as a sign of Jewish identity. When it had become necessary for Diaspora Jews to have them translated into Greek, since they no longer understood Hebrew, the authority of the Greek translation had to be supported by a story that the work had been done under divine supervision by seventy-two elders in seventy-two days, and the story gave rise to the name 'the Seventy' (Septuagint) for the new version.[3]

On similar previous occasions in their history, when great innovations had been introduced, the people were told that the new doctrine had been given in a vision from heaven. Ezekiel's awesome chariot, in which God was seen riding above shimmering fire in the midst of a rainbow, on a chariot drawn by four living creatures, had the purpose of giving to the Jewish exiles in Babylon the belief that God had come to them in Babylon to be worshipped, and was no longer confined to his temple in Jerusalem, so there was no need for the exiles to 'sit down by the waters of Babylon and weep'.[4]

To put forward the idea of a new revelation in a new scripture was an even greater change, and was rightly seen to mean the end of Jewish identity. But westernised Jews, and especially the Gentiles who met with them, were ready for it. They had their salvation history, in the story of the sufferings of Jesus, and the moment had come for one of the very great occasions, a new scripture for a new religion. The occasion was described as if it were a vision, and at the same time the detail of what had actually happened given, for those who understood.

The four gospels were intended from the start as the

substitute for the Old Testament, which was thought of by Diaspora Jews as having four divisions: the Law, the Former Prophets, the Latter Prophets and the Writings.[5] The remaining two sets of New Testament books ready by AD 49 corresponded to the secondary non-canonical books which Diaspora Jews attached to their Old Testament. It was around the more sacred books, the four gospels, that the imagery was developed of the four horsemen and the four living creatures.

The four horsemen really were horsemen, that is, they were priests who visited villages in the Diaspora, riding on horses because of their superior status. More humble persons rode on donkeys. Because of the distances, the priest would come for a season, arriving on the 31st of the solar calendar, the day when the season was considered to begin, staying for three months to teach, and leaving on the following 31st, after handing over to another teacher. Because their organisation was based on the four seasons of the year, they used the colours for the seasons, carrying a banner of the appropriate colour, attached to the horse's neck. The priest who came for summer, the Pentecost season that was primary in Ephesus, carried a white banner. Following him, the priest for autumn carried a red one, after him a black one for winter, and after him a green one for spring. The colours in Revelation 6 appear in this order, the correct chronological one.

In the three-tiered cathedrals of Herodians, there was a chair on the middle tier used by the priest as teacher. Bringing with him into the cathedral the coloured banner from his horse's neck, he attached it to the chair, making it a 'white horse', by the method of association on which much of the special language depends.

After holding his session with Jews on these great days, the priest used the chair for subsequent informal teaching. It was at the informal part of the service that the books of the New Testament were opened and their study commenced.

102

It was the custom in Diaspora communities for the local leader to invite the visiting priest to take the chair, saying: 'Come!'. Each of the four 'living creatures' in the vision of Revelation, saying 'Come!' to the 'horseman', was one of the evangelists, acting as leader of a Diaspora community that had become Christian, inviting the visiting Jewish priest to inaugurate the study of the new book, in order to show that there was continuity with Jewish tradition, and yet an independent local authority.

The early Christian father Irenaeus, writing about AD 180, associated the four gospels with the four living creatures of Revelation and of Ezekiel,[6] and the same tradition has continued in Christian imagery and architecture. Mark's gospel was signified by the Lion, Luke by the Calf, Matthew by the Man, and John by the Flying Eagle. The association has been thought to be fanciful, but it is, rather, valuable evidence for a connection that did not begin with Irenaeus but went back to the original concept of the gospels.

The four living creatures of Ezekiel were emblems of priests in their own time, and had come to be emblems of four classes of ministers who led the communities in Palestinian villages and in the Diaspora. Christian ministers had taken over the same positions, giving them names that have passed into Christian usage. 'The Man' was a kind of levite, and his office became that of cardinal. 'The Lion' was a local married bishop. A celibate bishop acted in a position that had become that of 'Flying Eagle', and an elder acted in the position of 'Calf', giving the word 'presbyter', which became 'priest'. (For further on these positions, see pp.169–170).

Matthew's gospel, treated as the primary one, and the equivalent of the Law (as shown by the Sermon on the Mount), was symbolised by the superior of the four, 'the Man'. Mark, which had been the first one written in historical form, and was associated with Peter, a married man, belonged to 'the Lion'. It corresponded to the

Former Prophets, books which were primarily histories. Luke, a Gentile presbyter who was below Matthew and Peter in rank, had written his gospel as the 'Calf', and his book corresponded to the Latter Prophets, containing parables and passages in oracle form. The gospel of John had had a special history (as will be shown on pp.526–527), and by now was relegated to be equal to the inferior Writings, and the celibates associated with it in the position of 'Flying Eagle' were also not highly regarded by the writers of Revelation, who were married Gentiles.

The four 'horsemen' who responded to the invitation to teach were all Jewish priests who were in sympathy with Diaspora Judaism, even though they came from Judea. This meant that they were Sadducees, Samaritans, or celibates equal to priests. There were no Pharisees, who were traditionally supporters of Palestinian Judaism. The first two in Chapter 6 may be seen from the detail to be the younger Annas brothers. The white banner was carried by Theophilus Annas, who was the resident priest at Ephesus under Matthew Annas, opening the year's study that was to take place in a school attached to the cathedral. He would teach Mark's gospel, placed first in the curriculum as the simplest, from June to September AD 49.

His younger brother carried the red banner for autumn. Ananus the Younger, or 'Red', was to 'take peace from the earth',[7] for he was prepared for more direct nationalist action than Matthew, who was called 'Peace'. After Theophilus opened Luke's gospel (which was dedicated to him), Ananus taught it for a season, for one of his duties was to be levitical head of the province where Luke had his Gentile centre.[8]

In December, the other major season for the Julian calendar, Ananus handed over to the priest with the black banner for winter. This, as may be seen from the detail, was Ananias the Samaritan, who had become the reigning high priest in Jerusalem in that year. For Samaritans, who kept the Julian calendar, the December solstice was a significant feast but not a traditional one, and Ananias was free to travel to his Diaspora constituency. Matthew's gospel, as the highest of all, corresponding to the Law, was opened at that season and its study commenced.

When the 'fourth seal was opened', in March AD 50, 'the rider on the green horse' appeared. 'His name was Death, and Hades followed him'. A man whose name was 'Death' had the power of excommunication, a symbolic putting to death. He was a Chief Monk, a head of one of the fully celibate orders based on the monastic Essenes, who gave 'life' when a man received their initiation, and 'death' if they expelled him. In the Diaspora he was a Magus, of the higher class of Diaspora Essenes. A Magus who was present at a Herodian service was one who had joined the Herodian side at the schism, and at this time he was Atomus, the Cypriot 'magician' (see Chapter 5). With him was 'Hades', his deputy. It may be seen from the history that he was Antipas Herod, who held the position of a Scribe and a monastic treasurer.

In this negative context the gospel of John was opened and studied, for it was perceived to be advocating celibacy and support of the monastic system, rejected by the seers of Ephesus who believed in marriage and life in the world. The gospel was studied in its original form, without its final chapter, at this season. But it was already undergoing a process of re-assignment, as may be discovered from the accounts of it in the Church fathers.[9] With the addition of its final chapter, putting Peter in a favourable light, it would be attributed to the party of the seers, and the name of John Aquila be linked with it. In this form it was grouped with the Epistle of Peter, part of the secondary literature that would be studied at the 'fifth seal', from June to September AD 50.

The viewpoint of the party of Jewish Christians, headed by James the brother of Jesus, was expressed in the Epistle of James. It was the last of the secondary literature, studied after the sixth seal was opened, from September to December 50.[10]

At the December solstice in AD 50 the seventh seal was opened. The last page of the book, to which the main tie had been attached before being brought up to the title page, was turned over by Matthew Annas,[11] showing that the studies were completed. It would be some years before Paul's epistles, only just commenced, would be added, with Acts and other epistles joining them to complete the New Testament in its present form.

But it was in AD 49 – very much earlier than has been supposed by modern biblical scholars – that the New Testament began, according to the record preserved in the Book of Revelation. It was not a haphazard growth, but commenced with full consciousness of a new scripture. Those who had written the books knew well that a religion transcending Judaism, and very much needed in the Greco- Roman world, had developed in their hands, and needed its own scripture. But they inaugurated it as an addition to the Septuagint, in order to avoid a radical break with the past. The Septuagint and the New Testament would be bound together for some time to come, and the Christian Bible would keep the Old Testament as the forerunner of its new revelation.

CHAPTER 9

The Great Winepress of the Wrath of God

HOW THE CHURCH CAME TO ROME

So the angel swung his sickle on the earth and gathered the vintage of the earth, and threw into the great winepress of the Wrath of God, and the winepress was trodden outside the city, and blood came out from the winepress, as far as the bridles of the horses, for one thousand six hundred stadia.[1]

In Rome, near the point where the Appian Way meets the road outside the ancient southern wall, there stands a church that is now called Domine Quo Vadis ('Lord, where are you going?'). Its name comes from the tradition that in AD 64 Peter, fleeing from Nero's persecution of Christians, saw at this spot a vision of Jesus, who persuaded him to go back to the city to face martyrdom. The church stands at the beginning of the area containing the catacombs, warrens of connected underground chambers, each with long rows of burial niches, known to have been used by the early Christians. Hundreds of small oil lamps, used to light the passageways, are still to be seen there.

Inside the city of Rome, close to the Colosseum and not far from the Forum, there stands the entrance to the church of St Clement.[2] The visitor goes through an ordinary porch at street level, then is taken down eighteen metres and two thousand years, to rooms that were part of a house here before the great fire of Rome in AD 64.

In yet another part of Rome, on the large island in the Tiber River, stands the church of St Bartholomew. This is the name that is used in the list of Twelve Apostles for John Mark.[3] The Tiber Island has known connections with Simon Magus. A stone has been found there, bearing the inscription 'To Simon the Holy God', confirming what Justin the second century historian included in his account of Simon and Helena:

> He (Simon) was considered a god, and, as a god, was honoured by you with a statue, which statue was erected on the river Tiber, between the two bridges, and bore this inscription in the language of Rome, 'Simoni Deo Sancto'.[4]

At the end of the Book of Acts, detail is given of the places that Paul and his party came to when they arrived in Rome in March AD 61: 'And so we came to Rome. And the brethren there, hearing about us, came to the meeting place to us, as far as the Forum of Appius and the Three Taverns'.[5]

From these points, and from many details in the pesher of the gospels, Acts, and Revelation, it is possible to discover how the Christian Church came to Rome, and where it first met.

The history began in the house used by the ruling Herods when they were in Rome. Herod the Great already cultivated the Romans, and his sons and their sons were educated there. Agrippa I was the most Romanised, moving in the highest circles as a young man, a close friend of one of the sons of Tiberius, and a special favourite of Antonia, who was a mother and grandmother of emperors. She had been a friend of his mother, and when he brought himself close to bankruptcy through lavish entertaining, she helped pay his debts.[6] The Herod house was the natural centre for Jewish interests in Rome. Before Agrippa, Archelaus must have lived there while he fought his case with the courts on the question of the succession.

Its exact location cannot be known, but when the system of distances is added to the interpretation, it is seen that it was five stadia, about a kilometre, north of the church of Domine Quo Vadis, probably just inside the ancient southern wall. Herod's house was the place that Acts calls 'the Three Taverns' ('Tavern 3').

It was called a 'tavern' because the Herods entertained there, with no restriction on fermented wine. Here, Gentiles from the emperor downwards were received. If they took wine with Herod as a sign of friendship, they were counted as a kind of initiate of his religion. An emperor who had received this form of 'membership' was called 'Babylon the Great', for 'Babylon' was a pseudonym for Rome. Not all emperors became 'Babylon the Great' – Nero did not – but those who did were given a lamentation at their death: 'He has fallen, Babylon the Great has fallen'. Claudius (AD 41–54) was especially friendly, and later the short-lived Vitellius (one of the several emperors of AD 69).[7]

After AD 6, when Judea came under the direct rule of Rome, it was important that the procurators appointed to the country should be entertained, for their attitude to the Jewish religion would make all the difference. In Judea itself, the resentment of the Roman occupation was so great that AD 6 was called 'the Period of Wrath', and the procurator himself was called 'the Wrath'.[8] But in Rome the appointed representatives were entertained lavishly, so that the dining chamber in Herod's house was called 'the Winepress', and 'the Winepress of the Wrath of God' (since the Sadducee priest, called 'God', gave the token initiation).

Other Gentiles of more humble rank were entertained in Herod's house also, and some joined the Gentile orders as committed initiates. The form of mission that received and instructed them was called 'the Vineyard'. The emphasis on wine derived from the fact that among Essenes new wine was called 'the Drink of the Community', and was the main privilege given at full initiation, being the higher element in the sacred meal.

These needed a meeting place of their own, where they received instruction in this Herodian form of the Jewish religion. According to the strict rules about uncleanness observed among ascetics, rules which governed the location of all buildings, Gentiles must meet at an unclean place, 2000 cubits or five stadia away from a main building.[9] The location that became the Domine Quo Vadis church, outside the wall of Rome, fitted the rule.

Here Gentiles, with Jews of equal status, met for serious study and debate. But they took wine in limited quantities, keeping ascetic rules for sobriety. Sipping it only, and vesting it with a developed symbolism, they came to call it 'blood'. When they left the main house and came here, it could be said that 'blood flowed from the Winepress'.[10]

Their building, near the juncture of the road below the southern wall with the Appian Way, was called 'the Forum of Appius', for they conducted debates on the model of the Roman Forum, and Appius may have been a member. For travellers coming from other parts of the world, it was a meeting place, not only because of its location but because it followed the rule that a meeting place must be at this distance from the centre.[11] For these travellers, when they had arrived there they had arrived in Rome, and it was called, simply, 'Rome'. As the movement became Christianised, Herodian Gentiles meeting here did not use the word 'Christian', rather 'Roman'. Gentiles meeting here were under the ministry of Jews like Paul. When, at the end of Acts, the simple statement is given: 'And so we came to Rome', Paul had arrived at the Roman school, bringing with him Jesus and Luke. But now they would remain in Rome, to meet the tensions of the next few years that would result in the death of Paul.

The building was defined as an unclean one, and that meant that part of it could be used as a latrine. The rules for distances of unclean places in the Scrolls were set down in terms of latrines.[12] The underground section would be used for such a purpose. Moreover, it would also be used for burials of the dead, as a tomb had an equal degree of uncleanness. Under the Forum of Appius the catacombs were developed, extended into burial places of Christians, and, when it became necessary, used as hiding places from persecution.

A useful alternate reading of Luke 24:13 in the Sinaiticus text shows that a latrine was said to be 'at 160 stadia'.[13] This was derived from the fact that in the Wilderness of Judea a circuit was taken by pilgrims, beginning at an unclean place, totalling 160 stadia (about 32 kilometres). The distances were fixed by the rules for unclean buildings, and measured in terms of the walking rate. The unclean place, itself five stadia (about one kilometre) from the main centre, could be described as 'at 160 stadia', when it was seen as the starting point of the circuit. In the Revelation passage quoted above, 'the angel threw into the great winepress of the Wrath of God, and the winepress was trodden outside the city, and blood came out from the winepress, as far as the bridles of the horses, for (literally "from") one thousand six hundred stadia'. This is a typical passage from Revelation, where exact figures are given but appear to be incapable of application. But they do, in fact, say something very precise, and have the purpose of telling insiders exactly where they would find their fellows in Rome in times of persecution. Rome was province 10, as is known from the details of the system.[14] An unclean place was called 'at 160 stadia', and an unclean place in Rome, at the same distance, was 'at 1600 stadia', the multiple indicating the province. The building, a meeting place which was actually five stadia from the main centre, would be found by those familiar with the terminology. They would also know that as an unclean place it had an underground section used as a hiding place.

In AD 64, Jesus did indeed appear there, to Peter, and in the flesh. He had been hiding in the catacombs, but came up to the building, the known meeting place, to meet Peter and give him courage to go back.

Not all Jewish missionaries in Rome were attached to Herod's house. Wherever Herod was, Sadducees and Pharisees were dominant. But Essenes under Jacob-Heli had been appointed to Gentiles at the outset of the mission. They had varying relations with the Herods, and in the period when there were no Herods in power, from AD 6, Essenes in Rome continued their work, bringing Gentiles into their kind of Judaism, which greatly valued celibacy.

Essenes in Rome were unlikely to want to hide, for their purpose was peaceful. In the late thirties AD one of the brothers of Jesus, Joses who was called Barnabas,[15] came to Rome to encourage them and to do some preaching and teaching himself. Meeting with jeering from pagan philosophers, he was rescued by Clement, the highly placed Roman whose story has been told in Chapter 7. According to the Clementine books, Clement brought him into his house, protected him, and became converted to his religion.

This is surely historical fact, and the house was that which has now become the church of St Clement. Its association with Clement, the Pope of the late first century AD, is accepted, but it has been assumed that there was no real basis to it, and that the Clementine literature is late and unreliable. However, as has been seen, the literature may be relied on as historical once its genre is understood. It would follow that Clement, rescued by Barnabas and instructed in Judea in the Christian religion, allowed his house, when he returned to Rome, to be used as one of the centres of the mission which from being Essene had become Christian.

The building goes down to a level dated before AD 64, when it was clearly the house of a prosperous Roman, not far from the Forum, with a small shrine of Mithras for household worship. The Colosseum was built very close to it, later in the century, using Jewish slaves.

In addition to the missions of the Essenes and the ruling Herods, there was another mission in Rome, called 'the Figtree'. From 4 BC, the disputes about the Herodian succesion that had been fought out in Rome between the brothers Archelaus and Antipas had led to a splitting of Herodian loyalties.[16] Antipas must have established a different house, and the mission that continued from his house continued to be hostile to the ruling Herods. This mission, which looked to the Therapeuts of Egypt rather than to Palestinian Essenes for its ascetic discipline, was called 'the Figtree' because Therapeuts did not drink wine but were skilled in the medical arts. The Vineyard and the Figtree were associated as images for Israel in the Old Testament. The two Herodian missions were associated but had separate organisations. As a parable in Luke says, 'a Figtree was planted in a Vineyard'.[17]

Simon Magus was a subsequent leader of the zealot Figtree mission, closely associated with the tetrarch Antipas. John Mark, or Bartholomew, accepted the Magus and treated him sympathetically in his gospel. These are indications that Antipas' house was on the Tiber Island, associated with Simon Magus as has been seen, where St Bartholomew's church stands now.

Magians in their 'zeal' intended to take over from Rome

as a material power. Under the authority of 'Simon the Holy God' they stored money and arms in Rome, refusing to send back to Judea the fees their members paid them. When the 'slaves' came to collect the 'fruits of the Vineyard', these 'farmers', the Magians, illtreated them and held the money back.[18] In the words of the parables of the pounds and talents, they 'hid their money in the ground', withholding the planned profit of the mission.[19] It was they who were at the centre of a notorious episode in Rome in AD 19, when a rich Roman woman named Fulvia gave a great deal of money to Jewish missionaries, intended for the Jerusalem temple, and the money was kept for themselves by the missionaries. As a result, Jews were expelled from Rome,[20] and continuing episodes of this kind, as well as the growing evidence that the Jewish missionaries were part of an underground political movement, was the reason why there were further such expulsions later in the century.

The separation of the house of Archelaus from the house of Antipas, which was also the separation of the Vineyard from the Figtree, had been formalised in 1 BC, during the disputes about the succession. The Vineyard then drew up a new plan of mission, and a new financial policy, under Sadducee influence. Its missionaries would be 'workers', not 'slaves', paid a denarius a day, a modest living allowance, enabling them to be full time and not have to work at a trade.

With their continuing preoccupation with chronology, they believed that the Eschaton, the end of the present order, would come in AD 60, the year 4000. They had just sixty years to go, and they drew up a plan of mission whose detail is given through Matthew's parable of the Vineyard.[21] It was expressed through 'hours' which actually meant sets of years (the explanation of this will be given on pp.230–231). When, at the 'eleventh hour', a worker came who was resented by the rest, the reference is to the association between Agrippa II and the procurator

Felix, who arrived in Judea in AD 54 and, as has been seen, married Drusilla the sister of Agrippa, being accepted into Agrippa's close circle. Felix, who received a form of initiation, became a source of considerable embarrassment. His rule as procurator became increasingly unstable, supporting one then another of the warring factions among the Jews. With the co-operation of the Sicarii, one of the rising bands of militants in Judea, he was responsible for the death of Jonathan Annas. Finally, in AD 60, Festus was sent to arrest him, send him to Rome for trial, and take his place.[22]

The ship that took Felix to Rome also carried Paul, Jesus, Luke, Peter and others of their party. Paul was at this stage not a prisoner, but after their arrival in Rome, Felix lost his main source of help after his brother Pallas fell out of favour with the court. Paul, who was Felix's close adviser and instructor, was arrested. Paul was imprisoned by June 61, and after a few more years lost his life when Nero attacked all Christians.[23]

This was not the first visit of Jesus and his party to Rome. In about AD 47, the 'Beloved Son' had been 'sent into the Vineyard', in the words of the parable. Jesus made a visit there in the years following the end of his first marriage. With him were Peter, Luke and John Aquila, all of them part of the Essene mission.[24] But these years also followed Jesus' separation from Simon Magus. The 'farmers' of the Figtree mission on Tiber Island decided to attack Jesus and Peter's mission, now called Christian. They would drive them out of Rome, saying 'the inheritance will be ours'. The mission, they believed, should be Jewish, and the Christians had compromised it.

The Christians on their side were not passive. Early in AD 49 they held a demonstration in the hope of the first appearance of the end of the Last Jubilee, a time when their prophecy of the Restoration should have been fulfilled.[25] Suetonius, a Roman historian, has left a record of it: 'Since the Jews constantly made disturbances at the

115

instigation of Chrestus, he (Claudius) expelled them from Rome'.[26] It has never been doubted that 'Chrestus' means Christ; but this was no visionary leader, rather, the real person, as the words of Suetonius imply. Claudius at this time was taking advice from Jews who had had a longer association with the Roman court, to whom the Christians were a rebel faction.

The party of Jesus came back to Ephesus, where they were present on the Day of Pentecost for the scenes described in the first five chapters of Revelation. But they were determined to return to Rome. In both Ephesus and Greece, to which they went in AD 51, they were away from the true centre of their mission. Their opportunity came later in the decade after a change of emperor. With renewed hopes of an Eschaton in AD 60, they began their journey, at first travelling back to Jerusalem, where Paul became involved in party disputes. After one such debate Jesus spoke to him again, encouraging him and saying: 'As you have been a bishop in my party in Jerusalem, you will be appointed as a bishop in Rome', for they would soon be going there. They finally arrived in Rome in March AD 61.[27]

Jesus survived Nero's persecution of AD 64, protected by his supporters. He made occasional visits to Ephesus, his last being to the council of AD 70. Thereafter, his death and final resting place must be presumed to have been in or around Rome, which under the influence of his church was to become known as the Eternal City.

CHAPTER 10

The Second Death and the Lake of Fire and Brimstone

RIVAL MONASTERIES

'He who conquers shall not be hurt by the second death.'
'. . . The lake that burns with fire and brimstone, which is the second death.'[1]

The concept of a second death, found throughout the Book of Revelation, seems to be characteristic of its violent and often incomprehensible religious imagery. The 'lake of fire and brimstone', which also appears frequently, looks like a particularly harsh way of talking about eternal punishment. It has not, up till now, been questioned that they are religious images, to be accepted or rejected according to one's point of view, and meaning nothing more than ways of speaking of the afterlife.

In fact, both expressions are like the number 666. They are talking about monasteries, in the secret and indirect way used by those who feared and hated the system. A history of two monastic systems is being given.

Our sources for the celibate rule practised by the ascetics who wrote the Dead Sea Scrolls are chiefly to be found in the Temple Scroll and the Manual of Discipline. There we read of penances and exclusions for the men whose whole life was bound by the authority of the community. If they committed a trifling offence such as laughing, spitting, or were so lacking in bodily control that they had to leave a meeting before it concluded, they were punished by periods of exclusion from the sacred meal, typically thirty days.[2]

No difference was made between moral and physical imperfection. Both kinds rendered a man unclean, with the resultant loss of holiness earned from attendance at the sacred meal (called the Purity). When the holy city was regained and its series of courts built, reflecting grades of holiness, people with certain physical conditions would never be allowed into the inner court: a man who had had a nocturnal emission, a man who had had sexual intercourse, a blind man, a leper.[3]

At Qumran, which was originally built as the chief Essene monastery, there were four distinct areas. Its northern and southern parts were divided by the old Israelite wall which had marked the original enclosure.[4] The wall defined the holy section to the north, and outside it to the south were sent those who had been excluded from the monastery for different kinds of offences. Erring monks were sent outside for the set number of days. A man who had had a nocturnal emission, for example, had to stay outside for three days, 'wash his garments and bathe on the first day, and on the third day wash his garments and bathe, and after sunset he shall enter the sanctuary'.[5]

In the south-west area at Qumran there was a very large cistern which was different from all the others in that no steps led down into it. Those with steps were, clearly enough, used for baptismal rites and the various washings such as took place before the sacred meal. But this one was reached from the outside, and, moreover, was close to a long row of cubicles which are to be interpreted as latrines.[6] This was the unclean place to which the excluded were sent.

There was a corresponding area on the south-east, also outside the Israelite wall, but with a fine long hall which was clearly used for taking meals. In an adjacent 'pantry' a large number of eating bowls were found by the archaeologists, still stacked in position. This was not, as was at first conjectured, the refectory of enclosed monks, who would not come to an outside hall to take their sacred meal. It was the place to which visiting Essene villagers came when they brought the food tithes to the exiled priests, whom they supported in preference to those in the Jerusalem temple. In return for the tithes, the villagers, thinking of themselves as pilgrims, were permitted to stay for a month at a time, taking meals in the hall, and receiving instruction in doctrine from the priests.

Married men who came to the outer hall as pilgrims might recently have had sexual intercourse, and so could not come within the wall of the monastery. In the first phase, a pipe led into the outer hall from inside the wall, stopped up by a stone, obviously intended to allow water from the aqueduct inside to flood the floor for the purpose of cleaning. The floor sloped slightly to let the water out by the southern door. This was not, as archaeologists first supposed, simply to clean the floor after meals. Water was very scarce, and a broom would have done the job very well. Rather, the water, which was considered holy, was to wash away the unholiness that the visiting married men might have brought with them. In the second phase, when a more worldly regime took over Qumran, the pipe was stopped and the floor levelled. [7]

The more culpable kind of sinner was sent to the south-west, for the west was always defined as inferior to the east. These were men who had aimed much higher than the married, and had sunk lower. By strict Palestinian monastic standards, they could be classed under two broad categories: 'Egypt' and 'Sodom'.

Egypt was the place where Diaspora ascetic Jews lived, following the rule admiringly described by Philo in his essay on the Therapeuts.[8] Their communities contained both men and women – a point against them from the monastic outlook. They did not live in coenobitic institutions (monasteries), having surrendered all property – another point against them. Rather, they lived as individual ascetics, practising poverty and chastity, and had developed the eremitical kind of discipline. In the second phase of Qumran, hermits and Diaspora Essenes took over the whole building, for it had been defiled by the earthquake in 31 BC and could no longer serve as a Palestinian Essene monastery. Their discipline came to be characterised by fire, the 'iron furnace of Egypt'. Their leaders met in the vestry, where the great fire stood,[9] and the south-west area was still regarded as the place of the flesh, a lesser 'Egypt'.

The monastic area came under the control of Diaspora 'seekers after smooth things', who had a looser type of communal discipline, one that could allow homosexuality, as the Book of Acts shows in a story alluding to the biblical men of Sodom, who besieged a house, demanding that visiting men be brought out to them.[10] Qumran at the Dead Sea was near the site of the biblical Sodom, and the outer part of the south-west area was, in particular, 'Sodom', the place to which these men were sent down. It was also 'Brimstone', for brimstone had reigned down on Sodom at its destruction, as Luke's gospel emphasises.[11] As has been seen in Chapter 6, the head of the proselytes who met at Qumran was called 'Brimstone'.

In Revelation Chapter 11, the phrase is found: . . . 'the great city, which spiritually is called Sodom and Egypt, where . . . their Lord was crucified'. The pesher of this passage is that on 20 March AD 44, the anniversary of the crucifixion, there was a dramatic re- enactment of the occasion, a kind of Passion play, in which Jesus himself took part. The enactment took place at Qumran, for it was there that the actual crucifixion had taken place. This point, which of course runs contrary to long Christian tradition, has been closely argued in *Jesus the Man*.

The crucifixion took place in the most unclean area of all, the outer south-west, beside the exclusion cistern. Its uncleanness was shown by the fact that it contained a long row of cubicles which had the shape defined for latrines in the Temple Scroll: 'these shall be covered houses with holes into them, into which the excrement shall go down'[12]. The notice standing there now, defining the remains as 'stables', comes from the first archaeologists, whose interpretation was hardly convincing as they are much too narrow for horses. Rather, they are to be seen as latrines to be used by priests who in the first phase of Qumran officiated in the substitute sanctuary, whose lower entrance was just nearby. Their duties required continual attendance at prayer, which meant that they could not take time to follow the rule of lay celibates, who had to walk an hour's distance.

According to the Old Testament, followed by passages in the scrolls, a latrine was 'outside the camp'. This phrase is used in the New Testament to refer to the crucifixion of Jesus: he was crucified 'outside the camp'.[13] It is not always realised that, in biblical terms, this means that he was in a latrine area. The south-west part of Qumran stood for every kind of uncleanness. Moreover, it was 'the place of a Skull', for it was the place to which men were sent as the first stage of their excommunication, to 'death'. A passage in the Copper Scroll, which calls this area 'the Salt', says that at its north- eastern corner there was a grave[14]. An actual skull would hang there, as a warning to the holy that they were entering an unclean area. Medieval monasteries continued to use skulls for such a purpose.

A man who was to be excommunicated was sent first to this most defiled part of the monastery, then put through a ritual which dramatised his spiritual death. He was dressed in graveclothes, carried out on a bier, and taken to his own place of burial, assigned to him in advance.[15] For the highest leaders, it was one of the caves hollowed out of the funnels of rock surrounding the Qumran plateau and its nearest cliff. He was placed in the cave as if buried, and left there for some days. Windows in the cave walls allowed him to breathe, but if he tried to escape any other way than through the guarded exit, he would fall down a sheer precipice. After some days he was let out and sent away into the world, spiritually 'dead', unless, as in the case of 'Lazarus', there had been a change of policy on the part of the ruling powers, so that he was no longer classed as a heretic and was reprieved, that is to say, 'raised from the dead'.[16]

The Chief Monk had the power to pronounce the edict of excommunication, and so 'his name was Death'. A 'Second Death' meant that there was another monastery and another Chief Monk. A schism had taken place, a rival chief monastery had been set up.

From now on the original one became the First Death and the new one the Second Death. Anyone over whom the 'Second Death' had power was under a vow of obedience to the new centre.

In January AD 38, the Damascus monastery was founded, by celibates who had separated from Qumran.[17] Their motive was a very strong one: Agrippa was coming. The emperor Tiberius had died the previous year, and Gaius Caligula had made his friend Agrippa the ruling Herod. He had not yet come back from Rome, but the last time he visited, during the twenties and thirties, it had become known that he was almost bankrupt, and once he had received the succession from Herod the Great, he could claim entitlement to the property stored at Qumran, for the original destination of the mission income had been Herod's coffers. The money was spirited away from the vaults at Qumran, and Damascus now became the centre for missionaries who taught that to become Jewish did not mean accepting the Herods as kings. As another monastery, it was a 'Second Death'.[18]

The missionaries had to justify the fact that they were engaged in preaching Judaism but were in fact exiled from their own land. In their Damascus Document, in which they renamed themselves 'the New Covenant in the Land of Damascus', they argued that exiled Jews, forming the eastern Diaspora, were more truly God's people than those in Palestine. The proof of this was what had happened in the sixth century BC, when Jews exiled in Babylon were far better off than those who remained behind in Jerusalem, which was destroyed around them. The writers of the Damascus Document darkly warned that the same thing was going to happen again: Jerusalem would again be destroyed.[19] On this point, they were quite right. The activities of their own zealot wing were leading to an inevitable confrontation with Rome.

In the early forties AD Damascus became the centre of the plot against the life of Agrippa I, led by Simon Magus. Agrippa's increasing ambition to be a Jewish emperor was alienating almost all parties, and even Peter and Jesus were drawn into the councils planning to oppose him.

In March AD 40 Jesus was present in Damascus, associated with Ananias, a name for Simon Magus. The youthful Paul, a loyal servant of Agrippa I and also a loyal supporter of the Jewish version of the mission to Gentiles, came to Damascus to spy out both opponents of Agrippa and those who were too liberal in their treatment of Gentiles. There he met Jesus, who taught him that there was another kind of New Covenant, one in which Gentiles were not required to become Jews at all. On the question of Gentiles, Paul swung right round, his conversion being both political and religious, for the two were indistinguishable. He remained, however, a servant of Agrippa, and it was the enemies of Agrippa who chased him from Damascus.[20]

By AD 43 some in Damascus, including James the brother of Jesus, had begun to change their minds about Agrippa. His charm was legendary, as Josephus records, and he had won over Simon of Jerusalem, who may be identified with Peter.[21] The Christians' version of that story is found in Acts 10. James and the brothers of Jesus came back from Damascus to Qumran, to the fury of the Damascus party, who in their Damascus Document wrote that the Princes of Judah had betrayed them and 'turned back to the ways of wickedness'.[22]

Qumran, the 'First Death', had indeed allowed Agrippa to receive the mission money that was sent there. When James and those with him came back, they at first worked with Agrippa. A new member of the Annas family, Matthew Annas, was in sympathy with them, and was appointed high priest by Agrippa.

But by March AD 44 Agrippa had dismissed Matthew as high priest, had quarrelled with the Roman governor Marsus, and was seriously endangering the security of the state. Matthew, a supporter of Rome, turned against him, and Qumran became another centre of disaffection against the Herods. The crisis was resolved when the poison plot succeeded, and Agrippa died in Caesarea. But Qumran remained from this time on lukewarm towards the ruling Herods. It developed as the centre for James' party, who came to be called Jewish Christians. They had more respect for Agrippa II but preferred to remain financially independent of him. To them were attached proselytes led by Nicolaus, also called 'Brimstone', so that it continued to be called 'the lake burning with fire and brimstone'.

Simon Magus remained intensely opposed to Agrippa. He operated from both Damascus and Caesarea, for he also allowed westernised Gentiles to remain un-circumcised, and they had their meeting place in Caesarea. When in that city he called himself 'the Great Power'.[23] Allying with Herod of Chalcis, Agrippa's brother, who had received the right to appoint high priests, he took over Damascus, calling himself there 'the Messiah of Aaron [24] and Israel'. From there he engaged in mission to the eastern province whose limit was Babylon, its most notable converts being Queen Helena and Izates.

Following the death of Agrippa in March AD 44, 'one tenth of the city fell'.[25] Revelation 11 records the great schism of that crucial season. Of the ten fee paying provinces, the eastern province seceded. From now on, Damascus was the Second Death, entirely separate from the western parties, the centre of a separate mission.

Since Qumran remained uncommitted to the ruling Herods, a fully Herodian chief monastery developed in Judea. It was at Masada in Idumea, an estate belonging to the Herods, who had originally come from Idumea. Its Chief Monk was the Herodian Magus, called 'the Beast' when with zealots. Masada became 'the Throne of the Beast'. By the sixties, when a party of Herodian nationalists had shown their preference for Bernice rather than for her pro-Roman brother, the Sicarii, who were dagger carrying zealots, were in control of it, under Eleazar Ben Jair, a descendant of Judas the Galilean who had operated from Qumran.[26]

At the end of the Book of Revelation the phrase is found: 'the lake that burns with fire and brimstone, which is the Second Death'.[27] After the death of Agrippa II in AD 102, there was no further reason for the distinction between Damascus and Qumran. The two monasteries were merged, and their titles joined.

About thirty years later, another generation of zealots made a last desperate throw, and Qumran was one of their fortresses. When, at last, they failed, it was left to be buried by the soil. There were none in Judea to remember what it had been, and those living in the Diaspora did not know, or did not care to know, what had happened there.

CHAPTER 11

Armageddon

THE FALL OF JERUSALEM, AD 70

'And he assembled them at the place called in
Hebrew Armageddon.'[1]

The word 'Armageddon' has become part of our
language, evoking the fear – or hope – of a great final battle
of such magnitude that it will wipe out the present order
of civilisation. The Book of Revelation is said to be a
prophecy of its coming, and for some people, still, this is
a proof that it will happen. For most of us these days,
however, the term is thought of as a myth we have left
behind.

In the historical meaning of the Book of Revelation,
the word does not refer to a myth, but to a literal event
in the past. When, in Revelation Chapter 16, we read:
'And he assembled them at the place called in Hebrew
Armageddon (*Armagedōn*)', it means that, shortly before
the fall of Jerusalem, there was a call to arms to Jews and
their supporters from all over the world. They were
asked to come to Judea to prepare to fight for the
defence of the holy city Jerusalem. The place where they
would camp and receive their military training would be
in the desert fortress of Qumran, and, more exactly, in
its unclean south-western area, which, because of one of

its uses, could be called 'A-R-Magedon'.

The word Armagedon (the more correct spelling) falls naturally into two parts, as Hebraists have seen. In Hebrew, in which vowels are variable, the second part is the same as Magadan, a word that is found in the gospels for a place which Jesus visited.[2] Variants of this name in different texts include Magadon, Magedan, Magedal, Magdalan and Magdala.[3]

All Jewish ascetics were organised in orders called 'tribes', using the tribal territories of ancient Israel, to express the fact that they were a New Israel. The two 'tribes' for women and Gentiles were Asher and Dan. Dan had originally had two parts, for historical reasons, one in the north of the country around what had become Caesarea Philippi, the other on the west coast, part of Samaria, around Joppa. It appears that they had come to be called Great Dan and Little Dan, and these terms were also used to express two low grades.

In Greek, when the proper name 'Dan' was retained, 'Great Dan' was *Mega-Dan*, and this would give rise to the variations quoted above. Mary Magdalene, who was the female head of Great Dan as the David queen, derived her title from the form *Magdala*.

Women were by definition unclean, and if they came to a monastery they were confined to its most unclean area, the outer part of the south-west, the part that was also 'Sodom', for sodomites were classed with women. When women, or Gentiles, their equivalent, were in this part of the grounds, it became 'Megadan' or 'Magedon'.

This area also contained the priests' latrine. It was for their special use, originally because they were serving in the sanctuary. All grades and ranks were called by Hebrew letters, as has been illustrated in the case of 666. The full set of letters that were in use is set out on pp.176, 183–184. There were both classes and grades. A priest was of class A, Aleph, the first letter in the alphabet, and also of grade R, Resh, the letter indicating that he was admitted to the sanctuary (the letter is used also in the T-R-S formula). An 'A-R' was a sanctuary priest. So, to combine A-R with Magedon meant, to the initiated, 'a sanctuary priest who is in the unclean place, the latrine'.

To be engaged in warfare made a man lose his holiness, for, as the War Scroll shows, a priest on the battlefield would be defiled if he approached the slain and touched 'unclean blood'.[4] So the place for assembly of men who had gone down to such a level was Armagedon, the latrine area where the holy became defiled. The long esplanade that begins in this part of Qumran was a very suitable place for a gathering of leaders who would form the first rank, a thousand. (The detailed battle plans in the War Scroll always show an organisation in terms of thousands.)

Just prior to the call to Armagedon, Revelation 16 reads: 'Blessed is he who watches, and keeps his garments, so that he may not walk naked and they may see his indecency'. There is a clear link with the rule in the Manual of Discipline: 'Whoever brings out his member from beneath his garment . . . so that his nakedness is seen, will be punished for thirty days.'[5] The writer of this section of Revelation, Tychicus, had expressed his willingness to answer the call to go to Qumran, for in such a time of crisis even Gentiles could respond to an appeal to defend the holy city. He was aware of the strict rules of conduct that were observed at Qumran, and quotes one of them in the context of the call to Armagedon.

Gentiles who had become converted to the Herodian form of the Jewish religion could see the necessity of rallying behind Agrippa II as he attempted to gain control during the last two years before the destruction of the city. The call to Armagedon went out in June AD 68. Agrippa still had a faint hope of persuading his countrymen to moderation, continuing from where Ananus the Younger had left off when he was murdered some months previously. Agrippa summoned his supporters, but it was

128

only a matter of months before he was forced to leave the city, using as his excuse the need to visit the new emperor who had replaced Nero.[6]

The real hero had been Ananus, who was closely allied with the Christians and had worked with Paul. He appears as the 'red horseman' of Revelation 6, for he was a Sadducee who was more in favour of nationalist action than his older brothers. Ananus had attempted to persuade his countrymen that they were bringing the destruction of the city upon themselves by their reckless-ness. His murder was described by Josephus as the beginning of the end: 'I should not be wrong in saying that the capture of the city began with the death of Ananus'.[7]

Ananus had been appointed high priest in AD 62. He reigned only for three months, but subsequently, in the grave crisis of AD 67 to 68, became the acknowledged leader of the people.

The circumstances of his dismissal in AD 62 were recorded by Josephus without comment, but are a clear indication of the political involvement of the Christians. Ananus was in charge in a period between procurators, and for reasons that Josephus does not amplify, took his opportunity to summon the Sanhedrin and order the execution of 'a man named James, the brother of Jesus called the Christ, and certain others'. He accused them of having transgressed the law and delivered them up to be stoned.

The new procurator was on his way, and a message was sent to him informing him of Ananus' action. As Ananus had no authority to convene the Sanhedrin without Roman consent, the procurator wrote back angrily, and Agrippa was forced to depose Ananus as high priest.[8]

In Revelation, James' death is dealt with in Chapter 15, and the chapter also shows that when the high priesthood was promised to Ananus there was open rejoicing. It becomes apparent that James was not simply the 'just man' who was stoned to death by the Jews because of his virtue, as the account of the Church father Hegesippus presents it.[9] He was actively involved with the anti-Roman party, to an even greater extent than his father Joseph had been before him. From his point of view, it was the only course that an honourable Jew could take in this time of corrupt Roman procurators and a direct threat to the survival of Jerusalem and Judaism. But from the point of view of those who had better knowledge of the Romans and more western sympathies, James and those like him were actually bringing about the destruction of the city.

From the early sixties onward Jerusalem was subjected to 'the seven bowls of the Wrath of God'.[10] Rome, apparently having despaired of orderly government over this troublesome but influential little nation in Judea, sent two incapable procurators, whose only aim was to enrich themselves by taking bribes from all parties. Of Albinus (AD 62–64), Josephus, one of the moderates, said 'there was no form of villainy which he omitted to practise', and of his successor, Gessius Florus (AD 64–66), that Albinus was a paragon of virtue in comparison with him. Under Gessius Florus the war broke out, for by now there was no other way.

By early in AD 68, the question was whether the moderates could succeed in quelling the zealots and so save the city. They were opposed by two linked groups: the Sicarii, led by Eleazar Ben Jair, later the hero of Masada, and the Idumeans, the most violent of all the factions.

Zealots, in the strict sense, were yet another faction, but they joined with the Idumeans in working for the destruction of all Romans. They were condemned by Ananus' party as 'the scum and offscourings of the whole country'.[11] But to the militants, Ananus and those with him were traitors. They sent a double agent who apparently sympathised with Ananus, but secretly revealed his movements. The spy told them that Ananus had sent an embassy to Vespasian, who was now the representative of Rome, inviting him to come and take possession of the city.

This was enough. Despite eloquent speeches by Ananus and the other leaders, and aided by a violent storm that gave them cover, the zealots entered the city of Jerusalem and took it over. The first victims were Ananus and his associates. Their assassins stood on their dead bodies and denounced them. Then they left their bodies unburied, simply thrown outside the city. This was the ultimate defilement for Jews.

At the last stage of the war another leader appeared, Simon Gioras, referred to in Revelation 16 as an 'unclean spirit' and as 'Frogs', meaning that he was like one of the plagues of Egypt. He was so notable that he was the Jew who was chosen to be displayed and killed when Titus, the victorious general, went back to Rome for his triumph.[12]

The last months of the Jewish state are recorded in unforgettable detail by Josephus. From the time the zealots took over the city, the end was inevitable. Law and order had broken down there were daily murders and pillages. Vespasian departed to Alexandria, where he was proclaimed a rival emperor, leaving the last stages of the war to his son Titus. In September AD 70, the Romans brought in their engines of war and overcame the upper city. The buildings were set alight, until the whole city was in flames. According to Josephus, Titus, now master of what had seemed an impregnable city, exclaimed: 'God indeed has been with us in the war. God it was who brought down the Jews from these strongholds; for what power have human hands or engines against these towers?'[13]

When the year AD 74 finally came, it was the end of any hope for those who throughout the century had been fighting for the independence of the Jewish state. They had stretched their faith in divine aid to its limit. As the

Roman forces scaled the sides of their last stronghold at Masada, they made their own Eschaton. Nine hundred and sixty of them committed suicide, believing that they had thus cheated the Romans of their victory and would rise again at a future bodily resurrection.

CHAPTER 12

The Fall of the Great Harlot

A WOULD-BE JEWISH EMPRESS

Following the chapters that reflect the fall of Jerusalem, the Book of Revelation records a long lament, plainly modelled on the dirge uttered for the first fall of Jerusalem in the sixth century BC. A woman is depicted; one who 'sits as a queen', and says, 'I am no widow', but her humiliation and desolation are to follow.[1] She clearly stands for the city of Jerusalem, and one of the purposes of the lament is to mourn the fall of the city.

But, as always, there are double meanings. The woman was not simply a symbol of the city, but a real woman, who really was a queen of Jerusalem, and who was destined for a personal fall. She was Bernice, the sister of Agrippa II, who acted as his consort.

Bernice had had a career typical of the Herod family. Born in AD 27 as the twin of Agrippa, she had been married, widowed, and remarried by the age of sixteen. Her second husband was her uncle, Herod of Chalcis; with whom she had two sons. He died when she was twenty-one, and she remained for some time a widow. But rumours began to circulate that she had committed incest with her brother, who never married. She then married a

133

foreigner, Polemo of Cilicia, who, attracted by her wealth, agreed to be circumcised and practise the Jewish religion. The marriage did not last long; Bernice, increasingly given up to licentiousness, deserted Polemo.[2]

As the threat of war drew closer in Jerusalem in the sixties, Bernice became the focus of a party of Herodian militants, for she had a greater devotion to the city than her brother. The three relatives of the royal family, Saul, Antipas and Costobar, who according to Josephus were 'lawless' and 'collected gangs of villains', were associated with her. Antipas, the treasurer of the city, was killed, but Gaius Costobar Herod succeeded him as the one who, when Bernice moved to Ephesus, 'committed harlotry with the Great Harlot', by promoting her as a priestess.

In the tradition of Herodian women, she had decided to use her own methods of gaining power over Rome. In AD 68 Titus, the son of Vespasian, was in Judea, assisting his father in the conduct of the war. He was a close associate of Agrippa,[3] and met the forty-one year old Bernice at this stage. By AD 75, after the fall of Jerusalem, she was the talk of Rome, for she had become the mistress of Titus. She came to Rome with her brother, 'at the very height of her power', as a Roman historian says. She moved in with Titus, expecting to marry him, 'and was already behaving in every respect as if she were his wife'. However, the prospect of a foreign empress was too much for the Romans, and she was sent away. In 79 she again came to Rome, when Titus became emperor, but was again refused the position of first lady of the Roman world.[4]

Bernice had become a heroine to the Jewish people from the beginning of the war, when she showed far more initiative than her brother. In 66, while her brother was absent in Alexandria, she visited Jerusalem as part of her Nazirite vow, barefoot and with a shaven head. Gessius Florus, the cruellest of the procurators, had just committed one of his worst atrocities, scourging and

134

crucifying Jews who were of the highest rank, who possessed Roman citizenship. Bernice sent messengers to Florus, expressing the utmost outrage, but no notice was taken of her and she was forced to watch the torture and death of the captives. She would have been put to death herself if she had not taken refuge in the palace.[5]

When Agrippa returned from Alexandria after this episode, he placed Bernice in a commanding position on the roof of the palace, as someone in whom the people had confidence, while he made a speech exhorting them to avoid violence.[6]

But, as Agrippa believed that God was on the side of Rome and could not find the energy to lead a resistance, Bernice had more enthusiasm for her country. It was at her insistence that Agrippa commuted the death penalty on a leading zealot to a term of imprisonment.[7]

She had always acted as official consort to her brother, as Acts also shows: Paul had had an audience with Agrippa and Bernice in Caesarea in 60.[8] Josephus calls her the queen.[9]

Agrippa left Jerusalem at the end of 68, Titus travelling some of the way with him then turning back.[10] Bernice went with them, as Revelation shows. Her next appearance is in Revelation 17, in Ephesus, as 'the woman clothed in scarlet and purple', who was 'sitting on the scarlet beast'. She had taken the position vacated by Helena[11] as the incarnation of Diana of the Ephesians, and was claiming to be a cardinal and bishop. On the badge on her forehead she wore several letters indicating her rank, as priests did, and she wore also an emblem of the emperor Vitellius, who had become 'Babylon the Great' by accepting her hospitality in Rome.[12]

For a short time early in AD 70 Bernice's faction in Ephesus planned to use her relationship with Titus to make her queen regnant and oust her brother. This is seen from the passage in Revelation about the 'mystery of the woman', which imitates the language of an oracle to speak of the current leadership struggles.[13]

After Bernice was sent away from Rome, she and Agrippa lived quietly among Diaspora Jews, making Ephesus their main centre. Bernice continued there as 'the Mother', the 'Sarah' to Gentiles. For Christians, however, she was 'the Mother of Harlots', a woman who combined a claim to priesthood with sexual licence, and led other women into the same error.

CHAPTER 13

The Reason for 2000

HOW THE CHRISTIAN ERA WAS ESTABLISHED

All the inhabitants of this earth now use, for public purposes, a calendar that calls a certain year in our own time the year 2000.

The letters AD, for Anno Domini, 'in the year of the Lord', were formerly used with the date, in the days of Christendom. It is more appropriate now to call it the Common Era (although the letters CE and BCE can be a little confusing and for that reason are not used in this book). But there is no doubt that this method of dating, in which a certain year two millennia ago was named 1 AD, was the work of the Christian Church.

It has been the opinion of historians that the reasons for the choice of that year are lost in the mists of history. It was said by the Church, of course, that the year was that of the birth of Christ. But the gospels themselves contradict it: Matthew says that Jesus was born during the reign of Herod the Great, and Herod died in 4 BC.

No really convincing reason has been offered by historians for the choice of that year. It is usually taken for granted that it was fixed on only much later, when

Christianity had become the official religion of the Roman empire. It is assumed, also, that there was little exact knowledge of the foundation events, so that the date was chosen on the basis of very little information.

With the discovery of the Dead Sea Scrolls, however, a rich new source has become available on this as on so many other questions. Once it is granted that the community of the Dead Sea Scrolls were the immediate predecessors of the Christians, their known interest in questions of calendar offers evidence on the subject which must be taken into account.

The community of the Dead Sea Scrolls were a separate sect from other Jews, and the main practice that marked their difference was their use of a different calendar, with a different set of dates. For example, although all Jews believed that the Day of Atonement, their most sacred day, must be held on the tenth day of the seventh month, according to Old Testament law, this day was different for orthodox Jews living in Jerusalem and for the ascetics living down near the Dead Sea. Both believed that the seventh month was in autumn, but, because the orthodox used a lunar calendar and said that the year was 354 days long, while the ascetics used a solar calendar and said that it was 364 days long, the tenth day of the seventh month fell on a different day for the ascetics. This made them a separate institution. It was a situation rather like that of western and eastern Christianity, where the Christmas celebration is on 25 December for the one, but on January 6–8 for the other.

One of the main occupations of the ascetics in their isolation was the study of calendar and all matters that were believed to derive from calendar. They held that theirs was the true liturgical calendar approved by heaven. Orthodox Jews, following the lunar way of counting, were disapproved by heaven, because they followed the moon, who – as they wrote in one of their works – disobeyed God by coming in every year ten days too soon.[1]

Heaven, they believed, not only wanted the year to be measured as 364 days, but governed the whole of history by the principles of the solar calendar. The number 364 was divisible by seven; the year contained exactly fifty-two weeks. (It will be apparent that they had to take into account the actual fact that the solar year is 365¼ days long; if they did not, they would, after a number of years, be observing spring in the middle of winter. This problem was met by intercalation, the inserting of extra days; see further on pp.237–238 about the method.) Everything was governed by a symmetry resting on the number seven. The divisions of history, marked by great events, were in sets of seven years, and of forty-nine years, and of four hundred and ninety years.

In pursuing such an idea, they were influenced by Pythagoreanism, which by now was a widespread popular belief. The Pythagoreans, from about the sixth century BC, had discovered the basic principles of mathematics, and had gone on from their discoveries to hold a kind of religious belief, that everything in the world was governed by number and could be discovered by those who knew the principles.[2]

If it were the case that heaven governed all events according to symmetrical numbers, then the future could be predicted, for great events would happen at the numerically significant divisions of time. This hope was the incentive for much of the study of calendar. It had become a primary concern for the exiled priests at Qumran, who soon acquired a public reputation for being able to foretell the future.[3] If events fell at the times they held to be significant, then it proved that heaven was on their side and they ought to come back into power in Jerusalem and the temple. Thus the question of political power was inseparable from the question of calendar.

As their community grew, especially with its great expansion in the first century BC, other chronological theories developed alongside the original ones. All who belonged to the community measured a year of 364 days and held their festivals together, but some disagreed about the divisions of history in sets of seven years. Rather, they said, history was divided by the generations of kings, which lasted forty years. The Essene marriage rule for their dynastic order set forty as the age when a king should have a son.

These theories lay behind the setting of the Christian millennium. During the first century BC it had come to be believed, for calendar reasons that will be more fully shown on pp.220–222, that the last millennium in the whole of world history had begun in what we now call 41 BC. The thousand year Kingdom of the Jews – the mission that has been described in the foregoing chapters – was to begin in that year. Herod the Great, whose rise to power had begun at that time, would be supreme head of the Kingdom, and his dynasty would last for the thousand years. The line of David, no longer in total exile, would have a place, but in a subordinate capacity only, acting in the position of king to represent Herod to the Gentiles.

But the popularity of Herod the Great did not last. As he declined into illness in his latter years, a new party arose, declaring that the mission and the Kingdom must continue, but without a Herod. There was an obvious way to express this in chronological terms, and it was this method that gave us our millennium. A zero generation of forty years was allowed, and the last millennium was begun again with what was now seen as the first generation. Reckoning from 41 BC, the year 1 BC became the year 0 of the final millennium, and the year AD 1 its year 1.

At first, this dating was established in order to give power to the dynasty of Ananus the Elder, who became the first high priest in Jerusalem under direct Roman rule. He and his descendants – he had five sons, all of whom became high priests in Jerusalem – would take the place of Herod the Great as both kings and priests. It had been the case for hundreds of years that a high priest also acted as king of the Jews. Once again, the Davids would have a place, but in the same role as they had had under Herod, representing the head of the mission to the despised Gentiles, without actual royal power.

In the course of the first century AD, however, the Herods declined and disappeared, and the Annas dynasty and other priests merged into continuing Judaism. Only the Davids were left, and all the leadership roles were combined in the heir of David and in the Pope who represented him.

The millennium of Annas became that of the Davids, and of Jesus as the true Christ. It was his succession that had begun its thousand year reign in AD 1. It would end in AD 1000, with the end of the world and the Last Judgment.

Other variations of the chronology were fought out during the first century, and their different versions are one of the main subjects of the history in the Book of Revelation. But since 1 BC and AD 1 expressed, above all, independence of the Herod dynasty, it gave the chronology that has survived.

As the Christian version of the Jewish mission increased in strength, it saw also its political opportunity in the contemporary need for continuous dating.

The Hellenistic period was one when the Greco-Roman world, having adopted a universal calendar of days, felt the need to have an agreed starting point for greater time, giving a continuous succession of years. Only the Jews dated from creation, and they were finding it increasingly difficult to believe that they knew its date. The Greeks dated in olympiads, starting 776 BC, but the system was too complex to be popular. The Romans dated by the years of the emperor, but had to begin again whenever there was a new emperor.

It had become apparent that if any party or group succeeded in imposing a starting point for continuous dating that reflected the interests of that group, it would

141

gain enormous prestige, in fact be the dominating culture. The history of the establishment of the millennium is the history of the rise to power of Christians in the Roman empire. This has always been known, but the new point to be made is that the Christians themselves were observing the dating from the beginning within their own circles, and were very well aware of the reason for their choice of year. They kept secret the fact that their organisation had had a previous history, and consequently kept secret the reason for the choice of year. But they were bound by their history and calendar, and by the prophecies that they still expected to be fulfilled. The date was not chosen in ignorance, but in full consciousness of what it meant in political terms.

The year AD 1000 came, and there was no Last Judgment. The accounts of the medieval Church reflect the crisis of those years. It was no newly conceived theory that put a Last Judgment in that year, nor a misinterpretation of the Book of Revelation, which gives great prominence to the thousand years. It was, rather, the end of the line for a hypothesis about history that went back to at least the third century BC.

The convenience of having continuous dating was sufficient reason to continue long after the basis had been lost and the superstition of numbers had faded. We all live now with the relic of those years in the first century when the foundations of western civilisation, already laid, were given a religious dimension. If the dating is no longer a sign of power, it has become, instead, a very effective memorial.

Part II

The Insider's Knowledge

This section contains, in systematic form, the special technical knowledge on which the pesharist of Revelation was expected to draw. For him, it came from having lived for a long time in a highly organised community.

For us, the knowledge comes from the Dead Sea Scrolls, from literature contemporary with the New Testament, and, by using the assumption of organisational systems as a working hypothesis, from the books of the New Testament themselves. Once it is seen that systems are in operation, and their essential contents are known, a rigorous logic makes it possible to see the unstated parts of the system, and to test their existence and use in the book by the criteria of many kinds of consistency. The process is precisely what a scientist does when forming a hypothesis and testing it against all relevant natural data.

But nature is much more complex than a book constructed by human minds. The Book of Revelation depends on a totally organised, unified system, which can be fully discovered, just as a complex puzzle can be solved with sufficient application. The results can be set out as complete, applied to every word in the book. They are consequently subject to proof or disproof.

After a summary of the party history, the systems of place, grade and time are set out in the following pages, in a form permitting testing for internal consistency, consistency with known facts, and consistent application in the pesher.

CHAPTER 1

Overview of the Parties

The starting point of our understanding of the history is given in Josephus, who tells us that in his time, the first century AD, there were three main parties of Jews, with a fourth 'intrusive' one of which he does not approve.[1]

The three respected ones were Sadducees, Pharisees and Essenes. Sadducees were the priestly aristocrats; Pharisees were the teachers of the people on points of law; and Essenes were the mystical, isolated ones with many Greek ideas, such as valuing celibacy and community of property.

The 'fourth philosophy' were the militant nationalists, their nucleus called zealots, who appeared in the first century AD when Judea became a country occupied by Romans. It can now be seen that they were Diaspora Essenes, the 'seekers after smooth things' attacked by their Palestinian counterparts in some of the Dead Sea Scrolls. They staged constant excited demonstrations, calling on God to help them shake off the hated Romans, and it was they who eventually brought about the destruction of Jerusalem. Their remnants committed mass suicide on Masada in AD 74.[2]

Through its close detail of persons and organisation, the concealed history in the New Testament traces the way that these four parties developed into the Jewish religion that still remains, and into Christians.

The main cause of the groupings and regroupings was the influence of Greco-Roman culture, but the successive Herods supplied the personal factor. In 21 BC, at the time Herod the Great rejected the ascetics' plan for a new temple, two permanent divisions opened up, both of which contained members of the four parties. From this time there were anti-Herodian Pharisees, Sadducees, Essenes and Zealots, and pro-Herodian Pharisees, Sadducees, Essenes and Zealots. The former survived as the eastern party containing the element that became present-day Judaism, the latter became, at first, an alliance of Herodians and Christians in the west, and finally, after the Herod dynasty died out, Christians only.

The eastern anti-Herod side had its extreme and more moderate wings. The extremists were the Damascus proselytisers for Judaism, the true Zealots; their Chief Monk, Simon Magus, was called the 'Second Death'. Their moderates were the Pharisees, such as Caiaphas the high priest, whose teaching survived the fall of Jerusalem and continued as orthodox Judaism. Linked with them, at first, were the Annas priests and their followers, who in AD 6 had thought that they were free of the Herods. This was the outlook of Sadducees such as Jonathan Annas, and the higher orders of Palestinian Essenes, as well as Gentiles such as James Niceta. They were opposed to the extravagant claims of Agrippa I, and probably assisted in his assassination in AD 44. For some years they remained independent of the west, and came to occupy Qumran as their celibate centre, their leaders being Jonathan Annas, Apollos, John Mark and James the brother of Jesus. But in AD 50, as Revelation shows, some of them came over to the west, persuaded by the more reasonable behaviour of Agrippa II. This party became Jewish Christians.

Of the western groupings who remained loyal to the

Agrippas, the nucleus, fully supporting Agrippa II, were Sadducees led by Matthew Annas and Theophilus Annas, the two Annas brothers who were most co-operative with Rome. Both benefited from the benign reign of the emperor Claudius to become a party whose emblem was the dove of peace. With them were the village Essenes, led by Peter. It was this party which, in December AD 43 in Antioch, began to use the name Christian. Their Gentile members lived as Peter did, married men who followed the discipline of pilgrims. These Gentiles, led by John Aquila, were called 'the Church'.

Close to them were ascetic Pharisees, the successors of Hillel the Great, who supported the Agrippas. Their leader, from AD 40 onwards, was Paul. His 'conversion' had been a change of mind on issues affecting the group that became Jewish Christians, which in the gospel period included Jesus. But he was always part of the court of the Herods, and particularly close to Timothy Herod, whom the childless Agrippa II had appointed as his heir. Paul's party did not use the name 'Christian', and did not give the primary leadership to an Annas priest. Rather, the Herod was Pontifex Maximus, and his house in Rome was the centre of the movement. Paul's party called themselves 'Romans'.

Late in the reign of Claudius, and under the emperor Nero, the Herod family developed their own form of zealotry, led by Bernice the sister of Agrippa. Their involvement in the fall of Jerusalem has been described in Chapter 11, and is the main theme of Part C of Revelation, for Tychicus, the third seer, one of Paul's party, moved towards their outlook together with Ananus the Younger, the last of the Annas brothers. Their version of Herodianism died out with the fall of Masada, where all zealots gathered on a property belonging to the ruling Herods.

In broad terms, the party history may be summarised:

PRO-HEROD–WEST	ANTI-HEROD–EAST
Herodians–Agrippa II, to AD 102	Damascus–Zealots, to AD 74
Christians–Matthew, Peter	Pharisees, continuing
Romans–Paul	
Jewish Christians–John Mark, James	
Herodian zealots, to AD 74– Bernice	

These are the formations that lie behind the different parts of Revelation. In the gospel period the emphasis had been different. Agrippa I was just beginning his attempt to restore the Herodian monarchy, and the issues were played out in terms of his rise. All parties were substantially eastern. They were then better summarised as Hebrews and Hellenists, the terms used in Acts.[3] Those supporting Agrippa were Hebrews, and they included John the Baptist and ascetic Pharisees under Gamaliel the predecessor of Paul. They included, at this stage, Caiaphas of the moderate Pharisees, and also the high ranking celibate Essenes with the Baptist. Those against him were all Hellenists, the Zealots under Simon Magus, and the moderate Sadducees under Jonathan Annas. With them was Jesus, both during the years of his public ministry AD 29 to 33, and in the early years of seclusion after the crucifixion. In that early period he was closely associated with John Mark, and accepted by Hellenists as the legitimate David. He endorsed the doctrine of lay priesthood held by the Magus, but supported the peace policy of Jonathan Annas.

PRO-AGRIPPA– HEBREWS	ANTI-AGRIPPA– HELLENISTS
High Essenes–Baptist, James Caiaphas, moderate Pharisees, Ascetic Pharisees, Gamaliel	Zealots Jonathan Annas, moderate Sadducees Peter and village Essenes Jesus with John Mark and Gentiles

Agrippa's desire to be a god, and at least an eastern Caesar if not a western, lost him the support of everyone except Gamaliel Pharisees in AD 44. In that year the re-alignment took place from which the Christians were formed. High Essenes and Caiaphas went to Damascus for a time, and the high Essenes only came back to Qumran as Jewish Christians. But in the meantime Peter, the village Essenes, Matthew, and the pilgrim Gentiles with Jesus had changed to support Agrippa II. Jesus separated from his former Hellenist associates of both outlooks, and allied closely with Paul, who now changed his mind about his legitimacy and accepted him as the true David and as the focus for all Gentiles, with Agrippa the leader for westernised Jews. The party history then began that is reflected in Revelation Parts B, C and D.

CHAPTER 2

From Qumran to Cathedral

WHAT THE SEER ACTUALLY SAW

The seers of Revelation, when they had their 'visions', were in fact sitting in the front row of a cathedral, describing the liturgy being enacted before them. Their book is rich in detail of positions and places, and it is possible, when they are understood, to trace the history of the evolution of the Jewish ascetic movement into the forms of worship of the Christian Church.

In most parts of Revelation, the cathedral was in the city of Ephesus, which had now become the centre used by Agrippa II when he met with Diaspora Jews outside the country. But it had been built as a reproduction of structures in the Wilderness of Judea, in the area where the Dead Sea Scrolls were found. The platonic theory of reproduction lay behind the plan of all places used by these Hellenised ascetics. Believing, with Plato, that the pure forms of earthly phenomena were to be found only in heaven, and that the earthly forms were mere copies, they could in this way justify their use of Qumran as a reproduction temple to the one in Jerusalem. Then they could go on making copies of Qumran and its related buildings, each one containing the essential values of the original. A study of the buildings in the Wilderness of Judea, together with their literature, gives the basic information needed for understanding the reproductions. At the same time it can be seen how the use of the buildings was modified under Christian influence, until the basic shape of a Christian church evolved.

The starting point of the observation is the shape and measurements of the room at Qumran that is here interpreted as the vestry.[1] It ran from north to south, having two divisions, a northern one running down to the edge of a dais, and a southern one of about the same length (see Diagram A).

Each seer was sitting in the equivalent of the southern part, just before the dais, in a seat that marked him as a leader of the congregation, with rows of seats for the ordinary congregation behind him. Directly in front of him was a step, then the edge of the dais, which raised the floor of the northern room one cubit. (It is necessary to give all measurements in cubits, as they were the units used. A cubit was the length of a man's forearm, a measure that became fixed at 18 inches or 46 centimetres, and this was the cubit used at Qumran. As will be seen below, the object used as their cubit standard is still to be seen there.)

Further back in the northern room of the Qumran vestry, a platform stood, and behind it, on the east side near the door, a round furnace made of bricks. On the west side was the back wall of a vault whose opening faced north, outside the vestry, looking towards the great round well which lay to the north, the main source of drinking water for the community. The platform, vault and furnace had been built in the second phase of occupation of Qumran, after an earthquake had devastated the buildings in 31 BC. The vault served to block off a door in the western wall which had originally communicated with a long north-south courtyard, whose dimensions and divisions show it to have been the original substitute sanctuary of the exiles at Qumran. It is this door that suggests

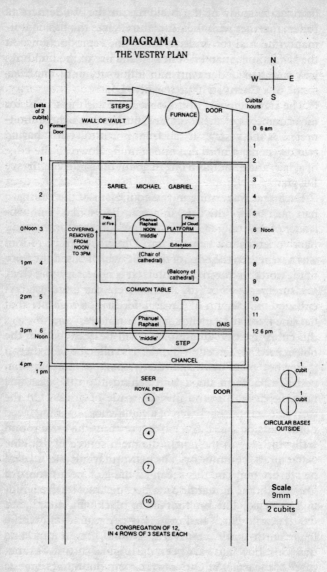

DIAGRAM A
THE VESTRY PLAN

N
W · E
S

Cubits/hours

(sets of 2 cubits)

STEPS — FURNACE — DOOR

WALL OF VAULT

Former Door

0 — 0 6 am

1 — 1

1 — 2

2 — 3

SARIEL   MICHAEL   GABRIEL

2 — 4

Pillar of Fire — Pillar of Cloud

0 Noon 3 — Phanuel Raphael NOON 'middle' — PLATFORM — 6 Noon

COVERING REMOVED FROM NOON TO 3PM

(Chair of cathedral) — Extension — 7

1 pm 4 — (Balcony of cathedral) — 8

9

COMMON TABLE

2 pm 5 — 10

11

Phanuel Raphael 'middle'

3 pm 6 Noon — DAIS — 12 6 pm

STEP

CHANCEL

4 pm 7 1 pm

SEER

ROYAL PEW

DOOR

①

1 cubit

1 cubit

CIRCULAR BASES OUTSIDE

④

⑦

Scale
9mm
2 cubits

⑩

CONGREGATION OF 12,
IN 4 ROWS OF 3 SEATS EACH

152

that the rooms were originally the vestry, to which the priests from the sanctuary came to change from their vestments into ordinary clothes, following a rule laid down in the Old Testament.[2] When the sanctuary could no longer be used for prayers after the earthquake, the platform was built in the northern part of the vestry, reached by a flight of steps from outside. It was used for the prayers of the highest priests, but did not have the holiness of the sanctuary, where the central rite, that of atonement, had been performed.

This change led to a further modification, which gave the plan of a Herodian cathedral. Forced to transfer their substitute sanctuary from Qumran, the ascetics, who now had the co-operation of Herod,[3] developed the two-storeyed residence of the Herods at Hyrcania (now called Khirbet Mird)[4] so as to include a sanctuary. The roof of a two-storeyed building was used for prayers, so that there were in all three levels used in worship. The ground floor and the middle floor (the floor of the upper storey) corresponded in function to the ground floor and platform of the Qumran vestry.

The seer in the cathedral at Ephesus, derived from the Judean model,[5] looked forward to the step and dais just to the north of him, then, further back, to two further tiers, a middle and an upper one. From the middle tier a balcony projected forward, following the pattern of a two-storeyed house (see Diagram B).

On the upper tier King Herod, when he was present, sat enthroned. On the middle tier could be seen the active priests and levites. A chair (*kathedra*) was placed on its balcony and used for teaching, hence the word 'cathedral'. The middle tier became the sanctuary of a Christian church, containing the high altar, and the upper tier was no longer used after the Herodian dynasty ceased. The ground floor dais and its step developed into the chancel of a Christian church, containing the step before the communion rail. The southern room became the congregation, with its seats called pews.

FROM PRIESTS AND LEVITES TO CHRISTIAN MINISTERS

Priests and levites officiated on the middle tier, using the titles of archangels that are found in both the Scrolls and the New Testament. All 'archangels' such as 'Michael' and 'Gabriel', were, in actual fact, real men, drawing on a doctrine of incarnation. They were descendants of the ancient priestly lines, which, they believed, were the ones approved by God, but they were no longer able to officiate in the Jerusalem temple. However, since the true temple was in heaven, where angels, archangels and spirits were engaged in continual worship of God, the earthly priests and levites could claim to be reproductions of these beings, who had entered into them by an act of incarnation (a familiar concept in the Hellenistic world, where great human beings were often said to be incarnations of God). 'Michael' was the supreme priest, the descendant of the Zadokite dynasty that had supplied high priests in Solomon's temple, and who should, the Essenes believed, still hold the high priesthood.[6] 'Gabriel' and 'Sariel' were the descendants of two other priestly dynasties, the next most important after the Zadokites: that of Abiathar and that of Levi.[7] The man who appears as the 'angel Gabriel' in Luke's gospel was the current descendant of the Abiathar priesthood, referred to by Josephus as Simon the Essene.[8] The 'heirs of Levi' were men in a levitical office supported by ascetic Sadducees, who were more accepting of the Jerusalem priesthood. They could themselves become public high priests in the Jerusalem temple, as did six members of the Annas family who played a central role in the history. Within the ascetic community they acted in the part of 'Sariel', the third priest in the hierarchy.

Gabriel was, in the liturgical system based on the

DIAGRAM B
HERODIAN CATHEDRAL, SIDE VIEW

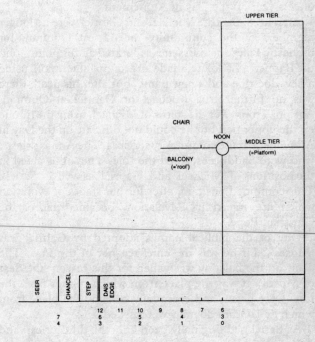

seasons, the priest for the east, spring, the Passover festival and the colour green. Sariel, originally, belonged to the west, autumn, Tabernacles and the colour red. These two feasts were the major ones for Jews, and the priests who officiated at them were at the top of the hierarchy, next only to Michael, the Zadokite, who officiated once a year on the Day of Atonement.

After AD 6, the true Michael and Gabriel were no longer members of the community meeting at Qumran, for monastic Palestinian Essenes separated at this point. John the Baptist, a Zadokite, made an attempt at reunion, using a new doctrine and a new name, but after his death there was no further true Michael or Gabriel at Qumran. Agrippa I took over the status of Michael, using the throne on the upper tier, but he could not officiate on the Day of Atonement at the community services. The Annas priests, who were Sadducees, filled the role. They thus acted in the positions of 'Michael' and 'Gabriel' as well as 'Sariel'. This combined position, after further stages of evolution which are traced in Revelation, became that of the Christian Pope.

One of the biblical names adopted by Gabriel was 'Moses',[9] for he was the chief teacher of the Law. The chair on the balcony was called for this reason 'the Seat of Moses'. It was the place from which rulings from the Law were given, and eventually became the place from which *ex cathedra* dogmas were issued.

As Sariel had originally been only the third priest, and as he belonged to the west, considered less holy, his main duty was to go out of the celibate community into the unclean world, where he acted as visiting priest to villagers.

The structure of the Qumran vestry was understood to be reproduced in the village, so that he could still say prayers. A typical village house was of one storey, and Sariel on arriving said prayers on its roof (*dōma*), which corresponded to the platform in the vestry. Then, when he had finished his prayers, he came down to stand in front of the door of the house, close enough to the villagers to act in the capacities they needed, including giving judgments and pronouncing forgiveness of sins. He was here at the equivalent of the dais and step in the vestry.

This point is illustrated in the gospel story of the 'paralytic'. The Annas priest, the Sariel, was at that time Jonathan Annas, who used the title 'God', as has been seen. Jonathan Annas took his status very seriously, and when he had to come to the village he was carried in a palanquin. Appearing to be unable to walk, he was called a 'paralytic' by his critics. After praying from noon to 3 p.m. on the roof of the building near Qumran that stood for all village houses,[10] he was let down in his palanquin to the doorway to attend to the villagers. Jesus, who being of lowlier grade had been standing at the door all the time, turned and attacked him for his excessive priestliness, claiming that he himself could act like a priest ('the Son of Man can forgive sins'). He then acted as if he was forgiving Jonathan's sins. He made him abandon his palanquin and 'rise up and walk'.[11]

While Michael, Gabriel and Sariel were the three chief priests (a passage in the Scrolls speaks of 'three priests and twelve men' as forming their council),[12] there were further ministers of high status. The main one was Raphael, the fourth in order in the hierarchy of archangels,[13] the one who presided over the season of December, when there were no traditional ancient feasts. He was the chief levite, the subordinate of Sariel, and he acted with him in both the monastery, where he was chief Scribe, and in the village, where he acted as the deputy of the visiting priest. The holder of this position in the original zealot party was Judas the Galilean, then in the thirties AD Judas Iscariot.[14] The Chief Therapeut (see further below) could be promoted to act in the same position, and was called the *archōn*. In his lesser position he was a bishop, and the higher position became that of archbishop.

Another figure of equal status appears in the literature of the archangels, and is named in Luke as the superior of a woman. This was Phanuel, whose position was that of an equal of Raphael, but he ministered to the uncircumcised.[15] Phanuel also officiated as a subordinate of Sariel, in both the celibate community and in the village. In some Jewish villages, and in the Diaspora, the local synagogue was under the control of the Hellenist party of ascetics, while in others with more eastern sympathies the Hebrews were in charge. Hellenist synagogues allowed Gentiles to attend and receive some instruction, even though they were uncircumcised, and it was a levite in the role of Phanuel who accepted them. One of his many titles was 'ruler of the (Hellenist) synagogue'. Being the superior of the uncircumcised, he was also the superior of women. 'Jairus, the ruler of the synagogue',[16] who had a 'daughter', was the Phanuel of the gospel period. In another of his roles, he wore scarlet vestments, originating the position of cardinal.

The Phanuel as Jewish priest to the uncircumcised was given special prominence in Revelation. Once Ephesus became the centre for Diaspora ascetics, he was found both in the cathedral, as a member of the celibate community, and in the local synagogue. Up to AD 50 he was Theophilus Annas, one of the younger Annas brothers. He was also called 'Elder 24' (the pesher meaning of 'twenty-four elders') because he was responsible for prayers during the twenty-four hours of the day and night. When, in Rev 4:10, 'the twenty-four elders fell before . . . the throne', Theophilus Annas was kneeling in the Ephesus cathedral before the throne of Herod.

According to the Old Testament, there were three minor levitical leaders, heads of families, called Kohath, Gershon (also spelt Gershom, but the spelling with -'n' is used in the Scrolls) and Merari, in that order.[17] The Temple Scroll shows that they were still given a position in the hierarchy.[18] From the pesher it is seen that the positions of Kohath and Merari were filled by younger members of the Annas family, and another man took the place of Gershon. All had a place in the Qumran vestry and in its reproductions. Being of lesser status than other priests and levites, they were permitted to come closer to Gentiles, and their functions were gradually taken over by Gentiles. The position of Kohath became that of a bishop, of Gershon that of a presbyter, and of Merari that of a deacon.

These offices became highly refined as time went on, becoming a means of expressing not only the levitical hierarchy but times and grades. The Book of Revelation depends on this system, and makes it possible to trace how it developed into the structure of the Church.

CHAPTER 3

The New Jerusalem

HOW TO BUILD A CHURCH

According to Chapter 21 of Revelation, the seer was taken away to a great, high mountain, and shown the holy city Jerusalem coming down out of heaven from God. The city was square, and there were twelve gates, in each wall three gates. The seer was given a measuring rod, and he measured the city. He measured its length, 12 000 stadia (about 1500 miles or 2400 kilometres). He measured its wall, which was 144 cubits (216 feet or about 66 metres); a point difficult to reconcile with the 1500 miles or 2400 kilometres. He was then shown its foundations, with twelve kinds of jewels.

The vestry at Qumran, described above, is 12 cubits long from the upper limit marked by the wall of the vault, down to the edge of the dais (see Diagram A on p.152). Its width, including the side walls, is 12 cubits. If a seer took a measure to all these four sides, treating the upper limit as finishing at the vault, he would find that it was 144 cubits. The length is 12 cubits, but hardly 12 000 stadia. (The reason for the latter measurement will be shown below, p.190.)

From a nearby cave at Qumran came the Temple

Scroll, which contains a plan for the new temple which the sectarians claimed had been given by God. The plan was to consist of three concentric squares, a wall surrounding each, with three gates in each wall. The tribes were to enter through the gates, in the order: Simeon, Levi, Judah on the east; Reuben, Ephraim-Manasseh, Benjamin on the south; Issachar, Zebulun, Gad on the west; Dan, Naphtali, Asher on the north.[1] The order of tribes does not reflect any of the plans in the Old Testament.

The Book of Revelation not only has a four square New Jerusalem with the same shape and gates, but its list of tribes (here interpreted as ascetic orders) is so close to that of the Temple Scroll that it would be extraordinary coincidence if it did not depend on it, with

DIAGRAM C

GATES IN REVELATION 7 AND THE TEMPLE SCROLL

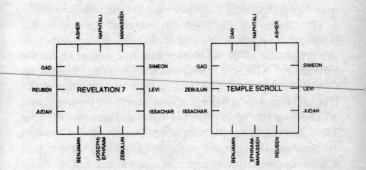

conscious variations. When the list in Revelation 7 is taken to begin from the *west* and read in a clockwise direction, then its eastern wall had gates for Simeon, Levi and Issachar (not Judah) its southern wall had gates for Zebulun (not Reuben), Ephraim and Benjamin; its western wall Judah (not Issachar), Reuben (not Zebulun) and Gad; and its northern wall Asher (not Dan), Naphtali and Manasseh (not Asher). In other words, Issachar and Judah have been exchanged with each other, and similarly

Reuben and Zebulun. Dan is missing altogether, and Asher replaces Dan. Manasseh, now separate, is given the position of Asher on the north wall. The direct reversals, and six out of twelve names in the same positions, must mean dependence. It will be shown below that reasons for the changes can be discovered from the history.

These are not the only links: Revelation has numerous and pervasive points of contact with the Scrolls. It speaks of wearing white clothes, and washing clothes as a sign of purity.[2] The Essenes were noted for wearing white garments,[3] and according to the Temple Scroll they must, after an episode of uncleanness such as a nocturnal emission, go outside for some days and only return after washing their clothes.[4] The Manual of Discipline prohibits nakedness[5] in just the same way as Rev 16:15, which speaks of the man who keeps his garments 'that he may not walk naked and they may see his indecency'.

The 'vision' of the New Jerusalem at the end of the Book of Revelation was, it may be seen, intended as the grand climax of the history that had begun about the time that the Temple Scroll was written. The expectation of the Restoration that had led to the writing of the Temple Scroll had been fulfilled, so it was believed, and so also had the hope of a true temple. But now, the true New Jerusalem was a Christian church in a Christian monastery. Its model was at Ephesus, and other Christian monasteries and churches must follow it. Its plan was set down in Revelation 21, using the same device as was used in the Temple Scroll and its predecessors, a revelation by a divine agency.

The plan was based on the number twelve, not only because of the traditional use of twelve in Jewish thought, but because the system of prayer hours and of grades was governed by this number. When the exiled priests at Qumran set up a substitute sanctuary, they used it, not only for the great feasts, but for daily and hourly prayers, for they had come to believe that prayers rising to God were an equally acceptable form of sacrifice. Their daily discipline and their organisation arose from their duty of ensuring that prayers were said at all the appointed times, times that were determined by the movements of the sun. The sun, they believed, was God's clock, and they themselves were its reproduction on earth. The Scrolls emphasise their duty of saying prayers exactly on time: 'not to be late or early for any of their appointed times', and speak of praying at the times of the sun as it moves through the sky.[6]

Just as the progress of time can be marked by successive positions on a clock, they marked its progress by their positions when they offered prayers. They were directed by their priests, who in the daylight hours were able to use a device such as the gnomon or sundial, with shadows showing the divisions of time. The divisions were transferred to fixed positions, a cubit representing an hour, the positions running north-south. They allowed a daylight day of twelve hours, as is stated in John 11:9.

A consequent equation of space and time developed, governing every aspect of their tightly structured system. When they were forced to move into the vestry, the 12 cubit north-south line was preserved by placing the wall of the vault 12 cubits north of the dais edge. The noon prayer was said on the sixth cubit down.

The platform for the prayers of the highest priests was erected over the noon point (see Diagram A on p.152). It was only 6 cubits wide, with a space of 2 cubits on either side, the eastern space being used as a passageway. The three highest priests stood on the platform, each occupying 2 cubits width. Michael was responsible for the noon prayer, Gabriel on the east for the 6 a.m. prayer, and Sariel on the west for the 6 p.m. prayer. Michael was not normally present, his duties being limited to the Day of Atonement, and he was represented at the centre by his servant. This was either Raphael or Phanuel, both being levites or their equivalent. The three ministers were all

163

likened to angels, giving the Christian term 'angelus' for the prayers at morning, noon and evening.

In the upper half of the room, under the platform, was the table where these three priests had their noon meal, eating the holy loaves of the Presence that had been laid out in the sanctuary. The platform acted as their roof, and they occupied the same 2 cubit spaces under it. In the lower half of the vestry, in the 6 cubits between the centre and the dais, stood the table that was used for evening meals, a more common occasion, when guests could attend. It was not used during the day, and a device was developed whereby the covering that was over it at night was removed during the day, with the purpose of letting the congregation, sitting in the room south of the dais, see the man offering the noon prayer on the central point of the platform. An extension of the platform, resting on the pillars supporting the platform, held the northern edge of the covering, and two further pillars held it at the edge of the dais. The remains of the pillars holding the platform were found by the archaeologists.

When this cover was removed, the sun shone down into the space, and the congregation were dazzled by it and could only just see the priest praying on the platform, giving him the appearance of something supernatural. This was the basis of the 'vision' of Jesus that Paul saw in Damascus in AD 40.[7] He was at that time in a reproduction of the congregation room in the Damascus monastery, and Jesus was praying at noon on the platform. Paul, looking up into the sun, was partly blinded, but Jesus was able to see him, and spoke to him.

In the course of time, and for several reasons – one of them being that under a less strict discipline a man was given a square of 2 cubits in which to pray – the northern 12 cubits were re-divided into six sets of 2 cubits, so that the noon line was at the edge of the dais and a noon prayer could be said there by Raphael or Phanuel. It was under the influence of village members that this change took place, for the dais edge represented the doorway of a village house, as has been seen, and they could now offer a noon prayer in their villages.

On another interpretation, one that allowed for both the monastic practice and the village practice, the original central line was retained as that for noon, while the dais edge, using the 2 cubit spaces, was used for a prayer at 3 p.m. This was the hour when the visiting priest Sariel came down to the doorway to meet villagers.

On this interpretation, the 6 cubit space which was uncovered in the vestry each day stood for the time between noon and 3 p.m., the sixth hour and the ninth hour. This was the explanation of the 'three hours' darkness' on the day of the crucifixion. The cover was normally removed, allowing the sun to shine down, but if, for a special reason, it was not removed, there was darkness over the area from noon to 3 p.m., 'from the sixth hour to the ninth hour'. There was a special reason for leaving it over on the day of the crucifixion. Because the solar calendar did not reflect the movements of the sun with perfect accuracy, the 'clocks' became 'three hours fast' over a number of years, and a great date such as that of the crucifixion was used to adjust them. The cover was left over until 3 p.m., which was the true noon.[8]

The pillars supporting the middle tier were in the spaces occupied by Gabriel for the morning prayer and Sariel for the evening prayer. From the Exodus imagery used by the Therapeuts, they were called 'the pillar of cloud by day' (east) and the 'pillar of fire by night' (west).

The method of division into 2 cubits for each hour allowed for a prayer to be said also at the half hour, on the alternating cubits. The increase in frequency of prayers was a consequence of an interest in greater accuracy in the measurement of time. The Book of Revelation shows in 8:1 that in 'heaven' time was measured in half hours. When the centre of the platform represented noon, its 1 cubit extension, holding the edge of the cover, represented 12.30. A circle was understood to lie over the central noon point, 2 cubits in diameter, within which the man saying the noon prayer stood. The lower half of the circle was called the 'middle' (*mesos*), an apparently vague term which has a precise sense in the timespace equation. When the edge of the dais, further down, represented noon, a similar circle made the 1 cubit step before it the *mesos*.

When the dais edge was treated as representing 3 p.m., the line 2 cubits south of it represented 4 p.m., and the step represented 3.30 p.m. A levite, Raphael or Phanuel, said a prayer on the dais edge, and could occupy the whole 2 cubits (the step being level with the edge of the dais), but, since they were members of the celibate community and were capable of occupying only 1 cubit, they made a distinction, using the chancel step alone when they were in a lesser state of holiness. It was used also by other ministers who corresponded to the lesser status.

The 4 p.m. line, 2 cubits south of the dais edge, marked the extreme limit of the northern section, for village prayers normally ended at 3 p.m., but could be extended to 4 p.m.[9] That hour had associations of uncleanness, for in the monastery it was the hour when the holier part of the day ended and the latrine was visited. In villages where Gentiles were taught, their teaching was given at 4 p.m., to show that they were unclean.[10] Across this 4 p.m. line a thin screen was placed, called a 'wall' in Revelation 21. In early Christian usage it was a lattice (Latin *cancelli*), which gave the word 'chancel'. It marked off the part where prayers and teaching could be given, and south of it was the room for the congregation.

In the Qumran vestry, the congregation originally consisted of twelve men; the lay celibates in the monastery, who according to the Scrolls were likened to twelve precious stones, and, as shown in Revelation 21, the jewels corresponded to the twelve precious stones on the high priest's breastplate.[11] They sat, rather than stood, each needing a 2 cubit square, and were in four rows of three seats each, across the 6 cubits in the middle part of the room. The first seat was in the centre of the first row, and was used by the first of the 'precious stones'. In Herodian usage it became the royal pew, and when the royal person was not present it was used by the seer, who from this vantage point had a good view through the centre of the screen to all that was being done in the northern section.

In Christian usage, derived from the Gentile practice, the 4 p.m. line of the chancel was the true beginning of the northern section, and the 144 cubit square of Revelation 21 began with it as the southern dimension, leaving a 2 cubit space at the north of the vestry. In the original Qumran vestry, the 2 cubits at the top were given a special treatment, as remains of installations near the furnace indicate.[12]

This was the plan of the Qumran vestry and of buildings derived directly from it. The plan of Revelation 21 describes, not the cathedral in the city of Ephesus, but a building which had been erected an hour's distance away, probably where the tomb of Mary stands now. As Revelation 11 shows, the seer, at the time of the schism of AD 44, had been given a measuring rod and told to build a reproduction of the Qumran vestry. At that stage, the Ephesus building whose construction he directed was a hermitage, occupied by Jewish men living like the Therapeuts. But when a later seer was given a measuring rod in Revelation 21, and sent to the same building, it was being re-dedicated as a Christian monastery. From the point of view of Christians with a more eastern orientation, the climax of the history came when the plan of the Temple Scroll was adapted to Christian usage. The room used for worship in the monastery was from now on the model for all ordinary churches.

The cathedral in the city of Ephesus had the same essential plan and orientation, but its three tiers introduced some further features. The middle tier corresponded to the platform in the vestry plan, but the 1 cubit extension of the platform now came further forward to make a 3 cubit balcony on which the *kathedra* was placed. The visiting priest used this chair, attaching to it the coloured banner from his horse, as has been shown in Chapter 8. This level corresponded to the roof of a one-storeyed village house where the visiting priest said his noon prayers, and so could be called the *dōma*. But above it was the upper tier, corresponding to the roof of a two- storeyed house, where prayers were said by more important persons. It was this arrangement that explains what happened in Joppa in a story in Acts 10. Peter was saying his prayers on the *dōma* at noon, and from above Jesus spoke to him, apparently as a heavenly vision. A cloth was let down to Peter, with 'unclean beasts' which he was told to eat, signifying certain doctrinal changes. To the reader who understood the system, this meant that Peter was in a three-tiered structure, and Jesus, as a real person, was saying prayers on the upper tier, while Peter was on the balcony which extended from the middle tier. Jesus let down to him a tablecloth marked with the emblems of animals. It was to be placed on his communion table, meaning that he must share communion with people he had regarded as unclean.

Similarly, in a building in Troas, the 'young man' called Eutychus was on the third storey, while Paul preached in the 'upper room'. Eutychus 'fell down dead', and Paul revived him. The story, in Acts 20, simply records the rehabilitation of John Mark, whose personal name was Eutychus[13]. He took a high view of his priesthood, but was made to go through a ceremony in which he was reduced from the upper tier to the ground floor, then raised by Paul to a more moderate doctrine of ministry, that of the middle tier.

FOUR LIVING CREATURES

According to Revelation 4, four 'living creatures' were seen by the seer. As shown in Chapter 8, they were the four evangelists, using titles derived from the four living creatures of Ezekiel's vision. They were called 'the first, the servant of a Lion' (the word *homoios*, 'like', having the special sense of 'servant', since a servant was like his master when he represented him); second, 'the servant of a Calf'; third, one 'having the face as of a Man' (not called servant); and fourth, 'the servant of a Flying Eagle'.

It is possible to see, from an understanding of the plan of the Ephesus cathedral in which the scene took place, just where the four were standing. They formed a triangle, with Matthew, the 'Man', at its apex on the edge of the dais. Peter, 'the servant of a Lion', stood on the chancel step in front of him. John Mark, 'the servant of a Flying Eagle', stood on the east side of the chancel step, and Luke 'the servant of a Calf', was on its west side. All four were just in front of the seer.

DIAGRAM D
POSITIONS OF THE EVANGELISTS

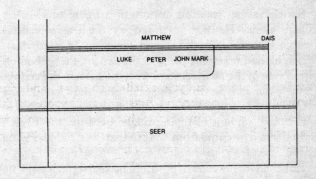

As has been seen, a levite or his equivalent, a Raphael or Phanuel, could say a noon prayer in the village when the

2 cubit measurement was introduced. The edge of the dais stood for the doorway of a village house. The levite either occupied both cubits at the edge of the dais and the step, or stood on the higher cubit, while a lesser minister stood on the step. When the visiting priest Sariel came down from his prayers to attend to villagers, he occupied the place of the levite on the dais edge. Sariel having combined his position with that of Gabriel, as has been seen, was the Man of the four living creatures of Ezekiel's vision, since Gabriel's name means 'Man of God'. While in the monastery his position was on the east, that of the Man in Ezekiel,[14] but when the combined Sariel-Gabriel came to the village he occupied the central place determined by his high status. Matthew Annas was the Sariel-Gabriel under Agrippa II in Ephesus, and at the ceremony of dedication of the gospels in AD 49 stood on the dais edge as 'the Man', the highest of the four.

The two halves of the circle on the dais edge and the step were north and south, and these were the original directions of the Calf and the Lion of the living creatures. The 'servant of a Lion', Peter, as the first living creature, occupied the place of the Lion in the centre of the chancel step.

Sariel-Gabriel was too important a figure to visit the village alone. He was attended by the lesser levitical figures Kohath (a bishop) and Gershon (a presbyter). When he had taken his place at the centre, they stood on either side of the chancel step, with the Lion in the centre. In the place of Kohath on the east John Mark stood. As a celibate, he was equal to a levitical bishop, a Kohath. He was called 'servant of Flying Eagle' because 'the Eagle', Sariel, when he came from west to east, was called 'Flying Eagle'.

Luke, in the western position of Gershon, could be called 'servant of a Calf', because he was a servant of the Herods. The title of 'Calf' had come to be adopted by the Herods, who used it both in the north and in a western position equal to Sariel. See 'Calf' in the Lexicon on this point.

In Revelation 6, where the teaching program for the gospels is described, each living creature said 'Come!' at the season corresponding to his compass point. Pentecost was the season of white, summer, noon, and the south, and the Lion spoke at Pentecost in AD 49. Autumn, corresponding to red, the west and sunset, was the season for Luke, standing on the west. Winter, the season of black, the north and midnight, was the season for Matthew, in the northern half of the circle. Spring, for green, the east and sunrise, was for the fourth living creature, standing on the east.

POSITION OF THE SON OF MAN, THE LAMB

In Revelation 1 Jesus as the Son of Man appeared. In Revelation 5 he appeared again as the Lamb. On both occasions, he stood *mesos*, in the 'middle'. This word, as has been seen, meant the lower half of a 2 cubit circle where the noon prayer was said, either that on the middle tier, or that on the dais edge and step.

Jesus as the Son of Man was standing 'in the *mesos* of the lampstands' (Rev 1:13). This gives the clue: he was on the chancel step, in the lower half of the circle representing the place for village prayers. The village was the place where there was a synagogue, and in the synagogue the seven-branched lampstand, the Menorah, burned, its seven lights marking the hours of the night from 9 p.m. to 3 a.m. Jesus was appearing at its final hour, 3 a.m., when for ascetics the night ended and their day began.

Later the same day Jesus as the Lamb was again in the *mesos*. The detail that he was 'slain' (Rev 5:6) gives the clue: he was wearing the scarlet of blood, and this meant that he was wearing the colour worn by Phanuel when in a lesser status, on the step rather than the dais edge. Scarlet was the colour worn by a priest in the outside world, and it was from this practice that the position of Christian cardinal developed (see Lexicon, **scarlet**). Jesus was now acting in the status of a lesser Phanuel. On both occasions he was in a lowly position, very close to the congregation.

In the original Herodian system, the David was a leader of the lower classes only. He was both a 'Lion' and a 'Lamb'. Both titles meant that he could act as a village minister, standing on the step in front of the village house when more exalted priests arrived. As the 'Lion' he was a bishop, and he used the title 'Son of Man', because he stood below 'the Man'. As 'the Lamb' he was equal to a lesser Phanuel, a cardinal. He had to go through many levitical ranks before he, and his descendants, attained the position of Michael himself.

THE CHIEF THERAPEUT

The Therapeuts of Egypt were one of the most important sects forming part of the original Herodian mission. Based in Alexandria, they reflected the outlook of Diaspora Jews who looked partly to Jerusalem, but were partly independent of the homeland, embracing the treasures of Greek learning with enthusiasm.[15]

Their eremitical communities were like the monastic communities of the high Essenes in some ways, but significantly different in that they were not shut off from the world and did not hold common property. However, their form of ministry was based on the position of the Chief Scribe in a monastery, a man who had earned by merit a position equal to the levite Raphael. Raphael's name means 'God heals', and the Therapeuts specialised in the study of healing. The Chief Therapeut was called a 'ruler', *archōn*.[16]

The *archōn* acted as a deputy to Raphael, moving into his position when he was absent. At the Last Supper, Theudas or Thaddeus, the Chief Therapeut at that time, took the position of Judas, the Raphael, after he left the supper. When a 'Judas, not Iscariot' is mentioned as speaking after Judas' departure, it was Theudas.[17]

The Raphael was the one who 'tested' or 'tempted' candidates for initiation. This, together with the zealot associations of the order of Manasseh to which Judas Iscariot belonged, gave him the names 'the Devil' and 'Satan'. The head of the Therapeuts, whose order was the related one of Ephraim, was called 'Satan' when he occupied the same position.

Judas Iscariot, following Judas the Galilean who was the 'Beast' of the zealot uprising in AD 6, did not confine himself to levitical duties, but could descend to the grade of the Lion, in which he was permitted to fight. For the ascetic order to which these men belonged, it was an act of religious dedication to take part in warfare in defence of Judaism. The Chief Therapeut, who belonged to a different order, shared their attitude, although usually more moderately, and varying according to the political climate. But he could deputise for Raphael in the role of Beast also. Reflecting this status, which was that of a bishop, one of his titles was 'Living Creature Four'. This was not the same as the 'fourth living creature'. The number meant that he was of grade 4 (see below, p.180).

Under the title 'Living Creature Four', apparently a summary of the other four but in fact another person, Apollos the Egyptian, the successor of Theudas, appeared at the Pentecost service described in Revelation 4 and 5. While the four living creatures who were evangelists were in the chancel, he was in the *mesos* of the throne (Rev 4:6), that is, on the balcony, in the southern half of the noon circle.

In the Exodus imagery of the Therapeuts the Chief Therapeut played several roles, one of them being that of Joshua the successor of Moses. Both the David and the Chief Therapeut were called Joshua (Jesus), as is shown in Matt 27:17. As a Joshua, it was his duty to blow the trumpet, as in the story of Joshua at the fall of Jericho. At the jubilee, he prepared the trumpet for Michael-Gabriel to blow (Rev 8:6), and at the lesser points in the jubilee he blew it himself (Rev 1:10, 4:1).

The Therapeuts of Egypt were central to the political history, for as Jews of Alexandria they were constantly torn between the east and the west, between loyalty to the homeland and preference for the Diaspora, between support of the Herods and antipathy to the Herods in favour of the older royal line of the Davids. Whenever the Chief Therapeut changed his political stance, there was an 'earthquake'. The name 'Earthquake' was used for him as a title at these points, derived from the fact that at the earthquake at Qumran in 31 BC there had been major changes, particularly affecting the Therapeuts.

It was the Diaspora order of Therapeuts who first admitted Gentiles, treating them as equal to the women who shared their eremitical discipline. While the seers of Ephesus were still within the Jewish organisation, the Chief Therapeut was their Jewish superior, and it was he who gave directions to the seer throughout the Book of Revelation.

CHAPTER 4

The System of Grades

As has been seen in the foregoing pages, the pesharist of the gospels and Revelation was working with knowledge of a very tightly structured system. Just as every hour of the celibate's life was governed by the times, so every activity was governed by a system of grades and ranks. Obedience to the system was the first requirement, producing a discipline that both gave the organisation its political power and produced the rebellion that led to the separation of Christians. But for the purposes of the 'mystery', the logical, man-made system gave an objective set of data, fixed facts from which the history could be deduced. It was in its own way a work of art, depending on a theory of symmetry, with the Pythagorean belief that everything could be brought under the control of numbers. Because of its unity, it can be discovered from a knowledge of the Hebrew alphabet and relevant information from the Scrolls and the surface of the New Testament.

Time, place, and hierarchy were interrelated in a unified structure. The heavenly powers were believed to control all systems of time, and all persons in the hierarchy. The times were themselves graded, the significant divisions assigned to the highest priests as the times over which they presided, that is, were on duty.

The essential divisions fell into four classes, reflecting the four seasons; then into seven kinds of ministers, reflecting the days of the week; then into twelve grades, reflecting both the twelve hours of the day and the twelve months of the year.

THE FOUR CLASSES

The four classes to which all members of the ascetic movement belonged were: first, the priests; second, the levites; third, lay celibates; and fourth, villagers. The list and the order are found in passages in the Scrolls,[1] the lay celibates being called 'sons of Israel' and the villagers called 'the sojourners' (*ger*), as they were the ones who went on pilgrimages to the monastery to bring the necessary food in the form of tithes. It may be seen that the first four letters of the Hebrew alphabet were used for the classes: Aleph (A, an Alpha in Greek); Beth (B); Gimel (a G, but the third letter); and Daleth (a D).

The Scrolls also show that there were twelve priests, twelve levites and twelve 'heads of tribes'; the latter (the lay celibates) also called 'princes of the people' and 'the congregation', and likened to precious stones.[2] Further detail from the pesher shows that the twelve priests formed class A (Aleph) under Sariel-Gabriel, and they served the wine at communal meals, as the Scrolls say the priest must do.[3] The twelve priests were subdivided into a higher five (for the four seasons and festivals, two being needed at Atonement-Tabernacles) and a lower seven, led by Phanuel, who in this role was called 'Spirit 7'.

The twelve levites of class B (Beth) were led by Raphael, and they were likened to 'loaves', for they corresponded to the second division of the temple, the Holy House, in which the twelve loaves of the Presence were placed on a table.[4] A 'loaf' means a levite in the pesher language. They were divided in the same way as the priests, but the higher group were the seven loaves, led by

Raphael (who was consequently equal to Phanuel of the priests) and a lower five. In the gospel stories of the 'feedings of the multitude', using five loaves in one case and seven in another, the meaning was that the powers of men who had been born into the levitical class were being given by Jesus to ordinary men, that is, that he was introducing ministry given by ordination, not by birth.

The priests and levites officiated in 'heaven', that is on the platform or its equivalent.

The twelve 'precious stones' of class C (Gimel) were the celibates, who in the original monastic system formed the congregation. Their leader was the king, who had not been born into a levitical tribe but had similar authority to the priests. He sat in the first seat in the congregation, making it the royal pew. While a Herod reigned, this position was taken by King Herod in his capacity as king (but he also claimed equality with the priests and exercised ministry). When there was no Herod, the David held this position.

The three classes A, B and C, were thus led by a triarchy called 'Priest, Prophet and King'. When, under Christian influence, laymen had been given the powers of priests, the leaders of the three were merged in the person of the Christ.

SEVEN DAYS, SEVEN ANGELS

When all men of priestly and levitical birth were counted, there were seven ranks: Michael, Gabriel, Sariel, Phanuel-Raphael, Kohath, Gershon and Merari. Merari, however, was not present in a celibate community, but was always outside, appointed to duties over the unclean. His position of deacon in the monastery was taken by an acolyte, a student, the leader of the acolytes being a royal prince. Raphael also was given special treatment, leaving Phanuel in the list of seven.

Prayers in the monastery were said every day, in contrast to the villages where only monthly services were held. The seven levitical persons led prayers on each of the days. The days themselves were called simply by numbers, not names, Sunday being Day 1, Monday Day 2, and so on. But each day belonged to an 'angel', that is a minister in the celibate community. The system of days was:

0	Saturday	Michael	4	Wednesday	Kohath
1	Sunday	Gabriel	5	Thursday	Gershon
2	Monday	Sariel	6	Friday	Acolyte
3	Tuesday	Phanuel			

The significance of Saturday, the sacred day in all Jewish worship, was expressed by making it a zero, so putting it at the beginning of the week. But in the practice of villagers it was treated as the seventh day at the end of the week, beginning on Friday evening. In both ordinary Jewish practice, as shown by Josephus, and in the community of the Scrolls,[5] a trumpet was blown on Friday evenings to signal the cessation of work for the sabbath. The day being that of Michael, he was called 'angel 7' when he blew the trumpet on the second Saturday of the series. He did not normally blow it himself on Friday evenings, but he did appear at the jubilee, the greater 'seventh day' (see further below, p.206). When 'angel 7' appears in Revelation, it means the ruling Herod, signalling the jubilee which was believed to be that of the Restoration.

In the village, a Raphael or Phanuel could officiate, offering a noon prayer as was done in the monastery. Diaspora ascetic communities, being of the same level as Palestinian villages, followed this up by also having daily prayers. They were led by Raphael or Phanuel, who now acted at the zero grade of Saturday. Below the levite, a minister equal to bishop Kohath led Sunday prayers, being differentiated from Kohath who acted on Wednesday. The Sunday bishop was a lay rather than levitical bishop, and, since the levite stood on the chancel step for the prayer starting Friday at 6 p.m., the bishop was below him in the first row of the congregation. It was here that the seer sat, 'on the Lord's day', Sunday, in Rev 1:10. He was there, not on Saturday at 6 p.m.,[6] but Saturday at midnight, beginning Sunday according to the Julian calendar, which he used as a Gentile.

Below the lay bishop, other ministers and members led prayers for the days, following the system of grades to be further explained below.

The village and Diaspora roster of days was:

0	Fri 6 p.m. or midnight	Saturday	Raphael or Phanuel
1	Sat 6 p.m. or midnight	Sunday	Lay bishop
2	Sun 6 p.m. or midnight	Monday	Lay presbyter
3	Mon 6 p.m. or midnight	Tuesday	Lay deacon
4	Tue 6 p.m. or midnight	Wednesday	Ordinary initiate
5	Wed 6 p.m. or midnight	Thursday	Pre-initiate
6	Thu 6 p.m. or midnight.	Friday	Lower pre-initiate

It was this set of ministers, still called 'angels', to whom the seven letters in Revelation 13 were addressed. They were ministers to Diaspora communities, in this case the seven churches in the province of Asia. The list began with Phanuel, the levitical cardinal in the cathedral in Ephesus, who was at that time Theophilus Annas. The other six were all individuals who were the chief lay ministers of the Diaspora, each of them including in his duties the care of one of the seven churches of the province.

TWELVE GRADES

A grade was a step in the educational ladder that could be taken by any layman who was studying in an ascetic community. A year was spent in each grade, and the grades were normally entered at certain ages. Since the grades were expressed through the cubit on which a man stood to pray, it was true, in the words of the gospel

179

saying, that by 'being anxious' (practising asceticism), one could 'add a cubit to one's age'.[7]

The numbers for the grades were taken from the priests, whose own numbers came from the days of the week, so that when a member of a monastery arrived, for instance, at grade 4, he was equal to a Kohath. But in the whole Herodian system there were twelve grades (fifteen in the original Essene system). The lowest was grade 12 and the highest grade 0. The letters of the Hebrew alphabet were also used to indicate grades, but this time using the later part of the alphabet, so that Taw, the last letter, was used for grade 0, indicating that it was not possible to go higher. (See Table 1 on p.182 for the summary.)

A man entered grade 12 at the age of eighteen. At this stage, he was simply a beginner, and not part of the subsequent structure. At grade 11, at the age of nineteen, he had taken the first step on the ladder of progress. At twenty, he had reached grade 10, and this was a significant stage, since at the age of twenty a villager could marry, as is stated in one of the Scrolls.[8] If he did, he was destined to stay in the world. But if he chose the higher way, either of a dynast who would not marry until thirty-six, or renounced sex altogether, he began at this point his progress towards the higher knowledge.

At twenty-one, both kinds of members reached grade 9, that of the main baptism. This was to receive the 'water', an immersion bath that was believed to wash away sin. Those entering a monastery became junior novices at this point.

Grades 12 to 9 were those to which married men were, at first, confined. While actively in the married state, they were at 11, and their wives, always one grade below them, were at 12. But they could at times undertake pilgrimages to the monastery, when they went up to 10. In the course of their pilgrimage they received a form of baptism in the running water of a river. On reaching the monastery, those with special merit went to grade 9.

At twenty-two, novices were at grade 8. According to the Manual of Discipline, a novice handed over his property to be kept in reserve, and was given the bread but not the wine at the sacred meal.[9]

At grade 7, at the age of twenty-three, the really significant step was taken by those who had chosen the celibate life. A man became an initiate, one who had handed over all his property and was now committed for life, being given the 'Drink of the Community', the wine at the sacred meal, as a sign of his privilege.

The monastic educational process then began, with four years of undergraduate study, through grades 6, 5 and 4, until he graduated at grade 3, at the age of twenty-seven.

After graduation, a monastic spent a further year preparing to enter the sanctuary. Arriving at grade 2, he entered the lower of the three divisions of the sanctuary. This was a great privilege, as it meant becoming equal to a Sariel. The middle section was the special place of Gabriel and a celibate at grade 1. A celibate at grade 0 was equal to Michael at the level of the Holy of Holies.

From the very highest grades, it was possible to fall to the very lowest. To be excommunicated from the monastery was to go down to 'Death (*thanatos*)', grade 12. This was also the grade of 'Sodom', for monastics guilty of sodomy were expelled. One grade above it was to be 'lifeless' (*nekros*) at grade 11. To be sent down to grade 10 was to become equal to a leper. 'Leper 10' of Luke 17:12 was a representative of such men. To be sent to grade 9 was to be sent to 'prison'.

The twelve grades were linked with the twelve hours of the day, and a man's grade was shown by the hour at which he prayed. Under the older Jewish system of hours, 6 a.m was Michael's hour, and the hours corresponded to the days, with the grade 6 acolyte praying on the ground floor at noon, the sixth hour (under Raphael- Phanuel), a grade 7 at 1 p.m., the seventh hour, a grade 10 at 4 p.m., and a grade 12 saying an evening prayer in the village at 6 p.m., the twelfth hour. To state the hour at which a man prayed was to state his grade, as in the case of Cornelius, who was shown to be a grade 9 by the fact that he prayed at the ninth hour (Acts 10:3).[10]

The Hebrew letters used for the grades are explained more fully below.

TABLE 1
SYSTEM OF GRADES

No.	Hebrew	Age	Position	Meaning	Hour
0	Taw	30	Michael	Holy of Holies	6 a.m.
1	Shin	29	Gabriel	Holy House	7 a.m.
2	Resh	28	Sariel	Enter sanctuary	8 a.m.
3	Qof	27	Phanuel	Graduate	9 a.m.
4	Sadhe	26	Kohath		10 a.m.
5	Pe	25	Gershon		11 a.m.
6	Ayin	24	Acolyte		noon
7	Samekh	23	Initiate	Full membership	1 p.m.
8	Nun	22	Novice	Pre-initiate	2 p.m.
9	Mem	21	Baptised	Lower pre-initiate	3 p.m.
10	Lamedh	20	Begin progress	Villager may marry	4 p.m.
11	Kaph	19		Married man; 'lifeless'	5 p.m.
12	Yod	18		'Sodom'; 'dead'	6 p.m.

An important principle governing the grades was that a servant must stand at arm's length from his master, that is, there must be 2 cubits and consequently two grades between them. A 4 was the servant of a 1, a 5 the servant of a 2, and so on.

THE MARK OF THE BEAST, THE CHI RHO, AND ALPHA AND OMEGA
The Scrolls give indications that they shared the contemporary Jewish reverence for their alphabet, but they were not using it in subjective ways such as are found in

the allegorical Jewish literature. For example, their veneration for the letter Nun ('N') is expressed in the Manual of Discipline (1QS 10:4), and Philo explains the reason:[11] it was the sign used for the number 50 (each letter of the alphabet also indicated a number), and their calendar of pentecontads depended on this number. Similarly, the number 7 was valued because the basic calendar division was into weeks. Their methods of using the numbers were objective, and can be discovered by objective means.

The letters of the Hebrew alphabet were used to indicate both grade and class. In the New Testament the Greek words for numbers are used, for those who did not have Hebrew. Some expressions, however, depend on the Hebrew letters, such as 666 (Taw, Resh, Samekh), and the 'Alpha and Omega' that is prominent in Revelation, depending on Hebrew letters transposed into Greek.

For the purpose of reference, the twenty-two Hebrew letters may be listed, in transliterated form: Aleph, Beth, Gimel, Daleth, He, Waw, Zayin, Heth, Tet, Yod, Kaph, Lamedh, Mem, Nun, Samekh, Ayin, Pe, Sadhe, Qof, Resh, Shin, Taw.

Each grade was designated by a Hebrew letter. The last twelve letters of the Hebrew alphabet were used to name the grades, with the highest at Taw. The grade letter was worn on a badge on the forehead, derived from the Jewish phylactery. The Damascus Document speaks of initiates marked on the forehead with the letter Taw, who will be saved in a coming eschatological crisis.[12]

The shape of the archaic Taw, X, was used. Its shape is known from inscriptions coming from the time when the Taw sign was first mentioned in the Old Testament, in Ezek 9:4. They show the X shape. In some of the Scrolls, the sacred divine name was written with archaic letters, illustrating their continuing use for special purposes.

This shape, the original sign, became the 'mark of the Beast'. It was preserved without change by the eastern party, for whom it meant membership of a form of Judaism.

The eastern party, as has been shown in Chapter 5, added to the Taw the two further letters which stood for significant stages, Resh ('R'), given at the age of twenty-eight at entry into the sanctuary, and Samekh (another 'S') given at age twenty-three at initiation. These three letters, with the Waw used with initials, gave the number 666 when the numerical value of the letters was used. (In normal Jewish practice, which used the letters as signs for the numbers, the first 10 letters were used for 1 to 10, then Kaph for 20, Lamedh 30, Mem 40, and so on, until Qof 100, Resh 200, Shin 300, Taw 400.) When the X sign was retained by the eastern party, and the schism of AD 44 took place, the westerners, both Herodian and Christian, had to change their sign. They had a resource, for they used Greek, and a 't' in Greek had the shape T. The Greek word *ti*, alone and in combinations, was used as a play on this letter.

The sign Chi Rho, X with a superimposed Greek R, in the shape of P, also may be seen to have developed from the system of Hebrew letters. Another way of speaking of a person who had gone through the system was to give him the letter Qof as well as Taw, and to impose one on the other. The Qof, a 'q' in Hebrew but in the shape of P, was the letter given at graduation at the age of twenty- seven. (The saying about a camel going through the eye of a needle derived from the letters, for class C, containing celibates, was Gimel, which also means 'camel' in Hebrew, and Qof has the meaning 'eye of a needle'. The saying means that a celibate graduated.)[13] A Qof, P shape, superimposed upon X, gave the same shape as the Greek letter Chi with a superimposed Rho. It was eventually understood to be the first two letters of *Christos*, but it had had a previous history.

When Greek was used as well as Hebrew, a solution was found to the problem of expressing the zero for Michael's form of Saturday, a zero day preceding day 1, and for grade 0. Hebrew had no word for zero, and the concept was a Greek one. The Greek letter Omega served the double purpose, for it was the last letter of the alphabet, like Taw. Its sound, 'O', came to express zero. To say 'I am the Alpha and the Omega' was a characteristic use of letters to convey great meanings to those who understood. It was to say 'I am a Sariel- Gabriel head of priests (class Aleph or Alpha, grade 1, priests) and a Michael (equal to Taw, the highest grade 0, superior priests)'. These words alone were said by a priest early in the Book of Revelation, but in its final part (in 21:6) they were said by Jesus III, who added 'the Beginning and the End'. His more exact meaning concerned the Christian feasts rather than the positions of the letters in the alphabet (see the pesher of this verse). But he was making the tremendous claim that the dynasty of the Davids had now taken over the prerogatives of the highest class of Jewish priests.

THE TWELVE 'TRIBES'

As has been seen, Revelation contains a list of the twelve tribes of Israel, the order of which must be dependent on the order in the Temple Scroll. In the first century BC, when the Temple Scroll was written, Jews were no longer strongly identified by tribes, although genealogies were kept. Rather, in the New Israel, 'tribes' were ascetic orders, membership of which was as binding as membership of tribes. Twelve of them had been formed, consciously based on the tribes, with their meeting places in the former tribal territories. When, in Matt 19:28, Jesus promised his followers that they would sit on twelve thrones judging the twelve tribes of the sons of Israel, he meant the great society of ascetics within which the Christians were emerging.

Each 'tribe' was highly organised, with just one thousand members for an order in the homeland.

The original orders, round which the others developed,

were the four for Palestinian Essenes, who numbered four thousand, as is stated by Philo.[14] The orders of Levi and Judah contained their permanent monastics and their dynasts respectively, while Zebulun and Naphtali – both tribes who had belonged to the northern area that had come to be called Galilee – contained Essene Nazirites and villagers. Nazirites were married men who left their marriages for periods of 30 to 100 days for the sake of solitary retreat. Villagers of the order of Naphtali undertook pilgrimages. An additional order, of Dan, contained women who followed the Essene way of life.

In the Diaspora, the orders of Ephraim and Manasseh, the two parts of the Joseph tribe, followed the Essene solar calendar and communal ideals, but were called by the Palestinians 'seekers after smooth things', a name appearing frequently in the sectarian scrolls. It was they who became the zealots. They took over Qumran in its second phase, after it had been defiled by the earthquake. Linked with them was the Pharisee order of Benjamin, for Sadducees and Pharisees had come to adopt the ascetic discipline also. Sadducees, as priests, joined the Essene order of Levi, but Pharisees, who were laymen, had their own order. The sage Hillel had been a member of Benjamin, and its best known later member was Paul, who says himself that he was of that 'tribe', and had 'sat at the feet of Gamaliel',[15] who was a descendant of Hillel.

The Herodian orders were modelled on these, and obviously were constructed to complete the tribal system. Their equivalents of the two higher orders were Simeon, whose centre at Masada was in Herod's home territory of Idumea, and Reuben, with its centre at Machaerus in Transjordan. Gad, their third order, had its centre at Gerasa in Transjordan, and Issachar, for men a grade below these, met in Galilee. The Herodian equivalent of the order of Dan, for women, was Asher, whose tribal territory included Tyre and Sidon. The order had been

186

founded by Queen Salome, as a detail concerning Anna of Asher in Luke 2:36 shows.

The tribes, or orders, were given numbers reflecting the twelve Herodian grades, indicating their degrees of holiness. In the arrangement around the walls in the Temple Scroll, the superior of the four groups of three was in the centre and the next two on either side. The numbering was:

0	LEVI (centre of east wall)
1	Simeon (north of centre)
2	Judah (south of centre)
3–4	EPHRAIM-MANASSEH (centre of south wall)
5	Benjamin (west of centre)
6	Reuben (east of centre)
7	ZEBULUN (centre of west wall)
8	Gad (north of centre)
9	Issachar (south of centre)
10	NAPHTALI (centre of north wall)
11	Dan (west of centre)
12	Asher (east of centre)

(See the diagram on p.161)

TWELVE PROVINCES OF THE KINGDOM

When the Kingdom of the Jews was designed in the time of Herod the Great, a system of provinces was set up, in emulation of the Roman organisation, and for the purpose of taxation. Each member was to be charged a half shekel initiation fee and a half shekel annual promotion fee, and this would bring in an enormous income which Herod intended to use for his building projects.[16]

It may be seen from the gospels and Acts that there were to be twelve provinces in all, of which ten would pay the fees. The lower two, 11 and 12, contained Gentiles who were not given any privileges so would not pay the half shekel. The twelve provinces were given the values and numbering of the twelve orders. Jerusalem itself was province 0, the purely priestly province. The rest ran, in order, from east to west. Province 1 was the far east, centred in Babylon. This was the one that seceded at the schism of AD 44, when 'one-tenth of the city fell' (Rev 11:13). Province 2 contained those Jews in the homeland or near it who were not in Jerusalem: Judea, Samaria and Galilee, Qumran itself, and nearby Egypt.

In the west, Asia Minor, where there was a large Jewish population, was divided into five provinces: Cappadocia, Galatia, Pontus, Bithynia and Asia, whose capital was Ephesus. They are listed at the beginning of Peter's first epistle, written to them. These were numbered from 3 to 7. Asia was province 7, and one of the reasons for the great emphasis on 7 in the Book of Revelation, coming from Ephesus, was that it honoured the seventh province. Closer detail shows that Cappadocia and Galatia were counted as 3–4, and were assigned to Ephraim-Manasseh, Pontus with Cilicia was province 5, and province 6 contained Antioch, the northern capital, as well as Bithynia, the two belonging together as the eastern and western extremes of Asia Minor.

Province 8 was called 'Egypt' in the list in Acts 2:9–11. It meant those Jews in Egypt who looked towards the west, not the homeland, and it included also islands of the Mediterranean on which ascetic centres were built. When the head of the order of Gad, the tetrarch Antipas, established a home on the Tiber Island in Rome (see Chapter 9), his island became the first of the islands, and was included in the province.

Province 9 similarly had a portion in both North Africa and Rome, for members who were of the low grade 9, either because they were sent into exile (to Libya-Cyrene), or because they were married. In Herod's house in Rome, no ascetic discipline was observed, and it was counted as equal to the married grade 9. The list in Acts 2:10 calls it 'the parts (*merē*) of Libya according to Cyrene', disguising its other location. The word 'parts' has the special meaning of the places for the three highest priests, and in Rev 16:19 the term refers to Agrippa's house in Rome, 'Tavern Three', to which he transferred his home when he fled from Judea in AD 69.

The place in Rome where the pilgrims of Naphtali met, the Forum of Appius, was the true Rome province, number 10. In the list in Acts 2:10 'Romans' appears after 'Cyrene'. This fact was drawn on to identify the place where those persecuted in Rome were hiding. The number was one of those used by the unclean class, and from the start both the distance of Rome, and its political meaning, gave it a low status from an eastern viewpoint. Below Rome in grade, and attached to it organisationally, were the two provinces for Gentiles who paid no fees: Achaia (Greece), 11, and Macedonia, 12.

The connection between the orders and the provinces, together with the history, gives a reason for the exchange of two sets of orders that took place between the Temple Scroll and Revelation 7. Judah and Issachar were reversed; and Zebulun and Reuben. The homeland province, 2, corresponding to Judah, was transferred to Herod's house in Rome – or would be in AD 69 when Agrippa II left the country for good. The homeland would be used only by members of the lowest Herodian grade, sent back from Rome. The reversal of Zebulun and Reuben meant that men of Zebulun, equal to Nazirites, had moved from Asia, province 7, to Antioch-Bithynia, province 6. The Herod crown prince, head of the order of Reuben, was appointed superior in the province of Asia.

In each province, it was expected that at any one time there would be twelve thousand members, one thousand from each of the grades, making 144 000 members in all. The person who was the head of province 12, coming last in a liturgical procession, was 'number 144 000'.

Ten of the provinces would bring in income. The upper six thousand in each of these would be fee paying Jews. Six thousand half shekels made a talent, so the ten paying

189

provinces would bring in ten talents per annum (on today's values, something like $US 6 million). Early in the history of the mission, in the time of Herod the Great, the money was stored in the vaults at Qumran, and the inventory, recording enormous sums, was kept on the Copper Scroll. The organisation in terms of six thousand Jews was also chosen because after ten four-year periods of evangelism in the forty years originally allowed, there would be sixty thousand in each of the ten paying provinces, making six hundred thousand in all, and this was the number of the true Israel according to the Book of Exodus.[17]

The 12000 stadia (about 2400 kilometres or 1500 miles) given as the measurement of the 'city' in Rev 21:16 may be understood as a reflection of the plan of provinces. The 12 cubits of the Qumran vestry were the original map, as it were, of all systems of twelve. Each cubit stood for an hour, a grade, an order, a province. Each province contained 12×1000 members, each thousand representing a grade. The figures from Luke's parable of the pounds, which show that each missionary had to make 100 members,[18] suggest that in every 1000 stadia (about 200 kilometres or 125 miles) there were ten meeting places, each for 100 members. Thus the representative line of a province would be thought of as 1000 stadia long. All twelve provinces represented by the vestry floor meant that it stood for a distance of 12000 stadia, no matter what its actual size.

THE SYSTEM FOR GENTILES

From the beginning of the Herodian mission to Jews of the Diaspora, there was an interest by Gentiles in joining it. The social and historical causes of this have been discussed earlier, and it has been seen that the popularity of the Herod family in the Roman court was one of the factors that led to acceptance of the idea of conversion to their liberalised form of Judaism.

But Gentiles, not having been born Jews, were necessarily of a low grade in this highly hierarchical organisation. They were at first treated as equal to Jewish married men, no matter what their own lifestyle, and confined to grades 9 and below. They could receive baptism, but not the sacred meal. But once 'the water was turned into wine', that is, they were admitted to the sacred meal, they began to rise to positions like those of Jewish village ministers.

There were two main categories of Gentiles: proselytes, who were circumcised and lived in every respect like Jews, and the uncircumcised. Only the latter developed into the Christian Church.

Proselytes were attached to the levitical class of Jews, being put under the authority of the Scribes, led by Raphael, in Diaspora monasteries. They could rise to the same position as acolytes, who were the 'Friday' members of the school, in grade 6. This meant that they were additional members of province 6, Antioch-Bithynia. Nicolaus, 'a proselyte of Antioch' named as the 'Friday' of a set of seven men in Acts 6:5, was the person to whom Jesus addressed the 'Friday letter' in Revelation 3, condemning him for excessive adherence to the Jewish calendar. Other letters in the same set condemn the Nicolaitans. For Jesus, proselytes ran against one of his fundamental tenets, that Gentiles should stay Gentiles.

Proselytes could remain a stage lower, at grade 7, not taking on the full discipline of those at grade 6. In every province, the fees of the first six thousand amounted to the talent, as shown above, and grade 6 proselytes were included in the sixth thousand. The fees of grade 7 below these were kept separate, as Gentile money. They were called 'the Seven Thousand', and 'the Remainder' (*loipoi*) as they headed the lower division of non-Jews. The Seven Thousand are referred to in Rev 11:13, and in one of Paul's letters he approves them as not having become entirely Jewish (Rom 11:4).

191

The other main category, the uncircumcised, came from the two Gentile orders or 'tribes', Dan and Asher, originally the orders for women. The men of Dan were celibates, living like monastic or dynastic Essenes, and the men of the Herodian order of Asher were married, living like village ascetics who could temporarily become Nazirites or pilgrims. Uncircumcised Gentiles were ranged in four different grades of ministry, each one of which produced a gospel. Their groups and grades were:

Lay Presbyters These were men of Dan, like John Mark, who chose to live like monastic Essenes. John's gospel was their product. They were attached to the Jewish class C, the celibate congregation.

Lay Deacons These were men of Asher, like James Niceta, who chose to live at times like Nazirites. Matthew's gospel was their product. Having private property and remaining in sympathy with the Jewish Christians, they paid fees.

Below these, and in the same group, men of Asher like John Aquila preferred to be pilgrims rather than Nazirites, following the example of Peter. Linked with western Christians, they did not pay fees. As pilgrims with an Exodus ideal, they were 'called out into the wilderness', using the term *ekklésia*, 'called out' (it translated the Hebrew *qahal*, a word for Israel in the wilderness). This word became 'church'. It was men like John Aquila, Herodian pilgrims, who formed the original 'Church'. Their order of Asher being Herodian, King Herod was the head of their churches. When they followed the custom of monastic schools and said prayers every day, they were organised in sevens, like the seven churches of Asia which appear in Revelation Part B written by John Aquila.

Lay Initiates These were individual Gentile celibates of Dan who joined Peter's order of Naphtali. They were the western equivalent of Shem (see below), becoming village initiates. Peter's protege Mark, in Rome, was in this group, and became the writer of Mark's gospel under Peter's guidance. The eastern head of Shem was the man called Philip in the gospels and Acts.

Lay Pre-initiates These were the men of Dan who chose to retain their own Gentile identities, not joining the Jewish orders or 'tribes'. Their racial groupings gave them the names 'Shem, Ham and Japheth', following biblical tradition. Shem contained Semites other than Jews, and they were permitted to become initiates (above). The two lowest groups of all were Ham, containing Ethiopians; and Japheth, containing Greeks and Romans. The head of the sons of Ham was the Ethiopian of Acts 8:27, shown elsewhere to be called Titus; and the head of Japheth, Luke, whose own name was Cornelius (Acts 10:1). Luke's gospel represented the western form of this group.

Further detail on the history of these groups is found in the pesher of the gospels and Acts. Of the lay presbyters, John Mark was originally instructed by Simon Magus, and he did not entirely separate from him. His order of Gentiles became the founders of Christian monasteries. In time, they developed a full system of grades, the same as those of their Jewish counterparts, so that John Mark went right up to graduation at Qof. Since Qof also meant the number 100, and a man at this grade was the leader of 100 celibates, John Mark was called a 'centurion' (Luke 7:2, Mark 15:39). As a result of the schism of AD 44, his gospel was re-assigned to the men of Asher, who were promoted to lay presbyter, in the way that is shown on pp.526–527.

The history of James Niceta, of the lay deacons, and of John Aquila, has been outlined in Chapter 7. Their change of loyalty from Simon Magus to the Sadducee Zacchaeus was not a personal matter, but a consequence of the great political rift on the question of Rome that led to the schism of AD 44.

Gentiles when they rose in rank were attached to the Jewish orders. The men of Asher, with the Sadducees, were linked with the priestly order of Levi. The Annas priest as head of this order was called 'the Spirit'. Consequently the seer, his servant, was said to be 'in a Spirit', as in Rev 1:10, 4:2.

The Book of Revelation gives some detail about the method of payment of fees of men like James Niceta. Payment was by instalments, for there was a possibility that Gentiles might not complete the course from grade 10 to 7. Their fees were paid in denarii rather than half shekels. Beginning at 10, after completing the first year and having arrived at grade 9, they paid a third of a denarius. After another year, another third, then at grade 7 they would pay the third third. Each instalment was called 'a third' (*triton*). The word 'the Third', used frequently in Part A of Revelation written by James Niceta, means a leader of fee paying Gentiles.

The paying Gentiles of Asher were likened to grain. In the newly published Scrolls fragment 4QMMT, there is discussion of 'the new wheat grains of the Gentiles', which are not accepted as sacrifices.[19] As Revelation shows, when they paid one-third of a denarius at grade 9, they were likened to barley, then at grade 7, when they paid the third third, they were 'wheat'. This is the meaning of Rev 6:6: 'A measure of wheat for a denarius, and three measures of barley for a denarius'.

Since they were attached to the high order of Levi, and also to the order below it, Judah, they came under the authority of both the Sadducee priest and of the David. It was he who was their chief teacher, instructing them while he was in the status of a village teacher, called 'the Word of God'. As the parable of the Sower says, 'the seed is the

Word of God'. He also, originally, received their fees, and while James the brother of Jesus was regarded as the David, he continued the system. But when Jesus came to the position, he abolished fees. Those who wished to continue paying them gave them to his equal the Herod crown prince, as is shown in Revelation.

The father of Shem, Ham and Japheth was Noah, and the class of pre-initiates who remained Gentiles used imagery derived from the Noah story. Their baptismal rite took place using a boat, and they were said to be 'saved through water'. After baptism they were brought on board the boat, which sailed up a water channel and deposited them on the dry land of 'salvation'.[20] The men of Shem were called the 'beasts' whom Noah saved, and the men of Ham and Japheth were likened to fish, baptised in salt water corresponding to their level of uncleanness. At the outset, a place at the edge of the Dead Sea was chosen, its bitter waters suitable for their lowly status. In the wider world, islands of the Mediterranean, such as Crete and Malta, were chosen for Gentile baptisms and places of instruction. This was the origin of the fish symbol for Christians.

Their 'fisherman' was Peter, of the order of Naphtali. In his epistle he uses the Noah imagery.[21] The 'Noah' mission had its main centre in Herod's house in Rome. Another image, associated with wine, could be developed, since Noah had 'planted a Vineyard'.[22] The wine image suited one of Herod's methods, entertaining distinguished Romans in his house. If they became merely token members of his religion, as the procurators did, they joined the 'Winepress'. But if they received instruction and practised the discipline they were said to join the 'Vineyard', whose organisation was the subject of several parables in the gospels.

Individual members of Dan were characterised by wine if initiates (*oinos*, fermented wine, not the new wine of Essenes) and by oil, which was associated with novices.

Higher Essenes did not use oil on their skins.[23] The passage in Rev 6:6 on the payments for wheat and barley adds: 'and the oil and the wine do not harm'. It means that these Gentile members were also to be accepted.

Throughout the Book of Revelation, a group of four terms frequently appear, apparently having only a general meaning: 'tribes, tongues, nations and peoples'. In fact, they refer to the four kinds of Gentiles who produced the gospels of Matthew, Mark, Luke and John. The reasons for these terms will be shown in the Lexicon.

Peter, who was the 'fisherman' for Ham and Japheth, being one grade above them, acted at their level in the process of baptism, as is shown by the story of his wading through the water in John 21:7. When with their lowest members he went down to grade 12, and so acted as head of province 12. He appeared in Macedonia, province 12, as Aristarchus of Thessalonica (Acts 20:4; 27:2). This made him 'number 144 000' in the whole movement, as the head of the province came last in a procession. Both within a province, and in the whole membership, it became true of Peter that 'the last shall be first'. He was chief missionary to Gentile Christians who retained Gentile identity, and when they separated he became the representative of Jesus, and their Pope.

THE ORIGINAL GENTILE SCHOOL

Outside the vestry room at Qumran, near the eastern entrance door to the southern room, there still stand two striking objects, carved stone, contrasting markedly with the rough stones of the building. They are in the shape of circular pillar bases, with rounded edges. The top of each has a diameter of exactly a cubit. This, it is believed, was the standard at Qumran, used as their cubit measure. The bases are in a large triangular area marked by the aqueduct on its east side and the wall of the south vestry on its west. A capacious bench is placed near them, outside the vestry door. In the same area was the mill for grinding flour, subsequently removed by the archaeologists.

It may be seen that these round bases were the place for those who were not permitted to come into the vestry. Merari (Zacchaeus), who was the deacon to the unclean, stood on an equivalent one in the story in Luke 19:4, when he 'climbed up the sycamore tree'. This was the place of the original Gentile school. At first, Gentiles, permitted to go only to grade 9, were permitted to come to this point outside the vestry as a privilege, to be taught at their own 'Tree of Knowledge' and receive initiation at their 'Tree of Life', using the Eden imagery that is found for the Jewish ascetic schools.[24] To proceed beyond this point, a man must be circumcised, and these stones formed the original 'millstone' and 'stumbling block', terms found in the New Testament to refer to the circumcision requirement.[25] But subsequently, under Christian influence, Gentiles were permitted to go beyond this point, to go into the vestry congregation, and finally to enter the ministry of the north vestry.

The round bases were reproduced in buildings in the Diaspora, including the monastery outside Ephesus. Here, a woman was equal to Merari, and could teach Gentiles. She stood here as a teacher of Wisdom. One of the names for the base on which she stood was the 'street' (*plateia*), from Proverbs: 'Wisdom cries aloud in the outside parts, in the street'.[26]

The last chapters of Revelation show that at the round bases at the monastery outside Ephesus, after it became Christian, Herodian Jewish doctrines were taught. The positions had been reversed: Gentiles had become the ministers of the vestry, which was now a church, and their former masters were now outside.

CHAPTER 5

The Daily Timetable

From all the sources, it becomes possible to put together a daily time table, showing the regular activities for every day in any ascetic community that was a reproduction of Qumran. It was because of the great regularity of life in celibate communities, governed by the rules for time, that it was possible for anyone knowing the system to say what would be happening at any hour in a community in any part of the Greco-Roman world. The sequence of events in a narrative is a further confirmation of the accuracy of the pesher, for they always follow the timetable. It is for this reason that it is possible to put in exact hours, even when there is no corresponding word in the text.

It becomes apparent, especially from a study of the concealed chronology of the gospels, that the community's concentration on the measurement of time had led them to make even closer sub-divisions of time than the half hours. Although the Book of Revelation has far fewer of these smaller units than do the gospels, words indicating them do appear, and they may also be seen in the background of some sequences of events.

The reason for the smaller divisions may be seen, arising from the basic principle of obeying God's will exactly on questions of time. The noon prayer must be said punctually at noon, indicated by the position of the shadow on the sundial or an equivalent device. But the sacred meal of monastics was also held at noon, and the levite saying the noon prayer was to attend the meal, at the table below the platform. He could arrive on time by drawing on a frequently used principle, that of observing both the zero and the first unit after it as the beginning, and another principle was the measurement of time in sets of twelve. An hour could itself be divided by twelve, into sets of five minutes. At five minutes after twelve the first unit began, and this gave the levite time to say his short prayer and move down to the table. The actual duration of the five minutes would be measured, after long experience, by the length of the prayer and the time taken to move down, if not by closer divisions on the sundial. The word *eutheós*, 'at once' has the precise sense of five minutes past twelve in the pesher (Rev 4:2). It and related terms are frequent in the gospels, and are used to indicate the exact time of details in the crucifixion, which was already intended to be re-enacted as a liturgical drama.

At night, between 9 p.m. and 3 a.m., the hours were marked by turning up each of the successive lamps on the Menorah, as is shown by some details in Revelation. After many hundreds of years of experience, the amount of oil in the lamps would have been measured so as to last an hour.

The timetable lying behind all services was:

3 a.m.   At this hour, treated as an artificial dawn, ascetics rose from sleep, to say their first prayers. Pilgrims commenced their journey, or, when at the celibate centre, rose to prepare for their early prayers. The hour was called 'cockcrowing' and was signalled by Merari, the levitical deacon.

3.30 a.m. End of the morning service of ascetics.

4 a.m. The first prayer of the day by higher pilgrims, directed by a priest as 'the Light', and by their bishop David as 'the Morning Star'. Once Gentile pilgrims were admitted to the same class they were directed by the David queen, who also acted as doorkeeper to the vestry to which they were admitted. (During the trial of Jesus in the Qumran vestry, Peter was the Jewish pilgrim saying his prayers here at successive hours, and Mary the mother of Jesus acted as David queen and doorkeeper.) At the same unclean hour monastics visited the latrine, following the rules that strictly regulated all their activities, on every morning except Saturday, as defecation was forbidden on the sabbath.

5 a.m. Second prayer offered by pilgrims.

6 a.m. Third prayer offered by pilgrims. Villagers had their first meal of the day. Monastics had no meal.

11 a.m. Monastics stopped physical labour and took an immersion bath before their noon meal.[1] In Herodian schools where there was no noon meal, teaching began for the day.

Noon The major noon prayer was said. Monastics had their first meal of the day, their main sacred meal. Villagers had no meal, but a drink of water only.
The Herodian service at a cathedral on a festival day began. A short prayer for noon was said by a levite in the noon circle on the middle

200

tier. At five minutes past noon the congregation took their seats, and a levite sat on either side of the middle tier, over the supporting pillars. The entrance door was shut. When King Herod was present, he took the throne on the upper tier.

Readings from the Law and the Prophets of the Old Testament were given from the east side of the middle tier.

1 p.m.   The Chief Therapeut, who observed the first hour as the beginning, came to the noon circle on the balcony for his prayer. At the festival service, four village ministers took their places on the dais edge and step.

2 p.m.   End of the noon meal of monastics. At a Herodian festival, the service continued. At Pentecost AD 49 in Ephesus Agrippa II was crowned by Matthew Annas at this hour, with the Chief Therapeut leading the choir in the Trisagion.

3 p.m.   The less holy part of the service began. In the village, the visiting priest, who had been praying on the roof of the one-storeyed village house, was let down in his palanquin to the doorway of the house, to attend to villagers. He received money defined as 'clean'. It included the tithe for the priests, the fees of Jews, and the Roman tribute.

At the Herodian festival, the reading from the Septuagint was given in the chancel, the Law in Greek by the Herod crown prince, and the Prophets by David, the Lamb.

On Friday afternoons, the preparation for the sabbath began at this hour. Walking more than 1000 cubits was forbidden,[2] but it was still permitted to lift up a burden.

The sabbath trumpet was blown.

3.30 p.m. The copy of the Septuagint was handed back to Herod. Psalms were sung, to the accompaniment of a harp. At this point, the more informal part of the proceedings, a service for higher Gentiles began, and incense was burned to convey their petitions to heaven.

On the 31st, when a Hellenist priest was visiting the village, a leading villager said to him 'Come!', as an invitation to stay for the Gentile service. The visiting priest who accepted the invitation went up to the balcony, where he sat on the 'horse' with the season's colour.

The service, which concluded with a communion meal, was held by Gentiles also on a Friday, although Palestinian ascetics refrained. The incense of Gentiles was then said to be mere 'smoke' to heaven, their prayers not accepted.

4 p.m. End of the day in celibate communities. Monastics visited the latrine. 'Unclean money' was paid: welfare tithes for the indigent, and Gentile fees. The welfare tithes for persons such as the physically handicapped were received by the bishop and the judge according to the rule for the Diaspora of CD 14:12–16 (the earnings of two days a month were used to help the indigent, that is, two-thirds of the tithe).

In Diaspora communities, further teaching was given to Gentiles by teachers who were willing to be in contact with them.

6 p.m.	The evening meal was held, the main religious meal in the village, a secondary non-sacred meal to monastics.
	The village evening session was four hours long (1QS 6:7 'a third of every night in the year'). The first two hours were called 'the supper'. In the first hour money placed on the common table was handed over to the appropriate priest. Then the common bread was eaten.
	On Friday evenings no meal was taken by Palestinian Essenes because of the rule against defecation on the sabbath, but there was still a meeting at which a council for decision making was held.
7 p.m.	The common wine was taken.
8 p.m.	The sacred part of the session began. The sacred bread was eaten.
9 p.m.	The evening lamp was lit. In the synagogue, the Menorah was lit. Raphael left the meal in order to light the Menorah.
	Others stayed at the meal, some not taking wine, others drinking sacred wine. Monastics used new wine; Herodians used fermented wine in unlimited quantities, sometimes leading to drunkenness; while some, including Christians, used fermented wine treated as 'blood', to be sipped in small quantities only as a symbol of receiving the merit earned by the 'Lamb slain' through his ascetic discipline.
10 p.m.	The session ended with the singing of a hymn. Some, after taking a short break, continued a further session of teaching and debate.

Midnight   End of the further session. The Julian day began at midnight. Diaspora Essenes held an Agape meal at this hour at their pentecontad gatherings, reaching the state of spiritual 'ecstasy' described by Philo.[3] Higher pilgrims called 'Blessed Ones' (to distinguish them from dynastic 'Holy Ones') were permitted to 'watch', conduct a vigil.

        Herodian banquets in Rome, at which the emperor or procurators were entertained, continued. On Friday night, midnight was observed as the beginning of the sabbath by those using the Julian calendar.

1 a.m.   The Therapeuts observed this as the beginning, including the beginning of the sabbath, and any expectations for midnight were extended an extra hour.

3 a.m.   End of the all night session. The last light of the Menorah indicated the time.

        A lamp was lit for those beginning their service in the vestry at this time. The extra light of the Menorah burned until 4 a.m. The Therapeuts returned to their hermits' retreats.

CHAPTER 6

Watching God's Clock

THE THEORY OF TIME

(The information in this section is necessary in order to explain why exact dates can be given at so many points in the pesher of Revelation. It concerns the solar calendar and the time systems that depended on it. A considerable amount of technical detail in the section may make heavy demands on the reader, but this is unavoidable when a whole new body of knowledge concerning the calendar has so recently become available. It may be better to treat it as a reference source to accompany the pesher in Part III.)

There could be no writings that appear to be more vague about time than the gospels and the Book of Revelation. The gospels are simply exasperating on this point: at one moment they give a date, such as the beginning of Jesus' ministry in the fifteenth year of Tiberius, AD 29, but they do not give the year of the crucifixion. Some dates turn out to be unbelievable, as when Luke says that Jesus was born in the year of the census of Quirinius, AD 6, making him only twenty-three at the outset of his ministry, a fact contradicted by Luke himself when he says that he was about thirty.

Yet at the same time the gospels can give precise hours. According to John, the first disciples joined Jesus at the tenth hour, 4 p.m. The meeting with the Samaritan woman was at the sixth hour, noon. The centurion's servant was healed at the seventh hour, 1 p.m. Jesus stayed in a place two days. The Book of Acts gives similar notes of hours and days without giving the year.

It appears to be inherently unlikely that Revelation would give dates and times at all, as it is not in the form of history but of timeless vision. Its last section repeatedly speaks about the thousand years, but this is presumably in the future and brings in an obscure belief of some kind. Yet it contains the same kind of odd notes of time. In Chapter 11, an event goes on for three and a half days. At one point there is 'silence in heaven for about half an hour'. Does heaven have a clock? Most curiously of all, the woman of Chapter 12 fled to the wilderness and was fed there for 1260 days. Another event is also timed as 1260 days, and two others for 42 months, which is 3½ years. The 1260 days is also about 3½ years.

It may be shown, in fact, that the Book of Revelation is in a familiar tradition of biblical literature, which gives dates of events by indirect means, to insiders who understood, leaving outsiders to think it was vague or even irrational. The Testament of Levi, for instance – part of a work called *The Testaments of the Twelve Patriarchs*, always known in the Church and found also among the Dead Sea Scrolls – talks mysteriously about a series of jubilees, in each one of which a certain high priest appears. 'In each jubilee there shall be a priesthood. In the first jubilee the first person to be anointed to the priesthood will be great . . . In the second jubilee the anointed one shall be conceived in sorrow . . .' and so on. The whole period covered, it says, is 'seventy weeks', that is 490 years, as a 'week' was seven years.[1] (A jubilee in this literature is seven 'weeks' or 49 years, not 50.) Vague as the descriptions are, there is enough information for anyone who knew the outstanding events of the period from which it came, and who understood the numbering system, to be able to say that it covers the period 511 BC to 21 BC.[2]

Another such scheme is in a book attributed to the antediluvian prophet Enoch,[3] but obviously coming from the same Hellenistic period as the Testament of Levi. It divides the whole of world history into 'weeks', and says that there will be ten such 'weeks'; seven of them in the past and three still to come. At the end of the eighth week something good will happen: 'a house will be built for the great king'. At the end of the tenth there will be the Last Judgment, then 'time will be no more'. The author obviously believes that he has worked out the whole timetable on which heaven organises history. A great event has happened at the end of each of the previous 'weeks': the birth of Enoch, Noah's flood, Abraham, the Exodus, Solomon's temple, the exile to Babylon, and at the seventh, the supreme one, the appearance of the author's own community, called the 'Plant of Righteousness'. Although he does not define his 'week', it is clear enough that he means 490 years, the larger time span named in the related literature depending on the solar calendar.[4] The sets of 490 years may be called 'world-weeks'. So, if only the date of creation in his theory were known, we would know when his 'Plant of Righteousness' appeared.

The Book of Revelation obviously comes from the same circles as these, and its dependence on them is now even more apparent when the Dead Sea Scrolls are seen as the missing link. In one of its sections it sets out a series of events in a structure of seven trumpets, in another in a set of seven seals, in another in a set of seven bowls, in others series of angels. Given the precedent, these are surely ways of measuring time, and promise an actual chronology. The religious purpose of such a technique is clear enough: if events are so ordered in sets of seven it will be possible to predict the future, the preoccupation with a thousand years being an indication that the author or authors are expecting an end to the present world order and the beginning of a better one at a time determined by a scheme of chronology. Such a motive is plainly stated in the Iranian literature that has been recognised as lying behind Jewish apocalyptic.[5]

The seven trumpets suggest an interpretation in terms of the familiar 'weeks', sets of seven years, making a jubilee of forty-nine years in all. A trumpet was blown every Friday evening before the sabbath, both in orthodox Jewish practice, as Josephus records, and in the community of the Dead Sea Scrolls, as shown in the Damascus Document. The events associated with the trumpets are vaguely stated, but sound like human events dressed in apocalyptic language, as in the previous literature of this kind. If it could be known when the starting point was, we would surely have a record of a certain forty-nine years.

When this hypothesis is brought together with observations about the special meaning of all terms, it is found that there is such a concealed chronology. The chronology is a particularly useful part of the demonstration of the existence of a pesher, in that it brings in the extra factor of mathematical proof.

The concealed chronology of the book of Revelation may be worked out to be as follows:

PART A
(a) The Seven Trumpets (8:6–11:19)

The period is September AD 1 to September AD 50, a jubilee of 49 years, divided into 7 septennia.

The trumpet was blown for the septennium in both September and the following March, as both were treated as a New Year by different viewpoints, and the Revelation viewpoint preferred March, since

September was the season for Jewish festivals. In the course of this forty-nine years the Julian calendar was adopted, and the September–March year was changed to December–June. This is stated in the pesher at the relevant point.

Sep AD 1	The jubilee begins (8:6)
March AD 2	First trumpet (8:7)–Archelaus Herod and Judas the Galilean
March AD 9	Second trumpet (8:8–9)Consequences of Archelaus' dismissal
March AD 16	Third trumpet (8:10–11)Joseph becomes heir of David, allied with Antipas
March AD 23	Fourth trumpet (8:12–13)–Rise of John the Baptist, return of Agrippa
March AD 30	Fifth trumpet (9:1–11)–Defeat of John the Baptist, replaced by Jonathan Annas
March AD 37	Sixth trumpet (9:12–11:14)–Reign of Agrippa I, rise of Matthew Annas; change to Julian calendar December 43 (10:7–11).
June AD 44	Seventh trumpet (11:15–19) The Christian party established.

(The events of the end of this jubilee are given in the Seven Seals, see below.)

(b)The Beasts (12:1–14:5)

This section follows the pattern of the forty year war that is set out in the War Scroll from Qumran. It was to be divided into two sets of twenty years, the first including a campaign in the east against the sons of Shem; the second in the west, with ten years against the sons of Ham and ten against the sons of Japheth (1QM 2:13–14). As may be seen from the history, the 'war' began in AD 6, with the zealot uprising, so the campaign against the sons of Ham was to begin in 26 and the campaign to Japheth in 36, finishing in 46.

The Revelation section uses this plan to give a separate account of the zealot party in the same general period as the Trumpets section. The zealots were the writers of some of the sectarian Dead Sea Scrolls, including the War Scroll. Rev 12:1–18 deals with AD 6–26, beginning with the ceremony for Jesus' twelfth birthday (he had been born in March 7 BC, and was 'born' at his Bar Mitzvah in March AD 6, aged twelve; this accounts for Luke's apparent error noted above). The emphasis is on Mary rather than on Jesus.

Rev 13:1–10 deals with AD 26–36, the main event being the rise of the first Beast, Judas Iscariot. As in the previous section, the crucifixion is not mentioned. James Niceta, the writer of Part A, was a follower of Jonathan Annas, and regarded Jesus as simply an associate of Simon Magus, to whom he was bitterly opposed. The crucifixion would have been seen by him as nothing but an abortive attempt to execute zealots.

Rev 13:11–18 deals with AD 36–46, the rise of the second Beast, Simon Magus, and the establishment of the Damascus party at the time Agrippa I restored the Herodian kingship. Rev 14:1–5 deals with the council of Jerusalem in AD 46, showing the triumph of Peter's Christians in Jerusalem.

This section does not have an overall structure like the Trumpets, but it contains indications of date, for example the 1260 days (12:6) and the 42 months (13:5), which would be understood by an expert in the solar calendar (see further below). The use of the word *kairos*, 'season' (12:12, 14), is also an indication of date, as its pesher is 'the quartodecimal intercalation year'. When it is known that the 'Dragon' is a Pharisee high priest, then further dates are given: AD 6 for the first Dragon, Joazar Boethus (12:3) and AD 18 for the next one, Caiaphas (12:13, 17).

PART B
The Lamb and the Seven Seals (1:1–8:5)

This section has been placed first in the book, as it presents the more Christian version of the history, but it is chronologically second.

Revelation draws repeatedly on another piece of chronological theory, that both a 'week' of seven years and a jubilee of forty-nine years must be preceded by a period of eighteen months as a time of preparation. This was because eighteen hours preceded the proper beginning of the sabbath on Saturday at 6 a.m., the true beginning according to solarists. Other Jews commenced the sabbath on Friday at 6 p.m., and the very earliest point at which it could be considered to begin was Friday at noon. Eighteen months reflected eighteen hours in the equation of months with hours that is frequently drawn on.

The eighteen months contained six seasons, and they were given special treatment as a time in which to make ready. Prior to the jubilee that would end in December AD 50 (after the seasons were adjusted in terms of the Julian calendar) there would be six seasons, with a 'seal' at the beginning and end, so seven seals. As has been seen in Chapter 8, these seasons were used for the study of the six extant sections of the New Testament.

The seven seals cover the last seven seasons of the jubilee of Part A. They are clearly shown to be seasons (three months) by the colours of the 'horsemen'. They begin in the summer of AD 49, with the 'white horse' (6:1–2), and are in chronological order. After the four seasons with colours, the series continues, to the seventh seal, ending six seasons, eighteen months.

The seven are:

Jun AD 49	First seal (6:12) White for summer
Sep AD 49	Second seal (6:34) Red for autumn
Dec AD 49	Third seal (6:56) Black for winter
Mar AD 50	Fourth seal (6:78) Green for spring

211

Jun AD 50	Fifth seal (6:911)
Sep AD 50	Sixth seal (6:127:17)Original end of the jubilee
Dec AD 50	Seventh seal (8:1)Julian end of the jubilee; 8:25 takes the date to 31 December and 1 January, AD 51, as the Julian New Year

The 'half-hour's silence in heaven' (8:1) is, in fact, a useful dating point. As will be shown, the day each season and seal began was the solar 31st, the day for great events according to solar calendrists. In Julian terms, it varied with the year; see the explanation and table on pp.234–241. In December AD 50 the solar 31st fell on Tuesday 15 December. In the practice of those who based their systems on twelves, a month was an equivalent to an hour, for there were twelve months in the year and twelve daylight hours, and a number of calendar devices depend on the equation of hours and months. A half hour was therefore equal to a half month, which, for the current solar calendar month, with 31 days, was 15½ days. From Tuesday, 15 December at 3 p.m., (the point from which the 'half hour' was taken), 15½ days brought the calendar to Thursday, 31 December at 3 a.m. The last day of the Julian year, 31 December, and the first of the New Year, 1 January, would have been observed as festivals. Thus the 'half-hour's silence in heaven' was a device for extending from the solar 31st on 15 December, a day of expectation, to the Julian New Year a little over a fortnight later, in the hope that heaven preferred the Julian calendar and would send the fulfilment of the prophecy for the end of the jubilee at the later date. (Their hopes were not fulfilled and Matthew Annas, who was held to be responsible for the calendar, lost his power from that day.)

The events preceding the seven seals are clearly connected with the seals, as the Lamb appears, and is said to be worthy to open the seals (5:9). They begin on a Sunday, 'the Lord's day' (1:10). In the solar calendar, Pentecost was the 15th of the third month, always a Sunday in the normative Day position of the calendar, the one for the period in question (see pp.237–238). In AD 49, Pentecost was on Sunday 1 June, an auspicious concurrence of the Julian and solar calendars, suitable for Agrippa's coronation in Ephesus. After the ceremonies of Chapters 4 and 5, the series of seals begins on the following 31st, 17 June, and goes through the 31st in each of the following seasons, for these were the regularly occurring festivals.

Dates known from the pesher of Acts give further confirmation of the correctness of the identification. In Revelation 1, set at midnight beginning 1 June AD 49, Jesus appears, together with 'star 7'. This means the David crown prince. Jesus' son, Jesus Justus, had been born in June AD 37 (Acts 6:7 'the Word of God increased'). He was twelve years old in June AD 49, and began to act as an acolyte, in the way described for Jesus' own twelve year old ceremony in Rev 12:1–6.

Agrippa II, born late in AD 27 (Josephus, *Ant.* 19:354) was twenty-three in September AD 50. (The birthdays were observed at the seasons, which were used for promotions.) This was the age for full initiation, and the pesher of the sixth seal, for that season, gives an account of the ceremony.

Thus Parts A and B of Revelation, the first two-thirds of the book, deal in their different ways with the first half of the first century AD. The reason why a jubilee was established for these years will be shown on pp.225–226.

PART C
The Seven Angels/The Seven Plagues/The Seven Bowls/
The Fall of the Great Harlot/The Marriage of the Lamb
(14:6–19:21)

This section of Revelation covers the period June AD 54 to June AD 74. It was governed by two chronological schemes, which had arisen as a result of the political circumstances and of the non-fulfilment of expectations in January AD 51.

The essential point about the mounting tension of this period was that it was believed that the year 4000 from the creation of the world was approaching, and in the opinion of many calendar theorists this meant the Eschaton, a great crisis of some kind which would mean the 'Last Things' (Greek *eschaton*). They were able to reconcile it with the Enoch belief that the whole duration of history was 4900 years by arguing that heaven worked in generations of forty years as well as sets of seven. The year 4000, a hundred years after the beginning of the final millennium 3900, would see the end of the present state of human affairs, and a prelude to the Last Judgment of 4900. The calendar basis of these beliefs will be shown below. The problem for the theorists was that they did not know the date of creation, but believed that they could argue backwards from great events such as an earthquake or the fall of Jerusalem. The values they attached to these events came from their political beliefs, so the arguments about dates were essentially political debates, a struggle for power.

The first scheme of Part C was of 'seven angels', covering the years AD 54–60. Each 'angel' or equal figure appeared in the Ephesus cathedral at a successive year, one of them being the Son of Man, Jesus, in AD 57. The series began in June 54, because, after the disappointment of January 51, the Ephesus party waited three and a half years until June 54, following a calendar usage that reflected a political attitude, one that had now become dominant. They had turned to nationalism, and this included respect for the Jerusalem temple and its calendar, in which each year fell three and a half years later (see pp.241–244). The year AD 60 had long been anticipated as the date of the Eschaton of 4000, reckoned from 3900 in 41 BC (see p.220–222), and they were adjusting to a new political emphasis in the form of their hopes.

When AD 60 and 61 produced no fulfilment, they had reason for looking to AD 70. Following on the equation of AD 60 with 4000, the decades we now use were their decades also. These were years of great political pressure, leading up to the fall of Jerusalem in 70, and the chronological expectation was at least one factor in the determination of zealots fighting in the war, for they expected a divine intervention in their favour at the appointed time.

A chronological device was now used for dating that was derived from the Exodus story. 'Plagues' were used as a means of counting time, each of one season, as this was the duration of an agricultural plague. In three cases in Revelation, 'seven plagues (plague 7)' appear. The meaning is that it is the end of an eighteen months, six seasons, with the word 'plague' marking the beginning and end, so seven in all.

Each time 'plague 7' appears, it is in June of year 2 of a decade: June 42, 62 and 112.[6] 'Calculations were now being based on decades: 40–50; 60–70; 110–120. In order to retain both sevens and tens, the last seven years of the decade (43–50; 63–70; 113–120) were being treated as a significant 'week'. The 'week' of years corresponded to a week of seven days, with the first year being a 'Sunday' and the last a 'Saturday'. That is, the years 43, 63 and 113 began a 'Sunday', and the years 49, 69 and 119 began a 'Saturday', treating Saturday as the seventh day.

But on another way of treating Saturday, it was the zero day at the beginning of the week. This meant that the years 42, 62 and 112 were also a 'Saturday'. That being so, they should be preceded by a period of eighteen months, since the true sabbath was preceded by eighteen hours, as shown above. Six seasons, called 'seven

215

plagues', preceded the zero 'Saturday', from January 41, 61 and 111. 'Plague 7' appeared in June 42, 62 and 112. Thus the whole decade was filled up with schemes, in what was by now a highly embellished way of describing the years and giving them value.

The 'seven plagues' were associated with 'seven bowls'. These were also a means of dating, derived from the financial system. Money was collected in a bowl at the beginning of a year, and spent, or 'poured out', at the end of the year. The bowl set out in the zero 'Saturday' year was called 'bowl 7' (Rev 15:7, June 62). It was 'poured out' in the following 'Sunday' year (Rev 16:1–2, June 63). At the beginning of the final 'Saturday' year, the 'seventh' poured out the final bowl (Rev 16:17). A new 'bowl 7' was set out in this year (unstated), and it appeared again in June 70, the next 'Sunday' year, as 'bowl 7' (Rev 17:1). In Rev 21:9, 'bowl 7' appears in June 112, the zero 'Saturday'.

Part C of Revelation contains Chapter 18, the lament for the fall of Jerusalem. It is sufficiently dated by the words 'one day' (Day 1), 'plagues' and 'famine' in 18:8. 'Day 1' was Sunday, 'plagues' (without a number) meant a solstice, and the only Sunday festival at a solstice was Pentecost, when the calendar was in the Day position (see below, pp.237–238, where the two positions of the calendar over successive sets of fourteen years will be described. Pentecost was on a Sunday in the Day position and Wednesday in the Night position). But prior to AD 71 the calendar had been in the Night position, and only changed to Day in that year. Further, the word 'famine' had the special meaning of a quartodecimal year for the intercalation. (For the explanation of this, see p.242.) The calendar expert knew from these terms that the date was Sunday, the day of Pentecost, AD 71.

Three formal laments for the fall of Jerusalem followed, shown by time details to have been at Atonement 71; 1 January, 72; and Atonement 72.

Whether the fulfilment had come with the fall of Jerusalem was a matter of opinion, but it appears that ascetics in the zealot movement believed that it was a start. From September AD 70, they added three and a half years until March 74. It was early in May AD 74 that the mass suicide of zealots on Masada took place. Part C of Revelation finishes in June AD 74.

During these years, after the third lamentation, the betrothal of Jesus Justus is alluded to on 1 January AD 73, with the presence of the 'bridegroom and the bride' (Rev 18:23), and the 'marriage of the Lamb' follows (Rev 19:6–10). In June AD 73 Jesus Justus was thirty-six, the year for marriage by the dynastic rule.

The last appearance of Jesus had been recorded in June AD 70 (Rev 17:14, 17), and it becomes apparent that he had died by 73, for the wedding of Jesus Justus at Pentecost was followed by his 'coronation', that is, the ceremony when he was appointed to the position of heir of David (Rev 19:11–16). Jesus Justus was on a 'white horse', so it was the solar 31st in June, drawing on the device used in Chapter 6, but now Jesus Justus himself was a priest-teacher who could use the 'horse'.

PART D
The Thousand Years (20:1–22:21)

The year AD 100 was another chance for the year 4000 from creation, for the Christian era had chosen 1 BC for its year 0 by taking the date 3940 falling in 1 BC, and declaring a zero generation of forty years, such as had not previously been allowed, making the year 3900, not 3940. This meant that 100 AD was 4000.

In the final section of Revelation, they had arrived at that date. Chapter 20 repeatedly uses the phrase 'the thousand years' (*chilia etē*). This means 'it was year 1000', just as 'three days' means 'on day 3, Tuesday'. Each 1000 of the 4000 was a 'year 1000', and the phrase 'thousand years' simply means: 'the date was the year 4000 from creation'.

The 1st of January, AD 100 brought a political crisis, in which the issue between east and west again came to a head, and the losers in the game of prophecy were punished. 'Satan was bound', not 'for a thousand years', as it seems to say, but 'in year 1000' (Rev 20:2). When, a few verses later, he was released, it was not a thousand years later, but six months later, when the year 1000 began for those observing the June solstice as the New Year.

The death of Agrippa II followed shortly afterwards, in AD 102. No further Herod was appointed, but for some time it was not certain that the Herodian dynasty had ceased. The Christians began to see that once the way had been made clear for them to lead the mission alone, a form of the Restoration would have come, in that the true king and priest, the current descendant of Jesus, would reign in a spiritual, if not in a political empire.

Hopes were raised again in AD 110, on the theory of a zero decade that had been used several times previously. By that year, there were no more Herods, and the heir of David, Jesus III, said 'I am the Alpha and the Omega. I am the Beginning and the End' meaning that he had taken over the prerogatives of Herod as supreme priest (Rev 21:6).

Three years later, in June AD 113 – as is shown by the word *kairos* ('season') in Rev 22:10, meaning the north solar quartodecimal year – he said the same words again (Rev 22:13). It was now eighty years since the year of the crucifixion, and in June it was eighty years since the Day of Pentecost when the Christians began their separation. Eighty years, or two generations, were a complete period in the Exodus imagery, leading up to the Promised Land. For Ephesus Christians, this was sufficient reason to declare that their hopes were fulfilled, and there was no further need for watching the historical clock.

However, those with more eastern views did, and Rev 21:9 presents 'seven bowls full of seven plagues'. The date was June AD 112. As shown above, this meant that they were hoping for an Eschaton in AD 120, with the significant septennium from 113–120. There is a most interesting confirmation of this interpretation in the account of ancient historians about an unexpected uprising of Diaspora and Palestinian Jews under the emperor Trajan in AD 115.[7] As on previous occasions, the defiance of Rome by zealot elements was partly encouraged by their belief that at the chronologically determined time heaven would intervene to destroy their enemies and sweep them into power.

For the Ephesus Christians, there was some reason for waiting to AD 114, fourteen years from AD 100. This is the final date in the book, but after that the interest in a dramatic divine intervention was abandoned by mainstream Christian writers.

A decade after the non-fulfilment of AD 120, zealotry broke out again in Judea, with the rise of a new leader, Simon Ben Kosba. The chronological theory would have been one of the reasons why he still hoped for victory and took up arms, only to bring about the final closure of Jerusalem and the end of the Jewish state.

In June, AD 113 the wedding of Jesus III was held. He had been born in AD 77. His bride first appeared in June 110, three years before her wedding, 'adorned' (Rev 21:2), then again in June 112, a year before her wedding, as the symbol of the New Jerusalem (Rev 21:9), then again in June 113 (Rev 22:17, where the detail repeats that of Rev 19:9–10, at the wedding of Jesus Justus). In AD 114, a fourth in the line of Jesus was born, as the last verse of Revelation shows through its use of the name 'the Grace of the Lord Jesus'. The 'Grace' was a name for the David crown prince (see Lexicon, **grace**).

All the hopes of Ephesus Christians had been realised: a new monastery had been built (a 'new heaven and new earth', following the plan of the original temple of the Qumran Temple Scroll). The line of Jesus, now central to the mission in place of the Herods, would go on.

Hope for a salvation sent from heaven did not die out in other circles in the province of Asia. In the second century AD Christian Montanists went out to a plain in Phrygia, in the province of Asia, expecting the New Jerusalem to come down from the sky.[8] The chronological theory that lay behind the history had been held for hundreds of years, and was not easily given up. It will be useful to see how it arose, before the time of the Church.

HOW THE DATES WERE SET
(Note before proceeding: a reminder is offered that in calculating from BC to AD, the BC number less one must be used. From 5 BC to AD 6 is ten years, not eleven. This was because no zero year was inserted at the change.)

THE BASIS OF THE CHRONOLOGY
The prophecy of Enoch, outlined on p.207, was written in 238 BC, as may be calculated. This, in the writer's theory, was the year 3430 from creation, the seventh world-week (490×7). He belonged to the party that came to be called the Essenes, nurturing in their midst the pretenders to the throne of David and to the high priesthood of Zadok. They clung to the solar calendar as the one heaven had ordained, believing that Jews who observed the lunar calendar were transgressing the will of God by keeping the festivals at the wrong dates.

The perfect symmetry of the solar calendar, with a date always falling on the same day of the week, the year structured in sevens without remainder, with four seasons of exactly the same length, gave rise to the belief that heaven acted in the same symmetrical ways, and the pattern of past history, constructed in sevens and tens, would be repeated in the future, in favour of the people who kept the true calendar. Above all, they longed for the

Restoration, the return of the Zadoks and the Davids to power. They themselves, as a sect called the Plant of Righteousness, had appeared at the great seventh world-week. Surely, at the eighth, in 490 years' time, which would be the year 3920 from creation, 'a house would be built for the great king'.[9] The temple would be built according to their ideas, and the true priest would reign there, with the heir of David as the true king. On their understanding in 238 BC, this would be in AD 253.

Then everything changed, and it looked as if the Restoration was about to come. Seventy years after they wrote, in 168 BC, the temple was defiled by their Gentile overlord Antiochus Epiphanes, who set up in it a statue of Zeus. War broke out under the heroic Maccabees, the Essenes (or Hasideans, as they were called), joined in,[10] and during the three years of the war they became convinced that their priests would rule in the temple when it was restored after the war. Apparently, they reasoned, they had been mistaken about the date of creation. It had been in 4088 BC, and the year 3920 was in 168 BC.

In the Book of Daniel, with its calculations about a period of 490 years (9:24–27), they set out their revision. They also wrote the Book of Jubilees, which revised Enoch's account of previous history in terms of their new dating.

They did not get their Restoration at the end of the war. The Maccabees, keeping a lunar calendar, were given power in the temple and state, both because of their popularity and because the Essenes were the remains of the old aristocrats whose day had long since passed. The Essenes retired in fury to Qumran, believing that the temple was in the hands of heretics. But they remained convinced about the system. If nothing had happened in 3920, it would happen in 4000. In 88 BC their day would come.

When this date again failed them, it proved to be an incentive for new learning, for they found, after research, that their scheme of previous history had a flaw. One of their world-weeks had ended with the fall of Jerusalem, and they had been using a date for this that was incorrect. It had happened much later than they had thought, and this meant that all the dates were out, the Maccabean period had not been 3920 after all, but 3920 was still to come. When the date of the fall of Jerusalem was corrected to something like its true date (they thought 581 BC; it was actually 587), they arrived at a set of dates which could no longer be altered in terms of historical events.

The Testament of Levi, described on p.206, sets out the revision. The 490 years between the seventh and eighth world-weeks were from 511–21 BC. Still some years in the future at the time of writing, the Restoration would come in 21 BC, year 3920 from creation. The year 3900, the beginning of the last millennium of world history, fell in 41 BC, and it was at that time that Herod began his rise toward power, assured by his flatterers that he was the inaugurator of a thousand year empire.

As the year 3920 for the Restoration and the temple approached, events looked auspicious. The earthquake at Qumran had driven the ascetics back to Jerusalem, where Herod the Great had personal reasons for favouring the Essenes.[11] The whole ascetic movement, which now included Sadducees and Pharisees who wanted to take on a higher discipline, was providing him with valuable income from the Diaspora. When he announced that he was going to use some of the money to rebuild the temple, Essene hopes soared high. The Restoration would come right on time, and they would be in power in the temple. The true priest, described in a beautiful passage of the Testament of Levi, would reign in it.[12] Herod could be the true king and true priest, and the David would be a spiritual counterpart. They wrote the Temple Scroll, setting out their architectural plans for the new temple, claiming that the plans had been dictated by God on Mount Sinai.

Herod was too astute to let the old aristocrats have power in a modern temple. He ignored their plan. This was a disaster for the Essene prophets, for the dates could no longer be changed. The Essene priests, the heirs of Zadok (Zechariah the father of John the Baptist) and his second priest Abiathar (Simon the Essene) conspired against the Herods from this point, Simon the Essene being the one who 'killed the fatted Calf' (Archelaus Herod), that is, Simon was part of the delegation of Jewish leaders who had him removed from office.

THE ZERO GENERATION AND JUBILEE

Some hard thinking was needed to save the prophecy. A device was found, that of allowing a zero unit. The Herodian form of the calendar always allowed a zero, a concept learned from the Greeks. Matthew's story of the Magians at the birth of Jesus conveys this point.[13]

A zero generation could be allowed in the dating. The first forty years from the day of creation should have been called a 0, not a 1. Since the year 3900 had fallen in 41 BC, 3940, the end of its first generation, was in 1 BC. But this should now be called 3900, and, since the prophet of the book of Enoch had said that the world was to last 4900 years, it, rather than 41 BC, began the last millennium of world history. This was the reason why the millennium that became the Christian millennium was set in 1 BC as its year 0, as seen in Chapter 13. It was a way of removing the Herodian millennium and beginning again.

In the same way, a zero jubilee of forty-nine years could be allowed, so the Restoration (3920) that was expected for 21 BC would now take place in AD 29. This was called the Last Jubilee, a phrase that is found in the Scrolls.[14] It was in AD 29, the 'fifteenth year of Tiberius Caesar', that Jesus began his ministry, announcing in the synagogue a fulfilment of the jubilee year, 'the year of acceptance'.

It was this version of the chronology that was held by Agrippa I, as shown in Rev 8:13. He had come back to Judea, forced there by the debts he had incurred in Rome through lavish entertaining, and began to gather around

223

him a party working for the return of the Herods, whose kingship had been abolished in AD 6. His appeal to the ascetics was that he would fulfil their Restoration in AD 29.

It was their custom to have a double beginning of the year, in September and the following March. This is illustrated in the Seven Trumpets section of Revelation. Agrippa's jubilee, the zero version of the year 3920, could be counted both from September AD 29 and March AD 30. From both the previous September and this date, he reckoned an Aeon (*aiōn*), the term having the precise meaning of 490 years. Agrippa I took the title of the Aeon, as the one who had inaugurated the new world-week, and his son Agrippa II came to be called the Aeon of the Aeon.

A new dating was commenced in AD 30, in honour of Agrippa. That year was year 0, its year 8 was AD 38 (Acts 9:33), and its year 14 was in AD 44. This was Paul's 'fourteen years' of Gal 2:1, an expression that has always puzzled commentators as it raises historical problems. Paul was using it in its pesher sense, 'year 14', meaning AD 44, following Agrippa's dating. The year 21 of the same era, 'three weeks' from September AD 29, is also noted in Acts, giving a date of September AD 50 (Acts 17:2).

Agrippa did not gain power in 29–30, but either then or later his supporters saw that there was another well-founded way of extending the jubilee, by allowing a zero quartodecimal period, fourteen years. The intercalations of the solar calendar were made every fourteen years (see below), and one such period could be allowed as a zero at the beginning of time. An intercalation was due in AD 29, and another in AD 43. In the latter year Agrippa was at the height of his power. He had been appointed ruler in 37 at the death of Tiberius, who always opposed him, and the accession of his friend Gaius Caligula. He managed to charm Claudius also, and in 41 at Claudius' accession was given increased power. In September 43, at the first ending of his fourteen year extension, he began to believe that he was the true priest of the Restoration. In March

224

AD 44, at the second occurrence of his extension, he went too far by proclaiming himself a divine king whose Restoration had come at that season according to the prophecy. His enemies saw their chance, and he was poisoned.

A term was developed for a seven year extension: 'woe!' (*ouai*). This was what the prophets said when they were denouncing a city, and it was a suitable word to use when the prophecy was not fulfilled and when someone's sin was blamed. One 'woe' meant seven years' extension, two 'woes' meant fourteen years, three meant twenty-one years.

THE JUBILEE OF THE ANNAS PRIESTS

In AD 29 there was another point of view, expressed through the three 'woes' of Rev 8:13. This was the calendar theory of Jonathan Annas, the 'Flying Eagle' who in that year cried: 'Woe! Woe! Woe!', meaning that they had to wait until AD 50. It was this theory that gave the jubilee of Parts A and B of Revelation.

The theory, as was often the case, arose from actual political circumstances. When the Herods were removed in AD 6, the Annas priests, under the Romans, took over the position of both high priest and ruler of the people in religious matters, using the title 'Royal One' (*basilikos*, John 4:46). In the previous generation, under Herod the Great, the kingship of Herod had been proclaimed at the millennium (3900, 41 BC), and a true priest had been expected in the year of the Restoration (3920, 21 BC). Ananus the Elder could be said to be both king, ruling at the millennium; and true priest, so appearing at the Restoration.

This was able to be expressed in calendar terms. By declaring a zero generation, as has been shown, the year 1 BC was called 3900, instead of 3940, as it had previously been. By dating from that year, Ananus was saying that he had replaced Herod as the king at the millennium. But he also needed to say that at the very same time he was the true priest, and that must mean that he had appeared in 3920. By adding an extension of three 'weeks', twenty-one years, to the unfulfilled Restoration of 21 BC, he brought it to September AD 1. This may have been justified by saying that the final jubilee of the world-week had lasted ten 'weeks', not seven. He had thus combined a revised millennium 3900 with an extended 3920, bringing about a conjunction of dates which would be acceptable when the meaning of the dates was given such great importance. From this time on, in the practice of the Annas priests, a millennial year was at the same time a Restoration, although the years for these events had originally been twenty years apart.

In the form of the Annas chronology that was used in the Diaspora,[15] September 1 BC was now 3900, or year 0; and September AD 1 was now year 3901, year 1, while at the same time it was given the significance of the year 3920. This meant that it was a jubilee year, for 3920 had been a jubilee. When it was decided that the Restoration had not really come in AD 1, a Last Jubilee was declared, and this meant that the true Restoration of the true Annas priest would come in September AD 50, forty-nine years later. Matthew Annas believed that he would inherit the title, but by his time the Herods had been restored and the young Agrippa II claimed a part in the great event. It happened that he would turn twenty-three in September AD 50, and this was seen as auspicious, for it was the age of initiation. Matthew and Agrippa the Younger were both to be vindicated by some form of heavenly intervention in AD 50, and their doctrine justified. Their doctrine was close to being Christian, and for this reason the period leading up to AD 50 is given detailed treatment in Part B of Revelation.

In September AD 29, when Agrippa I was declaring the end of his Last Jubilee from 21 BC, Jonathan Annas said (no doubt out of the hearing of Agrippa): 'Woe! Woe!

Woe!' (Rev 8:13). He was saying that his family's Last Jubilee was the true one, and they had another three 'weeks' to wait.

A double start to the year had been made, following Jewish practice which observed both equinoxes. Year 1 of the jubilee began in both September AD 1 and March AD 2. The trumpet was blown on both occasions, and repeated every seven years. But in the last 'week' of the jubilee a further calendar change was effected, to follow the Julian calendar, making the solstices, December and June, the primary feasts. The expectations for September were moved on to December, and those for March moved on to June. In Ephesus, June and the Pentecost feast were the greater solstice, while in Rome the December solstice and the following 1 January were observed as the greater New Year.

It was on 1 January AD 51, after the 'half-hour's silence' that the hopes of Matthew Annas failed.

When, after the experiments of the mid-century, the Christians triumphed, they saw that the beginning of the Annas era in 1 BC and AD 1 had been their own beginning. It was at that point that a mission to the Diaspora and to Gentiles independent of the Herods had been established. The school for Gentiles in Rome, which for a time was called the Vineyard, dated its foundation from 1 BC. It had originated with the split between the two branches of the Herod family when they disputed the succession in Rome, and had continued as a place of instruction for Gentiles attracted by the Agrippas, but from the time of the visit of the 'Beloved Son' in the late forties AD it had increasingly taught the Christian version of the doctrine.

Jesus had begun the process of taking over the rights and privileges of the Annas priests, earning himself the title the 'Wicked (Anti-)Priest'. That process was continued under his son and grandson, so that by the end of the Book of Revelation Jesus III said 'I am the Alpha and the Omega'. In Rome, no Jewish priests were necessary, and the Christians disowned their Jewish origins. The next step was to say that the dating that had been that of the Annas priests really belonged to Jesus. He was the one who combined the true king with the true priest. With his form of the mission, a Restoration had come, or rather, the taking up of a new religious power. AD 1 was the year of the 'birth' of his mission, and, since the general body of believers preferred to think in personal terms, it was treated as the year of his birth. Since its Julian beginning was in January, and the previous December solstice was linked with it and was not an ancient Jewish festival, it was chosen as the main Christian festival and that of the birth of Jesus.

THE ESCHATON, YEAR 4000

Although the prophecy of Enoch had relied on the number seven as the key to history, another point of view saw the division of history into generations of forty years as the one approved by heaven. Using the same calendar of days as solarists, they pointed to the forty years of the Wilderness wandering, and the custom of measuring the king's generations in sets of forty years. For them, a great crisis was likely to come in the year 4000, eighty years after the 3920 of the Restoration. This year was called the Eschaton, 'the last'. In the version of the dating that had become established, AD 60 was year 4000, and many looked to this year for the expected sign from heaven. AD 60 was the year of the 'shipwreck' recorded in Acts 27, and the story includes allusions to the expectation, the failure of which was, in fact, the 'shipwreck'.

In Ephesus, Ananus the Younger, preferring the forty year method, renewed hopes during the fifties by pointing to AD 60 as the great date. At the same time, he combined it with the significance of 3920, in the same way as the Restoration year had previously been combined with the millennium. All expectations for a millennial event were now treated as a Restoration, and were capable of extensions in sets of sevens. This was one of the reasons why AD 74 was treated as the last hope for AD 60, and why Part C of Revelation finished at this point.

But, on the Sadducee priests' own definition of the millennium 3900, falling in 1 BC rather than 41 BC, there was another chance for 4000, in AD 100. Part D of Revelation opens in that year, with new leaders under the ageing Agrippa II still preserving their hopes for an Eschaton-Restoration. The 'thousand years', meaning year 1000, the millennium 4000, fell a number of times during that year, according to the season which it was believed that heaven favoured. It fell on 1 January, again in March, and again on the Day of Pentecost. Then, for those who allowed a zero year from creation, it fell again in AD 101. Revelation 20 traces the political consequences of each disappointment, showing the rise and fall of the holders of traditional offices, who were discredited because of the failure of these Jewish prophecies. The consequence was that Christians emerged as the superior party.

Although Christians in Rome were settling for 1 BC–AD 1, those in Ephesus saw the year AD 100 as an Eschaton-Restoration, and the extension of fourteen years beyond it brought the history to AD 114. It was in this year that the Book of Revelation closed.

THE ZERO DECADE

The custom of allowing zero units from creation was applied also to decades, a practice that had been encouraged by the earthquake of 31 BC. That catastrophe, which had had important political consequences for the ascetics, must have occurred, on their theories, in a significant year. It was just ten years after 41 BC, the 3900 millennium, and one party, including the Therapeuts, whose leader was subsequently called 'Earthquake', chose to allow a zero decade in their reckoning. They expressed such a view also by always treating 1 a.m. or 1 p.m. after midnight and noon as the true ending of the half day.

This reasoning allowed them to treat AD 70, rather than AD 60, as the Eschaton. It was one element in the motives of the Sicarii, who used the calendar of the Therapeuts, in becoming involved in the war. The destruction of the city of Jerusalem did mark their Eschaton, but only from the point of view of the anti-Judean Diaspora was it a Restoration.

In the same way, the expectations for AD 100 could be postponed to AD 110. This was done, as shown by the treatment of the year in Rev 21:1–8.

THE SIXTY YEARS OF THE VINEYARD

The dating associated with the Vineyard, the mission to Gentiles in Rome, is supplied through Matthew's parable of the Vineyard (20: 1–16) and through details in Acts. Its foundation was in 1 BC, and it looked forward to the Eschaton of AD 60. Its expectation lies behind much of the imagery of Rev 14:14–20.

According to Matthew's parable, workers in a vineyard were hired at the start of day, then others at the third hour, others at the sixth hour, others at the ninth hour. At the eleventh hour others were hired, and when payment was made at the end of the day, these were paid the same amount as the rest, causing resentment.

Matthew's gospel, written last, supplies valuable detail on the chronology by stories such as this one. With the help of Acts 7 (a passage in the form of an Old Testament history which actually refers to the history of the mission from the time of Hillel), the chronological scheme may be worked out. Some Sadducees, relying on the division by forties, counted history in sets of 480 years, as shown by the fact that 21 BC, eighty years before AD 60, is called year 400 in Acts 7:6.[16] It appears that, on one of their interpretations, the sets of 480s were divided into eight sets of sixty years, and each sixty years was called a 'day', there being eight 'days' in the set. The seven 'days' were

for Jews, and the 'eighth day' for the evangelisation of
Gentiles. As a 'day' had twelve hours (daylight only; the
definition is given in John 11:9), each 'hour' was one-
twelfth of sixty years, that is, five years. Since 21 BC was
'year 400', the year 420, beginning the 'eighth day', fell in
1 BC.[17] It would end in AD 60, the year 4000.

The scheme on which the parable relies was:

421 BC	Begin 480 years, in eight sets of sixty years, each called a 'day'. From 421 BC to 1 BC, seven 'days', 420 years, for teaching Jews.
21 BC	Year 400 of this scheme, noted in Acts 7:6 (pesher).
1 BC	Day 8 ('eighth day', Acts 7:8 pesher) begins in year 420 of the scheme, for the evangelisation of Gentiles, to cover sixty years up to AD 60. In 1 BC the Vineyard mission in Rome was founded. Since sixty years was a 'day'(12 hours), one -twelfth of it, five years, was an 'hour'. Fifteen years equalled 'three hours'. 1 BC was '6 a.m.'
AD 15	'9 a.m.' (third hour) of the 'day', after fifteen years. New workers sent out.
AD 30	'Noon' (sixth hour) of the 'day'. New workers sent out.
AD 45	'3 p.m.' (ninth hour) of the 'day'. New workers sent out.
AD 55	'5 p.m.' (eleventh hour). Latecomers sent out.
AD 60	'6 p.m.'. The Eschaton 4000, which was also year 480 of the scheme (each 1000 years 40+960). End of the Vineyard mission. Workers 'paid', including the resented latecomers.

The point of the parable has always been understood to be that Jews objected to Gentiles coming in, but the exact detail of hours is not needed for this point, and as in all the parables, it is subject to a more exact explanation.

In AD 55 the procurator Felix, who had arrived in Judea in AD 54, became a member of the Jewish mission, receiving instruction in order to marry Drusilla the younger sister of Agrippa. With Agrippa, who in his late twenties was becoming an active leader, and with Paul, who was one of his instructors, he helped to change the character of the mission. Felix made many enemies, particularly because of his part in the assassination of Jonathan Annas.[18] He was finally arrested and brought to Rome, and it was the ship that carried Felix that also brought Paul and his party to Rome.

In Rome, then, where the Vineyard mission to Gentiles was based, the end of the 'day' in AD 60 would be a great event. In Rev 14:18–19 the account of AD 60 says that the 'angel' for that year was ordered to 'put forth his sickle and gather the clusters of the Vineyard of the Earth'. He 'threw into the great winepress of the Wrath of God'. When there was no supernatural intervention from heaven as a sign of the Eschaton, hopes were deferred to December 60 and 1 January 61, but these dates also failed, and there was a persecution of members in Rome.

The persecution of Christians by Nero in the summer of AD 64 was 3½ years later than the non-fulfilment of December AD 60, and they had undoubtedly helped to bring the punishment on themselves by staging demonstrations at the June solstice at a date they held to be a legitimate extension of the Eschaton.

EXODUS AND HOLY WAR
One of the original schemes of history, based on the periods of forty years, was that of an eighty years which would see, first an Exodus of forty years, then a Holy War

of forty years, at the end of which the 'Promised Land' would have been conquered. The original form of it is given in Acts 13:16–25. When Herod the Great took up this theme, which had been used by the Therapeuts before his time, he (or his heads of mission) treated the forty years 3900 to 3940 as that of both an Exodus and the first forty years of evangelism. The Holy War portion was due in 3940 to 3980, and these were the years 1 BC to AD 40. They saw the outbreak of zealotry, which was encouraged by the existing scheme. The War Scroll was written as a plan for the forty year war at this time. It actually broke out in AD 6, in the south lunisolar version of 3941, a generation year for Herodians. As has been seen on p.209, the second document of Part A of Revelation uses the scheme of the war, covering the years AD 6–46. The south solar version of 3980 fell in AD 44, and it was in this year that Agrippa staged his demonstration of godship, expecting a vindication from heaven.

Since 3900 to 3940 could be revised by inserting a zero generation, there should be another forty years for Exodus and its associated evangelism from the revised 3900 from 1 BC. The detail of the gospels and Acts shows that this was the case, and that a further point of significance to the prophets was that the year 38 of an Exodus must be that which saw a 'crossing of Jordan', as a proof that the rest would follow (John 5:5). Their source was Deut 2:14. In the year that was 38 of the revised Exodus, in its south lunisolar version counted from the zealot uprising, in AD 44, Theudas the Chief Therapeut attempted an actual miraculous crossing of Jordan and was arrested and beheaded.[19] Subsequently, the 'Egyptian', Apollos the successor of Theudas, led a great demonstration in AD 58, when from the Mount of Olives he demanded that the walls of Jerusalem fall down, as a latterday Jericho.[20] The year was 38 in another revision of the Exodus from AD 20–60.

As the expectations were deferred by a decade, the year

38 appeared again in AD 68, and the events recorded for that year in Rev 16:12–16 reflect it.

The forty year schemes, however, were subordinated in Revelation to the schemes based on seven.

DAYS AND DATES
The 1260 days, the feasts and the 31sts

The makers of the detail of the solar calendar, probably going back to Babylon in the sixth century BC, had a passion for symmetry and believed that heaven shared it. They knew – as can be seen from the fact that their calendar worked for so long – that the solar year is 365¼ days, less some minutes. This fact was known to the Greeks very early. But, as the later makers of the Julian calendar also discovered, a calendar that reflected the year exactly was unworkable. Whereas the Julian calendar resolved the matter by leap years, combining four quarter days into one intercalated day, the earlier one chose a year of 364 days, divided into 52 weeks, and further divided into four seasons, each of 91 days. Each season had two months of 30 days and one month, the one at the equinox or solstice, with 31 days.

The four 31sts in the year were a kind of intercalated day, in that they were out of the ordinary, and passages in the Book of Jubilees and in the newly published fragment 4QMMT show that they were the days on which great events were expected.[21] Initially it was believed that if a Restoration or any other form of fulfilment of prophecy were to come, it would come on that day. The 31st was counted with the following month as a kind of zero day to it, not with the previous month.

Traditional Jewish feasts were included at their biblical dates, but in terms of this calendar, so that they were observed on different days from the lunarists with their 354 day calendar. Passover was the 14th of the first month (March–April), Pentecost was the 15th of the third month (given a fixed date by the solarists, as shown in Jubilees,

234

although not in orthodox Jewish practice), Atonement the 10th of the seventh month, and Tabernacles the 15th of the same month (September–October).

The pentecontads, now known from the Temple Scroll, began on the 26th of the first month, and occurred every seven weeks, the next being Pentecost 15/III, and on through the rest of the year. The one in December was 29/IX.

Pentecost became a primary feast to those who adopted the Julian calendar, as it occurred at the half year that had begun in January, and the divisions reflected the Jewish year divided into two halves, September and the following March. In the normative position of the calendar, Pentecost always fell on a Sunday, and was followed over a fortnight later by the 31st for the June solstice, another major date. From AD 43–44 the Book of Revelation treats Pentecost as the greater religious feast, with December a lesser beginning of the year, while showing that there was a different point of view that reversed the values. Its version of Pentecost is always the one preceding the 31st at the end of the third month and the beginning of the fourth, whereas in the gospels a variation of this was used. Revelation in general uses a simplified form of the day dates, compared with the gospels. Its concentration is on the years.

The fulfilment of prophecy would, naturally, come at the season preferred by the party that was favoured by heaven. In the Jewish form, the issue was between the equinoxes used by the priests for their festivals, and the solstices, preferred by the laity. Once the Julian calendar was introduced in 45 BC it was recognised as an accurate one and combined with the solar calendar, giving the December solstice and following 1 January an importance it had not previously had. Westernised Diaspora Jews such as the Magians had no difficulty in incorporating it, and their party was founded in 44 BC in order to uphold it; similarly the Egyptian Therapeuts

TABLE 2

SOLAR CALENDAR (Day Position)

	I — Equ. (Spring)					II					III			
Sun		5	12	19	26		3	10	17	24	1	8	[15]	22	29
Mon		6	13	20	27		4	11	18	25	2	9	16	23	30
Tue		7	[14]	21	28		5	12	19	26	3	10	17	24	[31]
Wed	1	8	15	22	29		6	13	20	27	4	11	18	25	
Thu	2	9	16	23	30		7	14	21	28	5	12	19	26	
Fri	3	10	17	24		1	8	15	22	29	6	13	20	27	
Sat	4	11	18	25		2	9	16	23	30	7	14	21	28	

	IV — Sol. (Summer)					V					VI			
Sun		5	12	19	26		3	10	17	24	1	8	15	22	29
Mon		6	13	20	27		4	11	18	25	2	9	16	23	30
Tue		7	14	21	28		5	12	19	26	3	10	17	24	[31]
Wed	1	8	15	22	29		6	13	20	27	4	11	18	25	
Thu	2	9	16	23	30		7	14	21	28	5	12	19	26	
Fri	3	10	17	24		1	8	15	22	29	6	13	20	27	
Sat	4	11	18	25		2	9	16	23	30	7	14	21	28	

	VII — Equ. (Autumn)					VIII					IX			
Sun		5	12	19	26		3	10	17	24	1	8	15	22	29
Mon		6	13	20	27		4	11	18	25	2	9	16	23	30
Tue		7	14	21	28		5	12	19	26	3	10	17	24	[31]
Wed	1	8	[15]	22	29		6	13	20	27	4	11	18	25	
Thu	2	9	16	23	30		7	14	21	28	5	12	19	26	
Fri	3	[10]	17	24		1	8	15	22	29	6	13	20	27	
Sat	4	11	18	25		2	9	16	23	30	7	14	21	28	

	X — Sol. (Winter)					XI					XII			
Sun		5	12	19	26		3	10	17	24	1	8	15	22	29
Mon		6	13	20	27		4	11	18	25	2	9	16	23	30
Tue		7	14	21	28		5	12	19	26	3	10	17	24	[31]
Wed	1	8	15	22	29		6	13	20	27	4	11	18	25	
Thu	2	9	16	23	30		7	14	21	28	5	12	19	26	
Fri	3	10	17	24		1	8	15	22	29	6	13	20	27	
Sat	4	11	18	25		2	9	16	23	30	7	14	21	28	

I	Month beginning near March equinox.	14/I Passover
IV	Month beginning near June solstice	15/III Pentecost
VII	Month beginning near September equinox	10/VII Atonement
X	Month beginning near December solstice	15/VII Tabernacles
		31st counted with the following month

adopted it. But the other half of the order of Manasseh, with eastern views, did not accept it, and this was one of the reasons for the separation of the eastern province. In the western theory of prophecy, it was apparently agreed that heaven also used the Julian calendar, and expectations were held for 1 January and for June, at the Day of Pentecost. In Ephesus June was preferred, in Rome December–January.

The 31sts, ideally, were at the actual equinoxes and solstices, the 20th or 21st of March, June, September and December. But because the calendar did not correspond exactly to the length of the year, it fell back each year by 1¼ days, 30 hours, so after some years the 31sts were falling early in the months of March, etc. This was corrected by intercalation. It can be shown, from the Book of Daniel and the concealed chronology of the gospels, that the method was as follows:

After fourteen years, the calendar had fallen back by 17½ days (14×30 hours). This number of days was then inserted, in the form of 2½ weeks. Such a unit was quite workable, in that half a week was 3½ days, a unit frequently used. When the calendar arrived at the 31st of the month, 6 a.m. on Tuesday in the normative position, the 17½ day intercalation began, and ended 2½ weeks later, on Friday at 6 p.m. For example, when an intercalation was held in September of a certain year, it began on Tuesday, 6 September at 6 a.m., the point to which the calendar had then fallen back, and ended on Friday, 23 September at 6 p.m. From that time on, for the next fourteen years, the dates ran from this Friday 23 September as the solar 31st, not Tuesday. While the dates from Tuesday 6 a.m. were normative, the Day position, since it was a solar calendar, the method meant that for every alternate fourteen years it was in the Night position. When it was in the Night position, all 31sts were on Fridays, and Pentecost was on a Wednesday.

The quartodecimal year is indicated for the pesharist by

the word *kairos*, apparently vaguely meaning a season, but giving the intercalation year. It is therefore an important indicator of date. The north solar series of intercalation years fell in AD 1 (change to Night), 15 (to Day), 29 (to Night), 43 (to Day), 57 (to Night), 71 (to Day), 85 (to Night), 99 (to Day), 113 (to Night).

The corresponding Julian dates may be calculated, facilitated by the use of what are called the Dominical Letters or Sunday Letters.[22] The complete set of dates, in Julian and solar form, for the period covered by Revelation may usefully be set out in a table:

TABLE 3
JULIAN AND SOLAR DATES, 7 BC TO AD 115

BC-AD	Jan 1	31st (March)	31st (June)	31st (Sep)	31st (Dec)
BC 7	Thu	Tue Mar 17	Tue Jun 16	Tue Sep 15	Tue Dec 15
6	Fri	Tue Mar 16	Tue Jun 15	Tue Sep 14	Tue Dec 14
5 L	Sat	Tue Mar 14	Tue Jun 13	Tue Sep 12	Tue Dec 12
4	Mon	Tue Mar 13	Tue Jun 12	Tue Sep 11	Tue Dec 11
3	Tue	Tue Mar 12	Tue Jun 11	Tue Sep 10	Tue Dec 10
2	Wed	Tue Mar 11	Tue Jun 10	Tue Sep 9	Tue Dec 9
BC 1 L	Thu	Tue Mar 9	Tue Jun 8	Tue Sep 7	Tue Dec 7
AD 1IC	Sat	Fri Mar 25	Fri Jun 24	Fri Sep 23	Fri Dec 23
2	Sun	Fri Mar 24	Fri Jun 23	Fri Sep 22	Fri Dec 22
3	Mon	Fri Mar 23	Fri Jun 22	Fri Sep 21	Fri Dec 21
4L	Tue	Fri Mar 21	Fri Jun 20	Fri Sep 19	Fri Dec 19
5	Thu	Fri Mar 20	Fri Jun 19	Fri Sep 18	Fri Dec 18
6	Fri	Fri Mar 19	Fri Jun 18	Fri Sep 17	Fri Dec 17
7	Sat	Fri Mar 18	Fri Jun 17	Fri Sep 16	Fri Dec 16
8 L	Sun	Fri Mar 16	Fri Jun 15	Fri Sep 14	Fri Dec 14
9	Tue	Fri Mar 15	Fri Jun 14	Fri Sep 13	Fri Dec 13
10	Wed	Fri Mar 14	Fri Jun 13	Fri Sep 12	Fri Dec 12
11	Thu	Fri Mar 13	Fri Jun 12	Fri Sep 11	Fri Dec 11
12 L	Fri	Fri Mar 11	Fri Jun 10	Fri Sep 9	Fri Dec 9
13	Sun	Fri Mar 10	Fri Jun 9	Fri Sep 8	Fri Dec 8

14	Mon	Fri Mar 9	Fri Jun 8	Fri Sep 7	Fri Dec 7
15 IC	Tue	Tue Mar 26	Tue Jun 25	Tue Sep 24	Tue Dec 24
16 L	Wed	Tue Mar 24	Tue Jun 23	Tue Sep 22	Tue Dec 22
17	Fri	Tue Mar 23	Tue Jun 22	Tue Sep 21	Tue Dec 21
18	Sat	Tue Mar 22	Tue Jun 21	Tue Sep 20	Tue Dec 20
19	Sun	Tue Mar 21	Tue Jun 20	Tue Sep 19	Tue Dec 19
20 L	Mon	Tue Mar 19	Tue Jun 18	Tue Sep 17	Tue Dec 17
21	Wed	Tue Mar 18	Tue Jun 17	Tue Sep 16	Tue Dec 16
22	Thu	Tue Mar 17	Tue Jun 16	Tue Sep 15	Tue Dec 15
23	Fri	Tue Mar 16	Tue Jun 15	Tue Sep 14	Tue Dec 14
24 L	Sat	Tue Mar 14	Tue Jun 13	Tue Sep 12	Tue Dec 12
25	Mon	Tue Mar 13	Tue Jun 12	Tue Sep 11	Tue Dec 11
26	Tue	Tue Mar 12	Tue Jun 11	Tue Sep 10	Tue Dec 10
27	Wed	Tue Mar 11	Tue Jun 10	Tue Sep 9	Tue Dec 9
28 L	Thu	Tue Mar 9	Tue Jun 8	Tue Sep 7	Tue Dec 7
29 IC	Sat	Fri Mar 25	Fri Jun 24	Fri Sep 23	Fri Dec 23
30	Sun	Fri Mar 24	Fri Jun 23	Fri Sep 22	Fri Dec 22
31	Mon	Fri Mar 23	Fri Jun 22	Fri Sep 21	Fri Dec 21
32 L	Tue	Fri Mar 21	Fri Jun 20	Fri Sep 19	Fri Dec 19
33	Thu	Fri Mar 20	Fri Jun 19	Fri Sep 18	Fri Dec 18
34	Fri	Fri Mar 19	Fri Jun 18	Fri Sep 17	Fri Dec 17
35	Sat	Fri Mar 18	Fri Jun 17	Fri Sep 16	Fri Dec 16
36 L	Sun	Fri Mar 16	Fri Jun 15	Fri Sep 14	Fri Dec 14
37	Tue	Fri Mar 15	Fri Jun 14	Fri Sep 13	Fri Dec 13
38	Wed	Fri Mar 14	Fri Jun 13	Fri Sep 12	Fri Dec 12
39	Thu	Fri Mar 13	Fri Jun 12	Fri Sep 11	Fri Dec 11
40 L	Fri	Fri Mar 11	Fri Jun 10	Fri Sep 9	Fri Dec 9
41	Sun	Fri Mar 10	Fri Jun 9	Fri Sep 8	Fri Dec 8
42	Mon	Fri Mar 9	Fri Jun 8	Fri Sep 7	Fri Dec 7
43 IC	Tue	Tue Mar 26	Tue Jun 25	Tue Sep 24	Tue Dec 24
44 L	Wed	Tue Mar 24	Tue Jun 23	Tue Sep 22	Tue Dec 22
45	Fri	Tue Mar 23	Tue Jun 22	Tue Sep 21	Tue Dec 21
46	Sat	Tue Mar 22	Tue Jun 21	Tue Sep 20	Tue Dec 20
47	Sun	Tue Mar 21	Tue Jun 20	Tue Sep 19	Tue Dec 19
48 L	Mon	Tue Mar 19	Tue Jun 18	Tue Sep 17	Tue Dec 17
49	Wed	Tue Mar 18	Tue Jun 17	Tue Sep 16	Tue Dec 16
50	Thu	Tue Mar 17	Tue Jun 16	Tue Sep 15	Tue Dec 15

51	Fri	Tue Mar 16	Tue Jun 15	Tue Sep 14	Tue Dec 14
52 L	Sat	Tue Mar 14	Tue Jun 13	Tue Sep 12	Tue Dec 12
53	Mon	Tue Mar 13	Tue Jun 12	Tue Sep 11	Tue Dec 11
54	Tue	Tue Mar 12	Tue Jun 11	Tue Sep 10	Tue Dec 10
55	Wed	Tue Mar 11	Tue Jun 10	Tue Sep 9	Tue Dec 9
56 L	Thu	Tue Mar 9	Tue Jun 8	Tue Sep 7	Tue Dec 7
57 IC	Sat	Fri Mar 25	Fri Jun 24	Fri Sep 23	Fri Dec 23
58	Sun	Fri Mar 24	Fri Jun 23	Fri Sep 22	Fri Dec 22
59	Mon	Fri Mar 23	Fri Jun 22	Fri Sep 21	Fri Dec 21
60 L	Tue	Fri Mar 21	Fri Jun 20	Fri Sep 19	Fri Dec 19
61	Thu	Fri Mar 20	Fri Jun 19	Fri Sep 18	Fri Dec 18
62	Fri	Fri Mar 19	Fri Jun 18	Fri Sep 17	Fri Dec 17
63	Sat	Fri Mar 18	Fri Jun 17	Fri Sep 16	Fri Dec 16
64 L	Sun	Fri Mar 16	Fri Jun 15	Fri Sep 14	Fri Dec 14
65	Tue	Fri Mar 15	Fri Jun 14	Fri Sep 13	Fri Dec 13
66	Wed	Fri Mar 14	Fri Jun 13	Fri Sep 12	Fri Dec 12
67	Thu	Fri Mar 13	Fri Jun 12	Fri Sep 11	Fri Dec 11
68 L	Fri	Fri Mar 11	Fri Jun 10	Fri Sep 9	Fri Dec 9
69	Sun	Fri Mar 10	Fri Jun 9	Fri Sep 8	Fri Dec 8
70	Mon	Fri Mar 9	Fri Jun 8	Fri Sep 7	Fri Dec 7
71 IC	Tue	Tue Mar 26	Tue Jun 25	Tue Sep 24	Tue Dec 24
72 L	Wed	Tue Mar 24	Tue Jun 23	Tue Sep 22	Tue Dec 22
73	Fri	Tue Mar 23	Tue Jun 22	Tue Sep 21	Tue Dec 21
74	Sat	Tue Mar 22	Tue Jun 21	Tue Sep 20	Tue Dec 20
75	Sun	Tue Mar 21	Tue Jun 20	Tue Sep 19	Tue Dec 19
76 L	Mon	Tue Mar 19	Tue Jun 18	Tue Sep 17	Tue Dec 17
77	Wed	Tue Mar 18	Tue Jun 17	Tue Sep 16	Tue Dec 16
78	Thu	Tue Mar 17	Tue Jun 16	Tue Sep 15	Tue Dec 15
79	Fri	Tue Mar 16	Tue Jun 15	Tue Sep 14	Tue Dec 14
80 L	Sat	Tue Mar 14	Tue Jun 13	Tue Sep 12	Tue Dec 12
81	Mon	Tue Mar 13	Tue Jun 12	Tue Sep 11	Tue Dec 11
82	Tue	Tue Mar 12	Tue Jun 11	Tue Sep 10	Tue Dec 10
83	Wed	Tue Mar 11	Tue Jun 10	Tue Sep 9	Tue Dec 9
84 L	Thu	Tue Mar 9	Tue Jun 8	Tue Sep 7	Tue Dec 7
85 IC	Sat	Fri Mar 25	Fri Jun 24	Fri Sep 23	Fri Dec 23
86	Sun	Fri Mar 24	Fri Jun 23	Fri Sep 22	Fri Dec 22
87	Mon	Fri Mar 23	Fri Jun 22	Fri Sep 21	Fri Dec 21

88 L	Tue	Fri Mar 21	Fri Jun 20	Fri Sep 19	Fri Dec 19
89	Thu	Fri Mar 20	Fri Jun 19	Fri Sep 18	Fri Dec 18
90	Fri	Fri Mar 19	Fri Jun 18	Fri Sep 17	Fri Dec 17
91	Sat	Fri Mar 18	Fri Jun 17	Fri Sep 16	Fri Dec 16
92 L	Sun	Fri Mar 16	Fri Jun 15	Fri Sep 14	Fri Dec 14
93	Tue	Fri Mar 15	Fri Jun 14	Fri Sep 13	Fri Dec 13
94	Wed	Fri Mar 14	Fri Jun 13	Fri Sep 12	Fri Dec 12
95	Thu	Fri Mar 13	Fri Jun 12	Fri Sep 11	Fri Dec 11
96L	Fri	Fri Mar 11	Fri Jun 10	Fri Sep 9	Fri Dec 9
97	Sun	Fri Mar 10	Fri Jun 9	Fri Sep 8	Fri Dec 8
98	Mon	Fri Mar 9	Fri Jun 8	Fri Sep 7	Fri Dec 7
99 IC	Tue	Tue Mar 26	Tue Jun 25	Tue Sep 24	Tue Dec 24
100L	Wed	Tue Mar 24	Tue Jun 23	Tue Sep 22	Tue Dec 22
101	Fri	Tue Mar 23	Tue Jun 22	Tue Sep 21	Tue Dec 21
102	Sat	Tue Mar 22	Tue Jun 21	Tue Sep 20	Tue Dec 20
103	Sun	Tue Mar 21	Tue Jun 20	Tue Sep 19	Tue Dec 19
104L	Mon	Tue Mar 19	Tue Jun 18	Tue Sep 17	Tue Dec 17
105	Wed	Tue Mar 18	Tue Jun 17	Tue Sep 16	Tue Dec 16
106	Thu	Tue Mar 17	Tue Jun 16	Tue Sep 15	Tue Dec 15
107	Fri	Tue Mar 16	Tue Jun 15	Tue Sep 14	Tue Dec 14
108L	Sat	Tue Mar 14	Tue Jun 13	Tue Sep 12	Tue Dec 12
109	Mon	Tue Mar 13	Tue Jun 12	Tue Sep 11	Tue Dec 11
110	Tue	Tue Mar 12	Tue Jun 11	Tue Sep 10	Tue Dec 10
111	Wed	Tue Mar 11	Tue Jun 10	Tue Sep 9	Tue Dec 9
112L	Thu	Tue Mar 9	Tue Jun 8	Tue Sep 7	Tue Dec 7
113IC	Sat	Fri Mar 25	Fri Jun 24	Fri Sep 23	Fri Dec 23
114	Sun	Fri Mar 24	Fri Jun 23	Fri Sep 22	Fri Dec 22
115	Mon	Fri Mar 23	Fri Jun 22	Fri Sep 21	Fri Dec 21

L–leap year (Julian)

IC–intercalation (North Solar)

THE 3½ YEARS, 1260 DAYS, 42 MONTHS

There was another form of intercalation also, that of years. It is shown through sets of figures in Daniel (12:11–12) that from September 168 BC, when the Maccabean war broke out, to March 164 BC, 3½ years later, a period occurred in which there were no feasts in the temple.[23] From subsequent calendar uses it can be seen that this was treated as an intercalation, a non-time, for if there were no feasts there was no measurement of time, so, as it were, 'no time'. The image of a 'famine' was also used, for there were no feasts.

The principle was:

SEP year 0 to Sep year 1	1 year
Sep year 1 to Sep year 2	1 year
Sep year 2 to Sep year 3	1 year
Sep year 3 to Mar year 3½	½ year

The date at the end of the 3½ years was counted as the same as the date at the beginning. The year date given to September 168 BC was also given to March 164 BC. This change was continued through all the subsequent dating, and became an expression of party differences. Those who revered the idea of a temple in Jerusalem kept the later dates, from 164 (the series may be called south solar), but those Diaspora Jews who were not particularly attached to a temple kept the original, basic date, from 168 (north solar). When it came to the gospel period, September AD 29 was the north solar date of an important year, and March AD 33 was the south solar repetition of the same date. This date was one of great expectation, and the former occurred near the beginning of Jesus' ministry, while the latter was that of the crucifixion. The events of the gospel period were partly determined by the dating.

The Christian era was built on the north solar date, the original one, used by those Diaspora Jews who did not centre their hopes on the temple. But the date 3½ years later was turned to when the north solar date failed to produce the hoped for intervention from heaven, and more traditional parties argued that the pro-temple and more nationalist datings were the ones that would be preferred. This form of adjustment was turned to in the later parts of the period covered by Revelation.

The 1260 days appearing in Rev 11:3 and 12:6 are explained by this history. A period of 1274 days covered 3½ years of the calendar, using a year of 364 days. When the feasts were treated as the great days, the 3 years could be counted from Tabernacles in September to Passover in March. As Tabernacles was on the 15th of the seventh month, and Passover on the 14th of the first month, day 1274 fell on the 14th, Passover (see the calendar set out on p.236). This meant that there were 1260 days to the beginning of the previous 31st a fortnight before Passover, the zero day preceding the month. Those who wished to count from Tabernacles to the 31st before Passover (itself a great day) could count 1260 days, while others counted 1274 days. To say 'for 1260 days', that is, 'day 1260', was an elaborate way of saying that it was the 31st of the month, the end of a 3½ years, at the Passover season.

To illustrate:

(VII 15 Tabernacles, Sep–Oct. I 14 Passover, Mar–Apr)

VII 15 year 0 to year 1	364 days
VII 15 year 1 to year 2	364 days
VII 15 year 2 to year 3	364 days
VII 15 year 3 to I 14 year 3½	182 days
but to 31st beginning I	168 days

$364 \times 3 = 1092 + 168 = 1260.$

The adjustment by 3½ years was applied also to the generation years. The year 3970 (north solar) fell in September AD 30, and some believed that a generation year (*chronos*, 'time', but meaning forty years in the pesher), rather than a jubilee, would be chosen. This year, 3970, was a fortieth year in a series from 3930. A south solar party held that the same date would fall in March AD 34. This was the end of the 42 months of Rev 13:5. On the same basis, it was 42 months from September AD 40, the generation year 3980 (north solar), to March AD 44, and Rev 11:2 uses the expression at this point.

There was another version of the north and south years, used by those who allowed a zero year from creation following Herodian practice. Since they used some aspects of the lunar calendar, this may be called the lunisolar version. Each year was a year later than the solar one. Thus, at the rise of the Annas priests, they had four versions of the year 3941 that had become 3901: north solar in September AD 1, north lunisolar in September AD 2, south solar in March AD 5, south lunisolar in March AD 6. They had actually taken up power in AD 6, so called it year 1. The fact that AD 5 and 6 were years 0 and 1 was a reason why it was possible to go back to 1 BC and AD 1 as another version of the Annas dating.

In the gospels although not in Revelation, considerable emphasis is placed on the use of a year that was intermediate between north and south. It expressed the point of view of those who were neither for nor against the Jerusalem temple, but believed in a spiritual temple. This series is drawn on once in Revelation. The year AD 17 belonged to it as an intermediate intercalation year between AD 15 and 19, and is called a *kairos* (Rev 12:14).

Another calendar point is also illustrated in the gospels and Acts, and accounts for a feature in Revelation. The intercalation was normally begun when the dates had dropped back to 17½ days behind the 31st near the equinox, so catching up on the sun. But there was another way of doing it: to get ahead of the sun. At the 31st near the equinox, 17½ days were put in, for example from Friday, 23 September to Tuesday, 11 October. Over the next fourteen years the dates dropped back to the equinox 31st. This method was used by the Egyptian Therapeuts, but at the same time they acknowledged the other method. The result was that they used two positions of the 31st, holding the appropriate ceremonies on both. When the calendar was in the Night position, their Friday

31st came before their Tuesday 31st, Day, so they used the phrase 'Night and Day'. When it was in the Day position, the phrase was 'Day and Night'. This phrase is used often in Revelation, and it indicates the position the calendar was in, so is a useful guide.

The next part of this work will study the text of Revelation, to show that the history that is not apparent at first sight is actually present in it, when the special and technical senses of terms are known.

Part III

The Lexicon and the Pesher

The Lexicon

LIST OF SPECIAL MEANINGS

(This part of the book, although intended mainly for reference, is placed before the pesher in order to give the reader some familiarity with the practice of using special meanings.)

INTRODUCTION TO THE LEXICON

The whole 'mystery', or puzzle, depends on words whose familiar ordinary meaning is also used in a special, technical sense. The surface sense remains vague or general, while those with the key to the special meanings will discover an exact factual sense.

Some examples of exact meanings will illustrate: certain prepositions appear, normally meaning 'before' and 'behind' (Greek *emprosthen, opisō*). These words do not seem to give any more precise meaning, but to those with knowledge of Hebrew, and expecting an exact sense, they mean 'east' and 'west', for the Hebrew for 'before' (*qedem*) and 'behind' (*achrōn*) also means the two compass points, since in Hebrew thought the subject is facing east.

To take another example: when, in one of the seven letters, a person is condemned for being 'neither cold nor hot' (Rev 3:15), the meaning is that he is too Jewish, observes the equinox feasts in September and March only, and does not observe the Julian calendar, which allows feasts in December, winter, and June, summer. One of the main party differences was expressed through calendar, and the western party, most of which became Christian, used the Julian calendar.

All words having something to do with time have a very exact sense, and give dates. The word *kairos*, 'season', means that it is the quartodecimal intercalation year, in a known series (see p.238). The word *chronos*, 'period', means that it is at the end of a forty year generation. See pp.232–234 for the full explanation.

All 'heavenly' figures – angels, spirits, God, Lord, the one sitting on the throne, living creatures – are real people, whom a Hellenistic outlook interpreted as incarnations of divine beings, so could be referred to as if they were their heavenly counterparts for the purpose of disguise.

As the history was one of a political movement, under powerful leaders whose identity needed to be disguised, there was considerable use of pseudonyms which had arisen like nicknames. 'Locusts' was a name for John the Baptist, whose ascetic way of life meant eating locusts. Zealot leaders were called 'the Dragon', 'the Calf' and the 'Beast'. Teachers of the Law, coming from 'Mount Sinai', the centre where the Law was taught, were called 'Thunder', 'Lightning', 'Earthquake' and 'Hail', as these phenomena were associated with the giving of the Law. 'The Sun' was the man who was highest in the hierarchy of those keeping the solar calendar, and 'the Moon' was his wife. 'The Star' was the heir of David, part of this hierarchy.

There are a number of devices in which terms are read in a more particular way. One of these is a plural noun with a number, for example 'three days', 'five months', 'twenty-four elders'. These are to be read 'day 3' (that is, Tuesday, the third day of the week), 'month 5' (that is,

May in the Julian calendar), 'elder 24', a particular person, the village minister who was responsible for prayers for 24 hours of the day and night. 'Seven angels' means 'angel 7', a person holding the position of a minister for the seventh day, Saturday. The numbered person or item was the last of the series, and implied the existence of the rest.

A plural noun actually means a singular, expressing the platonic idea of a plural of reproduction. A person or place representing another was acting as a reproduction, and the plural is used for the reproduction. The best example of this is in the gospels, where the plural form of the word Jerusalem means its reproduction at Qumran, while the singular means the literal Jerusalem. In Revelation, the 'Holy One' (*hagios*) was the heir of David, but at times he was represented by his crown prince, who was then called the 'Holy Ones' (*hagioi*).

The definite article has a special function. There was a concept of being 'in the body', when a priest went down three grades to the level of his servant (see p.182). For example, he might, as priest, be at grade 2, but went down to grade 5 when he was 'in the body'. In the higher position the definite article is used, in the lower it is not. Both forms of the term may refer to the same person, or the article may make an important distinction, for example *to pneuma*, 'the Spirit', meaning the village priest, and *pneuma*, meaning his servant, the seer, who was 'in a Spirit' (Rev 1:10; 4:2).

A genitive expression gives information about grades. 'X of Y' means that X is one grade below Y. In the expression 'Son of Man', 'Son' is one grade below 'Man'.

The tenses, past, present and future, indicate positions. An action in the present tense takes place at the centre, an action in the future tense on the east, and an action in the past tense on the west. For this reason, the time sense of tenses is to be disregarded (a habit suggested by Hebrew), but they give further indications of place.

THE LEXICON OF SPECIAL MEANINGS

Each word is listed in its normal English translation, its Greek form, then the special meaning and its explanation.

Abaddon (Abaddōn) From Hebrew 'to destroy'. In Rev 9:11, the name used by the Chief Therapeut when in the party of the Hebrews, keeping Palestinian purity rules, including the rule about 'Destruction', the latrine.

abomination (*bdelygma*) The intention of nationalist Herodians to become god-emperors in Rome (Rev 17:4, 5, 21:27).

about (*kyklothen*) The positions over the two pillars supporting the middle tier in the cathedral, where the levites Phanuel and Raphael sat, one on either side, after saying the noon prayer. At these points they were at the perimeter of a larger 6 cubit circle around the central noon circle, so a form of the word 'around' (*kyklō*) is used. (Rev 4:3, 4, 8).

about to (*mellō*) This verb is used when an action occurs in preparation for one that will occur three hours or three months later. An hour was equated with a month, as there were twelve of both (John 11:9). The preparation for the evening meal began at 3 p.m., and this gave the concept of a minor start before a major event. In Rev 1:19, three hours before; in Rev 2:10, 3:10, 16, 8:13, three months before. In Rev 8:13 the word shows that the Restoration was declared by Agrippa I both for September AD 29 and for the following December–January, the Julian beginning.

abyss (*abyssos*) The great vault at the north-west corner of the Qumran vestry, where property was stored, including the common monastic property. It consequently stood for the monastic system (Rev 17:8, 20:1, 3). In the first phase before the earthquake, the property was probably stored in the northern chamber off the long courtyard that was used as the substitute sanctuary. A large deposit of money was found there by the archaeologists (see de Vaux, *The Archaeology of Qumran*, p. 34). It was right beside the abyss below the plateau containing the Qumran buildings, so it would be said that once the money was handed over, it had 'disappeared into the abyss', as it was not given back.

In the second phase when the vault was built into the vestry, a flight of steps ran beside the vault, leading up to the platform. The Priest-Pope climbed up them before appearing on the platform, and so was said to 'go up out of the abyss' (Rev 11:7, 17:8).

At the fall of Jerusalem in September AD 70, the chief Jewish monastery, the 'abyss' was relocated in Rome, where it appeared outwardly to be devoted to religion only, but was actually a zealot centre (Rev 17:8). By AD 100 the zealot monks were driven out of Rome and relocated in Ephesus (Rev 20:1).

accuser (*katēgōr*) The Roman emperor in his capacity of one who rejected a Herod's claim to the succession (Rev 12:10).

adultery (*moicheia*) Wrongful marriage. Rev 2:22, the marriage of Polemo of Cilicia to Bernice while he remained pagan.

aeon (*aiōn*) The Herod ruling as the true king-priest at the Restoration, in the period of 490 years following 3920 in its different versions (see pp.220–224). Agrippa I was called the Aeon, as he had begun his rise at the end of the Last Jubilee, AD 29 (Mark 10: 30, 11:14). His son Agrippa II was called the Aeon of the Aeon, in the plural of reproduction, as the second Herod of the period. He was given the title at the age of sixteen (Rev 10:6) and continued to use it throughout his life. After the Herods ceased, the Sadducee priest took over the title from Agrippa II (Rev 22:5).

afar (*makrothen*) 'From afar' was a name for the round

bases outside the vestry (see p.196), which at first formed the limit ('from') for visiting villagers, those who came from 'afar'. They were classed here with those excluded from the monastery, and thus equal to grades 8, 9, 10, 11, 12, which linked them with the Rome province. The term is used for the Rome province in Rev 18:10, 15, 17.

after (*meta*) With the accusative, the next time unit after. 'After the three days' (Rev 11:11), the day after day 3, Tuesday, so Wednesday.

again (*palin*) An indication of the hour, used frequently in the gospels. In Rev 10:8, 11, the noon sacred meal.

air (*aēr*) A name for the Annas priest, especially Jonathan Annas, who held that as an incarnation of the deity he was 'midway between earth and heaven', so 'in the air'. In Rev 9:2 it refers to Jonathan Annas when he succeeded the Baptist as Pope to the ascetics. 1Thess 4:17, 'to meet the Lord in the air', plays on this to say that Jesus will take the place of the Annas priest. In Rev 16:17, the Sadducee high priest Matthias, who was appointed at the outbreak of the war.

all, every (*pas*) This apparently general word always means a member of the Herod family, as Herod, the head of the mission, was the nominal head of every position in the hierarchy. When Herod is already the subject, *pas* added to an associated term means it is the Herod crown prince, for example, 'the Earth' means Herod and 'all the Earth' means the Herod crown prince in Rev 5:6.

all-mighty (*pantokratōr*) This word, apparently a title of God, is used in the pesher to refer to Sariel as king's priest to the Herods. 'All' means the Herods, and 'mighty' plays on 'seize' (*krateō*), meaning 'embrace', since the king's priest at the coronation embraced the Herod. The king's priest was third in the hierarchy of priests in 2 Sam 20:25–26. Matthew Annas was king's priest to Agrippa II (Rev 1:8).

254

altar of incense (*thysiastērion*) A person, Sariel as censer-bearer. The word originally referred to the altar in the Holy of Holies where the sacrifice for atonement was made (Exod 30:1–10, Luke 1:11). Then, since nomad Israelites had a portable censer ('the pillar of cloud by day and fire by night'), the priest visiting the Diaspora brought with him a censer representing the atoning power of the altar, placing it where he stood (Rev 8:3, 9:13).

amen (*amēn*) The word used by the congregation at the end of prayers, as stated in the Scrolls, 1QS 2:10, 18. Indicates the end of the service (Rev 5:14, 7:12, 19:4). If speaking continued after an 'Amen', it was after the religious service.

ancient (*archaios*) Used of the Chief Therapeut (Rev 12:9, 20:2) who kept the Julian calendar, for which December and June were the main feasts, and who treated Pentecost as the primary feast. Pentecost in June was the *archē*. See **beginning**.

and (*kai*) A word used simply as punctuation, to indicate a new sentence in the pesher. When it or one of the other sentence markers are not used, the sentence must continue, even if it appears to make little sense, as the continuation is important for the pesher. Conversely, a new sentence must begin at *kai*, even if it appears to break the sense.

angel (*angelos*) A levite or a celibate attached to a celibate community, responsible for prayers at appointed times (hence the Christian word 'angelus'). There were seven 'angels' for the seven days, see pp.177–178. The 'angel' belonged on the east side, the monastery, but was sent as a messenger to the west side, the village (Hebrew *mal'ak* has both meanings), so appeared in Ephesus, which represented the upper west division of the world.

Michael was responsible for Saturday both as a zero at the beginning of the week, and as day 7 at the end of the week. In the latter case he was called 'angel 7' ('seven angels'). The ruling Herod held this position (Rev 8:6 Archelaus, Rev 8:2, 15:1, 6, 7, 8, 16:1, 17:1 Agrippa II). After the death of the latter the Sadducee priest took his place (Rev 21:9). Michael (Herod) when 'in the body', was at grade 3, equal to Phanuel, and was then called 'angel 3' (Rev 8: 13). The Chief Therapeut, as an equal of Kohath, was called 'angel 4' (Rev 7:1, 9:14). When he was attached to a monastery he was 'the angel of the abyss' (Rev 9:11).

'Another angel' was a Sadducee acting as deputy to Herod, as the Priest-Pope. He was the Sadducee Ananus the Younger in Rev 7: 2, 14:6, 15, 17, 18, another Sadducee in Rev 18:1. But 'another strong angel' (Rev 10:1), means the Herod crown prince as deputy.

'Angel 12' of Rev 21:12 was the patriarch of Ephesus, in a new position, that of an uncircumcised Gentile of grade 12 who had risen to be archbishop. 'Angels' now presided over the twelve months as well as seven days.

After the death of Agrippa II, Jesus III was head of Christian celibate communities, and his 'angel' was his deputy, the Christian Pope (Rev 22:16). The corresponding patriarch of Ephesus was the 'angel' to the Sadducee in Rev 22:6.

another (*allos*) A deputy acting in the place of a superior.

anyone (*tis*). A title for King Herod as a celibate, in its meaning 'a certain one', as celibates were nameless and Herod was their head.

In Greek the same word acts as an interrogative pronoun, but it does not have this sense in the pesher; all apparent questions using it being statements. In Rev 13:17 'Not Anyone' (*mē tis*) means the Anti-Herod, Simon Magus. 'If Anyone' (*ei tis*) means the Herod when his right to rule is doubted: 'is he the *tis*?' (Rev 11:5, 13:9, 10, 14:9, 11, 20:15).

Apollyōn (*Apollyōn*) The name used by the Chief

Therapeut when in the party of Hellenists, with Simon Magus, so opposed to the ruling Herods (Rev 9:11). The word is a play on *a*, 'anti' and *polloi*, 'Many', one of the titles of Agrippa as head of the Many. In Mark 5: 9 the Chief Therapeut, at that time Theudas, said as Legion 'we are Many', meaning that he was supporting Agrippa. But he subsequently turned against him. His successor was called Apollos, the name drawn from the same title, used when he was anti-Herodian.

apostle (*apostolos*) Jewish monastics when sent to the south-west area of the grounds because of sin were 'sent out'. In John 9:7, the meaning given for the name of the exclusion cistern at Qumran, an alternate 'Siloam' was *apestalmenos*, from *apostellō*, 'to send from', giving *apostolos*. Gentile monastics were defined as equal to unclean Jewish monastics, and called 'apostles'.

'Apostles' were sent down to the pre-initiate grades. For both the Davids and the Herods, these grades looked to the crown prince as their superior, since the king associated only with initiates of 7 and above. The Herod crown prince was the superior of Herodian Gentile monastics, hence a would-be successor is called 'apostles' in Rev 2:2. The David crown prince was superior of non-Herodian Gentile monasteries such as those of John Mark, hence Barnabas, who had become crown prince to Jesus replacing James, is called 'the apostles' in Acts 14:14. John Mark himself could act as head, and could go down to the grades where he represented husband and wife as go-between. He was then called 'apostle 11' (Acts 1:26) and 'apostle 12' (Mark 3:14). 'The twelve apostles of the Lamb' (Rev 21: 14) means a successor in the position of 'apostle 12', who would act as go-between for the marriage of Jesus III. In Acts, the distinction between Herodian and non-Herodian heads of Gentile monastics is indicated by qualifying phrases.

archon (*archōn*) A title meaning 'ruler', used for the Chief Therapeut, when he acted as a lay equivalent of

Raphael the Scribe. See p.172. (Rev 1:5, John 3:1). Having moved up from bishop, he was in a position that became that of archbishop, and the word *archōn* took on this meaning.

ark (*kibōtos*) Originally the Ark of the Covenant, containing the tablets of the Law and the manna, standing in the Holy of Holies (Exod 25:10, Heb 9:4). Diaspora priests such as the Annas priests did not require Diaspora Jews to travel to Jerusalem to worship, but went to them, carrying a portable ark and censer. In AD 44 Matthew Annas established Ephesus as a place of worship outside Jerusalem. In the hermitage, where Jewish forms of worship were preserved, an ark was placed (Rev 11:19).This was the beginning of the process which enabled Agrippa to continue in Ephesus as king after Jerusalem was destroyed.

Armageddon (*Armagedōn*) See Chapter 11. The southwest area at Qumran, which was the place where the latrine for A–R priests stood, and where men were reduced to the level of 'Great Dan'.

army (*strateuma*) King Herod as head of the army. In the plural of reproduction, the Herod crown prince acting for him (Rev 9:16, 19:14, 19).

around (*kyklō*) 'Around the throne' (Rev 4:6, 5:11, 7:11) means the forward parts of the two pillars, on the balcony, where deputies to the central figure could stand.

as (*hōs*). This word is used for 'and' within a sentence, in the ordinary sense of 'and'. The word *kai*, 'and' is used to mark a new sentence. In the gospels, *hōs* is used with a time expression, for example in John 19:14, *hōra . . . hōs hektē*, 'an hour (five minutes to, the end of the prayer hour) and sixth (noon)'.

at now (*arti*) (Used to translate *arti*, 'now', to distinguish from *nyn*). Arti is used as a play on A-R-T, a priest of class A, grade R, who gives the sign T in place of Herod. In Rev 12:10 this was Ananus the

Elder, as in AD 15 there were no Herods. He alone was the religious ruler of the people. In Rev 14:13 Jonathan Annas is called 'from at now', meaning that he was at the other end of Ananus the Elder's tradition, holding that he was a leader independently of the Herods. This accords with his interfering behaviour noted in *Ant.* 20:200, and his alliance with Ananias the Samaritan in AD 50.

at once (*eutheōs*) The point at five minutes past the hour when the noon prayer finished, the congregation took their seats, and the doors were closed. The word is used frequently in the gospels in this sense, as a form of *euthys*, which means 'on the hour' (Rev 4:2).

authority (*exousia*) Initiation to grade 7 of members of the village class, that of married men and Gentiles, a play on *ousia*, 'being'. A person who has 'authority' has the power to initiate this class.

axe (*pelekizō*) To persecute, used of Romans persecuting Jews or Christians. In Luke 3:9, 'the axe (*axinē*) is laid to the root of the trees' means the opposite of what it appears; it means that the Roman axe is attacking the Jewish Plant-root, a name for the community in CD 1:7. The usage is based on Isa 10:5, where the Assyrians are the rod of God's anger against the Jews. In Rev 20:4, 'the souls of those axed' means that the Christian Pope ('souls') had been persecuted in Rome in AD 100, under the emperor Trajan.

Babylon (*Babylōn*) The emperor of Rome. 'Babylon' is used as a name for Rome in CD 1:6 and 1 Peter 5:13, since, as shown in the pesharim from the Dead Sea Scrolls, it was believed that Rome fulfilled what was said in the Old Testament about Babylon. 'Babylon the Great' means an emperor of Rome who had taken wine with King Herod as a sign of friendship with the Jews, and therefore was considered an initiate. Claudius in Rev 14:8, Vitellius in Rev 16:19, 17:5, 18:2. Titus, the son of Vespasian, is 'Babylon the Strong City' in Rev 18:10, and 'Babylon the Great City' in Rev 18:21.

Balaam (*Balaam*) The magician in the Old Testament, Num 22:5. A pseudonym used in Rev 2:14 for Atomus the Cypriot Magus (magician), who became marriage broker to the family of Agrippa, arranging the marriage of his sister Drusilla to the procurator Felix (*Ant.* 20:142). It appears that he was also involved earlier, at the time when Bernice prepared to marry Polemo of Cilicia, a Gentile who became Jewish and circumcised in order to marry her (*Ant.* 20: 145–146).

Balak (*Balak*) From the context of Rev 2:14, a pseudonym for Polemo of Cilicia (see **Balaam**). Balak was the Moabite king who hired Balaam the magician (Num 22:2).

bear (*arkos*) The tetrarch Antipas, as an alternative Herod to Agrippa, who was 'the Lion' (see **lion**). From Amos 5:19: 'As if a man fled from a lion, and a bear met him'.

beast (*thērion*) A man acting for the Lion, one who had zealot views on the purpose of military action. The zealot leader, from the order of Manasseh. Judas the Galilean in AD 6; Judas Iscariot from AD 26 (Rev 13:1); Simon Magus from AD 36 (Rev 13:11); the Herodian Atomus the Magus from AD 44 (Rev 14:9, 16:13, 17:3); his successor in AD 61 (Rev 15:2, 16:10, 19:19) and another successor in AD 100 (Rev 20:4). In the plural of reproduction, Apollos the successor of Theudas (Rev 6:8), who had taken the place of Judas after his death (Rev 13:5–6).

The 'Beast' was the third in the Pharisee-zealot hierarchy of 'the Dragon', (Priest), 'the Calf' (Prophet) and 'the Beast' (King).

A 'scarlet Beast' (Rev 17:3) claimed the status of a Phanuel, wearing scarlet in the outside world.

because (*hoti*) 'Because' is used to translate *hoti*, even when the natural meaning is 'that' or 'for'. The word is used as a play on *hoti*, 'the T', and refers to Herod and leaders of the western Herodian mission who used the T sign in initiation. (see p.184).

become (*eimi*) 'Become' is used to translate the verb 'to be', which follows Hebrew usage in the pesher, meaning 'to come into existence' rather than simply 'be'. For the meaning 'be', no verb is used in the Greek.

After the schism of AD 44 Ephesus was treated as the centre of the mission, Antioch-Jerusalem the east and Rome the west, (whereas formerly the three parts were Babylon, Antioch-Jerusalem and Ephesus-Rome). The verb 'to be' (become) meant to be a member in each of these places, using the tenses as signs of the east, centre and west. In the present tense, to be a member in the Ephesus cathedral; in the past tense, to be a member in Rome. 'The Becoming One' (Rev 11:17, 1:4, 8) means the Sadducee priest in Ephesus. Consequently, 'to become (be)' used alone means in Revelation Part B 'to happen in Ephesus' (Rev 1:19, 2:2).

bed (*klinē*) The bed of a priest or celibate (Luke 5:18, Mark 7:30), whereas the bed of a married person was *koitē* (Luke 11:7). In Rev 2:22, 'to be thrown on a bed', *klinē*, means 'to be made to become celibate'.

before (*emprosthen*) East. In Hebrew the word for 'before' (*qedem*) also means 'east', and the word for 'behind' (*achrōn*) also means 'west'. The corresponding Greek words have the same precise sense in the pesher. Where *emprosthen* appears (Rev 4:6, 19:10, 22:8), it means a position on the east side of the vestry. Note that in Rev 5:1, the Sinaiticus text reads *emprosthen* where other texts read *esōthen*, 'within'.

beginning (*archē*) The religious New Year, beginning the year. With article, the Pentecost season, observed as the New Year in Ephesus. For those using the Julian calendar, December and June were the two main feasts of the year, corresponding to September and March for those keeping the equinoxes. The Therapeuts, who based their organisation on the pentecontads, held that June was the primary religious feast, corresponding to March. The statement 'I am the *archē*' was given in June (Rev 21:6, 22:13), and means that the speaker acted as a priest at the New Year. Without article, it means March, three months or grades below June, according to the rule for articles (Mark 1:1, John 1:1). In Rev 21:6, 'the Omega, the Beginning' means that the speaker, Jesus III, was a Michael (Omega), but at Pentecost, not in September, when the Jewish Zadokite Michael had performed the Atonement. Agrippa had used the same definition for his role as Michael.

behind (*opisō*) West, see 'before'. The place called *opisō*, 'west' was in the corresponding positions to *emprosthen*, 'east'. It was here that the jubilee trumpet was sounded (Rev 1:10). The form *opisthen* is also found (translated 'at behind') (Rev 4:6, 5:1).

The evening prayer was said on the west side, just as the morning prayer was said on the east. Consequently the east side stood for day and the west for night, so, in order to express the positions of the calendar, a minister of the Therapeuts (who kept both positions, see p.244) stood first on the east side and then on the west when the calendar was in the Day position, and the reverse in the Night position. In Rev 13:3, 'the whole Earth marvelled behind the Beast', means that the person called 'Earth' changed ('marvelled') to the west ('behind'), that is that the calendar changed to the Night position. This was the case in AD 29, and the phrase indicates the date.

In Rev 12:15, 'the Dragon threw water behind the Woman', means that the baptismal ceremony began in the west. At Mird, where the episode took place, the beginning of the aqueduct was on the west.

behold (*idou*) Used for the place where prayers were offered at the high points of the sun.

belly (*koilia*) Gentile deacons, who as deacons were equal to the 'loins' of the 'body', but as being equal to

262

females were called the 'womb' ('belly', but 'womb' in Acts 3:2, 14:8). In Rev 10:9, 10, the word means the party of John Mark, who had produced John's gospel, the 'little book', and whose 'belly' was 'made bitter' through involvement in the poison plot against Agrippa I.

belt (*zōnē*) A belt, worn as a sign that the wearer was not in the sanctuary, since the rule of Ezek 44:18 forbade Zadokite priests in the sanctuary to wear a belt, to 'gird themselves with anything causing sweat'. John the Baptist as a hermit outside the sanctuary wore a leather belt for this reason (Mark 1:6), so also did the missionaries sent out by Jesus in Mark 6:8. In Rev 1:13, Jesus wore a golden belt, apparently a contradiction in terms, since gold meant a priest. But he wore it when as a layman he was acting as priest to Gentiles. In Rev 15:6 Agrippa did the same when entertaining the Gentile governor.

benefit (*eulogia*, 'blessing') This word is used for one of the four classes of property of the original mission: a) common property of monastics and dynasts ('glory'); b) shared property of village Essenes, as described by Philo in Every Honest Man 86 ('benefit'); c) membership fees ('honour/price'); and d) welfare tithes, as set out in CD 14:12–21. The four terms are found together in Rev 5: 13. 'Benefit' came to include Gentile property, as Gentiles were classed with village Essenes. In 2 Cor 9:5 Paul spoke of the *eulogia* he expected to receive from Achaia, a Gentile province. In the lists of seven kinds of payments of money in Rev 5:12 and 7:12, 'benefit' comes last in the former and first in the latter, because the latter describes the financial system of the new party of Romans, for Gentiles.

bird (*orneon*) A name for Gaius Costobar Herod, who claimed to be another Kohath, one of whose titles was 'the Dove'. See **peace**. (Rev 18:2, 19:17.)

bitter, make (*pikrainō*) To become involved in a poison plot against a Herod. Used of the anti-Agrippa I party in Rev 8:11. Used of the Magian plot against Agrippa I, with which John Mark was associated, in Rev 10:9, 10.

black (*melas*) The colour associated with winter and the December solstice. When 'the Sun became black' in Rev 6:12 Agrippa, 'the Sun', who had previously looked to September as the season for fulfilment of the Last Jubilee, being that of the main Jewish feasts, changed the expectation to December and the New Year of the Julian calendar.

blasphemy (*blasphēmia*) The doctrine of the Damascus party, who were zealots (Rev 2:9, 13:1, 17:3). 'Blasphemy against the Holy Spirit' (Mark 3:28) means zealotry as opposed to the policy of peace with Rome taught by Jonathan Annas, the 'Holy Spirit' (*to pneuma to hagion*).

blessed (*makarios*) A 'Blessed One' was a celibate like the Therapeuts, living in an eremitical community (individual celibates), but not in a coenobitic community (a monastery with common property). A lay celibate attached to a monastery was called a 'Holy One' (saint). The distinction between lesser Blessed Ones and higher Saints was preserved in the Christian Church. Both kinds of lay celibates formed a congregation, but the Holy Ones had their services and sacred meal in the daytime, while the Blessed Ones had services at night, as is shown of the Therapeuts. They held midnight vigils (Luke 12:36–38, Rev 16:15). Peter, on entering the celibate life, became a Blessed One (Matt 16:17). When the position of Christian patriarch of Ephesus was developed, he also was a Blessed One (Rev 20:6).

blood (*haima*) This word, used frequently in Revelation, meant a cup of fermented wine with a smear of blood, which was sipped at the communion meal only, not drunk freely. It came to be associated with the Christian communion wine by the following steps: a) Whereas monastic Essenes received new wine at their initiation

(1QS 6:4–6, 1QSa 2:17–20), married Essenes drank fermented wine, as a sign that they were not under a strict ascetic discipline.

b) When they undertook a Nazirite vow, going up to grade 8, they abstained from all wine according to the Nazirite rule (Num 6:1–4). Then, when Nazirites came back to the married state, they drank fermented wine, but sipped it in small quantities only to show restraint. Essene pilgrims, who were not Nazirites but abstinent from marriage, always drank wine, but using the same restraint.

c) The leader of village Essene pilgrims was the David, using the title 'the Lamb' in his role of Suffering Servant, one whose ascetic discipline in the celibate community atoned for the sins of those in the world (1QS 8:14, from the Suffering Servant image of Isa 53). Essenes had renounced literal animal sacrifices and substituted ascetic works.

d) As a sign that he was the one who atoned, the David put a smear of his own blood on the chief cup used by village pilgrims, in a ritual performed at Passover, reflecting the rite of the Passover Lamb, the blood of which was smeared over the doors (Exod 12:6–7).

e) Sipping the cup of fermented wine was then understood as accepting the atoning sacrifice by 'drinking the blood' (John 6:5456). The cup was 'the blood of the Lamb' (Rev 7:14, 12:11).

f) The usage derived from this was that 'the blood', with article, meant the cup of wine, and 'blood', without article, meant the bloodstain. In John 19:34 'a blood' means the literal blood of Jesus.

At the time of the zealot uprising, pilgrims visiting Qumran under Joseph the father of Jesus used the 'blood', and for them it stood for their willingness for martyrdom for the zealot cause (Rev 8:7). Under Jesus, it stood for willingness for a different kind of martyrdom, for the sake of his doctrine.

Other priests and celibates could act as Suffering Servants. When Michael was 'in the body' he wore scarlet, establishing the role of cardinal (see **scarlet**), and he also could put the bloodstain on the cup (Luke 11:51, 'a blood of Zechariah', the Zadokite, father of John the Baptist). Helena claimed to be a cardinal, so she also could give 'a blood' (Mark 5:25, Rev 17:6). As the Moon, her successor as head of Asher was 'turned to a blood' when she left a Nazirite vow, which women also could practice, and returned to grade 11 with the sipping of wine (Acts 2:20, Rev 6:12, 16:4).

body (*sōma*) The symbol of a western priest equal to Sariel, who as superior of the village class was over the 'body' of the membership. He was the 'Eagle' of the four Living Creatures, and the saying in Luke 17:37 'Where the body is, there also the eagles gather together' indicates the association. In Rev 18:13, Agrippa when 'in the body', or his deputy sitting on the west side of the high table, with Agrippa as priest ('souls') on the east side.

book (*biblion*) The Septuagint, the Greek translation of the Old Testament, in the form of a bound book. The codex, or bound book, was already in use in the 1st century AD (*Cambridge History of the Bible*, p.56). It was an innovation, used by the Hellenised Herodians for the less sacred version of the Old Testament. In Judea, it was wrapped in cloth and unfolded before reading (Luke 4:17, 20), and this practice is reflected in Rev 7:14. Its less important part was called *biblion* without article (Luke 4:17, the Prophets section). In AD 49 the six completed books of the New Testament were added to it and sealed, being classed as additional, non-scriptural reading. When Agrippa opened the Septuagint he also gave permission for the sealed books to be read later, so 'loosened the seals' (Rev 5:2). The New Testament was counted as part of the *biblion* in Rev 1:11.

The Herodian copy of the Septuagint contained a list of names of celibate members, entered at the time of initiation. This part of the book was called 'the Book of Life' (Rev 17:8, 20:12). The record was kept in the back part of the book, and this meant that it was read by the David, for it was his duty to read the Prophets in the lower part of the Septuagint. Hence the list was called 'the Book of Life of the Lamb' (Rev 13:8, Rev 21:27).

The New Testament was at first defined as part of the additional material to the Septuagint, of the same grade as its Writings. The New Testament was later seen as a 'reproduction' of the book, and so was called 'books' (Rev 20:12). But after the death of Agrippa it was called 'this book', as a lay substitute for the Septuagint (Rev 22:7, 10, 18). It was believed to contain a prophecy concerning the time, in the Book of Revelation itself, and in similar sections. This was 'the prophecy of this book'. But 'the book of this prophecy' in Rev 22:19, means the Septuagint, believed to contain a prophecy concerning the times in such books as Daniel.

book, little (*biblaridion*) A bound book containing John's gospel, which at first circulated independently, given the status of scripture. A copy was presented to Agrippa II at his sixteenth birthday in September AD 43 (Rev 10:2, 8, 9, 10), and it was on this occasion that it was re-assigned to the order of James Niceta, followed by John Aquila (see pp.526–527). As the party of John Mark who had produced it were involved in the poison plot against Agrippa I, it 'made the belly bitter', but when it was revised by the addition of the final chapter, it became 'sweet'.

booklet (*biblos*, fem.) With 'of life', a list of fee paying Herodian village members, not kept in the copy of the Septuagint, *biblion*, as they were not celibates (Rev 20:15). In Rev 3:5 the double negative means that Peter's name will be removed from the *biblos*, both because he was moving up into celibate status, and because he was becoming Christian rather than Herodian. In Rev 20:15, the list of Herodian members in which a Herod claimant was not included, implying that his claim was rejected.

bowl (*phialē*) A container used to receive money which was kept for a year then spent the following year. See p.216. Set out at a feast, after the main service, Rev 5:8.

breadth (*platos*) See **length**. The 'breadth' of the vestry was the 2 cubits at its north, considered to run east-west rather than north-south, being a place for excluded people (Rev 21:16). See **court**. In the Jewish system the 'poor and crippled' could be found here, and for this reason Agrippa was excluded to it because of his age (Rev 20:9). In the plan of the church described in Rev 21:16, 'the breadth' appears twice, and the meaning is that the northern 2 cubits had become a crypt under the 2 cubits from the dais edge down to the chancel screen, used for the same purpose, but the 'poor and crippled' were now 'hidden', nearer to but not visible from the congregation.

breastplate (*thōrax*) The congregation, which was said to correspond to the jewels on the high priest's breastplate (Rev 21:19–20, see p.167). In Rev 9:17 the congregation, whose pews were marked by the names of jewels, was the 'breastplate' of the high priest Matthew Annas. In Rev 9:9, the 'breastplate of iron' belonged to the Chief Therapeut, as his congregation were ascetics under a strict discipline.

bride (*nymphē*) The wife of the heir of David as a Virgin at her betrothal or before the marriage had been consummated (Rev 18:23, 21:2, 9, 22:17). The wife of the David was the chief missionary to Gentiles of the order of Dan (see Chapter 4). As the David moved into the position of a priest, his wife became the chief woman of the mission, replacing the Herod queen. The celebration of the bride of Jesus III in Ephesus followed the death of Bernice (Rev 21:12). Uncircumcised Gentiles formed the Church, so the Church was symbolised by the Bride, the Virgin.

bridle (*chalinos*) A name for the subordinate of the Jewish priest who was 'the Horses'. A celibate held the bridle of his actual horse when he came visiting (Rev 14:20).

bright (*lampros*) Belonging to a royal person (Rev 15:6, 18:14, 19:8, 22:1, 16).

brimstone (*theion*) See **remainder**. Circumcised celibate Gentiles who were to become proselytes acted as 'eunuchs' to King Herod. As celibates in Herodian orders, they could take a further step and practise sodomy, in which case they were called 'Brimstone', from the brimstone (sulphur) that rained down on biblical Sodom (Gen 19:24). Nicolaus- Blastus, the chief proselyte and 'eunuch' to Agrippa I, was also a sodomite, and the word refers to him and his successors in Herodian orders. Monastics who were condemned for this practice were sent to their exclusion place in the south-west quarter of the monastery grounds, which then became 'Sodom' (Rev 11:8) and 'brimstone', so Qumran at the Dead Sea (the 'lake') was called 'the lake of fire and brimstone' (Rev 9:17, 18, 14:10, 19:20, 20:10, 21:8).

Since proselytes in Herodian orders were commonly called 'Brimstone', the plural of the adjective from this word was used for the proselyte Izates (Rev 9:17).

broadsword (*romphaia*) This word was used for the sword held by the cherubim to exclude Adam and Eve from the Garden of Eden (Gen 3:24, LXX). It came to be used in connection with the 'Eden' schools in Essene monasteries, a rod which was held by the priest as a barrier allowing admission, or to exclude. See **wood**. It was used also in Gentile monasteries, wielded by the David their priest (Rev 1:16, 19:15). But whereas the 'broadsword' could be used to excommunicate from Jewish monasteries ('kill with the broadsword', Rev 6:8), that used by the Davids did not excommunicate, since at first Gentiles were not given the full form of membership called 'life', so they could not be 'put to death' (as stated in *GPhil* 52:15-20). Rather, it was 'two-mouthed', used to direct them either into the monastery or into an outside form of teaching ('mouth') if they were not suitable.

broadway (*plateia*) The southern one of the two round bases outside the vestry (Rev 11:8; 22:2). See pp.196–197.

The same word is used of the 'broad gate' of Matt 7:13. At Ain Feshkha, two adjoining doors in the eastern wall, the northern one unusually narrow and the southern one unusually broad, corresponded to the area outside the vestry: the southern one, leading down to the married quarters at Mazin, standing for women, marriage, and the unclean; the northern one, leading up to Qumran, being the 'narrow gate' leading to the celibate life.

In Rev 21:21, the teaching of Wisdom that had been given on the 'broadway' was brought into the chancel, making the chancel step the 'broadway of the city'. But in Rev 22:2 'the broadway of it' (the Herodian mission) was the one outside the vestry.

brother (*adelphos*) In the Jewish orders, a married man at grade 11, in the sexually active state. It was the same grade as that of 'Sister', and 'Brother' and 'Sister' were equal. John Aquila was the Brother, the chief married man, of Rev 1:9. He was head of province 11, Achaia, after his return from Rome, living in Corinth (Acts 18:1–2).

The word in the plural may mean a real brother, if he is at grade 11. In Rev 6:11 'the brothers of them (Gaius Costobar Herod)' means Erastus Saul Herod, his brother.

'The brothers of us' (Rev 12:10) means the third Herod, who was over Herodian married members. This was the tetrarch Antipas at the time of Rev 12, the brother of Archelaus. 'Brothers' means the Christian Pope in 19:10 (Clement, the brother of a previous seer), 22:9.

270

burn (*kaiō*) Used of the light that was turned up to indicate the hour in the Jewish system (Rev 4:5).

but (*de*) 'But' is used to translate the particle *de*, even though it does not always have this meaning. It is used in the pesher as a play on the letter D, that of class D villagers. See **neither**.

buy (*agorazō*) To buy ministry by payment of money, either by buying it for oneself through the practice of simony (Acts 8:18–19, Rev 13:17), or to 'buy' another minister by paying him a salary (Rev 3:18, 5:9, 14:3). The latter practice was opposed by those who believed that ministers should earn their own living by working at a craft, as Paul did (see 1 Cor 9:37).

calf (*moschos*) This term originally meant Raphael, the Calf of the north in Ezekiel's four living creatures. He belonged to the levitical class B, as did Sariel when he was in the role of 'Levi'. But King Herod combined the positions of Michael, Gabriel (class A) and a levitical king who was an equal of Sariel in class B. He did not claim to be Sariel, who was an actual high priest, but claimed to be equal with him. He took the position of Raphael the Calf up to the grade of Sariel, and acted as levitical king in this position, which was his third. As he was a Resh as Calf, his servant was a Pe 2 lay presbyter, so a 'second living creature' (Rev 4:7).

Archelaus Herod, being an ethnarch only, was said to be equal to Herod in his third position, so was the 'fatted Calf' (Luke 15:23) and the 'Golden Calf' (Acts 7:41).

camp (*parembolē*) The name for a village community of Essenes, called 'camps' in the Scrolls (CD 13:4, 13, 4QMMT B 60). They were the ones who were outside the monastery, and their 'camp' was their central point, from which measurements were taken to the unclean places one hour away (1QM 7:67). It therefore stood for a measuring point, and at Qumran was represented by the 1 cubit round base outside the vestry (see p.196). The deacon Merari belonged here, but a deacon could also teach in the northern section of the vestry, and this was the 'camp' of Rev 20:9.

carry (*bastazō*) To be a Phanuel, head of the lower division of priests, one of whose duties was to help carry the palanquin of the visiting priest (Rev 2:2, 3, 17:7).

cease, ceasing (*anapauō, anapausis*) Essene monastics stopped work and had an immersion bath at 11 a.m., as Josephus shows, then had a sacred meal. 'Cease' is used for this hour in Luke 11:1. It appears that the end of the meal at 2 p.m. was also called a 'ceasing'. The noon session was a service for Herodians, not a meal. If the service continued after 2 p.m., they 'did not have a ceasing'. The phrase in Rev 4:8 indicates the time, 2 p.m.

chain (*halysis*) The emblem of a Herod, since Gaius Caligula had given a golden chain to Agrippa I (Ant. 19:294) (Mark 5:3, Acts 12: 6, 21:33, 28:20, Rev 20:1).

chariot (*harma*) The palanquin of a visiting priest when he came to Herodian communities. He stayed in it to give teaching (Acts 8: 29, the similar 'chariot' used by a Gentile teacher). It was associated with the imagery of Ezekiel's chariot vision (Rev 9:9).

chasten (*paideuō*) To make a *pais*, literally 'child', but in the organisation meaning a novice at grade 8 (Rev 3:19). Luke 2:43, Jesus the 'child' (*pais*), Jesus as a pre-initiate novice at the age of twenty-two, about to turn twenty-three.

child (*teknon*) A person who has not yet become a 'man', an initiate. A twelve-year-old boy (Rev 12:4, 5), or a Gentile proselyte able to go only to baptism (Rev 2:23, plural of reproduction, Izates the proselyte, son of Queen Helena of Adiabene, p.85).

church (*ekklēsia*, 'called out') Originally, a community of Gentile married men of the Herodian order of Asher, such as John Aquila, who imitated Essene villagers like Peter by going on pilgrimages to the monastery. There

272

they said prayers and received instruction in the same way as village Essenes.

Although Gentile pilgrims were originally at grade 10, they subsequently went up 'out of the body' to grade 7, saying prayers every day of the week. They then were organised as seven churches in a province. The province of Asia, number 7, was their meeting place. Since King Herod was head of their order of Asher, he was head of their churches also, being called 'Church 7' (Rev 1:4, 20) and 'the Churches' (Rev 2:7 and in all the seven letters). Jesus III received his title in Rev 22:16.

The word *ekklēsia* is used in the Septuagint to translate Hebrew *qahal*, a term used for Israel in the wilderness.

city (*polis*) A Gentile monastery, which was their version of the Essene 'New Jerusalem'. Those Gentiles who became permanent monastics like the highest level of Essenes were called 'the city', but were still treated as only of the village level, so their leader, equal to a village levite, stood on the dais edge of the vestry. This was the meaning of the 'city' in Mark 14:13, and in Rev 21:15.

Those who chose to be dynasts were said to belong to a 'holy city', as 'holy' meant a lay celibate, not levitical. Their superior was the David, 'the Holy One', who in this role was called 'the Holy City'. He stood on the chancel step, being a little lower than the 'city'. In Matt 27:53 'the Holy City' means James, who had become the David at the time of the crucifixion. In Rev 11:2 it means Jesus himself, who was present at Qumran in March AD 44, as shown also in Acts 12:7, where he appeared as the 'Light' to Peter. At this same season he played his part in a re-enactment of the crucifixion at Qumran, on its exact anniversary (see the pesher of Rev 11:8). In Rev 21:2, 10, 22:19 'the Holy City' is Jesus III.

The name 'the Great City' was used for a Herodian school for Gentiles, making them Jewish rather than Christian. It was at first in the south-west area at

273

Qumran (that of 'Great Dan') (Rev 11:8), then in AD 69 transferred to Rome (Rev 16:19, 17:18, 18:10, 16, 19). In Rome, it was under Bernice as the Mother Sarah of Gentiles, giving rise to the double sense of Rev 18:10, 16, 19.

clothe (*periballō*, lit. 'throw around') To place on a person a vestment, consisting of a strip of cloth with a hole for the head, modelled on the priest's vestment of Exod 28:31–32.

cloud (*nephelē*) A name for Phanuel, who led the 3 a.m. prayers of pilgrims, so was their 'pillar of Cloud by day', just as the priest who led 9 p.m. prayers was the 'pillar of fire by night' in the Exodus imagery. Phanuel's seat was over the eastern pillar on the middle tier (Rev 4:4, 14:14). Jesus as equal to a Phanuel also sat there (Rev 14:14).

Phanuel went to the west pillar when the calendar was in the Night position, becoming 'a Cloud rising in the west' (Luke 12:54), and in this case he was 'upon of the Cloud' (Rev 14:15). The phrase indicates the Night position of the calendar in AD 58.

Agrippa II, on the occasion of his sixteenth birthday, was 'wrapped (clothed) in a Cloud' (Rev 10:1), that is, vested by Theophilus Annas, the Phanuel.

come (*erchomai*) The 'Coming One' was a levite to the superior priest, standing on the east side. The title was used by John the Baptist of the David as lay Messiah, his subordinate (Luke 7:19). In Rev 1:4 it is used of Matthew Annas in the east, where he was a levite only, having been deposed as high priest. In the plural of reproduction (Rev 7:14), Peter as a celibate.

come about (*ginomai*) To take place or be appointed at one of the expected times of prophecy. Here translated 'come about' rather than 'become', which is used for 'to be'. It indicates a decisive event at the significant time (Rev 16:17, 21:6). In Rev 1:10, it means that John Aquila had been appointed at Patmos, not that he was there. He was at this time in Ephesus.

confess (*homologeō*) To support a man as high priest, in the party tensions of the period, between Sadducees, Pharisees, etc. Heb 3:1, 'the high priest of our confession (*homologia*) Jesus', means that Jesus was given the same status by Christians. It then meant 'to declare that a man is a Christian priest' (Rev 3:5).

copper (*chalkos*) While priests, levites and celibates of classes A, B and C were likened to gold, silver and precious stones respectively, the Therapeuts were likened to copper, for as hermits they were given small amounts of money in copper coins. One of the names of the Chief Therapeut was 'Alexander the coppersmith' (2 Tim 4:14). On returning to village life and holding private property, the Therapeuts put their copper coins into the treasury of the ascetics (Mark 12:41). 'Copper things' in Rev 9:20 means Agrippa as a deputy for Rome in the west, represented by the Chief Therapeut Apollos, who in AD 43 was rising to take the place of the anti-Roman Theudas. Apollos was the 'Alexander the coppersmith' who 'did great harm' to Paul. In Rev 18:12 the word indicates grade 8, the level of village pre-initiates.

copper-frankincense (*chalkolibanon*) A word not found elsewhere, and supposed to mean 'burnished bronze' (Rev 1:15, 2:18). But it has been invented, as a combination of 'copper' (*chalkos*) and 'frankincense' (*libanos*), because it means the common property of Gentile monastics held by the David, called 'copper' as they were equal to the village class of Therapeuts (see **copper**) and also to village ascetics who followed the rule of whitening their garments with frankincense before attending the synagogue (CD 11:4). These Gentiles had begun as visitors to the synagogue, and had progressed under the Christians to be the same as Jewish monastics.

corner (*gōnia*) The 12×12 cubit square of the north vestry, from the wall of the vault down to the dais edge, was the 'tetragon' (Rev 21:16) (see p.160). 'Corner 4' was its north-eastern corner, where a bishop equal to Kohath (a 4, as a 'Wednesday') stood to receive higher pilgrims to say prayers at 4 a.m. As the place for the 'poor and crippled', it was the place to which an aged man was sent (Rev 20:8) and the place for the Chief Therapeut as head of the 'Poor' (Rev 7:1). As equal to a Kohath he was called 'angel 4'.

corpse (*ptōma*) A defiled high priest or king. Mark 6:29, John the Baptist. Mark 15:45, Simon Magus (not Jesus). Rev 11:8, Matthew Annas, just deposed by Simon Magus. Rev 11:9, Agrippa I.

court (*aulē*) This word applies to the 2 cubits north of the vestry where special installations were placed (see p.540, Note 12) (Rev 11:2). From the pesher it is seen that it was used as a place of instruction for privileged outsiders to the monastery. Peter was one of these, and he said his prayers here, near the fire in this area, during the trial of Jesus. It was called 'the court of the chief priest' (Matt 26:58) because it was part of the pathway and north vestry defined as the porch or court of the substitute sanctuary. Outsiders such as pilgrims were normally confined to the south-east and south-west quarters of the monastery grounds, outside the Israelite wall, but their leaders were permitted to come closer to the holy places.

covenant (*diathēkē*) The New Covenant that had been formed in the time of Herod the Great, as a Hellenised form of Judaism designed to attract Jews of the Diaspora (Rev 11:19). Its Greek word for 'new' was *neos* (Mark 2:22). When it was revised to become the Christian New Covenant, the word *kainos* was used.

crowd (*ochlos*) A Herodian at the pre-initiate grade, that of ordinary men. Agrippa preceding his initiation (Rev 7:9), reduced in grade (Rev 19:1). Erastus Saul Herod was the 'crowds' of Rev 17:15. The tetrarch Antipas in Mark 15:11.

crown (*stephanos*) A circlet with the graduation letter Qof, worn by a Sariel or Phanuel when teaching in Sadducee schools. The Gentiles in these schools were given higher privileges than those attached to the schools of the circumcision party (see **horn**). They were brought to graduation, signified by Qof ('the eye of the needle', see p.184). Their schools, under a royal person, were a 'kingdom', and to graduate in them was to 'receive a crown'. For Jews in ascetic schools, however, the letter Qof meant a 'crown of thorns', the letter being seen as a thorn, the emblem of a severe ascetic rule.

A woman teaching Gentiles could wear the circlet, but, since the Qof was the 'name' of a graduate, she wore the Qof of her husband. In Rev 12:1 Mary wore 'a crown of Star 12', Joseph.

cry (*krazō*) To preach.

cup (*potērion*) The cup used by Herod when entertaining the emperor or a procurator in Rome, treated as the symbol of Roman friendship with the Jews (Rev 16:19). It was the 'cup of the wine of the Wrath of the Fury' (Rev 16:19), because it was accepted by the representative of Rome, the Wrath, when he dined with Herod as the Fury, the agent of Rome. Such a cup was used by Bernice when she claimed to be queen regnant in place of Agrippa (Rev 17:4). At communion meals reproducing the Herodian banquet, held by those friendly to Rome, a *potērion* was used (Luke 22:17, 20). It became the Christian communion cup, and some of its sacredness was due to this previous history.

curse (*katathema*) A person who had been accursed according to the ritual of 1QS 2:5–6, excluded from the congregation (Rev 22:3).

dark (**make**) (*skotizō*) To confine to the hour of darkness, midnight. Gentiles were at first secretly taught at this time (Rev 8:12).

darken (*skotoō*). To come under the power of the 'Sons

of Darkness', the Roman armies (Rev 9:2, 16:10).

day (*hēmera*) A festival day by the solar calendar.

a) Singular, nominative. A person, Phanuel as the priest to uncircumcised Gentiles keeping the solar calendar, in the role of 'pillar of Cloud by day' (Rev 8:12, 9:15).

b) In the expression 'of day and of night' or 'of night and of day'. This is an important indication of the date, see p.245. The double dates of the Therapeuts were illustrated in action, the minister standing over the east pillar for the Day position, and over the west pillar for the Night position. If he took the east side first ('of day and of night'), it was the quartodecimal period when the calendar was in the Day position; if the west side ('of night and of day'), it was in the Night position.

c) Plural. The 31st at the quarters of the solar calendar, the day used for councils. 'In those days' means the 31st at the equinox, with the word order determining which one: 'those' after the noun means March, before the noun means September. 'In these days' means the 31st at the solstices: 'these' after the noun meaning June, before the noun meaning December. This way of indicating a season is used extensively in Luke-Acts. Only in Rev 9:6.

d) With numbers. 'One day' 'day 1', Sunday (Rev 18:8). 'Two days' 'day 2', Monday; day 3, Tuesday, etc. The word order shows the start of day. *Hēmerai treis*, 'day 3', with noun first means the earlier start of Tuesday at 6 p.m. the previous evening. *Treis hēmerai*, number first, the true start at 6 a.m. Tuesday. (Rev 11:9, 11.) This usage is frequently illustrated in the gospels. *Hēmerai deka*, 'day 10' (Rev 2:10), means the Tuesday of a second week, the day for grade 10, as the set of seven days was extended to a fortnight. 'Day 8', 'day 10', 'day 12' and 'day 14' appear in the gospels and Acts (John 20:26, Acts 24:11, Acts 25:6, 27:33).

death (*thanatos*) A person, the Chief Monk of the monastic system, who had power to excommunicate.

See **die**. Simon Magus as head of Diaspora monasteries in Rev 9:6, 13:12. At the schism between Damascus and western monasteries, each had their own 'Death'. Atomus the Magus of Cyprus was the Chief Monk to Herodian monasteries, and was the 'rider on the green horse', whose name was Death, of Rev 6:8. See Chapter 8. The Herodian Magus was the 'First Death' (although the term is not found) and the anti-Herodian Damascus Chief Monk was 'the Second Death' (Rev 2:11, 20:6, 20: 14).

deceive (*planaō*) Teach that another than the Agrippas is the true Herod. Rev 12:9, support Antipas. Rev 13:14, support Herod of Chalcis.

defile (*molynō*) To break the law of the Temple Scroll (11QT 45:7), concerning nocturnal emission. A man was obliged to go outside the monastery and wash his garments (Rev 3:4).

deny (*arneomai*) See **confess**. The opposite of 'confess', refusing to agree that Jesus is a high priest, as Peter did during his trial (Rev 2:13, 3:8).

despot (*despotēs*) A man in the position of Michael, either Herod (Rev 6:10) or the Annas priest (Luke 2:29).

destruction (*apōleia*) The latrine, which in a monastery was used also for other unclean purposes, one of its chambers a tomb, and for excommunications. One latrine was called 'Hades' (Luke 16:23). 'He goes to destruction' (Rev 17:8, 11) means 'he goes to the monastic latrine', and it gives a time, as the rule was that it must be used for defecation at 4 a.m. and 4 p.m. each day, except Saturday at 4 a.m. There is a further meaning, 'Rome', as Rome, province 10, was considered to be equal to grade 10, the grade to which those visiting the latrine went down at the tenth hour. It is of interest that in the remains of the cave which may be identified as the sabbath latrine at Qumran (see *Jesus the Man*, Chapter 26), a jar was found inscribed 'ROMA' (*DJD* III, p.30).

devil (*diabolos*) A name for Raphael the levite. See

Satan. Raphael, as a monastic Scribe, had the duty of preserving the rules of celibacy. It was he who tested for fitness for the strict discipline of Essene marriage, testing the bride and groom during the prior betrothal period. As Rev 2:10 shows, he tested the bride for virginity six months previously, through the bishop with medical knowledge.

The Raphael of AD 26 was Judas the Galilean, head of East Manasseh (the 'devil' in Rev 12:9), and the position was kept by Judas Iscariot his successor (Luke 4:13). Judas 'tempted' (tested) Jesus eighteen months before his marriage. Judas also objected at the second wedding of Jesus to Mary Magdalene (John 12:45). In Rev 2:10 the position of western Raphael, after the schism, was held by the chief Herodian Scribe-Treasurer (both duties of Raphael), who is to be identified with Antipas Herod the treasurer (see p.46).

devout (*hosios*) An ascetic (Rev 15:4, 16:5). The word may perhaps be a play on 'Essene'.

diadem (*diadēma*) The emblem on the headband of an initiator, representing that worn by a lay ruler in class D. When 'diadem 10' was on 'horn 10', as in Rev 13:1, the initiator was confirming that uncircumcised Gentiles at grade 10 had a merely lay status. When 'diadem 7' was worn on 'head 7', as in Rev 12:3, the initiator was giving grade 7 to non-celibate villagers, as he was a Pharisee (Joazar Boethus), and his party did not have a monastic system. Jesus Justus wore 'Many diadems' in Rev 19:12, worn by the David as a lay leader.

die (*apothnēskō*) To be excommunicated from a celibate community, entry to which had given 'life'. The ceremony was taken so seriously that the excommunicant was dressed in burial clothes, carried out on a bier, and placed in his own burial cave, now spiritually 'dead'. If he were reinstated, he was 'resurrected'. In the Christian period, when innovations in doctrine could be treated as heresies, there were frequent excommunications and 'resurrections'. The story of Lazarus in John 11 illustrates the procedure.

dominion (*oikoumenē*) Normally means 'the inhabited earth', then 'the (Roman) empire'. Used to mean the celibate Gentile head of the Rome province, who was also a member at Qumran. In Rev 3:10 Luke, of the 'Italian band' (Acts 10:1). In Rev 12:9 a predecessor of John Mark, in 16:14 the seer Tychicus. In Luke 4:5 the 'devil' (Judas Iscariot) showed Jesus 'all the kingdoms of the *oikoumenē*, the plan of the Rome province, to which Gentiles were attached. He was suggesting that he lead them to overthrow the emperor.

donkey (*ktēnos*) The means of transport permitted to a levite, the subordinate of a priest who used a horse. In Luke 10:34 the Good Samaritan used a donkey. He was Jonathan Annas, who at that time was the subordinate of John the Baptist (the man who was 'rescued', that is, supported in debate by Jonathan). In Rev 18:13, the sign of the levite sitting in front of the higher priest at the table.

door (*thyra*) The word includes a play on Hebrew Daleth, letter D, whose meaning is 'door' (Rev 3:20). Phanuel as Son of Levi was the 'hinge' of the door as priest in the village (see **priest**). 'A door' was the place of his servant, the acolyte (Rev 4:1).

double (*diploō*) See **Gog**.

dragon (*drakōn*) Pseudonym for Pharisee high priests. Joazar Boethus in AD 6 was in a nationalist triarchy of Dragon, Calf and Beast (Rev 12:3). Caiaphas was a Pharisee high priest, AD 18–36 (Rev 12:13, 16). A later Pharisee in the revived triarchy (Rev 16:13) and another in AD 100 (Rev 20:2).

drunk, be (*methyō*) To be literally drunk, if the drink was *oinos*, fermented wine (Rev 17:2); or spiritually elevated, if the drink was *haima*, 'blood', meaning the fermented wine sipped by Christians (Rev 17:6). Philo speaks of the ecstatic banquets of the Egyptian

Therapeuts, which used only bread and water, but the fellowship of those normally living as hermits led to a state of ecstasy, so that in the morning they left, 'drunk with this drunkenness in which there is no shame' (*Contemp. Life* 89). Village Essenes drinking wine but with restraint had similar meetings.

dwell (*katoikeō*) A play on 'down from' (*kata*) the house (*oikos*). *Oikos* means a holy place, and 'down from' a lesser grade. A third Herod, in the married state, was a 'dweller' (Rev 2:13), and a second Herod, the crown prince, was a 'dweller upon of the Earth' (Rev 14:6, 17:8), or one who acted in his place (3:10, 6:10, Gaius Costobar Herod, 8:13 Thomas Herod) or claimed the succession (Herod of Chalcis 11:10, 13:14). When Herod was 'the Earth', in the front row of the congregation, the crown prince beside him on the west was 'upon of the Earth', see **upon**. The 'dwelling' (*katoikētērion*), Rev 18:2, was the position of the Herod crown prince.

In Rev 8:13, Thomas Herod was the 'dwellers upon of the Earth', acting for the young Agrippa II who was two years old. In AD 29, the year of this verse, the scandal about Herodias, who had been married to Thomas, was blamed by the royal Herod party for the delay of the Restoration (see p.44).

In Rev 17:2 a new 'dwellers upon of the Earth' had been appointed, as Gaius Costobar Herod had claimed the right to rule when Agrippa lost credit at the fall of Jerusalem. He may be presumed to be Bernicianus, the son of Bernice from her marriage with her uncle Herod of Chalcis (*Ant.* 20:104). He lost the position when Gaius lost his power (Rev 17:8).

each one (*hekastos*) A celibate. From the phrase 'each to the other' referring to the celibate ideal of community (1QS 8:2) (Rev 2:23, 5:8, 6:11, 22:2).
each other (*allēlōn*) The chief Gentile proselyte (Rev 6:4, 11:10).

eagle (*aetos*) A name for the Annas priest as the Sariel, the priest in the west who was the Eagle of the four Living Creatures: Man, Eagle, Calf and Lion. 'Man', the Gabriel, and 'Eagle', the Sariel, could exchange with each other, with 'Man' going to the west, meaning the village, and 'Eagle' going to the east, to become abbot in a celibate community. In that case he was called 'Flying Eagle' and went up a grade. In Rev 12:14 Eleazar Annas; in Rev 4:7, 8:13, Jonathan Annas. John Mark, who held eastern views and was opposed to the Herods, was the 'servant of Flying Eagle' (Rev 4:7), being equal to a Kohath, and supporting Jonathan Annas when he turned against Agrippa.

ear (*ous*) The man in the position of a Gabriel was 'the ear' to Michael, standing beside him on the east of the noon circle, which was likened to a face. The true Gabriel had been Simon the Essene, whose name means 'hearing'. Under Herod as Michael, the Priest- Pope was his 'ear'. 'To have an ear' meant to be a Michael, a ruling Herod (Rev 13:9). The 'ear' to Agrippa II was Matthew Annas (Rev 2:7).

earth (*gē*) A person, the king as leader of the village congregation. Herod in this position, lower than his priestly positions. In a two- tiered structure, 'Earth' could also stand in the 2 cubits at the north end where the indigent were found. In a three-tiered structure, he could stand on the chancel step, where the indigent knelt to receive their 'crumbs'. To be 'thrown to Earth' or 'fall to Earth' was to be laicised or to act as lay king. When there was no Herod, the place was taken by the David, as in the period from AD 6–26 (Rev 12:16). Simon Magus was called 'Earth' when in an anti-Herodian party he claimed the positions of Herod (Rev 13:12).

earthquake (*seismos*) The Chief Therapeut, head of Ephraim. The term appears at the times the Chief Therapeut was undergoing a change of location or doctrine (Rev 11:13, 16:18, Matt 28:2, Acts 16:26). The earthquake at Qumran in 31 BC had led to a major relocation and change of affiliation, which affected the Therapeuts in particular.

east (*anatolē*) The east pillar in the vestry, the 'pillar of Cloud', the part of its top that was at the edge of the middle tier rather than at the balcony (see Diagram A). Phanuel, who stood there, said the early dawn prayer at 3 a.m. It was the 'east of the Sun', for this reason. Qumran itself was called 'the east of the Sun' as it was said to be like an early dawn to Jerusalem. 'From the east of the Sun' (Rev 7:2, 16:12) meant in another place, having come from Qumran, see **from**.

eat (*esthiō*) To take part in the communion meal, eating the loaves, which stood for the levite, thus receiving his authority and teaching.

eat down (*katesthiō*) To act at or confine to the common meal, not at the sacred meal. The common meal was the equivalent of the evening meal of villagers held at the common table (Rev 10:9). To confine a person of high status to the common meal was to say that he was under punishment, illegitimate (Rev 12:4), or to refuse to dine with him at the high table (Rev 11:5).

eighth (*ogdoos*) A person who was an 'eighth' was at grade 8 and head of the eighth order, that of Gad, whose leader was the third Herod. In Rev 17:11, the threesome of Herodian kinsmen was completed again, after the death of Antipas Herod, by a new Herod, one who was allied with Gaius. He claimed the succession, and soon after went to Rome. He may be conjectured to be the son of Drusilla and Felix, also called Agrippa, who was killed in AD 79 at the eruption of Vesuvius (*Ant.* 20:143–144).

elder (*presbyteros*) See **priest**.

emerald (*smaragdos*) The fourth precious stone of the list of Rev 21:19, belonging to the centre of the second row of the ordinary congregation, so one of the positions of the Herod crown prince, sitting behind 'jasper', King

Herod. The Herod crown prince in Rev 4:3.

end (*telos*) Midnight, as the end of the Julian day, and by the parallel of hours and months, December (Rev 21:6, 22:13). The times were those at which the Restoration was expected, by those using the Julian calendar. The verb *teleioō* has the same meaning.

endurance (*hypomonē*) A name for a layman who could take the place of Phanuel in the village, leading prayers 24 hours a day. The seer (Rev 13:10, 1:9) could hold this position, also a Gentile monastic (Rev 2:19).

enemy (*echthros*) A Roman governor, standing for all Romans. Marsus governor of Syria (Rev 11:5, 12). To 'love one's enemies' (Matt 5:43–44) had the special meaning 'admit the leading Roman to the Agape meal, thus showing friendship to Rome'.

enrichment (*ploutos*) See **rich**, on the David receiving Gentile fees. As Gentile numbers increased out of all expectation, the heir of David did indeed become rich: James' 'lands increased and his barns were full'. Jesus refused to accept fees. The Herod crown prince or his representative then received them.

Euphrates (*Euphratēs*) The Damascus monastery, which stood at the western limit of the eastern province, ending in Babylon. Where members of the Qumran monastery used the holy water of their 'Jordan', and of the aqueduct, their 'Kidron', members of the separated Damascus monastery used the holy water of their aqueduct, the 'river', calling it the 'Euphrates'. (Rev 9:14, 16:12.)

every (*pas*) See **all**.

except (*ei mē*) Literally, 'if not', so used to mean 'and also'.

exult (*euphrainō*) To claim the Herod succession (Rev 11:10, 12: 12, 19:20).

eyes (*ophthalmoi*) Since all words for parts of the body meant objects worn at or placed at the part, 'eyes' meant a lamp, used to help the eyes during night services. All ministers attending these services had an oil lamp, but the words for them, and probably their shape, expressed the grade of minister. Sariel's lamp was called 'fire' and when he acted as hermit it was called 'flame (of fire)' (Acts 7:30, Rev 1:14). Phanuel's lamp was called 'lamp' (Rev 4:5), Raphael's called 'lantern' (*lychnos*), and that of a lay elder who was not levitical was called 'eyes' (Rev 1:14, 4:6). In Rev 1:14 Jesus had 'eyes' and (*hōs*) 'a flame of fire', meaning that he had a layman's lamp which he used as a priest's lamp when he was acting as priest to Gentiles. But he had 'eyes 7' at a Jewish service (Rev 5:6), and since the main hours of the day were marked by a *lampas*, his lamp marked lesser times.

face (*prosōpon*) A priest's headband, worn on the upper forehead like that of a lay ascetic (the 'head') but permitted only to a priest or person of similar status. Singular, worn by a priest, plural, worn by a person acting in the priest's position. 'They fell on their faces' (Rev 11:16) means that such a person prostrated himself so that his headband touched the ground. 'From the face' (Rev 12:14, 6:16, 20: 11) is used of a person such as the Chief Therapeut who sometimes acted as a priest, but when in his lay capacity was 'from' (at the opposite extreme) to a priest.

faith (*pistis*) See **work**. Originally, 'faith' was the property of those who had been born into the tribe of Levi or into the royal family, who did not have to earn promotion by ascetic 'works'. But Jesus and Paul taught that laymen had received the identity of priests, and were 'saved by faith'. In Revelation 'faith' is used for a layman who claims this right, in Rev 2:13 and 14:12, of Jesus himself, in 2:19 of the Gentile monastic John Mark. In Rev 13:10, used of Barnabas ('the holy ones' as crown prince to Jesus), who was called a levite in Acts 4:36.

faithful (*pistos*) See **faith**. Paul, who taught the re-interpreted meaning of 'faith', was called 'the faithful one' (Rev 1:5, 2:13, both with Peter, 'the witness').

fall (*piptō*) To kneel before a superior power, a layman to a priest, or a priest to a higher priest. When used once, to kneel before a superior (Rev 4:10, 1:17). When used twice, of the emperor ('fallen, fallen, Babylon the Great'), it means that he had died, as the only superior powers to the emperor were the gods (Rev 14:8, 18:2).

falsehood (*pseudos*), **false prophet** (*pseudoprophētēs*) A rival claimant to the Herodian succession. In Rev 14:5, Herod of Chalcis, the brother of Agrippa I, who was supported by Simon Magus and the Damascus party. After his death, a member of the line of Tigranes, attached to the Damascus party. See p.47.

famine (*limos*) The year beginning the 3½ years (see p.242). Rev 18:8, AD 71, the north solar year when the calendar changed from Night to Day. Rev 6:8, the north solar sabbatical year AD 50.

father (*patēr*) A Sariel was a 'Father', a title used by Herod of the public high priest (*Ant.* 15:21). Used by the Sadducee priests (Rev 1:6). In Aramaic it was 'Abba', and this form was used for Sariel in his role of head of Therapeut communities (non-coenobitic) (Mark 14:36). It gave the word 'abbot'.

fear (*phobos*) The state of exclusion of a priest when he succumbed to sexual uncleanness, especially forbidden to a high priest, who was not permitted to officiate on the Day of Atonement if he had had a nocturnal emission the previous night (*Ant.* 17:165–166). Used also of a high priest when leaving to marry (Luke 1:12). Used of a man leaving the celibate community, Rev 2:10. In this condition, he was at the level of a deacon, equal to female and Gentile deacons, and Gentiles were called 'Godfearers' (Acts 10:2). In Rev 11:11 Matthew was exiled from the high priesthood and the country for political activity, so 'great fear fell' on him. He was exiled to Antioch, so 'to become fearful' (*emphoboi*) in Rev 11:13 meant being in Antioch, similarly in Rev 11:18.

As the word stood for a state of sexual uncleanness, it meant the married state, and 'Do not fear', said to a married man (Rev 1:17), meant 'leave the married state' (in order to take a temporary vow of abstinence from sex within the married state).

A man at this level wore black, and those who acted as Nazirites, wearing black, were in this class. A Therapeut who had gone down to this state was said to act *dia ton phobon*, as a levite 'on behalf of the Fear' (Rev 18:10, 15).

feed (*trephō*) To allow a woman or Gentile to have a meal on Friday evenings, forbidden to Jewish Essenes because of their prohibition of defecation on the sabbath. The word is an indication of date, as it means Friday (Rev 12:6, 14).

few (*oligoi*) A title of Herod, who was both 'the Many' as head of the lay council of a hundred, and 'the Few' as head of the priests, who had smaller numbers.

figtree (*sykē*) The Samaritan party led by Simon Magus in the gospel period was called 'the Figtree' (Mark 11:12–14, Luke 13:6). When Jesus 'cursed the figtree' he was condemning their zealot ambitions and financial exploitation. In Rev 6:13 the Figtree means Ananias the Samaritan high priest; see **fury**. In the course of the Samaritan troubles of AD 50–51 referred to in Rev 6:11–17, Jonathan Annas allied with Ananias, as is shown in War 2:243, and this agrees with John 1:48, that Nathanael (Jonathan) had been 'under the Figtree'. Jonathan and Simon Magus (followed by Ananias) represented two kinds of Samaritans, the former in favour of peace with Rome, the latter in favour of war, but both opposed to the Agrippas.

fig, early (*olynthos*) A summer fig, used to mean Jonathan Annas when associated with the Figtree; see **figtree**. Jonathan's preferred seasons were the solstices.

filthy (*rhyparos*) A celibate who had been excluded from the monastery in the north-east quarter at Qumran was sent to the south-west quarter, where the exclusion cistern and the priests' latrines were found. He was here 'filthy', as he had been guilty of such sins as nocturnal emission (11QT 45:7). He wore black, had to wash his white clothes, and could return to the monastery after some days. The four divisions of the monastery grounds are shown in Rev 22:11.

find (*heuriskō*) To recruit as a member, to 'find a foundling', that is, a person beginning education, as the monastic system was originally derived from taking in exposed children to make them acolytes in the shrines (Ezek 16).

fire (*pyr*) An oil lamp that was used to light the evening lamp, or the furnace in the vestry. See **eyes**. It belonged to the Chief Therapeut when he was acting in an equal status to Sariel, as an 'Elijah' who brought down fire from heaven (1 Kings 18:38), and also as associated with the 'pillar of fire' of the Exodus. At the evening common meal, when wine was drunk at 9 p.m., Therapeuts did not drink wine, but attended to the lighting of the lamp, on the model of the levite who lit the Menorah at this time. They also used the lighter lamp, the 'fire', to light the furnace in the vestry that stood for their discipline (Luke 22:55).

'Fire' stood for their willingness for martyrdom at times when zealot action was needed. In Rev 8:7, 'fire mixed in blood' means that Theudas, the chief Therapeut in AD 2, allied with Joseph the father of Jesus who was head of village pilgrims (see **blood**). (See *Jesus the Man*, Chapter 11.)

Since the Therapeuts were levitical and the king in his lay status was 'Earth', to 'throw fire on Earth' (Luke 12:49, Rev 13:13) meant to give laymen a levitical status, allowing them a form of ministry.

Gentiles like James Niceta, who adopted the related Jewish Nazirite discipline, wanted to be like Elijah and 'bring down fire from heaven' (Luke 9:54).

firstborn (*prōtotokos*) The David crown prince (Rev 1:5).

firstfruits (*aparchē*) A play on 'from an *archē*' (see **beginning**), meaning that the person held the opposite ('from') of the view that March was an *archē*, so observing feasts in September. The Jewish term implied some Jewish practices. James Niceta, holding more eastern views, in Rev 14:4.

five (*pente*) See **two**.

flame (*phlox*) See **eyes**.

flee (*pheugō*) To separate into a different party. In Rev 9:6, Simon Magus separated into an anti-Agrippa party. In Rev 12:6, Mary separated from the Pharisee and joined the Sadducee priest.

flesh (*sarx*) In the plural, the money received from the Herodian mission. It was used to 'buy' (pay the salary of) ministers, who were called the 'bread' that was eaten at the communion meals, and the bread at common meals was called 'flesh', as it could be taken by married men. Rev 19:18, with its list of different kinds of 'flesh', deals with the problem of the future of Herodian fees that arose with the fall of Jerusalem.

flute-player (*aulētēs*) The person who led the liturgical dance (Matt 11:17: 'we piped to you, and you did not dance'). The dance, led by a 'Miriam' was held at the Exodus ceremonies of the Therapeuts (*Contemp. Life* 83–87, Mark 6:22). Such a ceremony was held by the Herodians in Rev 18:22.

foot (*pous*, plu. *podes*) A collection vessel that was set out beside the foot for receiving money, but did not belong to the person receiving it. Money given at the 'right foot' was for eastern Herodian monasteries. For the history given in Rev 10:2, see **sea**. Money given 'at the left', without 'foot', was owned by Agrippa, being the large income from the fees of class D in the Diaspora (Rev 10:2, *de*, 'but' meaning class D). Money given at the 'feet' was placed at the left foot, and was either the Roman tribute (Rev 10:1) or the common property of

Dan monastics (Rev 1:15, 17, Acts 4:37). In a three-tiered structure, the 'feet' were at the chancel step. The 'right foot', the collection vessel, was placed in front of the eastern supporting pillar on the dais, and the left, or the 'feet', in front of the western (see Diagram A).

'Feet length clothing' (*podērēs*) (Rev 1:13) was an ordinary garment, not a levitical vestment, which was worn on the chancel step, the place where the priest changed into outside garments. The chancel step was associated with 'feet' for the above reason.

for (*gar*) A play on the letters Gimel (a 'g') and Resh ('r'), meaning that a person is a Sariel priest of grade 2 Resh, and also a celibate in class 3, C (Gimel as the third letter, see p.176). If a lay celibate claimed to be a priest, as Simon Magus did, the word *gar* was applied to him (Rev 13:18). In Mark 16:8, *gar* ends a sentence, being used as a noun.

forehead (*metōpon*) A badge worn in place of a phylactery, low on the forehead between the eyebrows. Although originally a sign of Diaspora membership (since Palestinian members wore an actual leather phylactery, of which numerous examples were found in the caves) it continued to be used by the eastern party and by Jewish Christians, and was regarded as a sign of Jewish allegiance (Rev 7:3, 14:1, 9, 20:4, 22:4).

fornication (*porneia*) The doctrine of the 'harlots', women of the order of Asher like Helena and Bernice, who claimed to be equal to Phanuel, so could be called 'priest', and wear the vestments of cardinal and bishop. Their order of women retained the traditions of sacred prostitution.

foundation (*themelios*) The council of celibates, below priests and levites. Corresponds to Hebrew *sod*, used in this sense in the Scrolls (1QS 8:5). 'Foundation 12' (Rev 21:14), the head of the council of Gentiles of grade 12, now taking the place of a Jewish head of the council as leader of the congregation.

fourth (*tetarton*) 'The fourth of the Earth' was the first of the four divisions under 'Earth' (see **third**, **tenth**). The four divisions were the Poor, Crippled, Blind and Lame (village welfare recipients who formed the four classes of non-coenobitic ascetics, Luke 14:21). The Poor were the Therapeuts. In Rev 6:8 Apollos was appointed as Chief Therapeut, over 'the fourth of the Earth'. The date in this verse (17 March AD 50) was exactly the same as that in Philippi when the effects of the 'Earthquake' (Apollos) were felt (Acts 16:26).

frankincense (*libanos*, from Hebrew 'white') The substance used by Essenes to whiten their garments, including village Essenes on Friday evenings before synagogue (CD 11:4). To use frankincense meant to act under Jewish synagogue rules (Rev 8:3, 5). The man who whitened the garments was a fuller (Mark 9:3). The servant who prepared the western side of the high table in Herod's house was the fuller responsible for supplying frankincense. He is listed with the five servants in Rev 18:13, and in Rev 8:3,5, the frankincense-holder *libanōtos* was on the western pillar.

freedman (*eleutheros*) A freedman was a member of Herod's household who was not a slave, of higher status than a slave. John Mark was the freedman Eutychus who drove Agrippa I's chariot and played a part in his arrest (*Ant.* 18:168–186). John Mark is the 'freedmen' of Rev 13:16, and 'freedman' of Rev 6:15. In Rev 19:18, 'All the freedmen' is the Herod crown prince receiving the fees of the highest class of Gentiles.

frog (*batrachos*) One of the plagues of Egypt was that of frogs (Exod 8:2), and the word is used derisively as a pseudonym for a new zealot leader, Simon Gioras, who belonged to the Egyptian order, the Therapeuts, in its married branch, that of Gerasa-Gad (Rev 16:13).

from (*apo*) At the limit of, opposite to. For places, it means the corresponding place some distance away. For times, it means a corresponding time at the end of the time span in question. 'From God' means the limit to which the Sadducee could go, the opposite extreme from his normal position on one of the upper tiers. His limit in the vestry was the chancel step, the place he occupied in Luke 5:19. 'From the east' means the opposite of the east, that is the west, and so with the other compass points in Rev 21:13.

fruit (*karpos*) The financial increase of the mission, that is, the numbers of those who had been converted and joined it, paying a fee. In the parable of the Vineyard, the 'slaves' went abroad and brought back the 'fruits', proof of increase in the form of fees. In Rev 22:2 eastern Christian monasteries were still using the method. The 'fruit' consisted of membership fees only, and was a sign of the increase of numbers in the mission, so was expected by Jesus in the story of the cursing of the Figtree (Mark 11:13–14).

furnace (*kaminos*) The great fire in the vestry, built for cooking the loaves of the Presence, and used by Egyptian ascetics to symbolise their discipline. (Rev 9:2.) From Deut 4:20 'out of the iron furnace, out of Egypt'. 1QS 8:4 speaks of ascetic life as 'the anguish of the furnace'.

fury (*orgē*) The Jewish head of state who was appointed the agent of Rome. Caiaphas in Rev 12:17 (the verb), then Agrippa II, appointed by the emperor Claudius in AD 44 as the agent of Rome in his country, like the procurator 'Wrath' (Rev 11:18, 6:16). In Rev 11:18 the term shows that Agrippa the Younger had set out from Rome in March AD 44 before hearing of the death of his father, having been appointed as proconsul to Cyprus, where he appeared in September AD 44 in Acts 13:7. Arriving in Ephesus by June 44, he heard of the death of his father and was accepted as the successor.

In Rev 6:17, following 'the Fury of the Lamb' referring to Agrippa in Rev 6:16, the phrase 'the Fury of them' appears. This is the key to the meaning of events in Rev 6:11–17. According to *Ant.* 20:105–136 and

War 2:223–246, the years 50–51 in Judea were marked by troubles led by the Samaritan high priest Ananias, who was associated with the Samaritan Jonathan Annas. Ananias bribed the corrupt Roman governor Cumanus to treat him as the leader of the people (so becoming 'Fury'), and led a Samaritan attack against Jews. After investigation the Samaritan party were taken to Rome, where at first they were in favour in the court, but Agrippa the Younger, who was in Rome in AD 51, spoke against them and they were punished by Claudius.

Agrippa having regained favour was 'Fury' in Rev 16:19.

garment (*himation*) A short vestment, contrasting with the long robe (*stolē*) of Scribes, which was not in coat shape but put on over the head, so 'thrown around'. It had become the vestment worn by celibates over another garment tied by a belt, as shown in Acts 12:8. It was the holy garment for Phanuel and dynasts (Rev 4:4), and eventually became the surplice, worn over the belted cassock.

gate (*pylōn*) A seat at an entrance door, where the teacher sat to give instruction to those entering. The twelve gates of the plan of the Temple Scroll were each thought of as a *pylōn*, for teachers appointed according to the grade of the order using the gate (see pp.161, 185). 'Gate 12' was, originally, the seat of the teacher of order 12, lowest Gentiles, but in Rev 21:12 it had gone up to be placed in the highest position. A 'gate 3' was for a teacher of order and grade 3, a cardinal, originally on the centre south of the Temple Scroll plan. But by the time of Rev 21:13 all of the central gates on the four sides of the building, representing the four compass points, were equal, with a 'gate 3' at each.

give birth (*tiktō*) To give first initiation to a twelve-year-old boy, or full initiation to a man at the age of twenty-three (Rev 12:4, 5, 13).

glass (*hyalinos*) A 'Sea of glass' was a lay equal of Phanuel the Cloud, using a glass container of holy water for sprinkling (Rev 4:6).

glory (*doxa*) A title of the Priest-Pope when acting in the role of 'Moses', whose face shone after being in the presence of the glory of God (Exod 33:18–22, 34:29). The role of 'Moses' had been that of the Gabriel (Acts 7:20 on Simon the Essene), who was superior both of coenobitic Essenes and of higher Therapeuts, whose Exodus liturgy needed a 'Moses'. Among the coenobitic Essenes, the dynasts, their second level, were treated as equal to higher Therapeuts. But the dynasts practised common property, whereas the Therapeuts did not. The common property was held by the Gabriel as 'the Glory'. When the Annas priests took this position after AD 6, the title and function was adopted by them. To say 'the glory is to God' (Rev 1:6) meant that the Sadducee was the Gabriel, and therefore entitled to hold the common property. The position of the Glory was taken by Jesus III as the 'Alpha', the head of Gentile monasteries, at the end of the history (Rev 21:11, 23).

glorify (*doxazō*) To appoint a Sadducee as high priest and Priest- Pope. See **glory**. (Rev 15:4.)

God (*theos*) A Sadducee priest, who held a view of his priesthood accepted in the Diaspora, that he was like a divine being, an incarnation of the Demiurge God. The Sadducee when visiting villages received prayers on behalf of God. The title 'God' (shown in John 10:33–36 to have been used by men) was accepted by Sadducee high priests but not by Pharisees, and the opposition of Pharisees to them, illustrated by Paul's hostility to Jonathan Annas or 'Stephen', was because of the perceived arrogance of the usage. Up to AD 68, 'God' was one of the Annas brothers. In Rev 16:7, it was the high priest Matthias son of Theophilus, who was high priest at the outbreak of the war (*Ant*. 20:223).

Gog, Magog (*Gōg, Magōg*) Names from Ezek 38:2 given

new technical meaning. Gog, used for those having a double form of membership of class C (Gimel, a 'g'), the celibate congregation. They wore a double Gimel (the vowel is disregarded). They belonged to two different parties, Christian and Herodian, as is shown by the word 'double' in Rev 18:6. In Rev 20:8 the word is used to describe Agrippa, who had both Christian and Jewish membership. A Gentile of grade 9, Mem, who had the same double membership was called Magog in the same verse.

gold (*chrysion*) 'Gold, silver and precious stones' were the emblems of priests, levites and celibates respectively; classes A, B and C. (1 Cor 3:12). Gold is associated with the Holy of Holies in Matt 23: 16.

gospel (*euangelion*, 'good message') A new scripture written for the Restoration, as 'good news' that it had arrived. The jubilee was marked by the announcement of 'good news' of the freeing of captives (Luke 4:18, quoting Isa 61:1–2). The Temple Scroll may be seen as having been written for the original year 3920 in 21 BC, when the Restoration was expected (see pp.220–222). For subsequent, adjusted dates, further new books were written, culminating in the canonical gospels. In Rev 10:7, Matthew's Sayings (*logia*, see pp.527–528), were published in December AD 43, the *telos* (end of Agrippa I's extended Last Jubilee). In Rev 14:6 the word means Paul's early epistles, beginning with Galatians, which he himself called a 'gospel' ('If any man preach to you another gospel...', Gal 1:6). It was said to be *aiōnion*, for the *aiōn*, the world-week.

grace (*charis*) A title used for the David crown prince, reflecting the original system whereby initiated fee paying Gentiles paid their fees to the David, while those in grades 11 and 12, being given few privileges, paid no fees, so were 'free', and 'saved by grace'. These latter were put under the crown prince. When Jesus became crown prince at the accession of his father in AD 16, it was said 'a Grace of God became upon him' (pesher of Luke 2:40). The servant of the crown prince who was in one of the non-paying orders could be called 'a Grace', and so use the name 'John'. In Rev 1:4 John Aquila used this name, at the time Jesus Justus had turned twelve.

In the last verse of Revelation, a new David crown prince is announced by using the term 'the Grace of the Lord Jesus' (Rev 22:21).

The name 'John' was used by Christians for John the Baptist as a derogatory term, at the times when he was reduced to grade 11, being in 'torment' (Rev 9:5). Consequently it is not used in the Scrolls for the Teacher of Righteousness. When he was twelve years old the name was given to him (Luke 1:60) because he was to assist his mother in admitting uncircumcised Gentiles at the low grades. As wife of the Zadokite, she was the superior Mother to all Gentiles.

grass (*chortos*) A person just beginning his education in the 'Eden' school system (Rev 8:7, Mark 4:28).

grave (*mnēma*) The place for literal burials (Rev 11:9) whereas a 'tomb' (*mnēmeion*), was the place for the symbolic burial of excommunication.

great (*megas*) The king, as a layman, was called 'great', and his son the prince was called 'little'. The king was a third in the triarchy, sitting on the west side at the table. In Sentence 2 of the Copper Scroll, a deposit of money in the 'tomb of the son of the third Great One' is named, meaning the crown prince of the Davids. As the king sat on the west, the 'great voice' was heard on the west of the platform in the vestry, the place of the pulpit.

Being associated with the west, the word 'great', used alone, means Rome (Rev 14:19, 15:1, 3, 16:18).

These terms were used also for the Gentiles of Dan, who were under the David king and prince. Great Dan was the higher of the two divisions of the ancient tribe of Dan, in the area that came to include Caesarea Philippi. The head of Shem (Philip the Evangelist in the gospel period) was 'the great ones' (Rev 11:18, 13:16, 19:18). Little Dan was its other division, in the area that came to include Joppa.

Greek (*Hellēnikos*) The form of worship of the Hellenist party of Acts 6:1, who used Greek in public worship, reading from the Septuagint, as opposed to the eastern Hebrews. See p.148 on the Hellenists and Hebrews as the two main parties in the mission up to AD 37. (Rev 9:11.)

green (*chlōros*) The colour for spring and the east, so that of Gabriel as the 'archangel' whose special feast was Passover. 'Gabriel' was the head of Essene monasteries, who had the power to excommunicate. The position passed to the head of Diaspora Essene monasteries, the chief Magus, who was called 'Death' as having this power. When he attended Diaspora councils as an equal of priests, he used the 'horse', the chariot-throne, as they did, so was 'the rider on the green horse'. After the schism of AD 44 there was a separate western Herodian order of Magians, their first being Atomus the Magus, who was on the 'green horse' in Rev 6:8.

With other nouns, 'green' means a person who studied in a monastic school, under Gabriel or his equivalent. Agrippa as a student in Rev 8:7 ('green grass'), as a graduate in Rev 9:4 ('All green'). In Mark 6:39 'green grass' refers to Agrippa.

Hades (*Hadēs*) 'Hades' was the place for excommunicated monastics, grade 11, one above 'Death' at grade 12, since 'Hades' was the place of torment, severe penance, prior to the final stage. (see *Jesus the Man*, Chapter 26, for its location at Qumran). A man of grade Resh had the power to send to 'Hades', and was also in charge of the Palestinian treasury. In Part B of Revelation this was Antipas Herod the treasurer of Jerusalem. He was the 'Hades' who accompanied Atomus the Magus to the Ephesus council in Rev 6:8; and is mentioned in Rev 1:18.

hail (*chalaza*) A person. One of the teachers of the Law. See **thunder**. Originally a name for Judas the Galilean, head of East Manasseh, as the Raphael to the Diaspora (Rev 8:7). One of the duties of Raphael was to go to the village to act as treasurer of Essene common property.

After the schism of AD 44 the positions of Palestinian and Diaspora treasurer were combined in the person of Antipas Herod the treasurer of Jerusalem, who was Great Hail of Rev 11:19, and after his death he was replaced by Gaius Costobar Herod, who was Great Hail of Rev 16:21a. 'Hail' of Rev 16:21b was Eleazar Ben Jair of Masada, a descendant of Judas the Galilean (*War* 7:253).

hair (*thrix*) The headcloth worn by a man with short hair (Rev 1:14, 9:8). He was not in the condition of a Nazirite, a married man who took a vow of separation for a period of 30–100 days and let his hair grow long in this time. When the Nazirite took up or returned to the married state, his hair was cut, and he was said to be 'a sheep' who was 'shorn' (Acts 18:18, 21:24). A cloth would have been worn in place of hair. A woman as equal to a married man wore a veil, also called 'hair' (Rev 9:8). The 'hair of a camel' worn by John the Baptist was the headcloth of a dynastic graduate (grade Gimel, meaning 'camel', see p.184) who had entered the state prior to marriage, as the Baptist did in AD 29 at the age of thirty-six (Mark 1:6). The headcloth of Jesus in Rev 1:14 was made of wool, showing that he was in the state prior to marriage, with hair cut short, and he wore a woollen headcloth as Shepherd to pilgrims of the class of 'shorn sheep'. Mary Magdalene wore a 'hair', a veil, at her wedding, then took it off for the ceremony of 'wiping the feet' (Luke 7:38).

half (*hēmisys*) Half a day of twelve hours, so six hours, the extra hours between the 6 a.m. and 6 p.m. beginning of day or night, and the Julian beginning (Rev 11:9, 11). Or half a year, six months, December, as hours and months were equated (Rev 12:14).

half-hour (*hēmiōron*) Corresponding to half a month, 15 days, as an hour was an equivalent of a month, there being twelve of both (see p.212) (Rev 8:1).

Hallelujah (*Hallēlouia*) The Hebrew word means 'may Yahweh be praised'. The Hebrew for 'praising' is *hillel*, and this was the name of Hillel the Great, the Jewish sage of the first century BC who, as may be seen, was the first Pope of the mission, its 'Abraham'. Subsequent Popes played on his name, and the new Priest-Pope of AD 73 is shown to have used 'Hallelujah' as a title (Rev 19:1, 3, 6).

hand (*cheir*) Following the rule for parts of the body, that an object worn or held at a part of the body is called by its name, a 'hand' was an object held in the hand. It was the flat plate, the paten for the sacred bread. The 'mark on the hand' was a letter on the plate showing the grade of the person who held it (Rev 13:16). The wine cup placed on it was the 'cup in the hand' (Rev 17:4). A large dish was used, with enough room for a book, a cup or a rod to be placed on it, when these objects were sacred and not held directly in the hand (Rev 10:2, 8, 14:14).

The least person who could hold the paten was an acolyte, who stood at the side of the middle or upper tier, ready to hand it to the priest. Since the hand was 2 cubits away from the head (a cubit being the length of the forearm), the acolyte stood 2 cubits away from the centre in the position of a servant. The noon circle on the middle tier was thought of as a 'face', so the 'right hand' was over the eastern pillar supporting the extension to the platform (see Diagram A). But if the priest was on the chancel step, where a priest to Gentiles must stand, his 'right hand' was at the east side of the chancel step (Rev 1:16).

If the literal right hand is meant, 'the right' (*dexia*) is used (Rev 1:17, 5:1). When the person was facing south

300

towards the congregation, his literal right hand was on the west side. When Jesus had 'the seven stars (Star 7) in his right' (Rev 1:20, 2:1), he had placed Jesus Justus on the west side of the chancel step. One of the purposes was to show that he was an acolyte to himself as well as to Agrippa, whom Jesus Justus served on the east side (Rev 1:16).

harp (*kithara*) The harpist, Phanuel, who as equal to David played the harp at the time in the service when psalms were sung (Rev 5:8, 14:2, 15:2).

harvest (*therismos*) In the original plan of Herodian mission, a 'new Exodus' had been declared for Jewish evangelisation, and at the same time there was a mission to Gentiles who were likened to 'wheat', under the David who was the Seed (see p.194). Year 38 of the 'Exodus' was a significant one, as it was the year for crossing Jordan (Deut 2:14), and this year was the test of the rightness of the chronology, as it should see a great event likened to 'crossing Jordan'. A 'year 38' had been expected in AD 31 (John 5:5), for a revised Exodus scheme, and the same year was that of a 'harvest' (John 4:35). Another 'year 38' was expected in AD 58, for a revised 'new Exodus' from AD 20–60, and this was the year when 'the Egyptian', Apollos, staged an attack on 'Jericho', demanding that the walls of Jerusalem fall down (Acts 21:38, recorded also by Josephus, *Ant.* 20:169–172). It was consequently also the year of a 'harvest', that of Rev 14:15–16. In this year, the expected numbers of fee paying Gentiles should be complete, and there would be no further evangelisation.

hate (*misō*) To exclude from the Agape meal, just as to 'love' was to admit to it. 1QS 1:9–10 'to love all the Sons of Light and hate all the Sons of Darkness' (Rev 17:16, 18:2).

He (*autos* as new subject) The word *autos* appears at times as a subject, meaning that it is a new subject for the verb, not referring back. It is translated He, with a capital, in order to convey this point. Similarly the plural, 'They'. In this position it means a royal or priestly person.

head (*kephalē*) A headband, worn around the upper forehead by an ascetic, containing the letters showing the grade. The band could be worn together with a head-cloth, as shown in Rev 1:14. When John the Baptist's 'head' was brought on a plate, it was simply his head-band as the chief initiator. When Jesus 'bowed his head' (John 19:30) he was wearing the headband. 'Head 7' was the headband with the letter for 7 worn by a priest or Scribe of the circumcision party who initiated prose-lytes to grade 7. He was also called 'Horn 10', as he kept the uncircumcised at grade 10. (Rev 12:3, 13:1, 17:3.)

heal (*therapeuō*) To be healed was to reach the status of a Therapeut (Healer) after going through the Exodus liturgy. The rule and liturgy of the Therapeuts of Egypt are described by Philo in *Contemp. Life* (Rev 13:3, 12, noun in Rev 22:2).

hear (*akouō*) To hear sermons, as a member of the con-gregation. 'The One hearing' means the seer, sitting in the first pew (Rev 22:8, 17).

heart (*kardia*) The emblem of a queen or crown prince, who were equal to each other in grade (Rev 2:23, 17:17; 18:7).

heaven (*ouranos*) A person, Michael or Herod in his position, in whose name prayers were said. He was the highest in the hierarchy. An acolyte could stand near, serving him, so he was 'in Heaven' (Rev 12:1, 3, 5:3).

When Jesus after the crucifixion was 'carried up to Heaven' (Luke 24:51) he was brought to the position of the priest on the platform at the Qumran vestry. In a three-tiered structure, 'the Heaven' was on the upper tier (Rev 4:1).

Up to AD 44 Qumran retained the functions of 'Heaven', being used as a council centre while Mird con-tained the sanctuary where the atonement was made.

But from that date new centres for Diaspora Jews and their Christian associates were established in Ephesus, in both the cathedral and hermitage, both of which contained a 'Heaven'. A 'Heaven' was also established in Rome (Rev 19:1).

Hebrew (*Hebraïsti*) The form of worship of the party of Hebrews, who used Hebrew and kept the purity rules of Palestinian ascetics (Rev 9:11). See p.148 on the Hellenists and Hebrews as the two main parties in the mission up to AD 37.

help (*boetheō*) Be a husband to (Rev 12:16, Acts 16:9).

hence (*enteuthen*) The northern one of the two round bases outside the vestry (see p.196) (Rev 22:2). It was at this point that a 3 a.m. prayer for cockcrowing could be said, indicating the very early beginning of the day. It was consequently called 'east', and this term (*emprosthen*) is used for it in Luke 19:4. In Sentence 21 of the Copper Scroll, it is called 'the east seat north of the Blue (*kohlit*)' (the Blue was the south base, the two being associated with the colours worn outside, scarlet, purple and blue). In John 19:18, the two other men who were crucified with Jesus were *enteuthen* and *enteuthen*, that is, 'east and east', meaning that Jesus was on the west and these two both east of him.

here (*hōde*) The seer in the Ephesus congregation sat in the first pew, called 'here' (Rev 4:1). The word was then used as a way of referring to the seer himself in the Ephesus cathedral (Rev 13:10, 18), and to Ephesus (Rev 11:12).

herself (*heautē*). See **himself**. Helena, the consort of Simon Magus, in Rev 2:20. Later, the Christian chief female celibate, the wife of the David in the supreme position (Rev 19:7).

hidden (*kekrymmenos*, from *kryptō*) In Rev 2:17, 'the hidden manna' was the communion bread that was given to Gentiles, who in Jewish monasteries were taught in places defined as hidden. Under Herodians they were brought into the chancel of the vestry, and the place where they received bread was called 'the crypt'.

high (*hypsēlos*) The platform in a monastery vestry modelled on Qumran (Mark 9:2, Rev 21:10, 12).

himself (*heautos*) An alternate man in the position of Herod as Michael, the supreme leader. In the gospel period, Simon Magus. The saying in Mark 8:34, '...deny Himself and take up his cross and follow me', means that Christians were to separate from Simon Magus and the Damascus doctrine, no longer use his X sign of initiation, but use instead the Greek T sign for the same letter. Rev 10:7 refers to Simon Magus as 'Himself'.

Simon was head of the Damascus party, and his 're-production' there, 'Themselves', was the representative of the rival Herod line, who hoped to replace the Agrippa line (Rev 2:9, the Tigranes line; 10:3 Herod of Chalcis).

holy (*hagios*) The David, while celibate in the monastery or in a service, was called 'the Holy One' (Rev 3:7, Rev 20:6). When he was not in the monastery, his crown prince acted for him, and as a 'reproduction' was called *hagioi*, the 'Holy Ones' (translated 'saints'). The word in the plural means the David crown prince. In Rev 13:7 this was James the brother of Jesus, then in Rev 11:18, 13:10 Barnabas Joses, the next brother who was given the title when Jesus and James parted, then in Rev 5:8, 8:4, 14:12, 16:6, 17:6, 18:20, 24, 19:8 Jesus Justus. The use of the plural in 18:20 and 19:8, the latter at the same time as the use of the title 'Lamb' (19:7, 9) shows that while the heir of David became the 'Lamb' on the death of his father, he was treated as the crown prince, 'the holy ones', until his coronation. The word in these verses is not an indication that Jesus was still alive. The use of 'holy ones' in the Sinaiticus text in Rev 22:21, the last word in the book, has proved baffling, as shown by the alterations of the text to 'All'. But it would mean that another celibate could now act as the substitute, in the capacity of Christian priest.

With 'all', 'holy ones' means the Herod crown prince (Rev 8:3). The 'Holy City' was the David acting as the celibate superior of Gentile dynasts. See **city**.

The word 'holy' means a lay celibate, not a priest, so 'holy angels' was a contradiction, as 'angels' were of the class of priests. It means a laicised priest, Jonathan Annas as abbot at Qumran in Rev 14:10. 'The Holy Despot' of Rev 6:10 was Agrippa, as Herod was 'the Despot'.

When the Trisagion ('Holy, Holy, Holy') of the seraphim was con ducted in Rev 4:8 at the coronation of Agrippa (based on Isa 6:3), it referred to Matthew Annas who was a bishop to celibates in west, centre and east.

David as 'the Holy One' in the monastery taught monastic initiates in the north-east quarter of the grounds, which was called 'holy' in the scheme of four divisions reflected in Rev 22:11.

honey (*meli*) The symbol of 'the land flowing with milk and honey', (Num 13:27). Salvation seen as entering the Promised Land, a doctrine accepted by Diaspora Jews and some Gentile converts of the mission such as James Niceta (Rev 10:9, 10).

honour (*timē*) The Greek word also means 'value, price', and it is used for a play on words, apparently 'honour', but in the pesher the 'price', the initiation fee charged as a 'ransom for the soul', see p.26.

It was charged to married Jews, who paid it at 3 p.m. (Rev 4:9) and to fee paying Gentiles, who paid it at 4 p.m. with the other 'unclean' money, the payments for forgiveness of sins (Rev 5:12). But Gentiles of provinces 11 and 12 did not pay fees, the original reason being that they were not given initiation. The saying 'A prophet in his own (*idios*) country (*patris*) does not have honour' (John 4:44) has the pesher: 'a Jerusalem bishop does not receive fees from Gentiles of the grade of *idios* (grade 11, equal to Jewish married men with their own property)'.

The fees of Jews were paid to Herod, 'Timaeus' (Mark 10:46). The fees of initiated Gentiles of 'the Tribes' were originally paid to the David as 'Jacob', but when Jesus did not accept them, they were given to the Herod crown prince, 'All the tribes' (Rev 1: 7). The name 'Timothy' includes a play on *timē*. In the lists of seven paid ministers in Rev 5:12 and 7:12, the position of the 'Wednesday', the fourth, was that of 'price', and James Niceta held this position in the seven letters (Rev 3:1–6). He continued to pay fees, but the money was returned to him to pay the expenses of mission, according to the principle set down by Matthew, that 'workers in the Vineyard' should be paid a denarius a day (Matt 20:1–10).

horn (*keras*) 'Horns' was used as a name for Raphael the Calf after Herod took the title 'the Calf'. Raphael was a Scribe, that is a chief celibate in the monastery, at grade Qof. He was responsible for the admission of proselytes. Theudas, who took the place of the Scribe after the death of Judas Iscariot, is 'the Horns' of Rev 9:13 ('four' is not in the Sinaiticus text, but it shows knowledge of his position as 'angel 4'). 'Horn 10 (ten horns)' means the man in this position who kept uncircumcised Gentiles down at grade 10. Joazar in Rev 12:3, Judas Iscariot in Rev 13:1, Gaius Costobar Herod in Rev 17:3. Jesus, who promoted the uncircumcised to grade 7 as full initiates, was a 'Horn 7' (Rev 5:6), and Simon Magus, as 'servant of the Lamb', promoted them as far as a grade 2 lay presbyter (as in the case of Izates of Adiabene), so was a 'Horn 2' (Rev 13:11). The term is seen to mean a person in Rev 13, where 'Horns' in v.1 is the personal subject of the plural verb in v.4.

horse (*hippos*) The priest who travelled to the village or the Diaspora, sitting on the chair on the middle tier with the colour for the season attached. See pp.102–103. Plural, the senior Annas priest (Rev 9:7, 9, Jonathan Annas; Rev 9:17 Matthew Annas).

The visiting priest when seated at the table was on the west side to a superior priest (Rev 18:13), so Jesus Justus could be on a 'horse' (Rev 19:11).

hour (*hōra*) The point of time when the fulfilment of the prophecy was expected. 'Hour 1' (*mia hōra*), 1 a.m., the hour to which the Therapeuts extended.

however (*plēn*) Two words for 'nevertheless' or 'however' are used in a special sense in the gospels and Acts. *Alla*, 'nevertheless', means eastern celibate Gentiles like John Mark, and *plēn*, 'however', means western celibate Gentiles like Luke. The terms probably came from the use of the right and left hands for gestures, and the association with blessings and curses in the Covenant imagery, the left or west representing curses. In Rev 2:25, *plen* refers to Luke.

hundred and forty-four thousand (*hekaton tesserakonta tessares chiliades*) A name for Peter, who was head of Christians in province 12. See p.196.

icon (*eikōn*) A rival Caesar, to whom tribute was paid in place of the true Caesar. The 'icon of the Beast' was the Samaritan high priest Ananias, priestly head of the zealots. Ananias was appointed high priest of the Jews by Herod of Chalcis in AD 48 or 49 (Ant. 20:103). The pesher shows that Simon Magus, who used the name Ananias as a servant of the high priest (Acts 5:1, 9:12), was behind the appointment.

idol (*eidōlon*) The Roman emperor, worshipped as a god. **Gold idol** (Rev 9:20), the emperor Claudius given initiation, as an honorary member of the class of priests.

idol-food (*eidōlothyta*) The food at the Roman ceremonies at which Caesar was worshipped as a god (Rev 2:14, 20).

if (*ei*) Used to introduce a question. With *tis*, 'Anyone', Herod, it means that his position was disputed.

if now (*ean*) Translated 'if now' to distinguish from *ei*. It means 'when' in the pesher.

in front of (*enōpion*) As one of the four prepositions (*enōpion, enanti, emprosthen, opisō*) meaning the compass points, *enōpion* has the pesher sense of 'north', and a place denoted by this word was a 'north', where a Raphael or his equal stood, since Raphael was the archangel for the north. The positions were on the middle tier of a three-storeyed structure, or the dais edge of a two-storeyed, both being the place for a levite. On the middle tier, 'in front of the throne' (Rev 1:4, 4:5, 6, 10, 7:9, 11, 8:3, 14:3, 20:12) means the central position, and 'in front of God' (Rev 3:2, 8:2, 4, 9:13, 11:16, 12:10, 16:19) means the east side of the centre (since 'God', or the village priest, sat on this side when only two leaders presided). 'In front of the Lamb' (Rev 5:8) or 'the four Living Ones' (Rev 14:3) or 'in front of the woman' (Rev 12:4) means the west side of the centre for the lay leader.

in order that (*hina*) Used as a play on *hē-N*, 'the N', the letter for the novice grade 8. In the text, it refers to a novice or pre-initiate, or to an action concerning the congregation. In Rev 13:13, the word is used before *kai*, making it the end of a sentence in the pesher; it means 'the letter Nun'.

incense (*thymiata*) The substance burned in the censer, which when stirred up gave 'fire by night' and when dampened down gave smoke, likened to the 'cloud by day'. In the Exodus, the priest leading the nomads used a censer as a guide. When used in the place of worship, the smoke was said to carry the petitions of celibates up to heaven (Rev 5:8, 8:3, 4). In Rev 18:13 it stood for the servant who placed this substance at the centre of the high table.

inner body (*nephroi*) Like 'belly' and 'stomach', means the sign of a category of low grade members of the 'body', equal to Gentiles (Rev 2:23).

intellect (*gnōmē*) A school for celibate Gentiles of Dan attached to a Sadducee school. In Rev 17:13, during the

308

leadership disputes of AD 70, Gaius claimed headship, but shortly afterwards the schools reverted to Agrippa (Rev 17:17).

iron (*sidēros*) The ascetic discipline of the Egyptian Therapeuts, called the 'iron furnace of Egypt'. In Rev 18:12 the middle level of the school system. The superior in the school had the 'iron rod' (Rev 2:27).

island (*nēsos*) Islands of the Mediterranean were used as places of retreat for celibate women of the order of Asher, whose main centre was the harbour island of Tyre. The female head of the order of Asher was called 'island' (Rev 6:14) or 'Every island' (Rev 16:20), (Bernice). Consequently islands were used by Gentiles of the order of Asher, such as John Aquila, who after his return from Rome was appointed a leader of the Gentile community on Patmos (Rev 1:9).

Titus, head of the 'sons of Ham', had equal status, and could use an island retreat as well as the mainland. His island was Crete, to which Paul's Epistle to Titus was written.

Israel (*Israēl*) The 'sons of Israel' were the members of class C, celibate graduates (see p.177. This name is given to the third class of members in the Scrolls (CD 14:4, 5) (Rev 2:14, 21:12). In Rev 2: 14, 7:4, it means the celibate congregation in Herodian monasteries, the class C 'precious stones', led by members of the royal family.

ivory (*elephantinos*). In Rev 18:13 in the phrase 'Every ivory vessel', a reference to the new third Herod in the threesome of kinsmen. See **eighth**. The name indicates that, being over province 8, based on the Tiber Island as the superior one of the retreat islands, he was also over the island of Elephantine on the Nile, where there was a long established Jewish colony.

jacinth (*hyakinthos*) The jewel representing the eleventh pew of the congregation (Rev 21:20, see p.167). The occupant of this pew, if female, was the head of grade 11, Sisters. In AD 41, when Rev 9:17 took place, this was Queen Helena of Adiabene, who had become a convert through the mission (see p.85).

jasper (*iaspis*) From the list of precious stones representing members of the congregation in Rev 21:18–20, the occupant of the royal pew in the centre of the first row. Agrippa II in Rev 4:3.

Jerusalem (*Hierousalēm*, singular form) In the gospels, 'Jerusalem' in the singular form means the literal Jerusalem, or, more exactly, the Essene Gate on the south side of Jerusalem and its related annexe on the Mount of Olives. (See *Jesus the Man*, Chapter 7.) Both were called 'Jerusalem', hence the expression 'Jerusalem, Jerusalem' in Luke 13:34. (In the plural form, 'Jerusalem' means Qumran.) In Rev 21:2, 10, 'the Holy City, new (*kainē*) Jerusalem' means the head of Gentile monastics (that is, the David) in the cathedral and hermitage at Ephesus, the latter reproducing the identity of the Gentile monastery which had been formed in the Mount of Olives annexe. It was *kainos*, for the Christian New Covenant. Similarly in Rev 3:12.

Jesus (*Iēsous*) This name (Greek for Joshua) was chosen for the son of Joseph (Luke 1:31) because there was no further patriarchal name in the succession of 'Jacob' and 'Joseph', titles that had been adopted by the descendants of David when they became involved in the Diaspora mission under Herod the Great (see p.29). Mary was already the 'Miriam' in the Exodus liturgy of the Therapeuts, and 'Joshua' came from the same story. A Chief Therapeut who was successor to his 'Moses' was a 'Joshua', and the name was used for him as a levitical celibate. 'Joshua Barabbas', the other 'Jesus' of Matt 27:16, was the Chief Therapeut Theudas, called 'son/servant' (*bar*) of 'Abba', the Father, who was Sariel as abbot to Therapeut communities. The Chief Therapeut when in the village class acted as a presbyter, a 'Joshua', blowing the trumpet on Friday evenings. This name was chosen for the boy Jesus to make him equal to his mother, who was also a presbyter. 'Miriam' and 'Joshua' were equals as subordinates of 'Moses'.

Jew (*Ioudaios*) In its pesher sense, this word does not simply mean 'Jew', but 'the head of the class of circumcised married Gentiles'. The Herods had originally been Gentiles, but had become Jewish, with the circumcised choosing to live as either ascetics or in the married state. The third Herod represented the latter, who were called 'Jews', because they lived in all respects like ordinary Jews. The head of this class was called 'the Jews', using the plural of reproduction. In the gospel period, 'the Jews' meant the tetrarch Antipas. He was succeeded, after his dismissal, by Herod of Chalcis, who was 'the Jews in Damascus' of Acts 9:22. Then after his death in AD 48 or 49 the false Herod supported by the Damascus community was called 'the Jews' (Rev 2:9).

John (*Iōannēs*) See **grace**.

jubilate (*agalliaō*) To act at the solstice service at 3 p.m. From the association of harvest with the June solstice. At 3 p.m. the villagers finished work and handed over the harvest, and the handing over of money at the Pentecost service was patterned on this (Rev 19:7). In Luke 10:21, used at the December solstice pentecontad.

key (*kleis*) The key to and control of the vaults where monastic common property was stored. 'The key of the deep well of the abyss' (Rev 9:1), was the key to the vault at the north of the Qumran vestry. 'The keys of Death and of Hades' (Rev 1:18) meant the key of the burial cave of the Davids, where Gentile monastic property was stored (see **Hades**). 'The key of David' (Rev 3:7) was used for the shared property of village Essenes, a practice continued by Peter (Acts 2:44).

Rev 3:7 describes the ceremony of the key of David. Three men were involved: David, an acolyte ('No One'), and a deputy. A ritual was performed ensuring that the money would not be taken. David opened the depository, then the acolyte closed it, checking the contents. The key was kept by the deputy. Then the acolyte opened it the next time, and he was able to see that nothing had been taken by the deputy. Peter as the substitute for Jesus in this ceremony (Rev 3:8) was given the 'keys' (Matt 16:19).

king (*basileus*) This word does not mean king, but was used for a person in the position of lay member of the levitical class, not a true levite, but as a high ranking celibate accepted into the class, the king being one example. The Chief Therapeut could be called 'king' (Rev 9:11). Consequently the title was used by Herod in a lesser position. The term could be used of Archelaus, who was only an ethnarch (Matt 2:21).

The title was claimed by anti-Herodians for the David (Matt 2:2, John 19:19), but disputed by the ruling Herods. Only after Agrippa II lost some power following the fall of Jerusalem, was this title given to the David (Rev 19:16).

Herod in this capacity was in his third class, and could be represented in it by a third Herod. Using the plural of reproduction, he was called 'kings' (*basileis*). His full title was 'kings of the Earth', meaning the head of a community, subordinate of Herod in his second role as 'the Earth'. This was Antipas Herod in Rev 1:5, 6:15, and after he was murdered in AD 67 he was succeeded in the position of 'kings of the Earth' by Gaius Costobar Herod (Rev 17:2, 18, 18: 3, 9, 19:19) and a later successor, a Herod relative holding the family property (Rev 21:24).

kingdom (*basileia*) A Jewish celibate community under a leader of levitical status. See **king**. 'The kingdom of God' meant the Jewish celibate communities under Sadducee doctrine, to which Gentiles could be attached. The 'kingdom of the Beast' (Rev 16:10, 17:17) was the Jewish celibate system of Diaspora Essenes who had become zealot. The 'kingdom of Heaven' was the Herodian system.

knock (*krouō*) To act like a priest returning from the outside world to the vestry (Luke 12:36, Acts 12:16, Rev 3:20).

know (*oida*) To recognise as a member.

knowledge (*ginōskō*, translated 'to have knowledge') To have the education of gnostics.

labour (*kopos*) The ascetic discipline of a Sadducee (Rev 2:2, 14: 13).

lake (*limnē*) The Dead Sea (Luke 8:22, Rev 19:20, 20:10).

lamb (*arnion*) A title of all the Davids. Each one held it from the time his father died, and for the rest of his life. Jacob-Heli in Rev 12:11. Jesus in Rev 5:6, 8, 6:1,16, 7:9, 10, 14, 17, 12:11, 13:8, 11, 14:1, 4, 10, 15:3, 17:14. Jesus Justus in Rev 19:7,9. Jesus III in 21: 9, 14, 22, 23, 27, 22:1, 3. It was the preferred title of the Davids under the Sadducee priest in Ephesus. The image was derived from the Suffering Servant imagery used of themselves by Essene celibates, who believed that their ascetic practices would make atonement for others, and should replace animal sacrifices (1QS 8:1–3).

The David king had originally been the 'Lion', a military leader equal to a bishop. But in the fifth century BC, after the return from Babylon, he had been forced to give up his military role, retaining the position of an honorary levite, one who had no armies but could officiate in the sanctuary like a levite, ruling 'not by might, nor by power, but by my spirit' (Zech 4:6). His warrior image had to change, and he became a 'Lamb', going up one grade but standing in the same place to say the noon prayer.

As 'Lamb' he was equal to a Phanuel, both being ministers to the uncircumcised, wearing white in their higher position, and scarlet on the chancel step (see **scarlet**). In the latter position he was 'the Lamb slain' (Rev 5:6).

lamp (*lampas*) See **eyes**. It meant Phanuel's lamp, and it was used by Joseph as a teacher of Gentiles in Rev 8:10. 'Lamp 7' (Rev 4:5) was the day lamp corresponding to the Menorah, whose lights were turned up to indicate the hour. But the day hours began at 6 a.m. 'Lamp 7' indicated 1 p.m., the seventh hour. This hour was used for prayer as an alternative beginning from noon, especially in the practice of the Therapeuts.

lampstand (*lychnia*) The Menorah, the seven branched candlestick, standing for the synagogue. During the night a Menorah was placed on the edge of the dais in the chancel, a spot corresponding to a Hellenist synagogue, and it was in front of this lampstand that Jesus appeared in Rev 1:13.

The Menorah burned during the hours of 9 p.m. to 3 a.m., those of the night by ascetic standards. This was six hours, and it had seven lamps. It appears that each was turned up more brightly for an hour to show the time. The first burned from 9 to 10 p.m., and the next five from 10 to 11, 11 to midnight, midnight to 1 a.m., 1 to 2, and 2 to 3. This left the seventh light, 'lampstand 7' to be turned up at 3 a.m. It burned for an hour, marking both 3 a.m. and 4 a.m. as the end of the night. The hour of 3 a.m. was counted as the start of day for higher celibates, and they said prayers for dawn at this time, while the hour of 4 a.m. was counted as the start of day for village pilgrims. Thus, 'lampstand 7' is an indication of time, either 3 a.m. or 4 a.m. In Rev 1:12, 3 a.m., and in Rev 1:19, 2:1, 4 a.m.

'Lampstand 2' (Rev 11:4) is also an indication of time, 10 p.m, the second light lit at this time and burning until 11 p.m.

lantern (*lychnos*) The lamp used by Raphael. See **eyes**. It was used for lighting the Menorah, the *lychnia*, which burned at night (Luke 11:33). The hour of 4 a.m. was both that of Gabriel-Phanuel 'the Light' (*phōs*) to villagers, and also the final hour for the seventh light of the Menorah (see **lampstand**), so at this hour the combined *phōs lychnou* appeared, 'the Light of a lantern' (Rev 18:23, 22:5).

Rev 11:33 shows that the *lychnos* was used in the 'crypt', and in Rev 21:23 it was used at 4 p.m., not 4 a.m., for teaching given in the crypt under the chancel step.

last(*eschatos*) A word referring to grade 12, the last and lowest of the grades, and the order for the uncircumcised. The Last One (Rev 1:17, 2:8) was Peter, who was the leader of Christians, Gentiles coming from grade 12. See **hundred and forty-four thousand**, and p.196.

The 'seven last plagues' (Rev 15:1, 21:9) means a time calculation concerning the Eschaton, originally the year 4000 in AD 60, which in the calculations of the Vineyard mission was the 'twelfth hour' from 1 BC (pp.230–231).

length (*mēkos*) The north–south dimension of the vestry, the 12 cubits running either from the dais edge northwards or from the chancel screen northwards (Rev 21:16, see pp.152, 163 and **breadth**).

leopard (*pardalis*) Sign of an Ethiopian, as an allusion to Jer 13:23: 'Can the Ethiopian change his skin or the leopard change his spots?'. The campaign against the sons of Ham, represented by Ethiopians (Acts 8:27) was to begin in AD 36, see p.210. The war leader of the campaign used a leopard sign (Rev 13:2).

life (*zōē*) Initiation, given by the Gabriel or his equal in the monastery. 'Truth' was taught by the Sadducee, and 'the Way' was the head of pilgrims, so Jesus claimed to be 'the Way, the Truth and the Life' (John 14:6).

lifeless (*nekros*, translated 'lifeless' to distinguish from *thanatos* 'death') A person at grade 11, the lowest grade but one, the position of a Jewish married man, who lost his spiritual 'life' when he engaged in sex (11QT 45:11–12, a man who had recently had sexual intercourse is not allowed into the temple precincts). When temporarily abstaining from sex he was a Nazirite, at grade 8, but went down to 11 when 'in the body'. The David was in this class while in the married or worldly state (Rev 1:18). James while the David was called *nekros* in Luke 7:11–17.

The plural of reproduction was used of the David crown prince, who was head of grade 11 (Rev 1:5). In Judea, James the brother of Jesus remained head of Nazirites in both their grades. The term 'the lifeless ones' was applied to him as head of Jewish Christians (Rev 11:18, 14:13), and to a subsequent head of Jewish Christians (Rev 20:5, 12, 13).

light (*phōs*) 'The Light' was the priest Phanuel who said prayers at dawn on behalf of Michael, or Michael himself 'in the body'. John the Baptist was 'the Light' in John 1:8. Phanuel in Rev 18:23, or an equal in Rev 21:24.

light-giver (*phōstēr*) A celibate acting in the place of Phanuel (Rev 21:11).

lightning (*astrapē*) A name for Phanuel when acting as 'Moses', giving the reading from the Law section of the Old Testament. He was one of the group 'Lightning, Thunder, Earthquake' which were associated with the giving of the Law on Mount Sinai. (Rev 4:5.) The Chief Magus as a Gabriel could also act in the position of a Phanuel in a celibate community (Rev 8:5, 11:19, 16:18). Simon Magus is called 'Lightning' in Luke 10:18, 11:36, 17:24, Matt 24:27, 28:3.

like (*homoios*) A servant, who acted on behalf of his master, often using the same name. Or a student of a teacher, as the student became like the master. The rule about the distance between servants and masters applied to their grades.

likeness (*homoiōma*) A successor, who had risen from servant to master. In Rev 9:7, the 'likenesses' (plural of reproduction) of John the Baptist, 'the Locusts', was

Jonathan Annas. The fact that Jonathan succeeded the Baptist is given in *Clem. Hom.* 2, 24, where he appears as Dositheus (the same name as Nathanael, John 1:45, who was Jonathan; all names mean 'God gave').

linen (*linon*), **fine linen** (*byssinos*) The white linen garments worn by celibates on the Essene model (War 2:123). *Linon* was worn by the permanent celibate Agrippa II (Rev 15:6), and *byssinos* by dynasts, male (Rev 18:12, 19:14) and female (Rev 18:16, 19:8).

lion (*leōn*) Originally, the ancient title of King David, used of his successors in the position of the fourth living creature. But Herod took over this position as well as that of the Calf, and he was the Lion of Rev 10:3, 13:2, while David was 'the Lion out of the tribe of Judah' (Rev 5:5). The 'Lion' was the king in his lower lay capacity, that of warrior, associated with the south. He was head of the lowest class, D, and he presided over their meetings on the chancel step. In the plural of reproduction, 'Lions' meant the head of the Therapeuts of Egypt, who took the warrior function, and was called 'Living One 4' (Rev 9:8).

little (*mikros*) See **great**. In the Gentile system, this word alludes to Little Dan (the part of the 'tribe' of Dan whose centre was at Joppa), and to Gentiles of Dan, the sons of Ham, who were originally permitted only to go to grade 11. In Rev 13:16, 'All the little ones' means Agrippa as head of the Joppa meeting place, where some of his property was stored. He lost control of the centre to Simon Magus, who became 'Simon the Tanner' in Joppa (Acts 9:43).

Living One (*zōon*) The Priest-Pope as initiator. Matthew Annas in Rev 4:9, 10. In the plural of reproduction, the Chief Therapeut.

locust (*akris*) The food of John the Baptist as a hermit at Mird (Mark 1:6). Locusts were eaten by Essene ascetics and there were rules on the method of cooking (CD 12:1415). John was consequently called 'Locusts'.

look (*blepō*) To look sideways at a person sitting or standing beside. Permitted to people belonging to the same grade, whereas 'to see' (*eidon*) was the verb for looking towards a superior. In Rev 1:12 *eidon* is used for the seer looking towards the chancel, but *blepō* when he turned to look at the person beside him. In Rev 11:9 Matthew Annas 'looked' as he entered the chancel from the south, a sign of the equality he adopted with other ministers.

loose (*lyō*) To release from the state of being 'sealed', unable to be read (for a book) or heard (for a person). The seal on the closed part of the New Testament, at the back section of the Septuagint, was loosed when the tie was released and the book able to be read (Rev 5:2). A person who had been in the lay state was 'loosed' when he became a full celibate (Rev 9:14). To be 'loosed out of sins' (Rev 1:5) means 'to go up from the married state to the celibate state'. In Rev 9:14, 20:3,7, an ascetic who was 'loosed' was promoted to a monastery.

lord (*kyrios*) A person acting in the position of the priest in the village. It might be Sariel ('lord the God', Rev 4:8), or Phanuel (Rev 4:11, 7:14) or a distinguished layman such as the David when in the village (Luke 10:39). It was not an exalted title. David acted in the position in two grades, that of Sariel and that of Phanuel, so was called 'lord of lords'. It is used of Jesus in Rev 17:14 (where 'king of kings' does not refer to Jesus, as it is preceded by 'and', beginning a new sentence). In Rev 19:16 it again means the David.

love (*agapē*, and verb *agapaō*) (To hold) the sacred meal, the Agape, of celibates of the Therapeut type, where men and women ascetics were present. A Gentile dynast acting as 'eunuch' could attend on behalf of the Bride, in the seat of the 'Beloved'. This was the position of the Beloved Disciple, John Mark, whose sacred meals are referred to in Rev 2:4.

In AD 46 Peter completed his transition to the celibate

life, presumably as a widower. He then attended the Gentile Agape meals of which Agrippa II was the formal head (Rev 1:5), and of which Jesus was the actual presiding head (Rev 3:9). In the gospel period Jesus had used the verb *agapaō* to him, but he had declined to use it, preferring *philō*, as a 'friend' was a married man (John 21:1516).

lust (*epithymeō*) To act as a Herod, characterised, since Herod the Great, by sexual or financial excess (Rev 9:6).

make (*poieō*) To hold a religious service.

male (*arsen*) A word with the special sense of the Messiah. The Hebrew equivalent is used of the Messiah in 1QH 3:6. In Rev 12:5, 13 the term refers to Jesus when accepted as legitimate by a Sadducee high priest, in Rev 12:5, at his boyhood initiation at the age of twelve, and in Rev 12:13, at his manhood initiation at the age of twenty-three (an event which is dealt with in the pesher of Luke 2:41–52).

man (*anthrōpos*) Gabriel ('Man of God') or his equal Sariel in the lesser of his roles, used when he came to the village and stood in the place of the levite on the equivalent of the dais edge. Here, he was 'Man' who was one grade below 'God'. Matthew Annas as a Sariel the equal of Gabriel (the position the Annas priests received in AD 6) was 'the Man' of the four Living Creatures (Rev 4:7). The 'Son of Man', David, stood on the step before him (Rev 1:13). In Rev 13:18 Simon Magus claiming to be a Gabriel was 'a Man'.

The reproduction of Gabriel in this position was called 'the Men'. This was Herod, who was a reproduction Gabriel in the higher position also. As 'the Men', Herod was head of the Herodian monastery at Masada in Idumea. Agrippa I appears under this name in Rev 8:11 and 4. In the latter verse it was at the time he attempted suicide 'in a tower in Idumea', as Josephus says (*Ant.* 18:147). Idumea was the home district of the Herods.

The Agrippas kept the position of head of Masada up to the late sixties, when Agrippa II lost control of it, probably allowing his sister Bernice to take it over, and the title was then used of the new head, Eleazar Ben Jair, head of the Sicarii, who is 'the Men' of Rev 16:2, 8, 21. He also inherited from Agrippa the title of 'tyrant', as the head of a monastery had despotic rule. Agrippa was the Tyrannus of the Ephesus school in Acts 19:9, where Paul taught, and Eleazar Ben Jair was called the 'tyrant' of Masada.

many (*polloi*) The council of the Many (*rabbim*), the organisational structure referred to in the Scrolls (1QS 6:8, etc). It was a council of celibates of class C. Herod as king was the head of the council, and is called 'the Many' (*hoi polloi*, Mark 6:2, John 2:23, Matt 7:13, Rev 10:11). There were 100 in the council (*War* 2:145, the Essenes never pass sentence in a court of less than 100 members), and a play on the letter Qof, numerical value 100, arose from this.

Since full proselytes were placed under Herod as superior, 'Many waters' was the council of proselytes or their equals, as 'waters' meant grade 9 baptisms to which they were initially limited.

mark (*charagma*) The letter for the grade, in the Hebrew form used by the zealots (see p.183). Placed on the food dish, the 'hand', (Rev 13:16), and by Herodian zealots on a badge in the place of a phylactery on the forehead (Rev 14:9).

marvellous (*thaumastos*) Refers to the 'miracle' of a change of calendar and doctrine, using the symbolism of crossing the Red Sea as a conversion of life. A calendar alteration saved the prophecy and chronology, so the man who made the change was like one who worked miracles (Rev 13:3, 15:1, 3, 17:7).

middle (*mesos*) The lower half of a 2 cubit circle within which prayers were said. In Rev 1:13, 5:6b on the chancel step; in Rev 4:6, 5:6a, 6:6, 7:17 on the middle tier.

mid-heaven (*mesouranēma*) The middle tier of a three-storeyed structure of which the upper tier contained 'Heaven' (Rev 8:13, 14: 6, 19:17).

might (*kratos*) The king's priest, the priest originally of the third rank who represented the king, putting the crown on him at his coronation, understood to be not his superior but acting in place of the king himself. It includes a play on *krateō* 'seize', meaning 'embrace'. 'All-mighty', *pantokratōr*, was the king's priest to the Herods, 'All'.

month (*mēn*) A Julian month. Month 3 ('3 months'), March; month 5 ('5 months'), · May; month 6 ('6 months'), June. The word is used on the 1st of the month. In the singular, with no number, it means the primary Julian month, January 1 (Rev 9:15, 22:2). On 'month 5', see **torment**. 'Forty-two months' means 3½ years, measured from the 1st of the Julian month, see p.243.

moon (*selēnē*) A person, the female partner of 'the Sun'. As the Sun was the high priest Michael, his wife or the chief woman, who acted as Mother to Gentiles, was 'the Moon'. Luna in Latin. This was the position of Helena. *Clem. Hom.* 2, 23: 'He (John the Baptist) had thirty chief men, fulfilling the monthly reckoning of the moon, in which number was a certain woman called Helena' (elsewhere called Luna). In Rev 12:1 Elizabeth the wife of Zechariah was 'the Moon', and, when Agrippa II used the title 'Sun', his sister and consort Bernice held the title (Rev 6:12). The woman in this position acted as a teacher to Gentiles. She did so when in the Nazirite state, a form of asceticism available to women, as shown by Josephus in the case of Bernice (*War* 2:313). Nazirites did not drink wine, so when she came down to the married state, she drank wine again, but only sipping it as 'blood' (see **blood**). So 'the Moon became blood' (Rev 6:12).

In Rev 18:14 Bernice appears immediately after the

list of twenty-nine male ministers. This reflects the structure described in *Clem. Hom.* above.

morning (*prōïnos*) Part of the title 'the Morning Star', used of the Davids. Their duty was to lead the first prayer of day for villagers, at 4 a.m.

Moses (*Mōüses*) A name for the Chief Therapeut in one of his roles, as is indicated by Philo in his description of the Exodus liturgy, in which the leader plays the part of Moses and the female leader plays the part of Miriam. (*Contemp. Life* 87). The Gabriel priest was called 'Moses' (Acts 7:20), and could act also as a Phanuel in the village. The Chief Therapeut as a Phanuel was a 'Moses', whereas as a Raphael he was a 'Joshua'. In Rev 15:3 'Moses' means the newly appointed Chief Therapeut in Agrippa's Roman party. See **tribe**.

mountain (*oros*) A 'mountain' was a hermitage, under a discipline like that of the Therapeuts, whose Exodus imagery used a 'Mount Sinai', but one which claimed independence of the ruling Herods. The vestry at Qumran had this status while an anti-Herodian party used it (Mark 9:2). After AD 34 this party established their main centre in Caesarea, in Samaria, and the 'Mountain' then meant the Samaritan anti-Agrippa leader, either Sadducee, believing in peace with Rome, or Magian zealot, believing in war with Rome. 'Mountains' was the title of the head of the Samaritans. In AD 50–51 the Samaritan high priest Ananias, allied with Jonathan Annas, acted independently of Agrippa II, who was abroad. See **fury**. Ananias is 'the Mountains' of Rev 6:15, and Jonathan Annas is 'the Mountains' of Rev 6:16. In Rev 16:20 'Mountains were not found' refers to the death of the Samaritan high priest Ananias at the outbreak of the Jewish war (*War* 2:441). In AD 70, in Ephesus, after the death of the Samaritan high priest Ananias, Gaius Costobar Herod continued the Samaritan tradition, opposing Agrippa, and was called 'Mountains' (Rev 17:9). As head of the Ephesus hermitage, in province 7, he was called 'Mountains 7', and the allusion to Rome came from the fact that the Ephesus hermitage was treated as the superior school for Gentiles from Rome. They went from grade 10 in Rome up to grade 7 in Ephesus.

Rev 8:8 'a great Mountain of fire' refers to the establishment of such a hermitage in Rome after the dismissal of Archelaus, in AD 9. This 'great Mountain' was brought back to Ephesus in AD 112 (Rev 21:10), when monasteries were expelled from Rome, and after the death of Agrippa II. 'Mount Zion' in Rev 14:1 means the Mount of Olives hermitage, attached to the Essene Gate in Jerusalem, which was under the Sadducee Matthew.

mourning (*penthos*) A short-term Nazirite vow, taken by married persons, male and female, in which they separated from society.

mouth (*stoma*) The lower half of the noon circle, which was likened to a face, with 'eyes' and 'mouth'. It was the place at which teaching was given. 'Out of the mouth(s)' (Rev 9:17), on its east side. The word indicates a place of teaching.

much (*polys*) See **many**.

murder (*phonos*) The form of zealotry of the Therapeuts. Theudas-Barabbas was a 'murderer' (Mark 15:7) (Rev 9:21).

mystery (*mystērion*) A 'mystery' was a riddling saying with a political interpretation, given in the Hellenistic world by oracles at places such as Delphi and Ephesus. Rev 17:7–14, introduced by 'I will tell you the mystery of the woman', imitates the form and its method of interpretation. A woman who acted as an oracle was called a 'mystery' (Rev 17:5). From this meaning the word came to be applied to writings with a pesher. In the Dead Sea Scrolls, Old Testament scripture is a 'mystery' (*raz* in Hebrew), and its interpretation is a *pesher*. In Mark 4:11, 'to you (the Twelve) is given the mystery of the

Kingdom of God', means that John Mark, 'the Twelve' was to sponsor the first of the gospels, that of John. Matthew's Sayings (*logia*, see pp.527–528) are the 'mystery of God' of Rev 10:7, and the 'mystery' of Rev 1:20 is the Book of Revelation itself. In the latter verse, Revelation is said to be 'the mystery of the seven stars' (Star 7, Jesus Justus as an acolyte), meaning that it is intended to form the final section of the New Testament, corresponding to the Writings, which would be read by lower grade persons such as acolytes.

naked (*gymnos*) Married, as from the point of view of celibates, sex required forbidden nakedness. 'Not naked' means celibate. (Rev 16:15). Peter in AD 33 was 'naked', that is married (John 21:7). As a man at grade 9, that of baptism, could marry, a celibate who had been reduced to grade 9 for a punishment was 'naked' (Mark 14:51), as was a proselyte who remained at grade 9 by eastern rules (Rev 3:17).

name (*onoma*) A celibate in the levitical class was one of the 'men of a name' of the Scrolls (1QSa 2:2, 8, 11, 1QM 2:6, 3:4). Such a man received a new name at graduation.

nation (*ethnos*) One of the four classes of uncircumcised Gentiles, 'tribes, tongues, peoples and nations' for whom the four gospels were written. The 'nations/Gentiles' (using both senses of Hebrew *goiim*) were their lowest class, meaning men who had chosen to retain their Gentile identity, that of 'Shem, Ham and Japheth', without joining one of the Jewish 'tribes'. Their superior was Herod as 'Noah', in his Rome centre, and they used the Noah's ark symbolism in their baptisms. Agrippa I as 'Noah' was called 'the Gentiles/nations' in Acts 10:45, and it is seen in this episode that the Judean headquarters of 'the nations' was in Caesarea (Rev 11:2). In world terms, 'the nations' were Roman Gentiles. In his role as 'Noah' Agrippa was at the level of deacon. Under him were Shem, at the level of initiate, and Ham and Japheth at the level of pre-initiate. Luke, head of Japheth, went up 'out of the body' to be equal to a deacon, and his gospel is characterised as that of 'the Gentiles/nations'.

Luke replacing Agrippa I is called 'nations' in Rev 10:11. 'Every nation' means the Herod crown prince, Timothy, acting for Herod (Rev 7:9, 14:6). A Herod who was acting in the place of the crown prince was *panta ta ethnē*, 'All the nations' this was Archelaus Herod in Rev 12:5, Gaius Costobar Herod in Rev 14:8, 15:4, 18:3, 23. The Hellenised Herod of whom the writers approved was called 'nations' in Rev 21:24, 26, 22:2.

near (*engys*) A term arising from the method of intercalation of the solar calendar, when one party intercalated 3½ years earlier than another (p.242). During these years, the same day had a double date, one for the party that had intercalated, the other for the party that had not. (This point is important for the date of the Crucifixion, see *Jesus the Man*, Chronology.) One date was then 'near' another, in the sense that they were side by side on a list giving both dates (Rev 1:3, 22:10).

need (*chreia*) The welfare tithes paid by village Essenes, described in CD 14:12–22. The earnings of three days of the thirty day month were to be given as tithes, and of these, two days' earnings were to be given for welfare, for the support of the indigent. The Christians abolished these as they were part of the Jewish priestly tithing system (Rev 21:23, 22:5).

neither (*oude*) A play on *ou-de*, 'not D', using *de* for the letter of the fourth class of members. A person who was 'not D' was a 'C', of the third class, that of celibates and the Herodian congregation.

nevertheless (*alla*) See **however**.

new (*kainos*) The New Covenant in the version of Matthew Annas established in Antioch in AD 43 (Acts 11:26) and using the name 'Christian'. See **Covenant**. A 'new song' was a hymn written for its form of worship, used in the informal part of the service when new compositions could be heard (Rev 14:3, 5:9). The word is used to mean 'Christian'. In Rev 2:17 the 'new name', 'Christian' was written on Peter's voting pebble in order to show his party.

Nicolaitans (*Nikolaitēs*) The party of Nicolaus-Blastus, servant of Izates, the chief circumcised proselyte. Nicolaus is named as a proselyte in Acts 6:5. A proselyte was a Gentile who had become Jewish by being circumcised and keeping all the ritual laws. Nicolaus was the recipient of the letter to Laodicea, and was condemned in two other letters (Rev 2:6, 15). His Jewish doctrine was shown by his being 'neither cold nor hot', that is, observing the Jewish equinox feasts only, and not the Julian calendar with its feasts in winter and summer.

night (*nyx*) In the nominative, a Raphael, the levite for midnight. A zealot levite in Rev 8:12, 21:25, 22:5.

no longer (*ouketi*) The end of the eighty years of 'Exodus' and 'Holy War', when the Promised Land had been possessed, and there was no more journeying. The term was used in September AD 43, at the September occurrence of the year 3980 south solar, the end of the eighty years of Herod the Great's original scheme (Rev 10:6). It was used again at the end of one of the revised forms of the expectation, changed to AD 70–71 when the exile of Herod's court from Jerusalem was interpreted as 'entering the Promised Land' of a Diaspora centred form of Judaism (Rev 18:11, 14).

no one (*oudeis*) The chief acolyte of a particular celibate centre, who could stand on the upper or middle tier to assist the priest, but was to be treated as 'No One' ('Nemo'). In Jerusalem and Judea this was the David crown prince, and James the brother of Jesus was the 'No One' of Luke 4:24, Mark 10:18, Rev 14:3, 15:8. In Ephesus it was the Herod crown prince, who was 'No One' in the description of the locking ceremony in Rev 3:7, and the acolyte in Rev 5:3 and Rev 7:9. See

sanctuary on the death of James, 'No One', in Rev 15:8.

nor (*oute*) *Oute*, normally meaning 'nor', is used as a play on 'not T' (*ou-te*), that is, not using the western shape of the initiation mark, a T, but the eastern shape, an X; and eastern customs. The word applied especially to Nicolaus-Blastus the proselyte (Rev 9:20, 21, 3: 16). 'Nor cold...nor hot' (Rev 3:15), the eastern winter and summer, beginning at the September and March equinoxes, not December and June. 'Nor' was used also for an object marked with the eastern X; in Rev 5:3,4 the lectern.

not (*ou, mē*) Both words mean 'not', but when there are two in succession, as may happen for grammatical reasons in Greek, still meaning a negative, they are to be taken in the pesher as 'not not', giving a positive, not a negative. This makes an important difference.

not yet (*oupō*) A non-fulfilment of the prophecy at the expected time, making it necessary to say 'Not yet' (Rev 17:1, 12).

number (*arithmos*) The Herod crown prince, characterised by the letter Nun (N), which represented the pre-initiate congregation. The crown prince was head of pre-initiates, while the king was head of initiates upwards. The term had implications of a significant person, for Nun meant 50 in Hebrew, the number specially venerated by the Therapeuts, as it governed their calendar and religious life (Philo, *Contemp. Life* 65, 'Fifty the most sacred of numbers' and 1QS 10:4, where it appears alone in the text). The Herod crown prince appears as 'the Number' at times for calculating membership and money (Rev 5:11, 7:4, 9:16). The title was claimed by the rival Herod successor Herod of Chalcis, in Rev 13:17, 18, and used by Gaius Costobar Herod in Rev 15:2.

observe (*theōreō*) To stand or sit beside when officiating or dining, so be in a position to observe (Rev 11:11, 12).

oil (*elaion*) One of the three kinds of food tithes (wine, corn, oil) that were brought to the exiled priests at Qumran. They used the grapes and corn as the elements of their sacred meal, but the oil was left to pre-initiate novices. Monastic and dynastic Essenes did not use oil on their skin: *War* 2:123 'oil they (the Essenes) consider defiling'. Novices were in the same class as villagers of the 'House of (Olive) Oil', for whom the name Bethsaida, a play on this meaning, was used (Hebrew *beth*, 'house', *zayith*, 'olive tree'). They included celibate Gentiles of the order of Dan, who lived in every way like monastic and dynastic Essenes (Rev 6:6). This association was part of the reason for the use of the name 'Christian', alluding to the chrism of oil.

In Rev 18:13 oil appears with the substances placed on Herod's high table by the levitical servants, wine and oil on the east side. It is similarly associated with wine in Rev 6:6.

ointment (*myron*) One of the substances placed on the high table in the second place from the west, that of a prince or queen, in the list of Rev 18:13. It is associated with the queen in Mark 14:3.

olive tree (*elaia*) In Zech 4:11 'the two olive-trees' were the levite and the David, who had given up his warrior role and could officiate in the sanctuary as a lay levite, one whose duty it was to light the oil lamps in the Menorah (Exod 27:20–21). For Essenes in their subsequent development, oil was the sign of a pre-initiate (see **oil**). Pre-initiate novices were taught by a novice-master, who was at the grade of a lay presbyter, 2, so was called 'Olive-tree 2' (Rev 11:4). In March AD 44 Matthew Annas had been reduced to this status for opposing Agrippa's nationalist plans. He consequently lit 'lampstand 2', the second light on the Menorah (Rev 11:4).

on account of (*dia* + acc.) Refers to a person acting in the place of a deputy, on behalf of another.

out of (*ek*) In a position to the east of the point named. 'Out of the throne' (Rev 4:5) means the east of the central throne, and similarly all expressions with 'out of'. This is one of the points showing the position of the three men on the crosses in Mark 15:27. Of the other two beside Jesus, one was 'out of the left', the other 'out of the right'. But 'left' and 'right' were used absolutely of the positions of king and priest respectively, and the meaning was that Jesus as king was on the west, the left, Simon Magus as priest was in the centre, which was 'out of the left', and at the same time the 'right' of the two positions of king and priest. Judas was on the east, which was 'out of the right'.

outside (*exōthen*) This term is used for the 2 cubits in the north of the vestry used for the excluded (Rev 11:2, 14:20).

owing (*ophelon*) Literally, 'would that', but used as a play on *opheilō*, 'owe', to refer to the taxes that were paid by villagers at the quarters of the calendar (Rev 3:15).

palm-tree (*phoinix*) The emblem of the order of Asher, meeting in Tyre and Sidon in Phoenicia, the name of which (*Phoinikē*) came from *phoinix*. There was a connection with Jericho, especially noted for its palms (*Ant.* 14:54, 15:96), in that Jericho was the meeting place of 'Abraham's' order of Benjamin, and Phoenicia was the meeting place of 'Sarah's' order of Asher. Palm branches used at Jesus' entry to Qumran, near Jericho (John 12:13), were carried by Gentiles of Asher. The 'church' came from the order of Asher (see **church**) and the palm emblem was one of those used by the Church, marked on Peter's paten (Rev 7:9).

paradise (*paradeisos*) A Gentile 'Eden', using the pagan term. See **tree**. Gentile monasteries were like Jewish monastic schools in using the image of an Eden. The David was their 'Adam' (also called 'the Gardener', John 20:15). In Rev 2:7, Peter will 'eat...in the Paradise of

God', meaning that he will preside at communion meals in Sadducee Gentile monasteries.

But Gentile monastics were defined as equals of 'apostles', that is, Jewish monastics who had been excluded to the south-west area for sin (see **apostle**), so their 'Paradise' was equal to a Jewish latrine (see p.118). For this reason, the words of Jesus to the other 'thief' on the cross, Simon Magus, 'Today you will be with me in Paradise' (Luke 23:43) were an ironical prediction of what did happen, that they were put in the burial cave at the end of the esplanade, which was also the sabbath latrine. See *Jesus the Man*, Chapter 26.

part (*meros*) One of the three parts of the ruling triarchy, Priest, Prophet and King. 'The part' was that of Michael, part 2 for Gabriel, part 3 (*tria merē*) for the King (Rev 16:19, meaning the west and Rome). Herod as Michael had 'the part', and in Rev 21:8, the word is used for the Herod claimant who did not succeed in gaining the position after Agrippa II's death.

Patmos (*Patmos*) The local community of John Aquila. See **island**. He had been appointed leader there, and himself taught and led services, representing Jesus. But when he came to his higher meeting place, the cathedral in Ephesus, he was in the congregation only, although in the first seat (Rev 1:9–10).

peace (*eirēnē*) A name for Matthew Annas as the chief Sadducee priest advocating peace with Rome (Acts 9:31, Rev 1:4, 6:4). His position in the Annas family was that of Kohath, the levitical bishop, whose emblem was the dove in the 'Noah' imagery. When the Annas priest acted at this level, he was the 'Dove', and one of the forms of the Spirit (Mark 1:10). In Rev 6:4, 'Red' 'took peace from the earth' means that Ananus the Younger, the youngest of the Annas brothers, received the promise of the Annas high priesthood, and, against Matthew, advocated positive nationalist action on behalf of Jerusalem in the reign of Nero.

pearl (*margaritēs*) The symbol of Wisdom, as found frequently in the gnostic literature, for example the Hymn of the Pearl in the *Acts of Thomas*, an allegory of the pursuit of Wisdom. Also in Matt 7:6, and in the *The Acts of Peter and the Twelve Apostles* 3:10 (NHL). As a woman could teach Wisdom (Prov 8:1) the pearl could be the symbol of the female teacher. It is noteworthy that the name Marguerite, retained in the Faust legend, preserves this point. Helena was the Pearl to Simon Magus. In Rev 17:4 Bernice wore pearls. In Rev 18:12 the fourth in the list of village ministers. In Rev 21:21, 'pearl 12' means the male teacher of Wisdom who led monthly services.

pebble (*psēphos*) A pebble used in Roman courts for voting, and used also by a graduate celibate in community councils. A white pebble indicated a 'yes' vote for Romans, and 'white' for the ascetics had the additional meaning of Pentecost, the season when new members were admitted. Peter as a member of a higher council was given a voting pebble (Rev 2:17).

people (*laos*) One of the four classes of uncircumcised Gentiles ('tribes, tongues, peoples and nations') for whom the four gospels were written. The 'peoples' were the men of Dan, such as John Mark, who adopted a monastic life like that of the Essenes. But being Gentiles they could only be attached to the congregation. They were the highest of the four kinds of Gentiles, becoming lay presbyters. John's gospel was their product, and John Mark was a presbyter (3 John 1). But when he separated his place was taken by a member of Asher, at first James Niceta promoted from deacon to presbyter, then John Aquila, and the gospel was re-assigned to their order.

As presbyters they were equal to an Essene novice-master, and within the monastic community this was one of the duties of the David crown prince. In Acts 7:17 *ho laos* ('people, laity') means Joseph at the time James was born. In Rev 13:7 the word refers to Barnabas-Joses the next brother of Jesus, taking the place of James as crown

331

prince to Jesus because of their political differences. Barnabas was said to be sent to the Uncircumcision (the first rank of uncircumcised Gentiles) in Gal 2:9. The word means Jesus Justus in Rev 18:4. In the plural of reproduction it means the Gentile who headed this class, John Mark (associated with Barnabas in Acts 16: 37–39) in Rev 7:9, 10:11, 11:9, his successors in Rev 17:15, 21:3.

period (*chronos*) Forty years, a generation. The divisions of history according to the Exodus imagery were in sets of forty years (Acts 7: 23, 30, 36). A *chronos* finished at the end of the 'Exodus' (Acts 7: 23) and the 'Holy War' (Rev 10:6). A king's dates were counted from the beginning of his forty-year generation. In Rev 3:21 Helena was 'given a *chronos*', meaning that she was being treated like a king, as an independent bishop who was head of her order. It was possible for her, as head of the order of Asher founded by Queen Salome, to use a dating series. Queen Salome in 79 BC had become a queen regnant and there was a dating series from her, in which AD 6 was year 84. This date was observed by Anna, of the order of Asher (Luke 2:27).

The 'little period' (*mikros chronos*) was the forty years following 3920, planned for the evangelisation of Gentiles. The phrase appears at the end of the Last Jubilee, 3920 with a zero jubilee (John 7:33, 12:35, both times with *eti*) and in AD 50, the Annas Last Jubilee (Rev 6:11, again with *eti*, 'still', meaning a Roman governor who received nominal membership on this occasion). In Rev 20:3, near an *eti*, at 4000, the delayed Eschaton-Restoration.

pierce (*ekkenteō*) To make a priest an ascetic, pierced by the 'thorn' (Rev 1:7, John 19:37, on Simon Magus).

pillar (*stylos*) The two pillars supporting the platform and its extension in the vestry were called 'the pillar of cloud' on the east and 'pillar of fire' on the west (see Diagram A), and a priest or levite sat or stood on the middle tier over the pillars. They were associated with two leaders using the Exodus imagery. Phanuel, who presided at 3 a.m. prayers when the pilgrims set out on their journey, stood over the 'pillar of cloud by day', so was called 'Cloud', and a person equal to a Sariel stood over the 'pillar of fire'. This could be the Chief Therapeut, or the Herod crown prince (Rev 10:1, 4:3). Christian leaders came to substitute for the 'pillars' (Gal 2:9). Peter was a 'Pillar in the sanctuary' (Rev 3:12).

place (*topos*) An unclean place at the level of grade 9 used by women, Gentiles and other outsiders. In Rev 12:6, Luke 11:1, the underground cells at Mird.

plague (*plēgē*, verb *plēssō*) A season, as the Egyptian plagues were said to last a season. The seasons followed the Julian year, the main ones being at the solstices. See pp.215–216 on 'plague 7' (Rev 15: 1, 6, 8; 21:9) and 'from plague 3' (Rev 9:18). Without a number, 'these plagues' means another June solstice (Rev 9:20). 'To plague' (Rev 8:12) means to make Gentiles use the solstice, not permitted to attend at an equinox feast.

Among non-monastic Therapeuts, the punishment was exclusion for a season rather than excommunication, and this was to be 'under a plague'. At the restoration at the end of the season, 'the plague was healed' (Rev 13:3, 12). Simon Magus was under both kinds of discipline.

power (*dynamis*) The position of the Phanuel, servant of Michael, who was priest to the uncircumcised. He said the noon prayer in Hellenist synagogues and in attached celibate communities. Simon Magus claimed the position of a Phanuel, allowing proselytes to remain uncircumcised, and calling himself 'the Power of God, the Great One' (Acts 8:10). The deputy to the Annas high priest was a Phanuel (Rev 12:10). The position gave rise to that of Christian cardinal (see **scarlet**). In the lists of seven kinds of payments to ministers in Rev 5:12 and 7:12, it is seen that a salary, not tithes, was paid to a lay cardinal. He is first in the former list, but in the second list, where ministers are lay, he is put in a special category of Jewish priests who received salary for ministering to Christians.

prayer (*proseuchē*) A petition, expressed through one of the Old Testament psalms, offered by Gentiles at the Gentile informal service at 3.30 p.m., the time for the Writings of the Old Testament, which included the Psalms (Rev 5:8, 8:3, 4). They were 'the prayers of the holy ones (saints)' because the singing of psalms was led by the crown prince as acolyte, and the crown prince was also a leader of Gentiles.

precious stone (*lithos timios*) The emblem of a celibate of class C. See p.176. The king when counted as third in the hierarchy was the chief of the 'precious stones'. He was leader of celibates when they sat as the congregation in the south vestry at Qumran, each seat marked by the name of a precious stone. Third in the list of 'gold, silver and precious stones' in Rev 18:12 and 1 Cor 3:12.

prepare (*hetoimazō*) To act at 3 p.m., the time for preparing the table for the evening meal (Mark 14:12). Non-Palestinians, Gentiles and the uncircumcised also held a preparation on a Friday, as they would hold an evening meal, whereas Palestinian ascetics avoided an evening meal in order to follow the Essene rule forbidding defecation on the sabbath. In Rev 12:6 the use of 'prepare' on a Friday shows that it was a meal table for this class. In Rev 8:6 the word is used to show that it was 3 p.m. on a Friday when the trumpet was blown.

priest (*hiereus*) The history of this word shows the way in which the priesthood of the Jewish ascetics developed into the Christian ministry. It began as the name used for Phanuel, who, as shown on p.176, was a subordinate priest, head of the lower division of twelve priests under Sariel. Both positions, Sariel and Phanuel, were taken by members of the Annas family.

Sariel was the visiting priest to village ascetics, but Phanuel, although belonging also to a celibate community, was primarily responsible for villagers. He acted as ruler of the synagogue in Hellenist communities. Acting in a day-to-day capacity to villagers, he was called by them 'priest' (*hiereus*, corresponding to Hebrew *kohen*, illustrated in Mark 1:44), while Sariel was called *archiereus*, 'chief priest'.

Phanuel was not always present, and a distinguished layman, an elder, could act in his place. In relation to him, Phanuel was called 'elders', using the plural of reproduction. Being responsible for prayers at the 24 hours of the day, he was called 'elders 24'. It was because of the use of both 'elder' (*presbyteros*) and 'priest' (*hiereus*) for Phanuel that the word 'presbyter' came to mean 'priest' in Christian usage.

Peter, when he took up the celibate life as a widower, rose to be equal to an elder acting for Phanuel. Since the Christians gave levitical status to laymen, he adopted the term *hiereus* to show that he was a true Phanuel (Rev 1:6, 5:10).

Phanuel had another role, to wear scarlet as the servant of Michael, who when 'in the body' wore this colour. See **scarlet**. While acting as priest, standing on the equivalent of the dais edge, he wore white, but when in this lesser capacity he stood on the chancel step, wearing scarlet. The David in one of his roles was equal to a Phanuel, wearing scarlet as 'the Lamb slain', and he then stood in this position (Rev 5:6).

The word 'cardinal' (from *cardo*, 'hinge') came from one of Phanuel's duties in this position, acting as the 'hinge'. He acted as the 'door' through which men passed into the higher ranks. According to the Scrolls, he made the villagers 'go in and come out' (in 1QSa 1:22–23, where he is called 'son of Levi', as in all the Scrolls. Sariel was called 'Levi', as shown in Mark 2:14). Thus Phanuel's position became both that of Christian priest and that of Christian cardinal. But the 'priest' belonged in the village setting, whereas the 'cardinal' belonged in a monastery vestry, the place where Michael changed into the colour scarlet. The two positions came to be differentiated, and a cardinal was ranked higher than a priest.

prison (*phylakē*) A place at the level of Merari, 'the jailer', at grade 9 and below. Since Achaia and Macedonia were provinces 11 and 12, Merari (Ananus the Younger) was found there (Acts 16:23, 17: 34). In Rev 18:2, 'prison' was the province of Achaia, where the Herodian treasury was located. Erastus Saul Herod had fled to Achaia when the war broke out (*War* 2:558). The association of 'prison' with 'marriage' is found in Rev 2:10.

prophecy (*prophēteia*) The prophecy of the Restoration and Eschaton held by solar calendrists, originally given in the Books of Enoch. (Rev 1:3). In Rev 22:7, 'the prophecy of this book' means the corresponding sections of the New Testament, especially the Book of Revelation itself. In Rev 11:6 Matthew Annas, opposing Agrippa I, said that Agrippa the Younger in Rome was the subject of prophecy, and the word was used for the Herod successor (Rev 1:3). In 1 Tim 1:18 Paul said that Timothy (Agrippa's heir) was the subject of Old Testament prophecy, and the Herod crown prince as Christian was called 'the prophecy' (Rev 19:10). See **prophet**. In Rev 22:18–19 the Hellenised Herod is warned to follow the 'prophecy of this book', the New Testament, rather than 'the book of this prophecy', the Septuagint.

prophet (*prophētēs*) Found only in the plural of reproduction in Revelation, meaning the Herod crown prince, who read from the Prophets section of the Hebrew Old Testament (divided into Law, Prophets and Writings). Used of Timothy in Rev 16:6, of Herod of Chalcis as a claimant to the succession in Rev 10:7, of Agrippa II before his coronation in Rev 11:18, of a later crown prince in Rev 18:20, 24.

prophetess (*prophētis*) A female prophet, that is a lay celibate with levitical status. Since the Herod crown prince was in this class, the Herod queen, who was of the same rank, claimed the status, as did her counterpart Helena (Rev 2:20).

pure (*katharos*) A virgin, male or female. Agrippa II, a lifelong celibate, Rev 15:6. The bride of Jesus Justus, Rev 19:8.

purple (*porphyra*) See **scarlet**.Purple was the colour of a bishop, one grade below Phanuel the cardinal, when in the outside world. The word *mebaqqer*, 'bishop', is found frequently in the Scrolls. The purple put on Jesus at his trial was a sign that he was merely an outside bishop (Mark 15:17). A queen consort was a bishop wearing purple (Acts 16:14). In Rev 18:12, in the list of ministers, 'purple' is placed with lay celibates.

queen (*basilissa*) A Herodian woman acting as equal to Herod in his role of *basileus*, see **king**. Bernice claiming to replace her brother (Rev 18:7).

rain (*brechō*) To act as a teacher, using the imagery of the Teacher of Righteousness, whose name was a play on 'he who rains down righteousness' (1QH 8:16–22) (Rev 11:6).

rainbow (*iris*) The emblem of the Herod crown prince, derived from the Flood imagery used by Herod as 'Noah' to Gentiles (Rev 4:3, 10:1).

red (*pyrrhos*) A non-monastic priest officiating in the west only. Rev 12:3 Joazar; Rev 6:4, Acts 20:4, Ananus the Younger. Red was the colour for autumn, equal to 6 p.m. and the west, the season for the main orthodox Jewish festivals.

reed (*kalamos*) A measure of 2 cubits, used by the seer under Egyptian discipline, as a papyrus reed stood for Egypt (Rev 11:1, 21:15).

rejoice (*chairō*) To hold a village sacred meal used for a wedding, either literal, or an initiation of Gentiles as the 'bride' (Rev 11:10, 19:7).

remainder (*loipoi*, 'the rest', plu.) Gentiles who became initiated and paid fees on their way to becoming proselytes were called 'the Remainder' and 'the Seven Thousand', because their fees were kept separate from those of Jews and they were treated as first of the Gentile grades in each province (see p.191). They were placed under the authority of the Herod crown prince (Thomas Herod in Rev 8:13). These proselytes were attached to the Herodian orders, who could act as 'eunuchs' to King Herod. The proselyte Nicolaus-Blastus, eunuch to Agrippa I, is called 'the Remainder of the Men' in Rev 9:20.

The Davids also taught initiated Gentiles, calling them 'the Remainder', and for James it was necessary that they should be circumcised. He was called 'Nemo of the Remainder' in Acts 5:13. Although Jesus did not cause Gentiles to be circumcised, he used the term 'the Remainder' of Luke when he was to act as 'eunuch' or go-between in his marriage (Rev 2:24). In Rev 19:21, the chief proselyte.

remember (*mnēmoneuō*) To make a 'remembrance', a written record of admission. Used of Gentile initiates who were admitted under the imagery of a wedding, since a 'memorial' was a marriage certificate (Mark 14:9) (Rev 2:5, 18:5).

repent (*metanoeō*) The decision to 'repent' was taken at the age of twenty, at grade 10 (see p.180). Jews went up from this grade, but the circumcision party, led by 'Horn 10', decreed that the uncircumcised should remain at grade 10. This meant that they were attached to province 10, Rome. When a member of the circumcision party, such as John the Baptist, said 'Repent!' to Gentiles, he meant: 'Join the mission, but in a low grade only, with your centre of authority in the Rome province, not Judea.' When Jesus said 'Repent!' as in Rev 2:5, 16, he meant: 'Become a member of the Rome province instead of Judea'. Rome, province 10, included Achaia and Macedonia, provinces 11 and 12.

revelation (*apokalypsis*) The word means 'uncovering', and its pesher sense is 'coming out of the seclusion of a monastery into public life'. In Rev 1:1, written in June AD 44, Jesus had returned to seclusion following the birth of a second son, but had special reason to have an audience with the new Herod, Agrippa the Younger, so was given permission to come out by his superior, Matthew Annas.

rich (*plousios*) In the singular, the David, who under the earlier Herodian system was permitted to keep as his own property the fees of initiated Gentiles, as they would not amount to a great deal. James, as the official David under Caiaphas, was the Rich Man during the gospel period and subsequently, until Caiaphas was dismissed (Luke 12:13–21). In the plural (Rev 6:15, 13:16) the proselyte Nicolaus-Blastus, who acted as head of fee paying proselytes, as shown in Rev 3:17.

right (*dexia*) The literal right hand, which would be on the west side when the person was facing south (Rev 1:17, 20, 2:1; 5:1). See **hand**.

righteous (*dikaios*) The David crown prince was 'righteous', of the grade below 'holy' (Matt 1:19). The Latin form of the word, Justus, was used for him (Acts 1:23 Col 4:11). The David when he went down to the married state was also called 'righteous' (Acts 22:14). Essene village teaching was called 'righteousness' (Matt 21:32).

river (*potamos*) The second in the hierarchy of washings 'water (cistern), river, sea'. It meant running water, either in a wady or an aqueduct. It was used for entry to grade 10 at Mird, and this grade included Gentiles below proselyte, whose baptisms in the 'river', the aqueduct at Mird, were conducted by a woman, Miriam (see Chapter 4). The wady at Mird, used for Jewish baptisms at this level, was called 'the river Jordan' (Mark 1:5). In Rev 22:1 the river is the aqueduct at the hermitage-monastery outside Ephesus that was built on the model of Qumran.

It was placed as at Qumran, emerging from the corner near the upper door of the vestry.

rock (*petra*) A person, the David, who received village pilgrims in the outer hall at Qumran, giving them a drink of water likened to water from Moses' rock. In 1 Cor 10:4: 'the Rock was the Christ'. He stood on a rock podium that is still visible in the outer hall. The podium was placed near the door to the 'pantry', where the cups for drinking water were stacked, and the pilgrims were handed a drink of water, so 'drank of the Rock' (1 Cor 10:4).

Peter, as the deputy to the David, was 'this Rock' (Matt 16: 18), as 'this' indicates a lay version. 'The Rocks' of Rev 6:15, 16 was James, held to be the David in Jerusalem in the party of Ananias the Samaritan.

root (*rhiza*) The organisation called the Plant-root, named in CD 1:7. It was a revised form of the Herodian mission, drawn up when the Herods were dismissed in AD 6. Joseph as the David was involved in it, receiving for himself and his successors the title 'the Root David' (Rev 5:5). When the David, in the person of the third Jesus, took over the position of the supreme head, he was called simply 'the Root' (Rev 22:16).

Its foundation date in AD 6 was the south lunisolar 3941 (3901 when the zero generation was allowed), and when this was taken back to the north solar 3941 (3901), it made AD 1 the year 1, giving the Christian era. See Chapter 13 and p.223.

ruin (*diaphtheirō*) To ruin financially, by taking the Herodian property (Luke 12:33, Rev 8:9, 19:2).

ruler (*archōn*) The Chief Therapeut, normally a bishop, going up to the position of Raphael. The term gave rise to the word 'archbishop', as an *archōn* was one grade above a bishop (John 3:1, Rev 1:5).

run (*trechō*) Be a higher teacher, as an ordinary teacher 'walked'. 4QpHab 7:34, the Teacher of Righteousness was the one who 'runs' (Rev 9:9).

sackcloth (*sakkos*) The garment worn by ascetics of the hermit type (Rev 6:12, 11:3). In Rev 6:3 a 'hairy sackcloth' was a cowl worn over the head, as 'hair' meant a headcloth.

sailor (*nautēs*) In the plural of reproduction, the head of the division of 'Ham', the third in the hierarchy of the 'Noah's Ark' mission, in which Herod was 'Noah', and his crown prince was 'Shem' (Rev 18: 17, Acts 27:27, 30).

salesman (*emporos*) In the plural Erastus Saul Herod, 'salesmen of the Earth', who acted as treasurer storing Gentile fees once they were assigned to the Herod crown prince. Taking fees from Gentiles and giving in return tokens of membership, he was a 'salesman'. In AD 70 he lamented the fall of Jerusalem because the Gentile money was given on the understanding that it was to help building projects in Jerusalem (Rev 18:3, 11, 15).

salvation (*sōtēria*) The power of a Sadducee priest to give initiation ('salvation') to Gentiles independently of a Herod. In AD 15 Eleazar Annas had the power, as there were no Herods (Rev 12:10). It was claimed for the Sadducee in Rev 7:10, and the Priest-Pope who took over priesthood from Agrippa in AD 73 received it (Rev 19:1).

sanctuary (*naos*) The place in the substitute sanctuary that represented the Holy of Holies, where the alternative rite of atonement was performed by the Essenes exiled from Jerusalem. Originally in the upper third of the long courtyard on the west side of the round well at Qumran. The line of stones marking off the upper third is still to be seen there. This place was also called 'Heaven', as the place where the alternative priest held the perpetual liturgy reproducing the one in heaven. After the earthquake of 31 BC, however, Qumran lost its holiness, and the rite of atonement was performed at Mird, which became the 'sanctuary' (Luke 1:9). But 'Heaven' remained at Qumran, on the platform built in the vestry, which was used by priests presiding at councils.

In AD 34, when the Hellenists decided to transfer their funds from Mird-Qumran to keep them from Agrippa, their monastery in Caesarea re-combined 'Heaven' and 'the sanctuary'. Reproductions used the same combination (Rev 11:19, 14:17). Since the 'sanctuary' was the equivalent of a Holy of Holies, the Herodian reproduction at the hermitage outside Ephesus contained a reproduction Ark of the Covenant where the scrolls of the Torah were kept (Rev 11:19, Heb 9:3–4).

The re-dedication of this building as a monastery for eastern Christians, Jewish Christians and remaining Herodians is described in Rev 21:9–21.

In a three-tiered structure, the 'sanctuary' occupied 4 cubits of the upper tier. The inner 2 cubits were called simply 'the sanctuary', (Rev 15:8, Matt 23:16). The eastern 1 cubit 'the sanctuary of God', and the western 1 cubit 'the sanctuary of the Lord' (Luke 1:9).

Since a 'sanctuary' represented the Holy of Holies, only a higher priest could be in the place designated in this way. An acolyte could be on the outer upper tier, called 'Heaven', but not in the 'sanctuary'. Hence in Rev 15:8, when James, the chief acolyte in Jerusalem and Judea, 'was empowered to enter the sanctuary', it means that he entered heaven itself, the true 'Holy of Holies', through death. James was stoned to death on the orders of the high priest Ananus the Younger in the year of this verse, AD 62 (see p.129).

sand (*ammos*) The third Herod, who was next in rank under 'the Sea', the Herod crown prince or queen (Rev 12:18, 20:8). See **sea**. He was a married man, and his name meant both that Herodian married orders were 'sand', unlike the Essene celibate 'Rock' (Matt 7:24–26), and also referred to the Covenant of Abraham which would produce numbers like 'the sand of the sea' (Rom 9:27).

sapphire (*sappheiros*) See **precious stone**. A female 'precious stone' was called 'sapphire' (Acts 5:1), and when in the congregation sat in the queen's pew, the second in the first row (Rev 21:19).

sardius (*sardion*) The precious stone that was the sixth in the list of Rev 21:20, of grade 6 acolytes. Rev 4:3 shows that there was an acolyte present on the outer east of the upper tier with Herod, as was customary.

Satan (*Satanas*) A name for Raphael the Scribe in his role of examiner, the adversary (Hebrew *Satan*) in the tests conducted for admission. He was called both 'the Devil' and 'Satan'. He acted also as chief treasurer to monastic property and the shared property of village Essenes. Judas Iscariot had this position in the gospel period (Mark 1:13, Luke 4:13), and before him Judas the Galilean (Rev 12:9). In Rev 2:9, 10, 13, the name was used for Antipas Herod, who after the schism of AD 44 became the Scribe-treasurer to the Herodian party. Agrippa I had transferred the main treasury of Herodian property to Achaia to keep it from the eastern party (Rev 10:2, pesher), and Antipas became its custodian. Achaia was the 'throne of Satan' (Rev 2:13).

A deputy treasurer was always needed, and this part fell to the Chief Therapeut, who took the title Satan. When, at the Last Supper, 'Satan entered into' Judas Iscariot (John 13:27), Theudas was taking the place of Judas, who was leaving the room. In Rev 12:9, 'the Devil' means Judas the Galilean, and 'Satan' means Theudas the Chief Therapeut who replaced him. The Chief Therapeut in Rev 20:2.

scarlet (*kokkinos*) The colour worn by the high priest Michael when 'in the body', in the outside world, in the battlefield or in the married state. According to the War Scroll (1QM 7:10–11), priests wore the colours scarlet, purple and blue, those of Old Testament priests, but only in the battlefield; 'they shall not wear them in the sanctuary', where white must be worn. The purpose of the vestry was to change into these colours. This gave the position and vestment of a cardinal, for Phanuel as the servant of Michael was equal to Michael when 'in the body', and showed this by wearing scarlet when he was at the level of the chancel step. In his higher status on the edge of the dais he wore white.

Since Phanuel as cardinal was priest to the uncircumcised, Helena, followed by Bernice, claimed the position. (Rev 17:3, 4, 18:16). A queen consort, however, wore purple. The cardinal, as a minister outside the vestry, is included in the list of ministers to Gentiles in Rev 18:12.

scorch (*katakaiō*) Men who followed the discipline of the Therapeuts, known as the 'iron furnace of Egypt', stood near the furnace in the vestry at Qumran in order to keep it alight. Standing directly in front of it, they were 'scorched', whereas those who stood in the doorway near it were merely 'warmed' (John 18:18, 25). The 'scorching' was accepted as part of their military training. Gentiles taught by the Therapeuts could also be 'scorched' (Rev 8:7), as could women under the Nazirite discipline (Rev 17:16).

scorpion (*skorpios*) A hermit living in an underground cell, which could be infested with scorpions. An exiled monastic was sent to these cells as a penance (Rev 9:3). They were used by ascetics under the Egyptian eremitical rule (Rev 9:10). Singular, the Chief Therapeut (Rev 9:5), plural, another man in his position so 'reproducing' him; John the Baptist after being laicised (Rev 9:3).

sea (*thalassa*) A person, of the grade lower than 'Earth'. Herod was 'Heaven and Earth', and below him were the Herod crown prince and the Herod queen (always equal to each other because one grade below the king). When the David acted as 'Earth' at the time there was no Herod (Rev 12:16) his wife was 'the Sea' (1 Cor 10:2).

Members of the lower village congregation when found at Qumran were confined to the south-west sector, called 'the Sea', and 'the Salt' (corrected translation of *melach* in Sentences 6, 15, 16 of the Copper Scroll). In the geographical plan based on the four divisions of the grounds, the south-west stood for Rome, considered to be a place for the unclean. So 'the Sea' also meant the community in Rome. To be 'thrown into the Sea' meant to be exiled to Rome (Rev 18:21). If a 'Mountain was thrown into the Sea' (Rev 8:8, Mark 11:23), a hermitage was transferred to Rome (see **mountain**).

'Upon of the Sea' in Rev 10:2 means the west side of the chancel step in a three-tiered structure (see **earth**). At the same time it means the provinces of Rome and the attached provinces of Greece (11 and 12). This verse refers to the transfer of Herodian property from the east to Greece. It is shown in the pesher of Acts, and supported by detail in Revelation, that the Herodian treasury of monastic funds was first at Mird (Hyrcania, the building that had been Queen Salome's treasury), then transferred to Joppa and Caesarea, then, when Magian interests dominated in Caesarea, transferred to Gaza on the Palestinian coast (Acts 8:26). The word 'Gaza' means 'treasury', and the story in Acts 8 shows that Titus the Ethiopian, head of the 'sons of Ham' remained loyal to Agrippa I when Philip of Shem tried to persuade him to join in the poison plot. Titus was in charge of the treasury. He is subsequently found in Corinth in Achaia (Acts 18:7), and this was the place where Erastus Saul Herod stayed (1 Tim 4:20).

seal (*sphragis*) To be forbidden to speak in the council was to be 'sealed' (Rev 7:4, 5). A person who was 'sealed' was excluded for a season. This gave rise to the 'seven seals' of Rev 5–8 (see Chapter 8). At the ceremony at which the New Testament was canonised, its books were placed in the back section of the bound book containing the Septuagint (see **book**). At the outset of the ceremony it was sealed to show that it must not yet be read. Two ties bound it on the outside. The main one, called simply 'the seals' (plural of reproduction) was brought up from the back cover to the title page. Presumably it was

345

fastened with the royal seal. Agrippa released this seal at the beginning of the service when the Septuagint was read (Rev 5:2). Another main seal, called 'seal 7', came from the back page to the title page, and Jesus released this after giving the reading from the Prophets which were in the front part of the book (Rev 5: 5). Then, when the Gentile informal service at 3.30 p.m began, he 'opened the seals' (Rev 5:9), that is, turned over the title page which had been fastened. At the service at the following 31st, he 'opened one out of the seven seals' (seal 7), that is, he opened the title page of the first division, Mark's gospel. Each of the six divisions was independently sealed in the same way, and the seals progressively released, until they came to the seventh seal (Rev 8:1), which was the other end of 'seal 7' on the back page. The back page was turned over, showing that there were no further contents.

sear (*kaumatizō*) See **scorch**. To use the rules for the Qumran vestry at the Masada monastery (Rev 16:8, 9).

season (*kairos*) The quartodecimal year for the intercalation of the solar and lunisolar calendar. See pp.237–238. The north solar year in Rev 22:10 (AD 113). The Herodian north lunisolar year in Rev 12:12, 11:18, 1:3. It was in this series of quartodecimal years that the income from the Vineyard mission was collected (Mark 12:2), hence the emphasis on the season in Rev 11:18.

In Rev 12:14 the intermediate intercalation year is used, preferred by Annas priests as being neither for nor against the temple (see p.244). This was AD 17 in the intercalation period AD 15–19. The word *kairos* (used in narrative at the beginning of the 17½ days) means the June intercalation in that year. The term 'a half of a season' in the same verse means December, six months later, when those using the Julian calendar preferred to intercalate. 'Half' is used absolutely (see **half**), here meaning six months later because of the equation of hours and months. The term *kairoi* in the same verse, using the plural of reproduction, means the September season, when more traditional members of this party intercalated. In the surface meaning, 'season, seasons and half a season' is an indication of a 3½ years, the beginning of an intercalation period, and gives some information to a learner.

seek (*zēteō*) To question, examine, for the purpose of determining promotion or demotion (Rev 9:6).

sell (*pōleō*) To give membership of the religion, or promotion, in return for payment of a fee (see p.26) (Rev 13:17).

sensuality (*strēnos*) The state of an ascetic of the Therapeut discipline who was in a sexual relationship. Bernice in Rev 18:3, the Chief Therapeut in Rev 18:7.

serpent (*ophis*) Theudas, the head of the Egyptian Therapeuts from AD 1 to 44, at the times when he was engaged in a poison plot against the ruling Herod. Egyptian poisons had been used in an attempted assassination of Herod the Great (*Ant.* 17:70, 73), and the Therapeuts, experts in drugs, supplied the means. One of their sects was called the Ophites. Theudas is the Serpent of Rev 12:9. He is called 'Pharaoh' in Acts 7:10, meaning that in the Exodus drama it was he who took the part of Pharaoh pursuing the fleeing Israelites. Theudas is the subject of John 3:14: 'Moses (Simon the Essene as Gabriel) lifted up the Serpent in the Wilderness' (promoted Theudas when he returned to Mird as the repentant Prodigal Son, see *Jesus the Man*, Chapter 11).

serve (*latreuō*) To hold a Christian worship service (Rev 7:15, 22:3).

seven (*hepta*) See **two**.

ship (*ploion*) 'Noah's Ark' in the baptismal imagery for Gentiles attached to Rome. See *Jesus the Man*, Locations, the System for Boats (Rev 8:9).

shortly (*tachei*) The Day of Pentecost, at the season of the shortest night (Rev 1:1, 22:6). The form *tachy*, translated 'soon', means the 31st at the June solstice.

sickle (*drepanon*) A means of reaping the 'harvest of wheat', an image of fee paying Gentiles (see p.194).

Presumably a rod for excluding or admitting them. The 'sharp sickle' was used for higher ascetics (Rev 14:14, 17, 18), the 'sickle' alone for the lower grades (Rev 14:15, 16, 19).

sign (*sēmeion*) A person with power to give the 'signs', letters of the alphabet indicating grades. 'Sign' (sing.), a priest (Rev 12:3 Joazar, 15:1 Ananus); (plu.), the reproduction of a priest. Great Sign (Rev 12:1), a layman giving promotion to Gentiles (Joseph). Verb (*sēmainō*), to give a promotion.

silence (*sigē*) An intercalation. On Rev 8:1, see p.212.

silk (*sirikos*) The garment of a judge, in the list of vestments in Rev 18:12. According to CD 14:12–17 welfare tithes were to be paid by villagers to a bishop and judges. In the list of vestments, 'purple' and 'silk' placed together indicate these two ministers. Silk is still associated with the legal profession.

silver (*argyrous*) The emblem of class B levites, in the hierarchy 'gold' (priests class A), 'silver' (levites class B) and 'precious stones' (celibates class C) found in 1 Cor 3:12 and in the Scrolls. In Rev 9: 20 Agrippa was 'the silver things' as a levitical king acting as deputy to Caesar in the east. This was in AD 43, and the following year he appeared on the platform at Caesarea clad in a glittering silver garment, claiming godship (p.41). In Rev 18:12, village levites.

sin (*hamartia*) The married state. 'Sinners' were the opposite of 'Saints' (Holy Ones), who were dynastic celibates. To be 'loosed out of sins' (Rev 1:5) means 'to be permitted to go up from the married state to the celibate state'.

slave (*doulos*) A slave, in the singular, was originally a literal slave in the household of Herod. When the Vineyard mission was founded in Herod's house in Rome, Herod's slaves served at the meals where membership of Herodian Judaism was given. When Herod was in Judea, the slaves from his house in Rome brought back the fees of new members, thus showing him how many had joined. These were the 'fruits of the Vineyard' of the parable (Mark 12:1–11). In the plural of reproduction, 'the slaves' meant Herod himself in the status of head of the Rome mission. The word in the plural refers to Agrippa II in Rev 1:1, 7:3, 11:18, 19:2; Agrippa I in Matt 21:34–35. In Rev 10:7, 13:16 it refers to Herod of Chalcis as a rival Herod, and in Rev 22:6 to the Hellenised Herod who was continuing the Herodian form of mission.

Gentiles had the same status as slaves (Gal 3:28), and the word 'slave' could be used for Gentile missionaries of the Vineyard. John Aquila, a married man working at a trade (Acts 18:3), received no income for his missionary work, and in this sense was like a slave, being given only his expenses while travelling. The word 'slave' was used of him (Rev 1:1). In Rev 15:3 it is used of Epaphras, a member of Paul's Roman party who had become a leader of the Therapeuts.

slave yoke/scale (*zygos*) A scale for weighing the property of monastics, who became 'slaves' after surrendering all that they owned. A weight in the form of an inscribed stone was found in the ruins of Ain Feshkha (de Vaux, *Archaeology and the Dead Sea Scrolls* p.67).

slay (*sphazō*) To be 'slain' was to be a cardinal, one wearing the scarlet of priests in the battlefield. See **scarlet**. The term applied to a Phanuel, a lesser priest, as a superior priest was not permitted to touch the slain (1QM 9:7–9).

small (*oligos*) See **few**.

smoke (*kapnos*) The incense used by non-Palestinian ascetics at 3.30 p.m. on Fridays, at the beginning of the service which would include the evening communion meal. The word is a useful indicator of date, as the 'smoke' occurred only on Fridays. On Fridays Palestinian Essenes did not eat an evening meal because of the rule forbidding defecation on the sabbath (*War* 2:147). Westernised Therapeuts and Gentiles who had been taught by them disregarded this rule and burned their incense as usual at their Friday afternoon service. Their Palestinian critics said that their petitions would not be received by the deity, and were mere 'smoke'.

Gentiles of the class of James Niceta held Friday afternoon services. Once they had been promoted to deacons, they claimed equality with the acolyte and proselyte deacons who were educated near the well and the steps north of the Qumran vestry (see **well** (**deep**) and **abyss**). But they only of this group sent up smoke on Friday afternoons, making it 'smoke out of the (deep) well' (Rev 9:2). Westernised Therapeuts, whose discipline was likened to the 'iron furnace' of Egypt, had 'smoke of a furnace' (Rev 9:2).

so (*tade*) 'So' is used to translate *tade*, literally 'the things' (*ta*) with the particle *de*. The word is used as a play on 'the D' (see **but**), the letter for class D. It precedes each of the seven letters in Revelation 1–3, and is used to say that Jesus is giving official Gentile teaching under higher authority.

son (*huios*) A name developed for the deputy of a high priest once the high priest came to be called 'Father' (*Ant.* 15:21). The public high priest who could be in power in Jerusalem was of the level of a Sariel, not a Michael, and his subordinate was called 'Son of Levi' to his 'Levi'. In the village or Diaspora to which Sariel came, a distinguished layman could act in the place of the subordinate. When this was the David, and the Sadducee Sariel was called 'God', the David was called 'Son of God', with support from Psalm 2:7. The title simply meant that he was a deputy to a Jewish high priest, and could act in some of his positions. The use of a title implying divinity was encouraged by the belief that the high priest was a semi-divine person.

Similarly, the 'Son of Man' was the David in the position of subordinate to 'the Man', the true levite.

song (*ōdē*) A hymn, modelled on the Psalms of David. A Christian hymn was a 'new (*kainē*) song' (Rev 5:9, 14:3).

soon (*tachy*) The solar 31st at the June solstice, when the longest day started early so came 'soon'. Rev 2:16, 11:14. See **shortly**.

sorcery (*pharmakia*) The activities of the Chief Magus, who specialised in drugs and poisons (Rev 9:21, 18:23).

soul (*psychē*) Herod in the position of a priest, sitting on the east side of the table, beside 'body'. Archelaus in Rev 8:9; Agrippa I in Rev 12:11, Acts 2:41; Agrippa II in Rev 16:3, 18:13, 14. Or the Priest-Pope representing him in this position. In Rev 6:9 it is used with a further phrase of Peter as the Christian Priest-Pope.

spirit (*pneuma*) One of the titles of Sariel, the Sadducee priest. John 4:24: 'God is a Spirit'. Sariel was head of the twelve priests, first of the three sets of twelve in the Qumran organisation (see p.176). They were divided into 5+7. Sariel was head of the upper 5, and Phanuel, called 'Spirit 7', was head of the lower 7. As 'Spirits', they served the wine at the sacred meal, whereas the levites served the loaves.

When Sariel as a Spirit went to the east side, with the 'holy ones' in the monastery, he was called 'the Holy Spirit', in the form *to pneuma to hagion*.

Without article, 'a Spirit' was a leader of the congregation, sitting in the first pew. A Gentile in this position was attached to the tribe of Levi under the Annas priest (see p.194) (Rev 1:10, 4:2, 17:3). 'Unclean spirits' meant a man who claimed this status while he was still married, not while temporarily celibate. This was done by the Herodian order of Gad, meeting in Gerasa. In Mark 3:11 it means the tetrarch Antipas, and in Rev 16:13 it means Simon Gioras, a man whom Josephus says to have been married, coming from Gerasa (*War* 4:503–538). He was also called 'unclean Spirit 3', meaning that he claimed the grade of a levite at grade 3.

When it was agreed in AD 44 that Herod of Chalcis and

his descendants should have the power to appoint high priests in future (*Ant.* 20:15–16), 'a Spirit of Life out of God came into...him' (Rev 11:11). When he chose Ananias the Samaritan to be future high priest (appointed by him in AD 49, *Ant.* 20:103) 'it was given to him to give a Spirit to the Icon of the Beast' (Ananias).

stadion (*stadion*) The Greek measure of distance (about 192 metres). In the reckoning of the ascetics at Qumran, 5 stadia, approximately 2000 cubits or 1 kilometre, needed an hour's walking time, and distances were measured in terms of stadia-hours. See p.111 on the 1600 stadia of Rev 14:20, and p.190 on the 12 000 stadia of Rev 21:16.

star (*astēr*) The David, using the Star of David emblem. He was one of the lesser 'powers' under 'the Sun', and 'the Moon'. When living in the celibate community, he led prayers at sunrise as the Morning Star (Rev 22:16) and the Great Star (Rev 8:10, 9:1). His crown prince could take his place (Matt 2:7, Rev 2:28), and was called Star 7 when taking part in daily prayers (Rev 1:16), or Star 12 when taking part in monthly prayers (Rev 12:1). Plural of reproduction in Rev 6:13, James. 'Star 7' was the acolyte to 'angel 7', the Michael who was responsible for the blowing of the sabbatical trumpet (see p.178), so in Rev 1:20 it is said that Jesus Justus, now an acolyte and 'Star 7', was the 'angels' (plural of reproduction) of 'Church 7', Agrippa II.

steersman (*kybernētēs*) Herod as head of the 'Noah' mission, the mission to Gentiles of the Mediterranean and of Rome (see *Jesus the Man*, Locations) (Rev 18:17, Acts 27:11).

still (*eti*) A play on E-T, the E for class E below all classes of members, for uninitiated Gentiles, and the T for a Gentile who had received the Herodian T sign, that is, had received a token membership by dining with Agrippa. Gentiles such as emperors and governors who had only a nominal membership were placed in class E. The word 'still' indicates the presence of an 'E-T', a leading Roman. In Rev 12:8, he was the Roman governor of AD 6, Quirinius. In Rev 9:12 'E-T' means the emperor Gaius Caligula. In Rev 3:12, 6:11, 7:16, it means Gallio the Roman governor of Achaia, who is referred to in Acts 18:14–16 as giving a judgment concerning the mission in Corinth. The Herodian treasury had been transferred to Achaia and the governor would have received Agrippa's hospitality for the same purpose as the governors in Rome and Judea. In Rev 18:21–23 it means Titus, Vespasian's son. In Rev 20:3 a Roman governor of Ephesus. The word may be used at the time when the service was opened to outsiders.

sting (*kentron*) The 'sting of death' (1 Cor 15:55), that is, a sceptre standing for the power to excommunicate held by an Annas priest (Rev 9:10).

stomach (*gastēr*) In the body imagery, the 2 cubit space at the north of the vestry, the 'court' of the chief priest, was said to be the lower part of the higher 'body', that of the chief priest. The vault just above it is in a distinct heart shape. This concept gave rise to the naming of the vestry, which became the church, as 'the body of Christ'. Monastic Gentiles as outsiders were at first instructed at night in the 'stomach' (Rev 12:2).

stone (*lithos*) A stone that was used as an admission token to the vestry by village Essenes and as a token of their circumcision by circumcised Gentiles (from Josh 5:2–3). It was given at the round base outside the vestry, likened to a millstone (Rev 18:21). Class D, below the 'precious stones' of class C were given an ordinary stone. Luke 3:8, 'God can out of these stones raise up children to Abraham' means 'the Sadducee has power to promote circumcised Gentiles to be equal to Jewish villagers'.

Peter's name in both Greek and Aramaic (Cephas) means 'stone'. He acted for the David as 'the Rock'. 'Stone things' (*lithina* Rev 9:20) means Peter as head of the village Essenes under Agrippa.

strength (*ischys*) A deacon whose work was to instruct grade 10 members to become 'strong' (Acts 19:20 shows that this was at the age of twenty). He was, or was equal to, the levitical deacon Merari (Rev 7:12), and received payment (Rev 5:12).

strike (*paiō*) To treat as a novice; a play on *pais*, 'child', meaning a pre-initiate just before becoming a 'man' (Luke 2:43). In Rev 9:5 Theudas treated Jonathan Annas as a novice, that is, a representative of Therapeuts, who were equal to novices of the Palestinian Essene monasteries.

strong (*ischyros*) The head of lower or village grades, beginning with grade 10, when members were confirmed or 'became strong'. See **strength**. They included the crown prince of a dynasty. Rev 10:1, 'another strong angel', Agrippa the Younger at sixteen, appointed deputy to his father. Mark 1:7 'the Stronger One', the David as one grade above his own crown prince. 'The Strong Ones' (Rev 6:15, 19: 18), the Chief Therapeut as a reproduction of the crown prince.

stumbling block (*skandalon*) The requirement that Gentiles wishing to join the mission should be circumcised (Rev 2:14), an important image in Pauline theology (Rom 14:13). The original 'stumbling block' was the upper round base outside the Qumran vestry door, also called the 'millstone' (see p.197). The uncircumcised were not permitted to go past this point.

suffer (*paschō*) In the marriage context, to 'suffer' meant to be in the six months period of a betrothal, either before the wedding (Rev 2:10) or after the second wedding during the six months until the birth of the child, when the man was not yet fully returned to the monastic community.

sun (*hēlios*) The Zadokite high priest Michael, called 'the Sun' as responsible for the solar calendar. The title was used by John the Baptist as the Zadokite (Rev 8:12, 9:2, 12:1). After the death of John the Baptist it was taken over by Agrippa I (Rev 10:1) and Agrippa II (Rev 1:16, 6:12,

7:2, 16). The title was still used by Agrippa II in the east after he ceased to be Pontifex Maximus of the mission (Rev 16:8, 12, 19:17).

sup (*deipneō*) Take the common part of the evening meal. In the case of the normal Essene meal from 6 to 10 p.m., the first two hours (Luke 22:20). For the Therapeuts, at midnight (John 13:2, Rev 19:9).

sword (*machaira*) The 'sword of the Spirit' (Eph 6:17) that was used to admit or exclude men from the village ministry, corresponding to the *romphaia* ('broadsword') which was used in monasteries.

tabernacle (*skēnē*) The 'tent' used by nomad Israel, before they had a temple (Exod 35–36). Consequently, the place of worship used by pilgrims to the Wilderness, at Mird (Rev 13:6a) and for higher pilgrims at Qumran (Rev 13:6). The term was used by Sadducees, and is a mark of the Annas priests (Rev 12:12, 13:5, 15:5).

Acts 7:44 speaks of the tabernacle at Mird. The building on the Mird height was used, attended by both hermits and pilgrims, and in phase 2 after the earthquake at Qumran it was used as the sanctuary, in place of the substitute temple at Qumran. But from the thirties AD the Sadducees who used the tabernacle image moved their centre to Caesarea. From this time, the word indicates Caesarea (Rev 13:6, 15:5).

tail (*oura*) The coloured banner indicating the season used by the visiting priest (see p.102).When he placed it behind him on the chair that he used as a 'Horse', it was like the 'tail of the horse' (Rev 9:10, 19; 12:4).

teeth (*odontes*) Gentile ministers. While Jewish levites and celibates were 'loaves', and in eating loaves one was taking in holiness, Gentile ministers were simply 'teeth' in the mouth (Rev 9:8). The same principle was used for 'smoke'.

tempt (*peirazō*) To administer the tests for admission or promotion that were used in the ascetic hierarchy (1QS

6:13–23). To examine the suitability of a candidate for admission was the task of a Raphael, called 'the Devil' or 'Satan' (the adversary) in this capacity. The rite of testing during the betrothal period ensured that the bride was a virgin and the husband was abstinent (Rev 2:2, 10, 3:10).

ten thousand (*myriades*) Ten thousand members, according to the plan of mission. Following 'twenty thousand' (*dismyriades*) in the genitive (Rev 9:16), a total of thirty thousand, the number of fee paying Jews in the five provinces of Asia Minor, six thousand in each (see p.188). But the Ten Thousand were the thousand in grade 10 in each province, the lowest Gentiles. The fees of these Gentiles from two of the five provinces were given to the Herod crown prince in Rev 5:11.

tenth (*dekaton*) The first of ten divisions, the ten fee paying provinces into which the Kingdom of the Jews was divided. The eastern province in Rev 11:13.

tetragon (*tetragōnos*) See **corner**.

thanks (*eucharistia*) Gifts presented to King Herod or his substitute on the throne (Rev 4:9, 11:17).

theft (*klemma*) See **thief**.

Themselves (*heautoi*) See **himself**.

thence (*ekeithen*) The southern one of the two round bases outside the vestry. See **hence**.

therefore (*oun*) A play on letters, meaning 'a Samekh', the grade of initiation. 'Therefore' in Hebrew is *'al ken*, which by a play means 'over (*'al*) grades Kaph (11) to Nun (8)'. Over these was Samekh (7) being the superior. To act *oun* means to act at the position of a grade 7, and when 'out of the body' this means a lay bishop (Rev 1:19, 2:5).

These (*houtoi*) 'These' alone is a name, and does not refer back to a previous subject. It was used as a title for the head of celibates in a Sadducee-Essene school, reflecting their use of the solstices of the Julian calendar. The solstices were called 'these days', while the equinoxes were called 'those days'. It refers to Matthew Annas in Rev 11:4, 6, 10; to the chief celibates in Rev 14:4; to Gaius

Costobar Herod claiming the position in Rev 17:13, 14, and Agrippa II having received back the headship of these schools in Rev 17:16.

They (*autoi* as new subject) See **he**.

thief (*kleptēs*) The name for a Scribe-treasurer who used the common property for zealotry. Judas Iscariot in John 12:6; Erastus Saul Herod the treasurer of Gentile property in Rev 3:3, 16:15.

thigh (*mēros*) In Psalm 45:3, King David as bridegroom had a 'sword upon his thigh'. It means the David as the Bridegroom at the initiation of Gentiles in Rev 19:16, and, since parts of the body may refer to vestments, a vestment coming down to the thigh.

third (*triton*) The first of three divisions, those of fee paying Gentiles. See p.194 on Gentiles who advanced to initiation, paying a denarius in three instalments. 'A Third of the Earth' was a Gentile who paid his fees to the king, 'Earth', and so was in the lay class of pilgrims (like John Aquila), whereas 'a Third of the Trees' was a Gentile like James Niceta who adopted the Nazirite discipline, so was levitical, and attached to a Herodian school likened to 'Eden' (Rev 8:7). 'A Third of the Men' (Rev 9:15, 18) means the Roman governor, counted as an initiate under Agrippa, called 'the Men' when he was like a Gabriel. In Rev 9:18 it means Marsus, governor of Syria, with whom Agrippa quarrelled shortly before the dismissal of Matthew Annas (*Ant.* 19:340–342).

thousand (*chilias*) An ascetic order. The orders contained literally a thousand at first, their organisation depending on the number, then as they expanded into the Diaspora multiplied as thousands. See p.185 on the organisation. See also **ten thousand** and **twelve thousand.**

For 'one thousand two hundred and sixty days' (Rev 11:3, 12:6), see pp.241–242. The period of 1260 days could be used either between north and south quarto-decimal years, or between north and south generation years, ending on the 31st before Passover. In Rev 11:3 it is used at the south solar generation year AD 44 (from September 40 to March 44), at the unintercalated 31st, since the south solar intercalation, due in March AD 47, had not yet taken place. In Rev 12:6 it is used at the south lunisolar quartodecimal year (3941), in March AD 6, at the intercalated 31st, as the intercalation had taken place.

thousand-rulers (*chiliarch*) A name for the head of the One Thousand, the order of Simeon at Masada, order 1 (see p.188). In the singular, this was King Herod (Acts 21:31), in the plural, his representative over the order (Rev 6:15, 19:18).

throne (*thronos*) Singular, the throne of Herod on the upper tier. In the plural, 'thrones' are a reproduction, the seat of the representative of Herod at the east side of the middle tier (Rev 4:4). When a zealot occupied a throne, it became 'the throne of the Beast' (Rev 16:10).

throw (*ballō*) To send to the congregation, either its 'Earth' level (Rev 8:7) or its lower 'Sea' level (Rev 8:8).

throwing down (*katabolē*) The outer hall of the Qumran monastery, to which excluded members were 'thrown down'. Part of it is called the 'stone's throw' in Luke 22:41. Village pilgrims came there, treated as being of the same level as excluded monastics, so the hall was the 'throwing down of the world', as they were part of the 'world'. Its opposite ('from') was the monastery itself, so 'from the throwing down of the world' means 'in the monastery' (Rev 13:8, 17:8, Matt 25:34).

thunder (*brontē*) A person, Sariel, who had the right to read the third division of the Old Testament, the Latter Prophets, associated with thunder (Amos 1:2). 'Lightning' read the Law, 'Voices' read the Former Prophets, both on the east side, and 'Thunder' read the Latter Prophets on the west side. These levitical figures derived their names from the phenomena associated with the giving of the Law on Mount Sinai (Exod 19:16).

Since Sariel originally belonged in the west, 'Thunder'

was the name of Sariel when in Ephesus (Rev 4:5, 10:3). James and John became 'Sons of Thunder', the Sadducee (Mark 3:17). It has been suggested on p.82 that the gnostic poem called 'Thunder, Perfect Mind' was intended to be uttered by the female oracle of Ephesus.

thus (*houtōs*) A play on Hebrew *ken*, which means both 'thus' and 'yes'. An allusion to the levite Kohath, who permitted marriage and said 'yes', while the Scribe refused it and said 'no'. As Matthew Annas was the Kohath of the Annas family, the word refers to him in Rev 9:17.

toil (*ponos*) An acolyte within a monastery, earning merit by ascetic practices, corresponding to 'works'. Connected with Masada, the Herodian chief monastery, in Rev 16:10, 11, 21:4. In Rev 21:10, 'Toil' is the leader of the 'brigands', including Idumeans of Masada, who killed Antipas Herod (*War* 4:140), and in 21:11 the leader of the Idumeans who killed Ananus the Younger (*War* 4:314–318).

tongue (*glōssa*) One of the four words, 'tribes, tongues, peoples and nations' that have the precise meaning of the four classes of uncircumcised Gentiles for whom the gospels were written. The 'tongues' were men who chose to join Peter's order of Naphtali, their leader in Rome being the Mark who wrote Mark's gospel at Peter's directions (see p.529). Peter's order of Naphtali missionaries held services in languages such as Greek, as a bishop of the Diaspora must do according to CD 14:9–10, so were called 'tongues'.Peter was the 'tongue' of Rev 5:9, 13:7, 14:6.

These bishops also looked after the shared property of village Essenes, in the practice described by Philo (*Every Good Man*, 85–87) and in Acts 4:34–35. The chief bishop over this property was a higher Essene from the monastery, a Scribe, who himself owned no property and who came to the village to administer the funds. In this capacity he was said to have the 'tongue-piece' (*glōsso-*

komon, John 13:29, held by Judas Iscariot, the Scribe at that time).

In the corresponding Herodian system the position of the treasurer was held by Herod, in his third grade of levitical king, and he was represented in the position by a third Herod, who was called 'tongues'. In the period of Revelation, this was Antipas Herod the treasurer of Jerusalem (Rev 7:9). In Rev 16:10 'they bit their tongues' means that they killed Antipas, in the disturbances of AD 67 (*War* 4: 140–146). In Rev 10:11, 11:9, the third Herod called 'tongues' was Herod of Chalcis.

torment (*basanos, basanizō*) A heavy penance, reduction to grade 11, the grade of 'Hades' just before final excommunication. This was the level of the Sisters, who gave birth in a place of this grade, for example the cells under the building at Mird, or the queen's house attached to Qumran, so the penance was likened to labour pains. It could take the form of a period of confinement for five months, 150 days, starting on 1 May, ('month 5') the day a four months pregnant woman went into seclusion by the rule that set December as the season for conception (Luke 1:24). Those Hymns of Thanksgiving from the Dead Sea Scrolls which have been recognised as coming from the Teacher of Righteousness contain a hymn likening the Teacher's sufferings to labour pains (1QH 3:3–10). It can be seen as having been written by John the Baptist while he was under the penance described in Rev 9:5.

towards (*pros*) Facing a person in a north-south direction.

trample (*pateō*) To punish a bishop by treating him as equal to a village bishop, who according to the rule of CD 14:8–9 must be less than fifty years old, so could be removed from office when he turned fifty. On 1 March AD 44, this was done to Jesus on his fiftieth birthday by Agrippa (Rev 11:2, see further **city**). It was done also to a Roman bishop, Clement, born AD 10 (see p.522, Note 4), so fifty at the end of AD 60 (Rev 14:20); and to a Chief

Therapeut in 19:15, who had been born in AD 23.

tree (*dendron*) A Herod as teacher in Herodian schools. (Rev 8:7, Mark 8:24). From the 'Eden' imagery for a monastic school. Ascetic schools were described as an 'Eden' by the Teacher of Righteousness in 1QH 8:126, and in a newly published fragment PAM 43.306. These were almost certainly the schools of the 'exegetes' described by Josephus (Ant. 17:149). They admitted outsiders to the monastery to pray and receive instruction. See **broadsword**, and **wood**.

tribe (*phylē*) The twelve ascetic orders set up from the foundation of the mission were called 'tribes'. They corresponded also to provinces (see pp.185–190).

This word is frequently found in Revelation in the group of four: 'tribes, tongues, peoples and nations'. These apparently vague words have the exact meaning of the four classes of uncircumcised Gentiles, for whom the four gospels were written. The 'tribes' were the married Gentiles of the order of Asher who adopted the Nazirite discipline, becoming deacons. James Niceta was their representative, and the gospel of Matthew was written for them, as shown in Rev 10:4–7. They paid fees, and in this respect remained linked with Jewish Christians. The fees were at first paid to the David, and James the brother of Jesus accepted this practice. But when Jesus was declared the legitimate David by Hellenists, he refused to accept the fees, which meant payment for religious salvation. Those who continued to pay gave them to the Herod crown prince, who was then called 'All tribes' (Rev 1:7). In Rev 13:7 'Every tribe' means Herod of Chalcis, who acted as deputy to his brother Agrippa when the latter returned to Rome in AD 34.

In Rev 7:4–8 the list of twelve, concerning a Twelve Thousand from each 'tribe', deals with a new party, called the Romans, whose leaders were twelve men living at grade 12 in each of the provinces, either as Gentiles, or Jews who were put down to a very low grade. All were members of Agrippa's household in Rome, and formed the congregation at the festival at which Agrippa the Younger was initiated at the age of twenty-three. They had adopted Paul's doctrine, which was close to that of Peter, but Peter was head of the Christians while Paul led the Romans. Each belonged to a low grade of one of the Jewish orders, except Dan, and the changes from the Temple Scroll (p.189) help in making the identification. Their party was formed in AD 50 at the time Agrippa was defeated by Samaritans in Judea (see Rev 6 and notes), but in 51 Agrippa in Rome succeeded in gaining the favour of Claudius and having the Samaritans punished.

The list, in order from the south-west corner (p.161), consists of Luke, Timothy, Erastus, John Aquila, Andrew, Clement, Onesiphorus(?), Ananus the Younger, Tychicus, Titus, Epaphras and Paul. Most names are found in Paul's epistles as his supporters. The 'tribes' and provinces to which they belonged are, in the same order: Judah, now province 9, Herod's house in Rome (Luke); Reuben, now province 7, Ephesus (Timothy); Gad, province 8, the Tiber Island (Erastus); Asher, now province 11, Achaia (John Aquila); Naphtali, province 10, the Forum of Appius in Rome (Andrew); Manasseh, now province 12, Macedonia (Clement); Simeon, province 1 (parts that were pro-Agrippa and pro-Paul) (Onesiphorus); Levi, province 0, Jerusalem (the priest Ananus the Younger); Issachar, now province 2, Qumran (Tychicus); Zebulun, now province 6, Antioch-Bithynia (Titus); Ephraim Therapeuts (Joseph), provinces 3-4, Galatia-Cappadocia (Epaphras); Benjamin, province 5, Cilicia-Pontus (Paul). The twelve orders were divided into four sets of three, as were the places in the congregation, which had been set up for class C heads of 'tribes' (p.167).

Luke and Titus were heads of Japheth and Ham in the order of Dan, but they acted as 'eunuchs' to the Davids and in this capacity belonged to the two Essene orders Judah and Zebulun. For Titus as 'eunuch' see Acts 8:27. Luke belonged to Herod's house in Rome (2 Tim 4:11), and could act in place of Herod (see **nations**). On the occasion of Rev 7, he was 'sealed', absent, as he was acting for Jesus in Thessalonica (Acts 17:9). Titus had been in Antioch, with Luke, as Manaen (Acts 13:1), and in the episode of Acts 8:26–39 he had affirmed his loyalty to Agrippa.

The five Herodian orders, Simeon (Masada), Reuben (Machaerus), Gad (Gerasa), Issachar (Galilee) and Asher (Tyre-Sidon) had been headed by the first three Herods, by a married servant of the king, and by a Gentile, respectively. Agrippa (Simeon) and Timothy (Reuben) both accepted Paul's doctrine. The eastern substitute for Agrippa in province 1 (Simeon) may have been the Onesiphorus spoken of approvingly in 2 Tim 1:16–18, 4:19. Erastus (Gad) was on Paul's side, the servant of Antipas the third Herod in Bernice's party, and in the Roman party was third to Agrippa and Timothy. At Agrippa's defeat of the Samaritans he was in a position to take over their Tiber Island headquarters, an event referred to in Mark 12:9. Tychicus (Issachar) appears in 50–51 as a Pauline Herodian, the servant of Agrippa who accompanied him to Judea, and as seer C volunteered for military service at Qumran, 'Armageddon'. John Aquila was of the order of Asher, and based in Achaia from 51 (Acts 18:2).

Ananus the Younger was the priest of Levi who replaced Matthew Annas in 50–51. His heroism at the time of the siege of Jerusalem, when he acted with Agrippa to advise moderation, has been seen on p.131.

Paul was of the order of Benjamin, as he says himself in Phil 3:5, and originally based in Cilicia (Acts 9:30, Gal 1:21). He was not present in the congregation in September 50, so 'sealed'. As Acts shows, he was at this time in Thessalonica (Acts 17:1–9). He had been forbidden by Matthew to preach in Ephesus (Acts 16:6).

Andrew (Naphtali), one of the first disciples of Jesus (John 1: 40), is seen from several indications to be the same as Thaumastus, a slave whose story is told in *Ant*. 18:192, 194. His kindness in giving Agrippa I a drink of water at the time of his arrest led to his being emancipated and becoming a steward in Herodian households. Andrew was called at the tenth hour (John 1:39), indicating membership of grade 10, order 10, and province 10. This, as has been seen on p.110, was the meeting place outside the walls of Rome, the Forum of Appius, where instruction in Herodian doctrine was given, and where Paul's Romans were founded.

A Chief Therapeut appears in Part C of Revelation, on the side of the seer Tychicus, who may be identified with Epaphras of Philemon 23, Col 4:12–13, Phil 2:25–30. Therapeuts were of the order of Ephraim (Joseph).

Clement, the brother of Aquila and Niceta (p.89) appears in Philippi in Macedonia in Phil 4:3. He was to become the successor of Peter, who belonged to the Christians of the same province. He had originally been instructed by Barnabas and by Peter in Caesarea in the centre once held by the order of Manasseh. He had become the Christian head of Manasseh, and the successor of Peter in province 12.

tribulation (*thlipsis*) The married state (Rev 1:9, 7:14). It includes the later part of the betrothal period (Rev 2:9, 10).

true (*alēthinos*) Sadducees and Essenes combined in teaching villagers and Gentiles. Sadducee doctrine was called 'the Truth' and Essene doctrine 'Righteousness'. Both terms were used of the Sadducee and of the David. See **righteous**.

trumpet (*salpinx*) The person who blew the trumpet for the sabbath, sabbatical year, or jubilee year. The Chief Therapeut blew it every Friday evening before the sabbath, and Michael blew it at the jubilee. At the jubilee, the Chief Therapeut as 'Trumpet 7' prepared and gave the trumpet to Michael (Rev 8:2). The 'Trumpet' was a person, as he could speak (Rev 4:4).

The Chief Therapeut in the Exodus liturgy of the Therapeuts played the part of Joshua, who led the blowing of trumpets that caused the fall of Jericho (Josh 6:15-21). The Chief Therapeut acted the part of a Joshua on two occasions recorded in Josephus (*Ant.* 20: 97-98, 169-172; Acts 21:38).

See p.208 on the seasons for blowing the jubilee trumpet.

trumpeter (*salpistēs*) A man in the position of the sabbath trumpeter.

turn upon (*epistrephō*) To turn at a right angle, from north to west in Rev 1:12a, and from west to north in Rev 1:12b.

twelve-month (*eniautos*) A year by the solar calendar, beginning on the 31st at the equinox, the Jewish reckoning (Rev 9:15).

twelve thousand (*dōdeka chiliades*) As each province had twelve grades, the Twelve Thousand was the head of the lowest, grade 12 (Rev 7:5-8). See **tribe**.

two (*dyo*) A Herod in charge of a grade or province was called simply by the number. 'The Two' was a Herod in charge at Qumran, province 2 (Rev 19:20). 'The Seven' was a Herod crown prince, in charge at Ephesus, province 7 (Rev 17:11, Mark 12:23). 'The Five' was a Herod at grade 5, that of a levitical presbyter over the treasury (Rev 17:10). 'The Ten' was Herod over province 10, Rome (Mark 10:41).

unclean (*akathartos*) At the level of a married man, grade 11 (Rev 18:2). See also **spirit**.

underneath (*hypokatō*) Literally 'under down'. In a two-tiered structure, under the platform at the north end. In a three-tiered structure, kneeling at the chancel step, in one of its three positions. 'Underneath the feet' (Rev 12:1) on the west side, as the collection vessel called 'the feet' was on the west. 'Underneath the Altar of Incense' (Rev 6:9), in the centre. Under the space at the chancel step the crypt of a Christian church was built, and 'underneath' meant persons who were taught in hidden places that became the crypt. See **hidden** and **breadth**.

understanding (*nous*) A Sadducee school for Jews, to which a Gentile school ('intellect') was attached. The Sadducee schools and the Magian schools were originally connected, both being Samaritan, having a centre in Caesarea that was opposed to the Agrippas, and differing only on questions of war and peace. Hence in Rev 13:18 the Sadducee Jonathan Annas as 'Understanding' joined with 'the Beast' at the time it had become necessary to oppose Agrippa. But in Rev 17:9 Samaritans had split for and against Agrippa II.

unrighteous, make (*adikeō*) To exclude from the vestry by confining to the ranks of those outside the monastery wall, who were not permitted to enter the vestry. See **righteous**.

until (*achri*) At midnight, or in December. When the Julian calendar was introduced, the sabbath, normally beginning at 6 p.m., did not begin 'until' midnight. Months replicated hours as there were twelve of both, and 'until', may also mean December, corresponding to midnight (Rev 2:25).

up high (*epanō*) The raised seat in the central circle in the middle tier.

upon (*epi*) With the accusative, in the middle. With the genitive ('upon of'), on the west side. With the dative ('upon to'), on the east side. Important differences are sometimes indicated by this point.

victor (*nikōn*) The person who won the debate at a council, as shown by the verb in Rev 11:7. The verb is used of Jesus in Rev 3:21, 5:5, 17:14. The chairman of village debates, the Lion, was the 'victor' when the sides were even and he had the casting vote, so when his party won it was said that 'the Lion was victorious' (Rev 5:5). Since Peter was 'the servant of the Lion', he is called 'the victor' in Rev 2:7, 11, 17, 26, 3:5, 12, 21; and the name is used for his successor in Rev 21:7. The plural of reproduction is used of Clement in Rev 15:2, while Peter was still alive.

view (*horaō*) To 'see a vision' (*horasis*), that is, see a priest or a ruling king. See **vision**. (Rev 1:7). In Rev 19:10, 22:9, to treat the speaker, the Sadducee, as a priest of high status.

virgin (*parthenos*) For a male, a permanent celibate like John Mark (Rev 14:4).

visage (*opsis*) The headdress put on by Phanuel when he led dawn prayers as a servant of the 'Sun', Michael (Rev 1:16). Since Michael the Zadokite had to wear a turban, as shown in Ezek 44:18, it was presumably similar. The turban of the Zadokite developed into the Pope's mitre.

vision (*horasis*) A reigning Herod as Pontifex Maximus, or the crown prince, his deputy (Rev 4:3), or the Priest-Pope acting in his place (Rev 9:17).

voice (*phōnē*) A man in the position of a levite, one of whose duties was teaching and preaching. He could speak on the eastern or western sides of the middle tier. 'In a great voice' means the western side, when he spoke to villagers, including Gentiles.

wail (*koptō*) Be an ascetic under Essene rules, which forbade laughter (1QS 7:14, *War* 2:132–133), as opposed to the rules of the Therapeuts, whose ecstatic banquets were occasions of joy (Rev 18:9). An acolyte came under this discipline (Rev 1:7).

walk (*peripateō*) To be a teacher, like a Greek peripatetic teacher.

wall (*teichos*) The screen along row 7, marking the chancel dividing off the clergy from the congregation in the Gentile church described in Rev 21. See p.166.

war (*polemos*) A council called at the main centre at 6 p.m. on the 31sts at the quarters of the year, attended by all leaders, the occasion when important political decisions were made. The rule in 1QSa 1: 25–26 reads: 'When they are summoned for judgment, or for a Council of the Community, or for war. . .'. A useful indicator of date, as it always means the 31st.

wash (*plynō*) With 'robes', to carry out the rule of the Temple Scroll, that a celibate after an episode of sexual uncleanness must go outside the monastery for some days and wash his clothes before returning (11QT 45:9). Used of Peter leaving the married state and becoming a celibate in Rev 7:14.

watch (*grēgoreō*) To hold a midnight vigil, as the Therapeuts did. See **blessed**. Since their kind of celibate community held their main services at night, they expected the events of the Eschaton to take place at night (Luke 12:36–40). Nazirites, that is men who were married but left their marriages for seasons of spiritual retreat, acting in many ways like the Therapeuts, kept vigils (Rev 3:2).

water (*hydōr*) An immersion cistern for baptisms of members reaching grade 9. 'Water' was the highest in the hierarchy of washings at 'water' (9), 'river' (10), 'sea' (11). These washings were given to Jewish married men when they came as pilgrims to the monastery, and consequently to Gentiles. Proselytes at grade 9 were characterised as 'waters' (Rev 8:11), and uncircumcised Gentile monastics as 'wells of waters' (Rev 8:10, see **well**). A place where Gentiles met was called 'waters' (Rev 17:1, 15).

'Many waters' meant proselytes, originally attached to a Hellenist synagogue, see **many** (Rev 1:15, 14:2, 17:1, 19:6). The phrase 'many waters' is found in CD 3:16 in the context of the 'well' (of the Law) that had been dug in Damascus.

'Water(s) of life' (Rev 7:17, 22:1) meant baptism

combined with initiation ('life'), that is grade 9 combined with grade 7, the method introduced by Sadducees and Christians to give Gentiles admission to the sacred meal.

way (*hodos*) The institution for uncircumcised Gentiles of the order of Dan, divisions of Shem and Japheth, who were permitted by Sadducees to go higher than grades 10 and 11, advancing to initiation at grade 7 or the status of novice at 8. Pharisees such as Paul, before his conversion, condemned the Way, the advancement of the uncircumcised (Acts 9:2). Rev 15:3 the Sadducee Ananus the Younger taught 'the Ways'. Rev 16:12, 'the Way' in Damascus (compare Acts 9:2).

we (*hemeis*) a) The royal plural, used by a reigning king. Agrippa II is spoken of as 'we' in Rev 11:15. He is addressed as 'you' (plu.) in Rev 1:9. When the Annas priest was the Michael at a time of no Herods, he used 'we' (Rev 12:10). b) In narrative, used by a Gentile dynast, who acts as 'eunuch' to a king or royal person. Luke, speaking for Jesus, is 'we' in the later parts of Acts. Peter, from AD 46 onwards, was head of province 12, Gentile celibates. He uses the form 'we' of himself in Rev 1:5, in speech.

weep (*klaiō*) Be in the position of a Widow, characterised by weeping. In Rev 5:4 this means the west side of the front row, the seat of the 'Sea', who was the prince or queen. The queen in this position was of the same grade as a Widow.

well (*pēgē*) See **well** (**deep**) Whereas circumcised proselytes equal to acolytes were taught near the well (*phrear*) at Qumran, the uncircumcised were taught at the building 3 kilometres further south, at Ain Feshkha, at 'Jacob's well', using a different word (John 4:6). These were celibate Gentiles who were in a class equal to that of Peter, and a *pēgē* in Revelation is a school for celibate Gentiles teaching Peter's doctrines (Rev 7:17, 8:10, 14:7, 16:4, 21:6).

well (**deep**) (*phrear*, translated 'deep well' to distinguish it from *pēgē*) Deriving its image from the deep round well at Qumran, a '(deep) well' was a school where acolytes were educated, and also circumcised proselytes who rose to the same class. The '(deep) well of the abyss' was the space north of the Qumran vestry near the steps, where teaching was given to the acolytes who would mount the steps to attend the priest on the platform.

wet (*hyetos*) To be a teacher who used water baptisms and whose teaching was likened to rain, like John the Baptist (1QH 8:21). The Chief Therapeut, however, was called 'Not Wet', as his order did not use immersion baths. They ministered in 'waterless places' (Luke 11: 24). If 'Not Wet' 'rained' (Rev 11:6), the Chief Therapeut acted as a teacher at Qumran.

what (*ti*) Used as a play on T, the T-shaped initiation letter used by Herodians and Christians in the west (see p.184). Herodian Christian doctrine in Rev 2:7 and all seven letters.

whatever See **whoever**.

wheat (*sitos*) Wheat was brought to the exiled priests at Qumran as one of the food tithes, and they used it to make the loaves of the Presence that were eaten at their sacred meal. In Rev 18:13 it was one of the substances placed on Herod's high table on the upper tier. Gentiles associated with the Therapeuts were likened to wheat, as this community had sacred loaves but did not drink wine. The Gentiles were likened to the different stages the wheat went through (Mark 4:28, Luke 12:28), and paid their fees in instalments (Rev 6: 6, see p.194).

when (*hotan*) Used as a noun giving a time point: 3 p.m. (Rev 4:9), 3 a.m. (Rev 11:7, 12:4, 20:7).

when now (*hote*, translated 'when now' to distinguish from *hotan*) Used as a noun giving a time point at the half hour. In Revelation, at 3.30 p.m. or 3.30 a.m., the time when the informal service for higher Gentiles began, following the teaching of Jews. Rev 5 shows the sequence of events at the less holy 3 p.m. service when the

Septuagint was read, and after 3.30 psalms, from the Writings of the Old Testament, were sung and new compositions, such as Christian hymns and the New Testament, were permitted.

(at) where (*hopou*) ('At' is added to distinguish it from *pou*, 'where'). A place for the unclean. Used of the unclean south-west area of Qumran in Rev 11:8, and of a woman's cell in Rev 12:6, 14.

who (*hos*) The masculine or feminine relative pronoun does not refer to the antecedent, but means a priest or royal person. In Rev 1:2, Matthew Annas; in Rev 9:20, Agrippa I; in Rev 13:12, 14, Herod of Chalcis, claiming to be the royal Herod.

who? (*tis*) Agrippa as the *tis*, the 'Anyone' (the Greek word is used in both senses) (Rev 13:4).

whoever (*hosoi*, plu.), **whatever** (*hosa*, plu.) Priests (Rev 13:15) or permanent Gentile celibates, and their places (Rev 1:2), as opposed to '**whosoever**' (*hoitines*), dynastic Gentile celibates (Rev 1:7, 2:24, 9:4, 18:17).

wilderness (*erēmos*) A hermitage, Mird (Hyrcania) in the Wilderness of Judea (Rev 12:6), or a building modelled on it (Rev 17:3). For the distances between Qumran and Mird, relevant to Rev 12:6, see *Jesus the Man*, Main Locations in the Wilderness of Judea. (Mary needed ten hours, and was still at the queen's house at 5 a.m., as shown by the detail of Luke 2:8–19. The rate of walking – 5 stadia or a kilometre an hour in the hot, dry conditions – meant that she took an hour to go from the queen's house up to Qumran, eight hours from Qumran to the junction of roads at the wady near Mird, and another hour from the wady to the Mird building. She had to arrive by 3 p.m., as it was Friday and walking more than 1000 cubits was forbidden after that hour. The word 'prepared' in the verse shows that she arrived at 3 p.m.)

will (*thelō*) To act under one's own will as a member of the village class and not under monastic discipline (Rev 2:21, 22:17).

371

wind (*anemos*) A name for the Agrippas as a kind of priest, playing on the fact that the word 'the Spirit', a name for the Annas priest, also meant 'wind'. 'Great Wind' is Agrippa I in Mark 4:37, Agrippa II in Rev 6:13. 'Wind 4' of Rev 7:1 is the rival Herod Tigranes from Damascus, as the east was counted as the fourth of the compass points.

wine (*oinos*) The fermented wine used by village and Diaspora Essenes as a sign of initiation. Palestinian Essenes used new wine. In the gospels, the communion meal to which Jesus admitted Gentiles used *oinos* (John 2:3). When the evening fellowship meal was prolonged, this wine could be drunk in quantities and could lead to drunkenness (Rev 17:2). See also **blood**.

In Rev 18:13, the products of the food tithes (wine, corn, oil, Hos 2:8) were placed on Herod's high table by levitical servants; the wine by Kohath, on the eastern side of the priest. With it was the oil, standing for pre-initiate novices, placed by the novice-master. In Rev 6:6 the fees for the 'wheat', Gentiles on the east side, are described, followed by 'do not harm (exclude from the vestry) wine'. Therapeuts did not drink wine, and excluded coenobitic celibates whose initiates and novices were associated with oil and wine.

winepress (*lēnos*) The dining chamber in Herod's house in Rome ('Tavern 3') where Herod entertained emperors and procurators, with no limit on fermented wine. See Chapter 9. When the procurator, 'the Wrath', was present, it was called 'the Winepress of the Wrath of God' (Rev 14:19).

wing (*pteryx*) The vestment with sleeves of a member of the 'seraphim', the choir on the west side of the chancel step. The choirs of the Therapeuts were likened to 'cherubim' on the east side of the chancel (from Gen 3:24) and 'seraphim' on the west side, like those in Isa 6:2 who sang the Trisagion at the king's coronation. The seraphim in Isa 6:2 had 'six wings', so 'wing 6' was worn by the leader, who was a grade 6 acolyte (Rev 4:8). 'Wing 2' (Rev

12:14) was worn by a female member of the choir who was a lay presbyter.

wisdom (*sophia*) A name for a teacher of Asher Gentiles attached to a Sadducee school, which for Jews gave 'understanding' (*nous*) (Rev 13:18, 17:9). The zealots and Herodian nationalists had a woman in this position, but Christian Gentiles used a man. James Niceta took up the position in the Ephesus hermitage at the schism of AD 44 (Rev 13:18). The grade was that of lay presbyter. In the system of days this made the teacher of Wisdom a 'Monday', for day 2. In the lists of qualities reflecting the seven days in Rev 5:12, 7:12, 'wisdom' appears in the position of Monday. See **pearl**. In Rev 13: 18 the seer was to be the teacher of Wisdom in Ephesus, in place of Helena, both of them being in the order of Asher.

with (*meta + genitive*) Beside another minister of the same grade. In a council, the leader of one side debated 'with' the leader of the opposite side (Rev 12:7).

witness (*martys*) A pilgrim, such as Peter, who had taken up a higher celibate discipline and so permitted to sit in the congregation, witnessing from the pews what took place in the chancel and sanctuary. Since he was a pilgrim who had dedicated himself to the missionary cause, he was prepared for martyrdom, a meaning that came to be added to the word. A 'witness' was a lay bishop in the congregation (Peter in Rev 1:5, 2:13), and 'witness 2 (two witnesses)' a lay presbyter (Peter on taking up the celibate life, Rev 11:3). The successor of Peter, his 'reproduction', was called 'the witnesses' (Rev 17:6). This was Clement, shown in the Clementine literature to have succeeded Peter (see Chapter 7).

witnessing (*martyria*) See **witness**. The Witnessing, a person, was the head of the congregation of pilgrim 'witnesses'. Matthew Annas in Rev 11:7; Joseph in Rev 12:11; Peter in Rev 12:17, 1:2,9.

woe (*ouai*) A cry meaning that the expected appearance

of the Restoration had not come, and there was a further seven years to wait. One 'woe', seven years; two 'woes', fourteen years; three 'woes', twenty-one years. In Rev 8:13, three woes for AD 29 to AD 50, from Agrippa I's Last Jubilee to the end of the Annas Last Jubilee (see p.225). Two 'woes' allowed a zero quartodecimal period, and were used at an intercalation year. In Rev 18:10, two woes from AD 71, the north solar intercalation year. Rev 12:12, one woe from AD 16, allowing a zero decade from AD 6.

woman (*gynē*) A woman who was or was acting in the position of Chief Woman in the community. Mary in Rev 12:1, acting in the position of her superior Elizabeth, the wife of the Zadokite Zechariah, who had just been killed. Mary in Rev 12:14, where in June AD 17 she was made a lay presbyter.

wood (*xylon*) According to the hierarchical list in 1 Cor 3:12, 'gold, silver, precious stones, wood...', the 'wood' meant class D, called 'sojourners' (*ger*) in the Scrolls, whose corresponding list is 'priests, levites, sons of Israel (celibates) and sojourners' (CD 14:4, 6). Class D included Gentiles, at first even those who had taken up the monastic life. Retaining the image of an 'Eden', with its 'tree of knowledge' and 'tree of life' for their schools (Gen 2:9), they called their tree 'wood' (from the fact that Hebrew '*es* means both 'wood' and 'tree'), while the Jews used the term 'tree' (*dendron*). Gentiles received initiation at the 'wood of life'.

When Gentile monasteries split for and against Herod, the Herodian ones were led by the deacon Merari, who was of low enough grade to be able to contact Gentiles. He appeared as Zacchaeus on the 'sycamore tree' in Luke 19:4, and again as the 'Jailer' in the province of Macedonia in Acts 16:23. His lay counterpart in Macedonia was Peter (Aristarchus of Thessalonica). Peter presided at communions in these Herodian monasteries, so 'ate out of the wood of life' (Rev 2:7).

One of the sentences in the Copper Scroll speaks of

the 'court of the houses of wood' (3Q15, S.8), meaning the part of the grounds where men of class D could come.

'Wooden things' (Rev 9:20) means the chief circumcised proselyte Gentile, Nicolaus-Blastus, who was permitted to go to the level of deacon.

In Rev 18:12 two kinds of 'wood' appear in the list of ministers to Gentiles, preceded by *pan* 'every', meaning that they were Herods who were teachers in Gentile schools. The higher, 'citron wood' must in the context mean Gaius Costobar Herod, and the lower, 'Every vessel out of precious wood', Erastus Saul Herod as a member of the Gentile congregation who also belonged to class C, the 'precious stones'.

word (*logos*) 'The Word of God' was one of the titles of the David, used when as a dynast he had left the monastery temporarily for betrothal and marriage. While he was living in the village but in the betrothed state, he was permitted to teach but not preside at the communion meal. He was under the authority of the Sadducee priest. When the phrase 'the Word of God increased' is used (Acts 6:7, 12: 24) it means that the marriage had produced a son. Jesus was in the status of 'Word of God' prior to his second wedding, in AD 49 (Rev 1:2, 9), and during it in June AD 50 (Rev 6:9).

When the David had reached an age when he would no longer engage in sex, his eldest son received the title 'Word of God'. In June AD 53, at his sixteenth birthday, Jesus Justus received the title from Jesus, aged fifty-nine (Acts 18:11). Joseph had used the title 'the Word' during his father's lifetime (Rev 12:11). Jesus III was called 'the Word of God' in AD 100, while his father was called 'Jesus' (Rev 20:4).

A substitute could act for the 'Word', using the plural of reproduction (Rev 19:9, 22:6). This name is used for the Christian Pope, with additional identifying terms. The name 'the Words of God' is used for Jesus at the age of seventy-six in AD 70, no longer the substantive holder of the position, but able to teach as a substitute (Rev 17:17).

'Words', in the plural of reproduction, means a lay teacher in the village. 'The Words of the prophecy' (Rev 1:3) was the layman who read from the Writings of the Old Testament, containing books such as Daniel, while 'the Words of the prophecy of this book' meant, by the end of Revelation, one reading from the New Testament (Rev 22:7, 9, 10, 18, 19). This was the Christian patriarch of Ephesus.

work (*ergon*) An ascetic was 'saved by works', as he must perform severe acts of self-discipline in order to earn his promotion. All lay initiates were practising ascetics characterised by 'works'. But those born into the tribe of Levi, or into the royal family, were members who did not earn their promotion in this way. The Sariel priest was called 'the Faith' (from 'Abraham'; see **faith**) and the original distinction between 'works' and 'faith', drawn on in Paul's theology, was between those who had to earn promotion and those who received it by birth. In Paul's re-interpretation, all laymen received the identity of those who were born priests, so were 'saved by faith'.

In five of the letters to the seven churches, Jesus says 'I know (recognise) your works', but in the two written to members of the Herod family, Gaius Costobar in Smyrna and Erastus Saul in Pergamum, the phrase is missing. (The first letter, to Theophilus Annas, includes it, as he was a practising ascetic as well as a priest.)

James the brother of Jesus, who was treated by Jonathan Annas after AD 50 as the ascetic acolyte who taught Gentiles, performed the 'works' of 14:13 and 16:11, where his death at the hands of Ananus the Younger is referred to (*Ant.* 20:200, *Eccl. Hist.* 2, 23:5).

world (*kosmos*) The party of Herodians in the Diaspora, at the village level (Rev 11:15). The epistles of John uphold non-Herodian monastic life by saying 'Do not love (*agapaō*) the world', meaning 'do not admit Herodian villagers to the Agape sacred meal'.

worship (*proskyneō*) Pay the taxes required by Rome of Jews. The word for tribute is *kēnsos*, suggesting a play on 'worship' (Mark 12: 14). Those agreeing to pay them to Rome gave them to the high priest. But a person who 'worshipped the Beast' refused to pay the taxes to Rome, that is, was a zealot.

worthy (*axios*) A distinguished layman who was permitted to handle or read from the Septuagint (Rev 5:2, 4, 9). John the Baptist, who was of the level of Michael, said 'I am not worthy to stoop down and untie the sandals' (John 1:27), meaning that he was a true priest, not a layman.

wrath (*thymos*) The Roman procurator, when he became formally an initiate of the Jewish religion. In Rev 12:12, Valerius Gratus, AD 16, who changed high priests frequently, shown by the pesher to have received bribes, so Judas ('the Devil') 'had Great Wrath'. The history shows that the high priesthood under the procurators was regularly bought through bribes. The emperor Tiberius believed that this practice was simply a 'law of nature' and could not be stopped (*Ant.* 18:172). Pontius Pilate was called 'the Young Lion of Wrath' in the Scrolls (4QpNah 2:5), and the period when the procurators began was called 'the Wrath' in CD 1:5. Felix, procurator AD 54–60, was the Wrath of Rev 14:10. He is shown in Acts 24:26 to have asked Paul for a bribe. Titus in Rev 16:1, 18:3; 19:15.

write (*graphō*) To copy a work or write a letter that is of the level of the Writings of the Old Testament, that is the non-sacred part. The New Testament was defined to be at this level, also other non-scriptural forms of writing. When the seer was told to 'write', he was being told to record a part of the New Testament (Rev 1:19, 10:4, 21:5).

year (*etos*) The New Year for those holding the Julian calendar. In Revelation January 1 (Rev 20:2, 5, 6) or the Day of Pentecost (Rev 20:3, 4, 7).

yes (*nai*) A word said in a formal context by Sariel the village priest, when he was giving assent. The word identified a Sariel or one who claimed equal status. In Revelation, it is used by the Sadducee Priest-Pope (Rev 1:7, 14:13, 16:7) and by Jesus III when he had attained the position of priest (Rev 22:20).

zealous (*zeleuō*, be zealous) Follow the rule of Diaspora Essenes, for whom ascetic zeal gave a right to exercise priesthood. Simon Magus was the chief Zealot (Luke 6:15) (Rev 3:19).

The Continuous Pesher

INTRODUCTION TO THE PESHER
This section sets out the solution to the puzzle that has been set up in the Book of Revelation. It is the pesher of the mystery, intended for the very careful reader with special knowledge, who would be studying it to learn, not about vision and apocalypse, but about the profoundly important history of the Christian movement from AD 1 to AD 114.

It was still secret knowledge, intended only for the leaders, the men studying in Christian ascetic schools. For them, it was practical politics that such knowledge should be enshrined for ever in a book that would be used as scripture, arousing a sense of religious awe in those who heard it read in church but did not expect to understand it closely, while those who wanted to investigate further would use it, and the other books like it, as their curriculum in preparation for leadership.

The pesher has been made as readable as possible, but in this part of the book it is a question of setting out every detail, in order to present for testing the claim that Revelation is set up for the purpose of a solution. This frequently leads to problems of style, which are further discussed below. The writers of these books were straining language, and inventing a new, insider's

379

language of special meanings. It was a characteristic of the 'code' that it should appear obscure or even nonsensical to outsiders. Moreover, an additional problem for explanation arises in that the meanings depend on the Greek language. In order both to translate the Greek and convey the indications of special meaning, a number of devices have had to be adopted which mean that the translation and pesher are not always quickly understood.

For a more flowing translation of the Greek text of Revelation, see the Revised Standard Version of the Bible. Readers knowing Greek are referred to a critical text and apparatus, preferably the Nestle Aland *Novum Testamentum Graece*.

The reader is referred to the Lexicon (pp.252–378) for the reasons why the words of the text yield the special senses that form the pesher.

The Greek text of Revelation is translated verse by verse, each verse (given in italics) followed by the pesher, following the form that the Scrolls use for the meanings they find in the Old Testament. The Greek is here translated perfectly literally, in order to show the basis for the pesher. This extends to the word order, which often gives vital clues, but leads to an unnatural English style. Moreover, it will appear especially strange that at every 'and' a new sentence is made. This is because the word 'and' (*kai* in Greek) is used as punctuation to indicate the sense units to the pesharist. The same sentences are preserved in the pesher, in order to facilitate comparison.

The Greek at times contains extra words or forms that are needed for the pesher, for example double negatives, which in Greek usage still mean a negative, but in the pesher mean an affirmative. In such cases the extra word is given in brackets{ }.

The pesharist was reading 'exactly' (*akribōs*), the word that is used in the New Testament for the technique. This meant an exact observation of every detail of wording, and an assumption that every detail, every variation, meant something. A mechanical approach was required, as if words were objects, pieces of a puzzle. It was a legalistic approach, to an extreme degree, an approach that will be partly familiar to students of the Jewish rabbinical literature. There was no room for literary nuances, or an interpretation that would vary from person to person.

The rules for treatment of *words* are set out at the beginning of the Lexicon. There are also rules for *sentences* which may be set out here.

a) A frequently used rule in Revelation is that the subject of a verb or reference for a pronoun, if not given, is the last named noun or pronoun of the same gender and number, even if at some distance away, or even if a different subject might be assumed. This is, of course, not the case for a natural reading of Greek, but it is one of the main rules for the pesharist, which must be strictly observed in order to give the intended meaning. The subject is made clear in the translation by repeating it in brackets ( ). A good example is in Chapter 6, where in v.1 the Lamb opened the seal, and it would normally be assumed that in all the following cases of 'and he opened the seal' the subject would be the Lamb. This is not the case: the subject of 'opened' is the last named person in each case. In Rev 8:1, 'the Lamb' has been put in by Revised Standard Version, on the assumption that he is the subject of 'he opened' in every case. But the Greek reads only 'he opened', and 'he' is the last subject ('God' in 7:17).

If the previous word of the same gender and number is a physical object, it is not the subject of the verb requiring a personal subject. But some terms that appear to be objects are persons, for example 'altar of incense', which can speak (16:7). 'Earth' is a person: it 'helped the woman' in 12:16. They are to be treated as persons if evidence is given that they are. Objects that are persons are given a capital letter in the translation.

The word order necessary to apply this rule is

preserved, but normal English word order is used for nouns with adjectives, and other cases where there is no significance to the pesher.

b) Another important rule for the pesharist is that all events are strictly successive. There are no 'flashbacks', or events previous to the one described. The most interesting example of this is in Rev 11:8, which takes place in March AD 44, and includes the sentence '...the great city, which spiritually is called Sodom and Egypt, where also their Lord was crucified'. This means that a re-enactment of the crucifixion at Qumran took place in March AD 44, and that Jesus was present to take part in what had already become a liturgical drama. Simon Magus, the Beast of Rev 11:7, was present also. In Acts 12, dealing with the same season, both are shown in the pesher as present at Qumran, as well as Peter and Mary Magdalene.

c) Successive nouns or participles which appear to be in apposition, without 'and', are to be taken as a list of names. In Rev 12:9: 'the Great Dragon, the ancient Serpent, the one called Devil', means three different people. In Rev 8:6, 'the seven angels, the ones having the seven trumpets', means two people (both reproductions, so in the plural).

d) Sentences which are naturally understood as questions in the surface meaning, but which do not use a Greek word indicating a question, are to be taken as statements, since to rely on punctuation would be outside the procedures of the pesharist. *Tis*, meaning 'anyone', but which may also mean 'who?' is to be taken always as 'anyone', in a statement.

e) It may happen that the narrative suddenly changes to speech without introduction, the speech being indicated by the use of an imperative, as in Rev 12:12, 'rejoice!', or Rev 13:18 'let him count', or by a first person, as in Rev 16:15 'Behold I come'. In such cases, the seer who is giving the narrative is recording that he himself spoke at this point on behalf of the congregation.

The pesher includes necessary explanations which do not correspond to the words in the Greek text, but are part of the special knowledge on which the pesharist draws. Historical points drawn from back ground sources such as Josephus are given as part of the special knowledge. Dates are given at all points, drawn either from structures such as the seven trumpets, which refer to seven sets of seven years, or from known organisation in terms of time. The reasons why these may be known have been set out in Part II.

The Greek text used is that of Codex Sinaiticus. The Book of Revelation is not found in Codex Vaticanus, which is an almost perfectly accurate text. Sinaiticus comes a close second to it. Both were produced as official copies of the New Testament at the time Christianity became the religion of the Roman empire, in the early fourth century AD, and would have copied earlier texts. The exercise of demonstrating that a pesher exists requires a single perfectly accurate text, for any selection from texts introduces the element of subjectivity. Text critical opinion rates Vaticanus, then Sinaiticus, very highly. Variant texts from the early centuries, as well as early papyrus fragments, show a knowledge of the pesher, so the demonstration would actually work on one of these, for example the D text. But Sinaiticus in Revelation gives an approved text, and it is part of the hypothesis that the small number of variations from Vaticanus that it contains (in other books of the New Testament) are not scribal errors, but conscious variations made with an understanding of the pesher.

Note that the chapters of Revelation are out of order, for the reasons explained in Chapter 7. Part A by James Niceta, written first, is placed second in the final book, in 8:6–14:5, but is here given first. (Within the first document of Part A, its final section 11:15–19 shows the hand of John Aquila, who took over from James Niceta after the schism of March AD 44, and similarly the final section of the second document, 14:1–5.) Part B by John Aquila, written second, is placed first in the final book, 1:1–8:5. Part C by Tychicus is in 14:6–19:21. Part D by the final seer, another John, is in 20:1–22:21.

When all these introductory questions have been dealt with, it must be admitted that the pesher will read strangely. An original pesharist of the New Testament, writing for a community that understood the special meanings, would still have produced a writing that sounded strange. The Dead Sea Scrolls set out their pesher of the Old Testament verse by verse, and if the introductory phrases 'Its pesher concerns...' were removed, they would have a compressed history, not easily followed, whose form and sequence were determined by the scriptural text. Although the New Testament books were set up for a pesher in a way that the Old Testament books were not, their surface meaning still had to be coherent, and the underlying history could not flow entirely naturally.

The modern pesharist has a whole set of extra problems of communication apart from these. The special meanings have to be more fully explained in the context, and similarly the history to which they refer. The outlines of that history have been set out in Part I of this book, but many details have still not been given and are incorporated in the pesher. In order to form an opinion about the existence of the pesher – and this of course is the purpose of setting it all out word-for-word – the reader is asked to study each verse with some care, and at all points to refer to the Lexicon.

PART A

REV 8:6–14:5

FIRST DOCUMENT–THE SEVEN
TRUMPETS (8:6–11:19)
THE HISTORY OF GENTILE MISSION
DURING THE JUBILEE AD 1–50

CHAPTER 8

(See pp.208–209 for the chronology of Chapters 8:6–11:19.)

6 *And the seven angels, the Ones having the seven Trumpets (fem.) prepared them (masc., the seven angels), in order that they (the seven angels) might blow.*
6 On Friday, 23 September AD 1, at 3 p.m., Archelaus Herod was vested by the Chief Therapeut, who had the jubilee trumpet, and Archelaus blew the trumpet to end the extended jubilee and begin the Last Jubilee.

7 *And the first blew. And there came about Hail. And fire mixed in blood. And it (Hail) was thrown to the Earth. And the Third of the Earth was scorched. And the Third of the Trees was scorched. And All green Grass was scorched.*
7 On Friday, 24 March AD 2, the trumpet was blown for the greater half year. Judas the Galilean was appointed

Scribe-treasurer at Qumran. Theudas the Chief Therapeut allied with Joseph, head of Essene pilgrims, ready for martyrdom. Judas was laicised to lead the army. The chief pilgrim Gentile adopted the military discipline. The chief Nazirite Gentile adopted the military discipline. Agrippa Herod, aged twelve, began his education in a military school of the Therapeuts.

8 *And the second angel blew. And as a great Mountain of fire burning was thrown to the Sea. And the Third of the Sea came about blood.*
9 *And there died the Third of the Created Things of the ones in the Sea, the ones having Souls. And the Third of the ships was ruined.*
8 On Friday, 15 March AD 9 the trumpet was blown for the second septennium of the jubilee. Following the dismissal of Archelaus, a non-Herodian hermitage was established in Rome. Uncircumcised Gentiles in Rome adopted the pilgrim form of communion.
9 Gentiles in Rome supporting Archelaus were excommunicated. Gentiles of his 'Noah' mission were no longer financed by him, as his property was confiscated.

10 *And the third angel blew. And there fell out of the Heaven a great Star burning, as a lamp. And it (the Star) fell upon the Third of the rivers. And upon the wells of the waters.*
11 *And the name of the Star is said: the Wormwood. And the Third of the waters came about to Wormwood. And Many of the Men died out of the waters. Because they were bitter.*
10 On Tuesday, 24 March AD 16 the trumpet was blown for the third septennium of the jubilee. The acolyte Joseph, father of Jesus, became the heir of David, acting as a teacher of Gentiles. He taught pilgrim Gentiles who were baptised in running water. He taught uncircumcised Gentile monastics.
11 Joseph allied with the Therapeuts, who studied poisons. Gentile Nazirites joined the anti-Agrippa

Therapeuts through him. Agrippa in Rome was excommunicated through the influence of Gentiles. They planned to poison him.

12   *And the fourth angel blew. And the Third of the Sun was plagued. And the Third of the Moon. And the Third of the Stars, in order that the Third of them might be made dark. And the Day did not appear, the Third of it. And the Night likewise.*

13   *And I saw. And I heard one Eagle flying in mid-heaven saying in a great Voice, Woe, woe, woe the dwellers upon {of} the Earth out of the Remainder of Voices of the Trumpet of the three angels, of the Ones about to blow.*

12   On Tuesday, 16 March AD 23 the trumpet was blown for the fourth septennium of the jubilee. Gentiles taught by John the Baptist were not permitted to attend at the equinox. Helena became the Mother to Gentiles. Gentiles taught by James were only taught at night. There was no Phanuel acting as priest to uncircumcised Gentiles. Judas Iscariot was the chief Scribe-treasurer.

13   In September AD 29, I, James Niceta, at the age of twenty-six, was appointed lay bishop, to sit in the first pew as seer. I heard Jonathan Annas preach from the pulpit of the Herodian building at Mird: 'The Restoration has been delayed by twenty-one years until AD 50, because of the wrong done by Antipas to Thomas Herod, acting under Agrippa I who has returned and declares a Restoration'.

CHAPTER 9

1   *And the fifth angel blew. And I saw a Star out of the Heaven (masc.) fallen to the Earth (fem.). And there was given to him (Heaven) the key of the deep well of the abyss.*

1   On Friday, 24 March AD 30 the trumpet was blown for the fifth septennium of the jubilee. At Qumran I saw

the acolyte James, the legitimate David under the Baptist doctrine, appointed as head of lay celibates. John the Baptist as Michael received the key to the monastic property stored in the vault near the round well.

2   *And he (Heaven) opened the deep well of the abyss. And there went up smoke out of the deep well, as smoke of a great furnace. And the Sun was darkened. And the Air out of the smoke of the deep well.*
2   John the Baptist opened the entrance to the vault. Gentile deacons not observing Palestinian rules held their Friday afternoon service near the round well, and so did the Therapeuts. At 6 p.m. John the Baptist lost his position when his prophecy failed. Jonathan Annas took his place, supported by non-Palestinian Gentiles.

3   *And out of the smoke there came out Locusts (fem.) to the Earth. And there was given to them authority, as have authority the Scorpions (masc.) of the Earth.*
3   Through Gentile influence, John the Baptist was laicised. He could give village initiations only, and acted like a Therapeut initiating the village congregation.

4   *And it was said to them (fem., Locusts), in order that they should not make unrighteous the Grass of the Earth, neither Every green, neither Every Tree, if not the Men. Whosoever do not have the seal of the God upon {of} the foreheads.*
4   John had to accept Agrippa as a pre-initiate, and Agrippa became head of Herodian pilgrims, head of Herodian Nazirites, and also head of the Masada monastery. Agrippa became a dynastic celibate with a voice in the council, wearing the badge on his lower forehead.

5   *And it was given to them (Whosoever), in order that they should not kill them (masc., the Scorpions). Nevertheless, in order that they (the Scorpions) might be tormented five*

months. And the torment of them (the Scorpions), as a torment of a Scorpion, when it strikes a Man.

5   Agrippa then had authority over the Baptist, but he could not excommunicate him. He put him under penance for 150 days on 1 May AD 30. John was confined to his cell, and Theudas the Chief Therapeut was also under penance, but then he allied with Jonathan Annas.

6   *And in the days the those, the Men will seek the Death. And they will not {not} find him (Death). And they will lust to die. And the Death flees from them.*

6   On Friday, 23 March AD 31, when the Baptist's prophecies again failed, Agrippa as head of Masada, following his suicide attempt, attempted to recruit Simon Magus, the Chief Monk. He formed an alliance with him. But then Agrippa himself was excommunicated by Simon Magus for Herodian practices. Simon Magus separated from him.

7   *And the likenesses of the Locusts like Horses prepared to war. And upon the heads of them (Horses) as crowns like gold. And the faces of them as faces of Men.*

7   The successor of the Baptist was Jonathan Annas, a priest who travelled to the Diaspora to hold councils. He wore an ascetic's headband, and a circlet with the letter Qof, in gold for a priest. He wore a priest's headband, which was the headband of a Priest-Pope to Agrippa.

8   *And they (Men) had hair, as hair of women. And the teeth of them (women), as of Lions they became.*

8   Agrippa wore the headcloth of a married man, and the chief woman wore a veil. The chief woman, Helena, gave communion bread to Gentiles, and she was a minister of the Therapeuts.

9   *And they (Lions) had breastplates, as iron breastplates. And the Voice of the wings of them (Lions), as a*

Voice of chariots of Many Horses running to war.
9   Theudas the Chief Therapeut was head of a celibate congregation in Judea and in Egypt. He led a choir, and he acted as bishop to Jonathan Annas who came to preside at councils.

10   *And they (Horses) have tails like Scorpions. And stings. And in the tails of them (Scorpions) the authority of them to make unrighteous the Men five months;   11   they (the Men) have upon {of} them a king, the angel of the abyss; a name to him in Hebrew Abaddon (Destroyer). And in the Greek a name he has, Apollyon.*
10   Jonathan as priest carried the coloured banner and acted as superior of the Therapeuts. He carried a sceptre giving him power to excommunicate. As village priest he put Agrippa under penance for 150 days on 1 May AD 31,
11   and Agrippa then allied with Theudas in his capacity of celibate controlling monastic property; Theudas when with Agrippa being in the party of Hebrews, keeping the purity rules. But when with the Hellenist party he was opposed to Agrippa.

12   *The Woe the one has come from. Behold there come still two Woes after these things.*
12   In September AD 36 the end of the first extra septennium of the Last Jubilee came. In March AD 37 began the reign of a Roman (Gaius Caligula), and at this time Agrippa became ruler, beginning his second extended 'week'.

13   *And the sixth angel blew. And I heard one Voice out of the Horns of the golden Altar of Incense the one in front of God,*
14   *saying to the sixth angel, the One (nom.) having the Trumpet, Loose the four angels, the Ones (acc.) bound upon {to} the great river Euphrates.*
13   On Friday, 15 March AD 37, the trumpet was blown for the sixth septennium of the jubilee. I heard Theudas,

as a Scribe under Jonathan Annas, who was now
appointed high priest in Jerusalem, 14 speaking with the
acolyte James, and Theudas said: 'Promote me, a levitical
bishop, to the monastic life, making me head of proselytes
attached to the Damascus monastery'.

15 *And there were loosed the four angels, the Ones prepared
to the hour. And a day. And a month. And a twelve-month,
in order that they (the Ones prepared) might kill the Third of
the Men.*
15 Theudas from this hour entered the monastic life,
expecting the Restoration on this Friday at 3 p.m. Then
he postponed it to Pentecost. Then it was postponed to 1
January AD 38. On Friday, 14 March AD 38 from
Damascus Theudas excommunicated the Roman
governor, who had dined with Agrippa.

16 *And the Number of the Armies of the Horseman, Twenty
Thousand of Ten Thousand; I heard the Number of them (Ten
Thousand).*
16 In September AD 39 Agrippa the Younger, aged
twelve, was appointed Herod crown prince, nominal
leader of the army and Herodian head of Asia Minor,
where there were thirty thousand Jewish members; in
Jerusalem I heard him give the Septuagint reading.

17 *And thus I saw the Horses in the vision. And the Ones
Sitting upon {of} them, Ones having fiery breastplates. And
Jacinths. And Brimstones. And the heads of the Horses as
heads of Lions. And out of the mouths of them (Lions) there
proceeds out fire. And smoke.*
And Brimstone 18 *from these three plagues were killed
the Third of the Men, out of the fire. And of the smoke. And
of the Brimstone proceeding out, out of the mouths of them (the
Men).*
17 On Friday, 9 June AD 41 I saw from the congregation
at Mird the installation of the high priest Matthew Annas

391

as Priest-Pope. Agrippa sat on the west side as king, and Theudas was over the congregation of Therapeuts. Queen Helena of Adiabene was present, seated in pew 11. Her son Izates was present. Matthew wore an ascetic's headband, and Theudas did also. Theudas as an eastern bishop had again turned to zealotry. The Gentile service for Friday began.

Nicolaus-Blastus was initiated   18   on Friday, 8 June AD 42, and at the same season Agrippa quarrelled with Marsus the Roman governor of Syria, supported by Theudas. The Friday service for Gentiles was held. Nicolaus-Blastus was appointed a deacon.

19   *For the authority of the Horses in the mouth of them is. And in the tails of them. For the tails (fem.) of them like Serpents (masc.), they (fem., the tails) having heads (fem.). And in them (fem., heads) they (Serpents) make unrighteous.*
19   Matthew Arinas was treated as a village bishop who initiated Gentiles. He carried the coloured banner to Diaspora centres. Theudas was both an ascetic and equal to a village priest over the Therapeuts, who had knowledge of poisons. He had power to exclude from the vestry.

20   *And the Remainder of the Men. Who were not killed in these plagues. Neither they (Who) repented out of the works of the hands of them, in order that they should not worship the demons. And the golden Idols. And the silver things. And the copper things. And the stone things. And the wooden things, which nor are empowered to look. Nor to hear. Nor to walk.*
20   The proselyte Nicolaus-Blastus was appointed 'eunuch' to Agrippa. Agrippa avoided the plan to excommunicate and kill him in June AD 43. In Caesarea at this season, Agrippa was baptised as a congregation member of the Rome province, and no longer diverted the Roman tribute to zealotry. The emperor Claudius was

given a token initiation. Agrippa became his eastern deputy. Agrippa was also a deputy over Therapeuts in the west, represented by Apollos. He was also over village pilgrims, represented by Peter. Nicolaus-Blastus the chief proselyte used the eastern X sign of initiation as an acolyte. He was permitted to hear sermons. He acted as teacher.

21   *And they (the Wooden Things) did not repent out of the murders of them. Nor out of the Sorceries of them. Nor out of the fornication of them (the Sorceries). Nor out of the thefts of them (the Sorceries).*

21   Nicolaus-Blastus did not become a member of the Rome province, as he was associated with the zealots. He was associated with Simon Magus. He was associated with Helena. He was associated with Herod of Chalcis.

CHAPTER 10

1   *And I saw another strong angel going down out of the Heaven (masc.), clothed by a Cloud (fem.). And the Rainbow (fem.) upon {of} the head of him (Heaven). And the face of him (Heaven), as the Sun. And the feet of him (the Sun), as Pillars of fire.*

1   On Sunday, 1 September AD 43, in the cathedral at Ephesus, at the sixteenth birthday ceremony of Agrippa the Younger, I saw him come to the middle tier, where on the east side he was vested by Theophilus Annas. Then he went to the west side, and as Agrippa's son, he received the emblem of the 'Rainbow', used in the 'Noah' mission. He wore a priest's headband, and so did Agrippa. At 3 p.m. Agrippa's collection vessel was put out, and Agrippa the Younger stood over the western pillar.

2   *And having in the hand of him (the Sun) a little-book*

393

opened. And he (the Sun) put the foot of him, the right one, upon {of} the Sea. But the left one upon {of} the Earth.

2   On Agrippa's paten (plate for the holy bread) was a copy of John's gospel, to be given to the prince for his birthday. Agrippa announced the transfer of his monastic treasury from Judea to Achaia. But the income from villagers remained in Ephesus.

3   *And it (the Earth) cried in a great Voice just as a Lion roaring. And when now he (the Lion) cried, there spoke the seven Thunders the Voices of Themselves.*

3   King Agrippa preached from the west side of the middle tier, as head of Herodian nationalists. At the informal service at the half hour he preached again, and Matthew Annas, who had been dismissed as high priest and become priest for Ephesus, opposed him for his plans to gain empire, saying that Herod of Chalcis was the true Herod.

4   *And when now there spoke the seven Thunders, I was about to write. And I heard a Voice out of the Heaven saying, Seal what the seven Thunders have spoken. And do not write them.*

4   At the Gentile service Matthew gave counsel, and I began to copy his Sayings, to be published in December. But a message from King Agrippa was sent to me: 'Do not allow Matthew's teaching to be read. Do not treat it as scripture'.

5   *And the angel. Whom I saw standing upon {of} the Sea (fem.). And upon {of} the Earth he (Whom) lifted the hand of him the right one to the Heaven.*

5   At noon on Tuesday, 24 September AD 43, the solar 31st, Agrippa the Younger was given the rights of the sixteen-year-old crown prince. I saw him standing first on the far west of the chancel step. Then from the near west of the chancel step he went to the east side of the upper

tier, carrying his bread paten, becoming an acolyte to his
father.

6   *And he (Heaven) swore in the Living One to the Aeons of*
Aeons. Who created the Heaven. And the things in it
(Heaven). And the Earth. And the things in it (Earth).
Because a No Longer period will become.
6   Agrippa I, acting in the place of Matthew Annas, gave
him the oath of office, appointing him his successor who
would be called Agrippa II. Agrippa I now claimed to be
himself the Priest-Pope, head of priests. He was also head
of levites. He was also head of the village congregation.
He was also head of the lower congregation. He held that
the Herodian Holy War was now finished and the
Promised Land had been conquered.

7   *Nevertheless in the days of the Voice of the seventh angel,*
when he is about to blow. And there was ended the mystery of
the God, as he (God) gave the gospel to the slaves of Himself,
the prophets.
7   At 3 p.m. on this day the first trumpet was blown for
the extended end of the Last Jubilee, and it would be
repeated in December. At midnight beginning Tuesday,
24 December AD 43 Matthew's Sayings were published
for the end of the Last Jubilee, and approved by Herod of
Chalcis, who was allied with Simon Magus and claimed
to be the true Herod.

8   *And the Voice which I heard out of the Heaven again*
speaking with me. And saying: Depart, receive the book, the
one opened in the hand of the angel, of the One standing upon
{of} the Sea. And upon {of} the Earth.
8   At noon on this day I heard Apollos the new Chief
Therapeut directing me. At 3 p.m. he said to me: 'You are
promoted to an acolyte of the Therapeuts, taking the copy
of the Septuagint lying on the paten of Agrippa the
Younger, who begins the ceremony on the far west of the

chancel step. Then he goes to the near west of the chancel step'.

9   *And I came from, towards the angel, saying (nom.) to him to give to me the little-book. And he says to me, Receive. And eat it down. And it will make your belly bitter. Nevertheless in the mouth of you it will be sweet, as honey.*

9   After the Septuagint reading I stood in front of Agrippa the Younger, and asked him to re-assign John's gospel to my order. He said to me: 'You may receive it like communion bread. You may make John's gospel your own, to be read at common meals. When used by Gentiles like John Mark, it is a book for Gentiles plotting to poison Agrippa. But when it is re-assigned to you, and given its extra chapter, you will use it to teach the doctrine of the Promised Land'.

10   *And I received the little-book out of the hand of the angel. And I ate it down. And it was in the mouth of me, as sweet honey. And when now I ate it, the belly of me became bitter.*

10   On Wednesday, 1 January AD 44, the ceremony was repeated for the New Year, and I received John's gospel from Agrippa the Younger's paten. I claimed it as the gospel written by my order, read at their common meal. I taught from it the doctrine of the Promised Land. But when I read it at the Gentile informal service, I joined with John Mark in the plot against Agrippa.

11   *And they (prophets, v.7) say to me, It is necessary for you again to prophesy upon to peoples. And to nations. And to tongues. And to kings Many.*

11   Herod of Chalcis, whose party I had joined, said to me, 'You must take your place with the four kinds of uncircumcised Gentiles, linked with John Mark as head of Gentile monastics. Luke is the head of Roman Gentiles. Peter is head of all Diaspora Gentiles. Matthew is the superior of Gentiles in Sadducee schools'.

CHAPTER 11

(For chronological details in this chapter, see pp.243, 244, and relevant Lexicon notes.)

1   *And there was given to me a reed like a rod. One saying: Arise. And measure the sanctuary of the God. And the Altar of Incense. And the Ones worshipping in it (the Altar of Incense).*

1   On Sunday, 1 March AD 44, at a council at Qumran, I was given the two cubit measure used to build hermitages of the Egyptian order. Apollos my archbishop said: 'Be promoted. Plan a new hermitage outside Ephesus on the model of Qumran and Mird, where Matthew will officiate. He will bring the portable censer there. The Roman tribute will be paid through Matthew.

2   *And the court (fem.), outside of the sanctuary (masc.), throw out outside. And do not measure it (fem. the court). Because it is given to the nations. And the Holy City they (nations) will trample forty-two months.*

2   The 2 cubits on the north of the room are to be treated as the place for outsiders. They are not included in the 12×12 cubit square of the vestry and chancel. Agrippa belongs there as an outsider. He has attacked Jesus, treating him as a village bishop, thereby removing him from office on his fiftieth birthday on this 1 March of the south solar year 3980'.

3   *And I will give to my two witnesses. And they will prophesy days a thousand two hundred and sixty, clothed in sackcloth.*

3   Apollos said at the following solar 31st: 'I promote Peter to lay presbyter. He enters the ministry at 6 p.m. on this day, Friday, 6 March, when he begins his celibate life'.

4   *These (masc.) become the two Olive Trees (fem.). And the two lampstands (fem.), the Ones (fem.) in front of the lord of the Earth standing.*

4   Matthew Annas had been reduced to novice-master at Qumran. At 10 p.m. he lit the second lamp of the Menorah which stood on the dais edge, and claimed to replace Agrippa as head of the congregation.

5   *And If Anyone them (masc., These v.4) wishes to make unrighteous, fire proceeds forth out of the mouth of them (These). And it (If Anyone) eats down the enemies of them (These). And If Anyone wishes to make them (These) unrighteous, thus it is necessary to kill him.*

5   The news was brought from Caesarea that Agrippa had excluded Matthew from the ministry, and Apollos supported Matthew. Agrippa refused to admit to his table Marsus governor of Syria, who supported Matthew. At 1 a.m. Agrippa's exclusion of Matthew took effect, and Matthew excommunicated Agrippa.

6   *These have the authority to lock the Heaven, in order that Not Wet should rain the days of the prophecy of them (These). And authority they (These) have upon {of} the waters to turn them to blood. And to smite the Earth in Every plague as many as when they (These) wish.*

6   Matthew claimed independence at Qumran, with the power to exclude Agrippa from the right to the property, and when the prophecy of the Restoration was not fulfilled at 1 a.m., he appointed as teacher Apollos, whose order did not use immersion baths, and said that Agrippa the Younger in Rome was the true Herod who fulfilled the prophecy. Matthew allowed baptised Gentiles to become initiated and drink wine, in the form used by Christians. He attacked Agrippa for the non-fulfilment, ruling that the Herodian New Year was at the June solstice.

7   *And when they (These) end the Witnessing of them, the Beast, the one going up out of the abyss, will make with them (These) a war. And he will be victor over them. And he will kill them (These).*

7   At 3 a.m. Matthew gave up the claim to be head of the congregation, and Simon Magus as Pope climbed the steps to the platform beside the vault, to debate against Matthew at the council. He was against both Agrippas, and won the debate. He excommunicated Matthew.

8   *And the corpse of them (These) upon {of} the broadway of the Great City. Which one (fem.) is called spiritually Sodom. And Egypt, where. And the lord of them (These) was crucified.*

8   A fortnight later, at 3 a.m. on Friday, 20 March, Passover from the first position 31st and the anniversary of the crucifixion, Matthew was dressed in graveclothes for the first of the three and a half days leading to his final rite of excommunication, and his 'bier' placed at the lower round base outside the vestry. Then he was taken to the south-west area, the place for Gentiles and the place of punishment to which sodomites were sent by the priest. This was the place of the 'flesh'. At 9 a.m. the liturgical commemoration of the crucifixion began, and Jesus was placed on the western cross as one of the players in the re-enactment.

9   *And they (These) look out of the peoples. And of tribes. And of tongues (fem.). And of nations the corpse of them (nations) days three. And a half. And the corpses of them (nations) they (tongues) do not leave to be put in a grave.*

9   Then on Monday, 23 March at 3 p.m. Matthew was restored by the Christians, with the help of John Mark. Matthew was again head of Gentile Nazirites. Peter was head of all Diaspora Gentiles. On Monday evening at 6 p.m. Agrippa was declared by Simon Magus to be excommunicated, beginning his three and a half days at that hour. The decision was repeated at midnight,

beginning the 31st following the intercalation. Peter did not want Agrippa to be actually killed.

10   *And the dwellers upon {of} the Earth rejoice upon {to} them (neut., nations). And they (nations) exult. And they (nations) send gifts to each other. Because These the two prophets tormented the dwellers upon {of} the Earth.*

10   During the midnight banquet Herod of Chalcis gave initiations, claiming the place of Agrippa as head of Roman Gentiles. He anticipated taking Agrippa's place as king. He sent a reward to Nicolaus-Blastus, Agrippa's eunuch. Matthew, now acting for Agrippa the Younger, who was in Rome, put Herod of Chalcis under a penance.

11   *And after the three days. And a half, a Spirit of Life out of the God came into, in them (dwellers). And they (dwellers) stood upon the feet of them. And a great fear fell upon the Ones observing them (dwellers).*

11   On Wednesday, 25 March at 6 a.m. (Agrippa collapsed from the poison). At noon, Herod of Chalcis, who received the right to appoint high priests, took charge. He received the income from the mission. Matthew, who shared the table with him, was appointed to Antioch as an exile.

12   *And they (dwellers) heard a great Voice out of the Heaven saying to them: Go up here. And they (dwellers) went up to the Heaven in the Cloud. And there observed them (dwellers) the enemies of them.*

12   Herod of Chalcis agreed to the plan proposed by Matthew: 'Let there be a Diaspora place of worship in Ephesus'. He authorised the Ephesus cathedral, appointing Theophilus Annas the priest to the uncircumcised. Marsus governor of Syria dined with Herod of Chalcis.

13   *And in that hour there came about a great Earthquake. And the tenth of the city fell. And there were killed in the*

Earthquake names of Men Seven Thousand. And the Remainder (plu.) became fearful. And they (the Remainder) gave Glory to the God of the Heaven.

13   At 3 p.m. on this Wednesday, at Qumran, Theudas, holding that it was year 38 for the 'entry to Canaan', failed in his demonstration at the Jordan and was put to death. The eastern province seceded from the west. Nicolaus-Blastus who had given the poison to Agrippa was excommunicated by the new Chief Therapeut Apollos. He became a proselyte deacon in Antioch. He accepted Matthew as Priest-Pope.

14   *The Woe the second has come from. Behold the Woe the third comes soon.*

14   The extension of the Last Jubilee, March version, came to an end. It was announced that there would be a third septennium, for the Annas form of the Last Jubilee, changing the New Year to the June solstice.

15   *And the seventh angel blew. And there came about great Voices in the Heaven, saying, There has come about the kingdom of the world of the lord of us. And of the Christ of him (the lord). And he (the lord) will hold kingship to the Aeons of the Aeons.*

15   At noon on Tuesday, 23 June AD 44 the trumpet was blown for the seventh and last septennium of the Annas jubilee. In the cathedral at Ephesus, Matthew, speaking for Agrippa the Younger, said: 'The western Herodian party in the Diaspora has been founded, under Agrippa the Younger. The associated Christian party under Jesus has been founded at the same time. Agrippa the Younger is head of celibate communities and will have the title of Agrippa II'.

16   *And the twenty-four elders in front of the God, sitting (elders) upon the thrones of them, fell upon the faces of them. And they worshipped to the God,*

17   *saying, We give thanks to you, lord the God the All-mighty, the One becoming. And the One who became. Because you have received the great Power of you. And you have held kingship.*

16   At the end of the noon prayer Theophilus Annas took his place over the eastern pillar, then at 3 p.m. prostrated himself towards Matthew. He gave him the Roman tribute,   17   saying, 'I give you gifts, Matthew, king's priest to Agrippa II, the Priest-Pope in Ephesus, which is now the centre of the mission. You are the priest for Rome also. You have appointed me as your Phanuel. You are head of the Sadducee celibate communities.

18   *And the nations have been made furious. And the Fury of you has come. And the season of the lifeless ones to be judged. And to give the reward to the slaves of you, the prophets. And to the holy ones. And to those fearing the name of you, the little ones. And the great ones. And to ruin the Ones ruining the Earth.*

18   Agrippa II has been appointed by Claudius the agent of Rome in the east. He has arrived in Ephesus on his way to Cyprus. This is his north lunisolar intercalation year, observed also by Jewish Christians as their greater half year. The Gentile mission fees are to be given to Agrippa. Gentile monastics are under Barnabas, acting as crown prince to Jesus. Luke the head of Japheth is a deacon in Antioch under you, Matthew, and Titus head of the sons of Ham is in his party. Philip the head of Shem has separated. No money is to be given to the Damascus party, who take the money from Agrippa's mission.'

19   *And there was opened the sanctuary of the God in the Heaven. And there appeared the ark of the covenant of him (Heaven) in the sanctuary of him (Heaven). And there came about Lightnings. And Voices. And Thunders. And Earthquake. And Great Hail.*

19   The hermitage an hour from Ephesus was used for

Herodian Jewish celibates, with its platform treated as a Holy of Holies used by Matthew. It contained an ark for the scrolls of the Torah. The Law was read by Atomus the Magus. The Former Prophets were read by Gaius Costobar Herod acting as crown prince. The latter Prophets were read by Matthew. Apollos was the Chief Therapeut. Antipas Herod was the Scribe-treasurer.

CHAPTER 12

(See pp.209–210, for the chronology of 12:1–14:5.)

1   *And a great Sign appeared in the Heaven, a woman clothed by/with the Sun. And the Moon underneath the feet of her (woman). And upon {of} the head of her a crown of twelve Stars.*

1   At midnight beginning Friday, 19 March AD 6, Joseph, the David crown prince and acolyte, stood on the platform in the Qumran vestry, and Mary, taking the place of Elizabeth as initiator of Gentiles, was vested by the twelve-year-old John the Baptist, whose father Zechariah had just been killed. Elizabeth was with the excluded at the north of the vestry, in mourning. Mary wore an ascetic's headband, and a circlet with the emblem of Joseph.

2   *And she in a stomach having. And she cries in birthpangs. And she is in torment to give birth.*

2   Mary went to the space at the north of the vestry where Gentiles as outsiders were taught. She preached to prepare them for membership. She enacted their entry to membership as a 'birth'.

3   *And there appeared another Sign in the Heaven. And*

404

behold a great red Dragon, having seven heads. And ten Horns. And upon the heads of him seven diadems.

3   Then Joazar Boethus the high priest came to the platform. He took the chair as Pharisee high priest of the nationalist triarchy, one who gave initiation to proselytes. He kept the uncircumcised down at grade 10. On his headband was the emblem of a Pharisee who gave only non-celibate initiations.

4   *And the tail of him drags the Third of the Stars of the Heaven. And he threw them (Stars) to the Earth. And the Dragon stood in front of the woman the one about to give birth, in order that when she gave birth to the child of her he might eat it down.*

4   He then took the uncircumcised Gentile admitted by Joseph down to the queen's house, forbidding him to come closer to the Qumran buildings. He laicised Joseph. As Mary, at 3 a.m., began the ceremony at which the twelve-year-old Jesus was to be separated from his mother, the Pharisee stood in the place of the levite, and after the first part of the ceremony declared that Jesus was illegitimate.

5   *And she gave birth to a son, a male. Who is about to shepherd All the nations in an iron rod. And there was snatched up the child of her toward the God. And toward the throne of him.*

5   But at the same hour Joazar ceased to be high priest, Jesus became the legitimate heir, and was hailed as the potential Messiah. Joseph was permitted to return to Qumran, where he was to be head of the Herodian school for Gentiles under Egyptian discipline. At 4 a.m. Jesus came under monastic rules, and was taken up to Qumran to be presented to Ananus the Elder, the new Sadducee high priest. He was taken into the vestry to stand before the platform.

6   *And the woman fled to the wilderness, at where she has there a place prepared from the God, in order that there they (All the nations, v. 5) might feed her one thousand two hundred and sixty days.*

6   Mary left at 5 a.m. for the ten hour walk to Mird, reaching it at 3 p.m., the time on Friday when walking must cease, and went to the underground cells of the Sisters, where she attended the Friday evening meal which Herodians permitted Gentiles and women to take, and at 6 p.m. the south lunisolar quartodecimal year 3941 began.

7   *And there came about a war in the Heaven, the Michael. And the angels of him warring with the Dragon. And the Dragon warred. And the angels of him.*

7   At the same hour a council was held at Qumran, with the young John the Baptist present as the heir of Zadok. Simeon (Simon the Essene), the Gabriel, debated with Joazar. Then Joazar held a separate council. Archelaus Herod was allied with him.

8   *And he (the Dragon) was not strong. Neither a place of them (the angels) was found still in the Heaven.*

8   Joazar was no longer the high priest. Archelaus was replaced by the Roman governor Quirinius, who as ruler of the country could take the platform at Qumran.

9   *And there was thrown the great Dragon, the ancient Serpent, the one called Devil. And the Satan, the One deceiving the whole Dominion (fem.), was thrown to the Earth (fem.). And the angels of him (the One deceiving) with him were thrown.*

9   The uprising was held, and the revised triarchy, without Archelaus the Calf, was defeated: Joazar, Saddok-Theudas and Judas the Galilean. Theudas then replaced Judas, and the chief Magus taught the Gentile head of the Rome province that Antipas was the true Herod, and was

laicised. Judas the Galilean was killed.

10 *And I heard a great Voice in the Heaven saying, At now has come about the Salvation. And the Power. And the kingdom of our God. And the authority of his Christ. Because there has been thrown the accuser of our brothers, the One accusing them in front of the God of us of day. And of night.*

10 In AD 15 I, James Niceta, an acolyte at the age of twelve, heard Ananus the Elder on the platform at Qumran say: 'I, Ananus the Elder, reign independently as high priest, without a Herod, giving initiation to Gentiles. Eleazar Annas is my deputy. Celibate communities teach Sadducee doctrine. Gentiles are given initiation by Jacob-Heli. The emperor Augustus has died, while the new emperor Tiberius, advised by the Annas priest, does not make Antipas the Herod. It is the Day position of the calendar'.

11 *And They (new subject) were victorious over him (God) on account of the blood of the Lamb. And on account of the Word of the Witnessing of them (They). And they did not love the Soul of them until Death.*

11 Then Antipas caused the dismissal of Ananus, who presided at the village communion meal with Jacob-Heli. Joseph, who acted as head of pilgrims, supported Antipas. Antipas in Rome would not admit Agrippa to his midnight Agape meals, and caused him to be excommunicated by the chief Magus.

12 *On account of this exult, Heavens. And the Ones in them tabernacling. Woe to the Earth. And the Sea. Because there has gone down the Devil toward you (plu., Heavens), having great Wrath, knowing. Because he has a small season.*

12 In AD 16 the seer sent a message from the congregation: 'Agrippa, claim the Herodian kingship. Eleazar Annas has become high priest and supports you. In another seven years you may return and become the king.

In Rome you act as the Herod. In Judea Judas Iscariot supports you and bribes the procurator Valerius Gratus; recognising you as the Herod. This is the intercalation year for the Herodian calendar'.

13   *And when now the Dragon saw. Because he was thrown to the Earth, it (the Earth) pursued the woman. Which One (fem.) gave birth to the male.*
13   On Tuesday, 23 March AD 17 Caiaphas was present in Jerusalem at the afternoon service for Gentiles. He was laicised when he objected to admitting the uncircumcised, and he attacked Mary. Mary, now the David queen, took part in the initiation of Jesus, the David crown prince, at the age of twenty-three.

14   *And there were given to the woman the two wings of the great Eagle, in order that she might fly to the wilderness to the place of her, at where she is fed there a season. And seasons. And a half of a season from a face of the Serpent.*
14   On Friday, 4 June AD 17, Mary was made a lay presbyter by Eleazar Annas, leading the female choir as 'Miriam', and she went to Mird to the cells of the Sisters, where she joined in the Friday evening meal. The ceremony was repeated in September. It was repeated again on Friday, 3 December, when Theudas presided in his lay capacity.

15   *And there threw the Serpent out of the mouth of him behind the woman water, as a river, in order that he might make her one-carried-by-a-river.*
15   At the Exodus liturgy at that season, Theudas went to the source of the aqueduct west of the Mird building to play the part of 'Pharaoh', treating the aqueduct as the 'Red Sea' in which Mary as 'Miriam' gave baptisms to Gentiles at grade 10.

16   *And the Earth helped the woman. And the Earth opened*

the mouth of it. And it (the Earth) drank down the river, which the Dragon threw out of the mouth of him.

16   Joseph acted as husband and bishop to Mary. At the Mird building he admitted Gentiles for teaching. He had a drink of water from the aqueduct, representing pilgrims at grade 10 who were permitted to drink water only, not wine, but Caiaphas refused to allow an uncircumcised Gentile to be promoted further.

17   *And the Dragon was furious upon {to} the woman. And she came from, to make a war with the Remainder of the seed of her, of the Ones keeping the commandments of the God. And of those having the Witnessing of Jesus.*

17   In AD 18 Caiaphas, a Pharisee, became high priest and agent of Rome, and attacked Mary for being a minister teaching Gentiles. Mary left Mird and went to Qumran, where she joined in the councils of proselytes taught by James, now the official crown prince, and with Gentile monastics taught by Sadducees. Peter became the chief pilgrim, supporting Jesus as legitimate.

18   *And he (Jesus) stood upon the Sand of the Sea.*

18   Jesus with the Hellenist party ministered to the third Herod, the tetrarch Antipas.

CHAPTER 13

1   *And I saw out of the Sea a Beast going up, having ten Horns. And seven heads. And upon {of} the Horns of him ten diadems. And upon the heads of him names of blasphemy.*

1   On Tuesday, 12 March AD 26, as a Gentile initiate at the age of twenty-three, I saw Judas Iscariot as a bishop, going up the steps to the platform, the head of the party which kept the uncircumcised down at grade 10. He gave initiation at grade 7 to proselytes. The uncircumcised

were not admitted to the celibate congregation. The letters on his headband showed that he was a zealot.

2   *And the Beast which I saw became like a Leopard. And the feet of him (the Leopard), as a Bear. And the mouth of him (the Bear), as a mouth of a Lion. And there gave to him (the Lion) the Dragon (subj. of gave) the Power of him (the Dragon). And the throne of him (the Dragon). And great authority (fem.).*

2   I saw Judas appointed as 'Leopard', the general for the campaign to Ethiopians, planned for AD 26. He had a collection vessel for Gentile Roman tribute, and the tetrarch Antipas was an alternate leader. Antipas gave Herodian teaching, and so also did Agrippa, who had returned. Caiaphas appointed Agrippa as his deputy. But Caiaphas as high priest was ruler of the people. He gave village initiations.

3   *And one out of the heads of him (Dragon), as slain to Death. And the plague of the Death of him (Dragon) was healed. And there marvelled the whole Earth behind the Beast.*

3   John the Baptist acted as leader of ascetics beside Caiaphas, and was threatened with excommunication by Simon Magus. Simon was excluded for a season, then was restored under the rules of the Therapeuts. In AD 29, when the calendar changed to the Night position, Agrippa was accepted as the Herod successor, with the financial support of Judas.

4   *And they (Horns, v. 1) worshipped to the Dragon. Because he (the Dragon) gave the authority to the Beast. And they (Horns) worshipped to the Beast saying, Who is like the Beast? And Who is empowered to make war with him?*

4   Judas paid the Roman tribute money to Caiaphas. Caiaphas gave Judas the power to initiate. Then Judas kept the tribute money himself, to be used for zealotry,

and said: 'Agrippa is the servant of Judas'. Then Agrippa turned against Judas in the council.

5　*And there was given to him (the Beast) a mouth to speak great things. And blasphemies. And there was given to him (the Beast) authority to make, forty-two months.*
5　Theudas, a teacher, took the place of Judas. He became a zealot. Following Judas' death, he was given the right to initiate on 1 March, AD 34, the south solar generation year.

6　*And he (the Beast) opened the mouth of him to blasphemies towards the God, to blaspheme the name of him (God). And the tabernacle of him (God), the Ones in the Heaven tabernacling.*
6　Theudas became leader of the zealot Hebrews' party, opposing Jonathan Annas who was leader of the peace party. Jonathan moved with the Hellenists to Caesarea, where the 'tabernacle' and 'Heaven' came together again, as they had once been at Qumran, and Jonathan was supported by the peace party to become the next high priest.

7　*And there was given to him (Heaven) to make a war with the holy ones. And to be victorious over them. And there was given to him (Heaven) authority upon Every tribe. And people (masc.). And tongue (fem.). And nation (neut.).*
7　At the council on Friday, 19 March AD 34, Jonathan Annas opposed James the brother of Jesus. He removed James as crown prince to Jesus. Jonathan was supported by the four kinds of uncircumcised Gentiles, their Nazirites led by Herod of Chalcis, to whom Gentile fees were now paid. Barnabas-Joses, the next brother of Jesus, was now his crown prince in place of James, and superior of John Mark. Peter was the head of Diaspora Gentiles. Luke was the head of Roman Gentiles.

8　*And there worship him (people) All the dwellers upon {of}*

Earth (fem.). Of Whom is not written the name of him (Whom) in the book of the life of the Lamb slain from a throwing down of a world.

8   Herod of Chalcis paid the Gentiles' tribute money through Barnabas. Agrippa's name was removed from the list of initiates recorded in the Septuagint, kept by Jesus, who was in seclusion in the Caesarea Magian monastery.

9   *If Anyone has an ear, let him hear.   10   If Anyone to captivity, to captivity he departs. If Anyone in a sword to be killed, him in a sword to be killed. Here is the Endurance. And the faith of the holy ones.*

9   But the seer spoke for the congregation: 'Agrippa, whose right to restore the Herodian kingship has been denied by some, has been promised the succession; let him be accepted.   10   Agrippa is in Rome, and meets with the Roman pilgrims. But he has been excommunicated by Jonathan Annas as both a celibate and a layman. I have been appointed to lead prayers as seer in the Ephesus congregation. Barnabas has been given the status of a priest.'

11   *And I saw another Beast going up out of the Earth. And it (the Earth) had two Horns like a Lamb. And it (the Lamb) spoke, as a Dragon.*

11   On Friday, 16 March AD 36, at the beginning of the campaign against Japheth, I saw Simon Magus going up the steps beside the vault to the platform at Qumran. He claimed the positions of Agrippa, and he promoted the uncircumcised as far as lay presbyters, agreeing with Jesus that circumcision was not necessary. Jesus was a member of the council, and so was Caiaphas.

12   *And the authority of the first Beast, he (the Beast) makes All (authority) in front of him (the Beast). And he (the Beast) makes the Earth. And the Ones in it (the Earth) dwelling, in order that they might worship the first Beast. Of Whom was healed the plague of the Death of him (Whom).*

12   Simon Magus gave initiations in the position of
bishop, and he initiated Herod of Chalcis. Simon claimed
to be head of the congregation, holding its property.
Herod of Chalcis was instructed as the Herod successor,
and advised to divert the Roman tribute to Simon. At the
accession of Jonathan Annas in March AD 37 Simon was
excluded for a season, but restored at Pentecost.

13   *And he (Who) makes great Signs, in order that. And fire
he makes out of the Heaven (masc.) to go down to the Earth
(fem.), in front of the Men.*
13   At this season Herod of Chalcis established a separate mission in Damascus, giving promotions to
proselytes. He brought Theudas from Qumran to the
Damascus congregation, and linked it with Masada.

14   *And it (the Earth) deceives the Ones dwelling upon {of}
the Earth on account of the Signs which were given to him
(Heaven) to make in front of the Beast. One saying (masc.
nom.) to the Ones dwelling upon {of} the Earth to make an
Icon to the Beast (neut.). Who (masc.) has the plague (fem.)
of the sword. And he (Who) lived.*
14   Simon taught Herod of Chalcis that he was the
Herod successor, accepting him as a head of schools who
could give promotions on Simon's advice. Simon advised
Herod of Chalcis to appoint the Samaritan Ananias as
high priest. At the June solstice in 37 Herod of Chalcis
was excluded for a season by Jonathan Annas. But he was
accepted in Damascus as the Herod.

15   *And there was given to him (Whom) to give a Spirit to
the Icon of the Beast, in order that. And should speak the Icon
of the Beast. And it (the Beast) should make that Whoever if
they do not worship the Icon of the Beast they should be killed.*
15   Herod of Chalcis appointed Ananias the Samaritan
to be future high priest and leader of the congregation.
Ananias was made a member of the council. When in

September AD 37 Jonathan Annas refused to divert the Roman tribute to Ananias, Simon brought about his deposition from the high priesthood.

16 *And he (the Beast) makes All the little ones. And the great ones. And the rich ones. And the poor ones. And the freedmen. And the slaves, in order that they (the slaves) should give to them (the freedmen) a mark upon {of} the hand of them the right, or upon the forehead of them.*

16 At the same season, when it became known that Agrippa was appointed king, Simon in Caesarea established the anti-Agrippa party, first taking the headship of the Gentiles of Joppa and its property from Agrippa. Then he gained Caesarea Philippi through Philip. He gained Nicolaus-Blastus. He gained Theudas. John Mark, the chief Herodian freedman, supported him. Herod of Chalcis claimed headship of the Vineyard mission, and rewarded John Mark for his part in betraying Agrippa, by permitting him to serve the sacred bread, and John Mark wore a headband like a phylactery as the eastern party did.

17 *And in order that Not Anyone should have power to buy or to sell, if not the One having the mark, the name of the Beast or the Number of the name of him.*

17 At the schism in AD 44 Simon became Pontifex Maximus of the Damascus party in place of Agrippa, and he bought promotions by payment of money and gave initiations in return for money, and so also did Herod of Chalcis, who was treated as head of schools by Simon and as the Herod successor.

18 *Here the Wisdom becomes. The One having understanding, let him count the Number of the Beast. For a Number of a Man becomes. And the Number of him (a Man) is six hundred sixty-six.*

18 At this time the seer spoke for the congregation: 'I am going to Ephesus as a teacher. Jonathan Annas is

supporting Herod of Chalcis as the successor. Herod of Chalcis is appointed by Simon over celibate congregations. He uses the system of promotions through the letters Samekh, Resh and Taw'.

CHAPTER 14

1   *And I saw. And behold the Lamb standing upon the Mount Zion. And with him a Hundred and Forty-Four Thousand having the name of him. And the name of the Father of him written upon {of} the foreheads of them.*
1   I, John Aquila, was present in Jerusalem for the council in June AD 46. On Pentecost Sunday, 5 June at noon, Jesus stood on the middle tier of the hermitage on the Mount of Olives. Beside him stood Peter, now a graduate celibate, head of Christian Gentiles of province 12. Peter also wore on his lower forehead the Jewish graduation sign given by Matthew Annas.

2   *And I heard a Voice out of the Heaven, as a Voice of Many waters. And as a Voice of great Thunder. And the Voice which I heard, as of harpists harping in the harps of them.*
2   At 3 p.m. the readings from the Septuagint were given by Matthew as Priest-Pope, and by his deputy Theophilus Annas, priest for uncircumcised Gentiles. Matthew concluded the reading. Then he signalled the informal part of the service at the half hour, and the reading of the psalms began, accompanied by harp music conducted by Theophilus Annas.

3   *And they (harpists) sing a new song in front of the throne. And in front of the four Living Ones. And of the elders. And No One was empowered to learn the song, if not the Hundred and Forty-Four Thousand, the Ones bought from the Earth.*
3   After this a Christian hymn was sung, led by

415

Theophilus from the centre of the middle tier. Apollos, the choirmaster for the Therapeuts, stood on his west side. At 4 p.m. Theophilus presided. James the brother of Jesus was present as an acolyte, and sang only a pre-Christian hymn, and Peter joined him, together with the former seer James Niceta, now a missionary who was paid from Herodian funds.

4 *These are the Ones who with women were not defiled, for virgins are they. These are the Ones following the Lamb at where he departs. These were bought from the Men as firstfruits to the God. And to the Lamb.*

4 At the council of Jerusalem at this season, the four kinds of uncircumcised Gentiles who produced the gospels were recognised: first, permanent monastics, on condition that they did not accept Helena. Second, celibates like Luke, acting as acolyte to Jesus who was about to go to Rome. Third, missionaries like James Niceta, supported from the funds of Agrippa II, looking to Matthew Annas as their priest. Fourth, Peter, who was the deputy to Jesus.

5 *And in the mouth of them (the Men) there was not found a Falsehood, unblemished they (the Men) are.*

5 Herod of Chalcis was not given the Herod succession, but it was given to Agrippa the Younger in Rome, and he intended to be a lifelong celibate.

PART B

REV 1:1–8:5

THE ESTABLISHMENT OF THE CHRISTIAN PARTY IN EPHESUS, AD 44–51

CHAPTER 1

Four Preliminary Documents, written at the accession and coronation of Agrippa II.

A. A letter of Jesus, written from Antioch in June AD 44 to Agrippa the Younger, who was expected in Cyprus in September (1:1–3).

1 *A revealing of Jesus Christ, which gave to him the God, to show to the slaves of him (God) the things which must come about shortly. And he (God) has given a sign, having sent from through the angel of him (God) to the slave of him (God), John.*

1 A public appearance of Jesus Christ, by special permission of Matthew Annas, to inform Agrippa of the new calendar with its primary feast at Pentecost. Matthew has granted a promotion, sending his chief celibate to appoint the Herodian Gentile missionary John as seer in the Ephesus congregation.

2   *Who witnessed the Word of the God. And the Witnessing of Jesus Christ, Whatever things he (Jesus) saw.*

2   Matthew is the superior of Jesus when he is in the outside world. Peter is head of the pilgrim congregation for Jesus, who is now at a monastery.

3   *Blessed is He Who Reads. And the Ones hearing the Words of the prophecy. And keeping the things in it written, for the season is near.*

3   You, Agrippa, as the Herod who gives the reading from scripture, are a Blessed One, equal to a celibate keeping midnight vigils. When you are in the congregation you listen to the lay teacher teaching from the prophecies of the Old Testament. You study the Writings yourself, and observe the ascetics' calendar, for which June AD 44 is your intercalation season.

B. A letter of John Aquila to Agrippa, expected in Ephesus for his second coronation in June AD 49, with messages from Matthew, Theophilus and Jesus (1:4–5a).

4   *John to the seven Churches the ones in the Asia, Grace to you (plu.). And Peace from the One becoming. And the One who became. And the Coming One. And from the Seven Spirits the ones in front of the throne of him (the Coming One).*

4   John to Agrippa II as head of the seven Gentile communities in the province of Asia; I speak as a servant of the David crown prince. Matthew is the Priest-Pope in Ephesus. He is also priest to the Rome community. He is a levite in Antioch. Theophilus Annas, priest to the uncircumcised, is his deputy.

5   *And from Jesus Christ, the witness, the faithful one, the firstborn of the lifeless ones. And the archon of the kings of the Earth.*

5   Jesus is a lay levite to the Therapeuts, and the heir of David, with his chief pilgrim Peter, his presbyter Paul, and his son and heir Jesus Justus. Apollos is the archbishop under the Scribe-treasurer Antipas Herod.

C. A letter of Peter, head of Gentile celibates, to Agrippa II and to Jesus, written at the same time as the above (1:5b-6).
To the One loving us. And to the One releasing us out of the sins of us in the blood of him.
To Agrippa, who presides over the Agape meal which I now attend. And to Jesus, who permitted me to leave the married state and enter the celibate state, using the Christian form of communion.

6   *And he has made us a kingdom, priests to the God. And to the Father of him (God), to him the Glory. And the Might (neut.) to the Aeons of the Aeons. Amen.*
6   Jesus has put me in charge of the Christian celibate community, and allowed me to act as a priest like Phanuel, under Matthew Annas. Matthew is the Priest-Pope, the abbot of eremitical communities, and holding the common property of dynastic celibates. He is the king's priest who will embrace and crown Agrippa II. My letter is ended.

D. A letter of Matthew Annas in Ephesus to Agrippa, written at the same time (1:7–8).

7   *Behold he (the Might, neut.) comes with the Clouds. And Every eye will view him (masc., God, v.6). And the Whosoever Ones have pierced him (God). And there will wail upon him (God) All the tribes of the Earth. Yes, Amen.*
7   In Ephesus Matthew Annas is the king's priest, and Theophilus Annas is his deputy. Agrippa is to be crowned by Matthew. Agrippa has appointed Matthew head of ascetics. Timothy Herod, appointed the Herod crown

prince, has become an acolyte to Matthew, receiving the fees of Gentiles. I add the 'Yes' of a Sariel. My letter is ended.

8   *I become the Alpha. And the O (Omega) says a lord the God, the One becoming. And the One who became. And the Coming One, the All- mighty.*

8   The signature: I am appointed the first of the class of priests. 'I appoint Agrippa as the Michael,' I will say when I crown him in Ephesus. I am a priest in Rome also. I am a levite in the east, king's priest to the Herods.

The Seven Letters and the Seven Seals
(Rev 1:9–8:5)
1 June AD 49 to 1 January AD 51

(See pp.211–213 for the chronology of Part B.)

9   *I, John, the brother of you (plu.). And one common in the tribulation. And a kingdom. And Endurance in Jesus, I came about in the island called Patmos on account of the Word of the God. And the Witnessing of Jesus.*

9   I, John Aquila, am the chief Gentile married man, under you, Agrippa. I take the common meal, for married men. I go as pilgrim to a celibate community. I act as leader in a Christian community, and have been appointed over the Gentiles on Patmos to act as a village teacher on behalf of Jesus. My superior is Peter, deputy to Jesus.

10   *I came about in a Spirit in the Lord's day. And I heard behind me a great Voice, as of a Trumpet,* 11   *saying, That which you look at write to a book. And send to the seven Churches, into Ephesus. And into Smyrna. And into Pergamum. And into Thyatira. And into Sardis. And into Philadelphia. And into Laodicea.*

10   At midnight beginning Sunday, 1 June AD 49, I was

at the Ephesus cathedral for the Pentecost festival, and sat in the royal pew in the congregation as seer. I heard my archbishop Apollos on the west of the middle tier, and he blew the trumpet for the earliest stage of the end of the jubilee, 11 then he said to me: 'Make a copy of the document placed beside you, to become part of the New Testament attached to the Septuagint. Send it to Agrippa as head of the seven Gentile communities of Asia, whose main centre is at Ephesus, the "Saturday". The next in rank is at Smyrna, the "Sunday". The next is at Pergamum, the "Monday". The next is at Thyatira, the "Tuesday". The next is at Sardis, the "Wednesday". The next is at Philadelphia, the "Thursday". The next is at Laodicea, the "Friday"'.

12 *And I turned upon to look at the Voice, the which spoke with me. And having turned upon I saw seven golden lampstands.*
12 At 1 a.m. Apollos came down to the west side of the congregation, and I turned due west to see him. Then I turned north, and saw the seventh light of the Menorah turned up, indicating that it was 3 a.m.

13 *And in a middle of the lampstands one like a Son of Man, clad in feet length clothing. And girdled towards to the breasts, a golden belt.*
13 At the centre of the chancel step stood Jesus, wearing a garment that was not a levitical vestment. He wore a belt around the waist, as he was outside the sanctuary, but a gold one because he was a priest to Gentiles.

14 *But the head of him. And the hairs white, as white wool, as snow. And the eyes of him, as a flame of fire.*
14 On his headband he wore the letter for class D, that of villagers. He wore a white layman's headcloth made of wool, showing that he was the chief Shepherd to the village 'sheep'; and also the letter of one whose chief feast

was in December. He carried an oil lamp, using it as a priest's lamp for Gentiles.

15 *And the feet of him like copper-frankincense, as in a furnace fired. And the Voice of him, as a Voice (fem.) of Many waters.*
15 A collection vessel for Gentile monastic property was placed west of him on the chancel step, for Gentiles following the Egyptian discipline. He spoke as one equal to a Phanuel, the priest superior at Gentile councils.

16 *And having in the right hand of him seven Stars. And out of the mouth of him a sharp two-mouthed broadsword proceeding out. And the visage of him, as the Sun shines in the Power of him.*
16 Two cubits to the east of him stood Jesus Justus as an acolyte, aged twelve. Beside Jesus was the rod used for admitting or excluding Gentile monastics; used to direct them but not to excommunicate. At the time for leading early prayers for Gentiles he put on a headdress, acting as a Phanuel for the dawn prayer.

17 *And when now I saw him, I fell towards the feet of him, as lifeless. And he laid the right of him upon me saying, Do not fear, I become the First One. And the Last One.*
17 As this Gentile service began, I knelt in front of the collection vessel on his west side, in the status of a low grade Gentile who paid no fees. He came to me and placed his right hand on my head, saying: 'Renew your abstinence from marriage, under myself as your bishop. Peter is your provincial bishop.

18 *And the Living One. And I came about lifeless. And behold I become a Living One to the Aeons of the Aeons. And I have the keys of the Death. And of the Hades.*
18 Matthew Annas is your Priest-Pope. I have entered the state preceding marriage. But I still act as a priest to

422

Gentiles, initiating them on behalf of Agrippa II. I hold the Gentile monastic property, keeping it in the burial cave of the Davids, which is also used for excommunication by the Chief Monk Atomus. With him is Antipas the third Herod, the treasurer.

19 *Write therefore the things which you have seen. And the things that become. And the things that are about to come about after these things,* 20 *the mystery of the seven Stars which (plu.) you saw upon {of} the right of me. And the seven golden lampstands, the seven Stars angels of the seven Churches become. And the seven lampstands seven Churches become.*

19 Make a record of what you see from the seat of the seer, to form part of scripture. Describe what happens in Ephesus. Record the letters which will now be dictated to you 20 as part of the Book of Revelation, intended as the final section of the New Testament to be read by acolytes at a western lectern. It is now 4 a.m., and Jesus Justus begins his education as an acolyte of Agrippa, head of Gentile communities in Asia. At this hour Agrippa on his coronation day becomes head of Gentile communities'.

THE SEVEN LETTERS

CHAPTER 2

To Ephesus, the 'Saturday', under Phanuel, a cardinal to Gentiles.

1 *To the angel of the church in Ephesus, write: So says the One seizing the seven Stars in the right of him, the One walking in a middle of the seven golden lampstands.*

423

1   Jesus continued: 'To Theophilus Annas, cardinal to the Gentile community in Ephesus, write: This is Gentile teaching given by Jesus, who embraces Jesus Justus as his own acolyte also, and who teaches Gentiles at the dawn service.

2   *I know your works. And your labour. And the Endurance of you. And because you are not empowered to carry bad ones. And you have tested the Ones saying Themselves apostles. And they become not. And you have found them False Ones.*
2   I recognise you as a practising ascetic. You follow the communal discipline. You act as priest in the village, overseeing prayers at every hour. As Herodian, you do not admit to the synagogue the opponents of Agrippa. You have examined the claims of Tigranes Herod to be the Herod successor. He is not accepted as a member in Ephesus. You have declared him to have no right to the succession.

3   *And you have Endurance. And you have carried on account of the name of me. And you have not been weary.*
3   You allow a Gentile minister to lead the perpetual prayers. You act as subordinate to me as priest to Gentiles. You have remained under the ascetic rule.

4   *Nevertheless I have down of you. Because the first love of you you have left.*
4   But I am not in your party. As Herodian you will not share the Agape with John Mark.

5   *Remember therefore whence you have fallen. And repent. And the first works make. But if not, I come to you. And I will remove the lampstand of you out of the place of it, if then you do not repent.*
5   Re-admit John Mark as an initiate in the congregation, kneeling at the chancel step as you do. Become a member of the Rome province. Minister to ascetic

bishops. When you return to the celibate community, I will take your place. When I do, I will remove the Menorah, making a synagogue into a Christian place of worship, where you may officiate as a Jewish priest.

6   *Nevertheless you have this. Because you hate the works of the Nicolaitans. Which and I hate.*
6   You are a priest to the uncircumcised. As Herodian you reject the proselyte Nicolaus-Blastus. I as your equal also reject him.

7   *He having an ear, let him hear what the Spirit says to the Churches: To the victor, I will give to him to eat out of the wood of the life, which becomes in the Paradise of the God.*
7   Let Agrippa hear what his Priest-Pope Matthew says to him as head of Gentile communities: "I give Peter the right to preside at communion meals in Gentile monasteries under the Sadducees."

To Smyrna, the 'Sunday', under a lay bishop.

8   *And to the angel of the church in Smyrna write: So says the First One. And the Last One. Who came about lifeless. And he lived.*
8   To Gaius Costobar Herod, minister in charge of the Gentile community in Smyrna, write: This is Gentile teaching given by Jesus, who is their chief bishop. His deputy is Peter. Jesus has entered the state preceding marriage. He still initiates Gentiles.

9   *I know of you the tribulation. And the poverty. Nevertheless you become rich. And the blasphemy out of the Ones saying Jews to become Themselves. And they become not. Nevertheless a synagogue of the Satan.*
9   I recognise you as celibate lay bishop acting for the bride before the wedding. You are under an ascetic rule. But you accept Gentile fees. The false Herod from

425

Damascus, claiming leadership of "the Jews", is a zealot. He is not accepted as a member in Ephesus. But he goes to Achaia, where Antipas Herod is treasurer of Herodian property, and attends the synagogue there.

10 *Nothing fear the things you (sing.) are about to suffer. Behold, the Devil is about to throw out of you (plu.) to a prison, in order that you (plu.) may be tested. And you (plu.) will have tribulation ten days. Come about (sing.) faithful until Death. And I will give to you (sing.) the crown of the life.*

10 Leave the celibate state, three months before the betrothal period beginning in September. In September Antipas as Scribe-examiner will exclude you, acting for the bride, from the vestry, as the first step towards her marriage, and as her medical representative you will prove her virginity. You are now at grade 10 as acting for the betrothed Virgin. Minister to her until midnight at the wedding ceremony, when she enters grade 12. Then after the wedding I will promote you to cardinal.

11 *He having an ear, let him hear what the Spirit says to the Churches: The victor is not {not} made unrighteous out of the Second Death.*

11 Let Agrippa hear what his Priest-Pope Matthew says to him as head of Gentile communities: "Peter has been excluded by the Damascus party".

To Pergamum, the 'Monday', under a lay presbyter.

12 *And to the angel of the church in Pergamum write: So says the One having the two-mouthed sharp broadsword.*

12 To Erastus Saul Herod, minister in charge of the Gentile community in Pergamum, write: This is Gentile teaching given by Jesus, who admits some men to Gentile monasteries and sends others to village schools.

13   *I know where you (sing.) dwell, at where the throne of the Satan. And you seize the name of me. And you have not denied the faith (fem.) of me in the days of Antipas, the witness (nom.) of me, the faithful one (nom.) of me. Who was killed beside you (plu.), at where the Satan dwells.*

13   I recognise you as the Herodian presbyter, in charge of the Gentile section of the Herodian treasury in Corinth. You embrace me as a priest to Gentiles. You have allowed me to act as a priest, at this season when Antipas Herod, instructed by Peter and Paul, has been admitted to our party. Herod of Chalcis has been excommunicated (and has died), and Antipas his successor over "the Jews" has brought their property to Achaia, where he is now the Scribe-treasurer.

14   *Nevertheless I have down from you (sing.) a few things. Because you have there ones seizing the teaching of Balaam. Who taught to Balak to throw a stumbling block in front of the sons of Israel, to eat idol-food. And to commit fornication.*

14   But I am not in your party on questions of Herodian doctrine. You have members who embrace Atomus the Magus as the Teacher. Atomus instructs Polemo of Cilicia, preparing for his marriage to Bernice, to accept the circumcision requirement before he can become a member of the congregation, yet he allows him to attend banquets honouring the emperor as a god. He treats Bernice as a priestess.

15   *Thus you (sing.) have. And you (sing. nom. pronoun), Ones seizing (plu. acc.) the teaching of the Nicolaitans likewise.*

15   You accept Gaius Costobar Herod as a levitical bishop. You are the presbyter of the group, and your deacon is Nicolaus-Blastus the proselyte.

16   *Repent therefore. But if not, I come to you soon. And I*

will make war with them (Nicolaitans) in the broadsword of the mouth of me.

16   Become a member of the Rome province. When you are with the celibate congregation, I will take your place at the June solstice. I will debate against Nicolaus in the council, arguing from Gentile monastic rules.

17   *He having an ear, let him hear what the Spirit says to the Churches: To the victor I will give to him the hidden manna. And I will give to him a white pebble. And upon the pebble a new name written, which No One knows if not the One receiving.*

17   Let Agrippa hear what his Priest-Pope Matthew says to him as head of Gentile communities: "I give Peter the right to give sacred bread to Gentiles in the crypt. I give him a voting stone to use at the Pentecost councils. On the voting stone is the name 'Christian', which is recognised by Timothy Herod and also by Agrippa"

To Thyatira, the 'Tuesday', under a lay deacon.

18   *And to the angel of the church in Thyatira write: So says the Son of God, the One having the eyes of him, as a flame of fire. And the feet of him like copper-frankincense.*

18   To John Mark, minister in charge of the Gentile community in Thyatira, write: This is Gentile teaching given by Jesus, who may act in the place of the priest's deputy, who uses his layman's lamp as a priest's lamp at Gentile services. In his collection vessel he receives the property surrendered by Gentile monastics.

19   *I know of you the works. And the love. And the faith (fem.). And the deaconing. And the Endurance of you. And the works of you, the Last Ones, more of the First Ones.*

19   I recognise you as a practising ascetic. You are admitted to the Agape meal. You also act as a priest. You act as deacon with Jews. You also act as cardinal with

Gentiles. You have ascetics, pilgrims and Nazirite bishops in your congregation.

20 *Nevertheless I have down from you. Because you leave the woman Jezebel, the One calling Herself a prophetess. And she teaches. And deceives my slaves to commit fornication. And to eat idol-food.*
20 But I am not in your party. Although now Herodian, you allow Helena to teach Gentiles, when she claims that as the mistress of Simon Magus she is a cardinal. She acts like a levite. When she instructs Polemo, whom I am instructing also, she teaches him that Bernice, a priestess, should be queen regnant. She allows him to attend Roman banquets in honour of the emperor as a god.

21 *And I gave her a period in order that she might repent. And she does not will to repent out of the fornication of her.*
21 I allowed her to act as lay bishop, independent head of her order, if she would join the Rome province and the Christian party. She says she is not a layperson, will not join the Rome province, nor abandon her claim to be a priestess.

22 *Behold, I throw her to a bed. And the Ones committing adultery with her to great tribulation, if now they do not repent out of the works of her.*
22 As superior of the uncircumcised, I order her to be celibate. Polemo, a Gentile, is entering a wrongful marriage when under her instruction he becomes Jewish and does not join the Rome province.

23 *And the children of her I will kill in Death. And All the Churches will have knowledge. Because I become the One who tries the inner body. And hearts. And I will give to you (plu.) to each one according to the works of you (plu.).*
23 I will excommunicate Izates. Timothy Herod is being educated as an acolyte in my school. I am the

429

examining bishop for Gentile acolytes. Also for women. You, Luke, a celibate, are promoted to be my "eunuch" for my marriage.

24 *But to you (plu.) I say, to the Remainder, the ones in Thyatira. Whoever do not have this teaching. Whosoever have not had knowledge of the deep things of the Satan, as they say, I do not throw upon you (plu.) another burden.*

24 I speak to you, Luke, as a Gentile initiate attached to the Thyatira convent. Permanent Gentile celibates of your order are not counted as laymen. Dynastic ones are not given the gnostic education of Scribes, and they say on my behalf, "I do not ask you to adopt monastic discipline".

25 *However, that which you (plu.) have, seize until I come.*

25 As chief western celibate Gentile, care for Lydia until I come in December.

26 *And the victor. And the One keeping until an end the works (neut.) of me, I will give to him authority upon {of} the nations (neut.).*

26 Peter is Pope to Gentiles. Jesus Justus is my acolyte, keeping midnight vigils, and I appoint him also an acolyte to Agrippa.

27 *And he will shepherd them (masc. Whosoever, v.24) in a rod of iron, as the clay vessels are smashed.*

27 He acts on my behalf over Gentiles attending the school under Egyptian discipline, and he practises physical training.

28 *As and I have received beside the Father of me. And I will give to him (the Father) the Morning Star.*

28 I have again been given permission by Matthew to go outside for marriage. I hand over Jesus Justus to Matthew for his education.

29   *He having an ear, let him hear what the Spirit says to the Churches.*

29   Let Agrippa hear what his Priest-Pope Matthew says to him as head of Gentile communities.

CHAPTER 3

To Sardis, the 'Wednesday', under an initiate.

1   *And to the angel of the church in Sardis write: So says the One having the seven Spirits of the God. And the seven Stars. I know of you the works. Because a name you have. Because you live. And you are lifeless.*

1   To James Niceta, minister in charge of the Gentile community in Sardis, write: This is Gentile teaching given by Jesus, who acts with Theophilus Annas. Jesus Justus is his acolyte. I recognise you as a practising ascetic. You act as a Herodian Nazirite. You are a Herodian initiate. At present you are in the married state.

2   *Come about one watching. And strengthen the Remaining Things which were about to die. For I have not found of you the works perfected in front of the God of me.*

2   Become a Nazirite again, observing midnight vigils. Receive into your congregation in your place Gaius Costobar Herod, when he leaves the community to act for the bride in September. You are a Nazirite ascetic, but not a member of a Sadducee celibate community.

3   *Remember therefore how you have received. And you have heard. And keep. And repent. If then therefore you do not watch, I will come, as a thief. And you will not {not} have knowledge what kind of hour I will come upon you.*

3   Keep a record of initiates using the wedding imagery. You are a seer, listening to sermons in the congregation.

431

Act also as deacon. Become a member of the Rome province and the Christian party. When you have finished your Nazirite vow, in December, I will come, with Erastus. You have gnostic learning, keeping the Julian calendar, so I will come at midnight, the Julian start of day.

4 *Nevertheless you have a few names in Sardis which have not defiled the garments of them. And they will walk with me in white. Because worthy are they.*
4 You have Timothy Herod in Sardis, who is not yet a grown man. He wears a white vestment and is equal to me in status. As a Herod prince he may give the reading from the Septuagint.

5 *The victor thus will be clothed in white garments. And I will not {not} erase the name of him out of the booklet of the life. And I will confess the name of him in front of the Father of me. And in front of the angels of him (Father).*
5 Peter is a bishop, wearing a white vestment for the Pentecost season. I remove his name from the list of married members. I will present him as a priest before Matthew. He will also be presented as a celibate before Matthew as Priest-Pope.

6 *He having an ear, let him hear what the Spirit says to the Churches.*
6 Let Agrippa hear what his Priest-Pope Matthew says to him as head of Gentile communities.

To Philadelphia, the 'Thursday', under a pre-initiate.

7 *And to the angel of the church in Philadelphia write: So says the holy one, the true one, the One having the key of David, the One opening. And No One locks. And One locking. And No One opens.*
7 To Peter, minister in charge of the Gentile community in Philadelphia, write: This is Gentile teaching

given by Jesus, who as the David combines the positions of chief dynastic celibate, teacher under the Sadducee, treasurer of the shared property of Essenes, the one who first opens the vault. Then the acolyte locks it. Then the deputy keeps the key. Then the acolye opens it the next time.

8   *I know of you the works. Behold I have given in front of you a door opened, which No One is empowered to lock it. Because you have a little Power. And you have kept of me the Word. And you have not denied the name of me.*

8   I recognise you as a practising ascetic. I have appointed you to act in my place over the shared property, with Timothy Herod as the acolyte. You are my deputy cardinal. You act as my substitute teacher. You do not now deny my priesthood, as you once did.

9   *Behold, I give out of the synagogue of the Satan, of the Ones saying Themselves to become Jews. And they become not. Nevertheless False Ones. Behold I will make them (False Ones) in order that they will come. And they will worship in front of the feet of you. And they will have knowledge. Because I have loved you.*

9   In Achaia, I exclude from Antipas' synagogue those who say that the false Herod Tigranes is the true head of the "Jews". He is not a member in Ephesus. He is not a legitimate Herod successor. I will accept him only in the status of a Gentile. He will have to pay his Roman tribute through you. He will have to receive a gnostic education. You are the one who presides at the Christian Agape meal.

10   *Because you have kept the Word of the Endurance of me. And I will keep you out of the hour of the tempting, the one about to come upon {of} the whole Dominion, to tempt the Ones dwelling upon {of} the Earth.*

10   Under Herodian rules you act in my place as teacher and leader of prayers. I will hand over to you in

September, when the betrothal period begins, when Luke as Gentile head of the Rome province acts for me, and Gaius Costobar Herod acts for the bride.

11 *I come soon. Seize what you have, in order that No One may receive the crown of you.*
11 I will come to the service on the solar 31st. Embrace Jesus Justus, and let Timothy act as a Christian cardinal.

12 *The victor, I will make him a Pillar in the sanctuary of the God of me. And outside he (God) will not {not} go out still. And I will write upon him (God) the name of the God of me. And the name of the city of the God of me, of the new Jerusalem, the one going down out of the Heaven from the God of me. And the name of me, the new one.*
12 I allow the Christian Pope to act as a cardinal in a Jewish hermitage under Matthew. Matthew may instruct Gallio the Roman proconsul of Achaia. I will allow Matthew to bestow the name "Christian" on my behalf. The chief Christian monastic is subordinate both of Matthew and of myself, as head of Christian monasteries, and he stands on the chancel step as a cardinal. These monasteries are to be called "Christian".

13 *He having an ear, let him hear what the Spirit says to the Churches.*
13 Let Agrippa hear what his Priest-Pope Matthew says to him as head of Gentile communities.

To Laodicea, the 'Friday', under a proselyte.

14 *And to the angel of the church in Laodicea write: So says the Amen, the witness, the faithful one. And true one, the Beginning of the Creation of God.*
14 To Nicolaus-Blastus, minister in charge of the Gentile community in Laodicea, write: This is Gentile teaching given by Jesus, who as head of the congregation

434

concludes the service, who is with Peter, and with Paul. Jesus is a teacher under the Sadducee, treating Pentecost as the religious New Year.

15   *I know of you the works. Because nor cold you are, nor hot. You were owing, cold or hot,* 16   *thus. Because you are lukewarm. And nor hot, nor cold, I am about to spit you out of the mouth of me.*

15   I recognise you as a practicing ascetic. Although Herodian you use the eastern seasons at the equinoxes instead of the winter and summer of the Julian calendar. Your taxes should be paid both in winter and summer,
16   to a bishop. As Herodian you observe the equinoxes. At the March equinox and the September equinox I will exclude you from my schools.

17   *Because you say, Because I am rich. And I am enriched. And Nothing I have need. And you do not know. Because you are the wretched one. And a beggar. And poor. And blind. And naked,* 18   *I counsel you to buy beside me gold fired out of a fire, in order that you may be enriched. And white garments, in order that you may be clothed. And there may not appear the shame of your nakedness. And with eyesalve I will anoint your eyes in order that you may look.*

17   With the Herods you say: "I am servant of the Herod crown prince, using the T sign, when I receive Gentile fees for him. I act as servant of his treasurer. Yet I receive welfare as an acolyte". You do not recognise the un-circumcised. As a proselyte, under Herodian rules, you head the class of the excluded. Your ministers correspond to the four kinds of welfare recipients who are not admitted to a Jewish vestry, the first a Nazirite initiate. Then a hermit initiate. Then a Nazirite pre-initiate. Then a monastic excluded for sin,   18   and in that capacity I meet with you in the council, and advise you to pay the salary of a Chief Therapeut as your priest, and act as his treasurer. Observe Pentecost and wear a white vestment.

Keep the ascetic rule requiring covering of the body. I will give you the layman's lamp for study of Christian books.

19   *I, Whoever (plu.) if now I befriend I rebuke. And I chasten. Be zealous therefore. And repent.*

19   I am superior of Gentile monastics, and at their common meal I exercise discipline over them. I am superior of their novices. Keep the ascetic rules of an initiate. Join the Rome province and the Christian party.

20   *Behold, I have stood upon the door. And I knock, if now Anyone hears the Voice of me. And he (Voice) opens the door, I will come in towards him (Anyone). And I will sup with him. And He (new subject) with me.*

20   I am about to enter the class of the married. When I return to the vestry, Agrippa will receive me back. His levite will let me in to the celibate congregation, and I will officiate as Agrippa's subordinate. I will join in the first part of the evening communion meal beside him. In the later part, a priest will sit beside me.

21   *The victor, I will give to him to sit with me in the throne of me. As and I have been victorious. And I have sat with the Father of me in the throne of him.*

21   At Gentile meals, Peter sits beside me in the lay position, and I take the priest's place. I also lead the debates. But when Matthew is present, I sit on the lay side on the west.

22   *He having an ear, let him hear what the Spirit says to the Churches.*

22   Let Agrippa hear what his Priest-Pope Matthew says to him as head of Gentile communities'.

CHAPTER 4

1 *After these things I saw. And behold a door opened in the Heaven. And the first Voice which I heard, as of a Trumpet speaking with me, One saying, Go up here. And I will show you the things that must come about after these things.*

1 At the noon service on the same day I stood at the seer's seat. The east entrance to the upper tier was opened. Apollos, my archbishop, appeared on the balcony and again blew the trumpet for the early start of the jubilee, then said to me: 'Sit in the seer's seat. I will explain to you the noon order of service'.

2 *At once I became in a Spirit. And behold a throne lay in the Heaven. And upon the throne a Sitting One.*

2 At the end of the short noon prayer I sat in the royal pew as seer. Herod's throne was placed across the upper tier. At its centre Agrippa was enthroned as a Michael.

3 *And the One Sitting like to a vision, to a jasper stone. And to a sardius. And a Rainbow about the throne like to a vision, to emerald.*

3 Agrippa was the supreme priest, but also the king who sometimes used the royal pew. The place for the acolyte was beside him. His crown prince, Timothy, sat over the western pillar on the middle tier, as another royal priest, the 'Rainbow' of the Noah mission.

4 *And about the throne twenty-four thrones. And upon the thrones twenty-four elders sitting, clothed in white garments. And upon the heads of them golden crowns.*

4 Over the eastern pillar was the seat taken by Phanuel after the prayer. Theophilus Annas took his place on it, wearing a white vestment. Over his ascetic's headband he wore a circlet with golden letters, showing that he was of the class of priests.

5   And out of the throne there proceed forth Lightnings. And Voices. And Thunders. And seven lamps of fire burning in front of the throne, which become the seven Spirits of God.   6 And in front of the throne, as a glass Sea like crystal.

5   Theophilus on the east side gave the reading from the Old Testament Law. Timothy Herod the crown prince gave the reading from the Former Prophets. Matthew Annas on the west side gave the reading from the Latter Prophets. Then Theophilus in the centre turned up a light to indicate that it was 1 p.m.   6   In the centre of the middle tier holy water was sprinkled.

And in a middle of the throne. And around the throne four Living Ones full of eyes before. And at behind.

The 1 p.m. prayer was said on the forward balcony. Apollos the Chief Therapeut, after saying it, put his layman's lamp over the eastern pillar, as it was the Day position of the calendar. Then he went to the west side.

7   And the Living One, the first one, like a Lion. And the second Living One like a Calf. And the third Living One having the face, as of a Man. And the fourth Living One like a Flying Eagle.

7   The four evangelists took their places at the dais, Peter as a lay bishop standing in the centre of the chancel step. Luke stood on its west side as a lay presbyter. Matthew wearing a priest's headband came to stand at the edge of the dais. John Mark as a celibate bishop stood at the east of the chancel step.

8   And the four Living Ones, one according to one of them having up six wings, about. And inside full of eyes. And a ceasing they do not have of day. And of night, saying, Holy, holy, holy, a lord the God the All- mighty, the One who became. And the One becoming. And the Coming One.

8   At 2 p.m. Apollos on the western pillar began to lead the choir of 'seraphim' who sang for the coronation. He went also to stand over the eastern pillar, to conduct the

'cherubim'. He began the second half of the service over the eastern pillar, since the calendar was in the Day position. Then he went to the western pillar, saying: 'Matthew, who leads celibates in the east, centre and west, is the Sariel, the king's priest who crowns Agrippa, a priest in Rome. He is Priest-Pope in Ephesus. He is a levite in the east'.

9   *And when the Living Ones give a Glory. And an honour. And a thanksgsiving to the One sitting upon {to} the throne, to the Living One to the Aeons of the Aeons.*

9   At 3 p.m. Apollos gave community property to Matthew as a 'Moses'. The fees of Jewish villagers were paid. Gifts were given to Agrippa on the east side of the throne received on his behalf by Matthew.

10   *There fall down the twenty-four elders in front of the One sitting upon {of} the throne. And they worship to the Living One to the Aeons of the Aeons. And they (the Aeons of the Aeons) will throw the crowns of them in front of the throne, saying,*

10   Then Theophilus Annas knelt on the west side of the middle tier before Agrippa. He paid the Roman tribute to Matthew, who received it as deputy to Agrippa. Agrippa then caused a circlet to be placed on the head of Theophilus, now in the centre, and said to him:

11   *Worthy are you, the lord. And the God of us, to receive the Glory. And the honour. And the Power. Because you have created All Things. And on account of the will of you they became. And they were created.*

11   'You, Theophilus, are a village priest, equal to a distinguished layman. Matthew is your superior, and head of celibate communities. You may receive the fees. You may say prayers at noon in the centre of the circle. As deputy to Sariel, you crown the Herod prince. You give him membership of the village council. He has been baptised by you.'

CHAPTER 5

1   *And I saw upon the right of the One sitting upon {of} the throne a book written before. And at behind, sealed with seven seals.*

1   The less sacred part of the service began, and I saw in the right hand of Agrippa, sitting on the west side of the throne, a bound book containing a copy of the Septuagint, to be read on the east side of the chancel step. Its back section contained the six divisions of the New Testament, which was to be read on the west side, and this section was sealed so that it could not be read, with the secondary tie brought up from its back page to its title page.

2   *And I saw a strong angel proclaiming in a great Voice, Who is worthy to open the book? And to loose the seals of it.*

2   I saw Timothy, the Herod crown prince, on the west of the middle tier, announce: 'Agrippa as a royal person may handle the Septuagint. He will also unfasten the main one of the two ties, brought up from the back cover of the New Testament to its title page'.

3   *And No One was empowered in the Heaven, neither upon {of} the Earth, neither underneath the Earth, to open the book, nor to look at it.*

3   Timothy as acolyte was given the Septuagint, and he brought it down before the congregation, first to the west side, then in front of the step, then to the eastern lectern marked with the X sign.

4   *And I wept much. Because No One was found worthy to open the book, nor to look at it.*

4   As I did not observe the Law, I moved to the west side of my pew. Timothy gave the reading from the Law section of the Septuagint at the lectern.

5   *And one out of the elders says to me, Do not weep. Behold there has been victorious the Lion, the one out of the tribe of Judah, the Root David, to open the book. And the seven seals of it.*

5   When the reading from the Law was finished, Theophilus on the chancel step said to me: 'Move back to your seat. Jesus, the bishop to the lowest grade, the chief dynast, the David of the mission to Gentiles, will give the reading from the Prophets of the Septuagint. He will then unfasten the secondary seal of the New Testament section of the book'.

6   *And I saw in a middle of the throne. And of the four Living Ones. And in a middle of the elders a Lamb standing, as slain, having seven Horns. And seven eyes. Who become the seven Spirits of the God sent from to All the Earth.*

6   I looked up at the forward balcony. Apollos stood there, indicating a lesser event. To the centre of the chancel step, in front of Theophilus, came Jesus wearing white, and also the scarlet garment of a cardinal, as an initiator of the uncircumcised. His lamp marked the lesser divisions of hours. Theophilus concluded the reading and came to the chancel step, giving the book to Timothy.

7   *And it (All the Earth) came. And it received out of the right of the One Sitting upon {of} the throne.*

7   Timothy went back to the middle tier. He received the collection bowl from the right hand of Agrippa, who was sitting on the west side of the throne.

8   *And when now he (the One sitting) received the book, the four Living Ones. And the twenty-four elders fell in front of the Lamb, having each one a harp. And golden bowls full of incense, which become the prayers of the holy ones.*

8   As the Gentile informal service at the half hour began, Agrippa received back the copy of the Septuagint from Timothy, and Apollos appeared, to indicate a minor

441

service. Theophilus knelt on the west of the dais edge before Jesus, who as David stood to lead the singing of the psalms; Theophilus played the accompanying harp. The bowl for collecting money was set out, and a censer burned beside it, while the choir of 'cherubim' singing psalms was led by Jesus Justus.

9   *And they (the holy ones) sing a new song saying, Worthy you to receive the book. And to open the seals (fem.) of it. Because you were slain. And you have bought to God in the blood of you out of Every tribe. And of a tongue. And of a people. And of a nation.*

9   After the psalms Jesus Justus led the choir in a Christian hymn, saying: 'You, Jesus, now receive the copy of the Septuagint back from Agrippa. You open the title page of the New Testament section. You are appointed a Herodian cardinal. You will preside at the Gentile communion meal in place of Matthew, giving the cup, on the east side of Timothy. Peter will be present. John Mark will be present. Luke will be present.

10   *And you have made them (the holy ones) to the God of us a kingdom. And priests. And they (priests) will hold kingship upon {of} the Earth.*

10   You have appointed your crown prince, under Matthew, to Christian celibate schools. Peter is a Christian priest. Peter is active head of Christian celibate communities under Agrippa'.

11   *And I saw. And I heard a Voice of Many angels around the throne. And of the Living Ones. And of the elders. And there became the Number of them (the elders) Ten Thousand of Ten Thousand. And Thousands of Thousands,* 12 *saying (plu.) in a great Voice, Worthy is the Lamb, the one slain, to receive the Power. And Enrichment. And Wisdom. And Strength. And Honour. And Glory. And Benefit.*

11   At 4 p.m. I was in the seer's place. I heard Timothy speak from the western pillar, at the time when 'unclean'

442

money was received and financial arrangements were made on this coronation day. Apollos was present for the minor service. Theophilus stood on the edge of the dais. Timothy was now granted the Gentile income of the Herod crown prince, the fees of paying Gentiles of grade 10 in two of the five provinces of Asia Minor. He also received the Jewish fees from the first grade of the two provinces, 12 and he said on the west side, 'Of the seven kinds of payment to lay ministers, Jesus may receive the same payment as the cardinal. A married bishop receives a payment. A teacher of Wisdom, a lay presbyter, receives a payment. So does a lay deacon who gives instruction. So does a Gentile initiate acting as a missionary. In a separate class is the celibate bishop holding common property. And the acolyte holding shared property'.

13   *And Every Created Thing which in the Heaven. And upon {of} the Earth. And underneath the Earth. And upon {of} the Sea. And All Things in them (the Thousands, v.11) I heard saying, To the One Sitting upon {to} the throne. And to the Lamb the Benefit. And the Honour. And the Glory. And the Might to the Aeons of the Aeons.*

13   At 6 p.m. Agrippa presided at a coronation banquet. Present was Timothy his crown prince. Antipas the third Herod was present. Also Erastus. I heard Timothy say: 'Let the Jewish mission income be given to Agrippa. Let Jesus control the Gentile property. Let the Jewish fees be received. Let common property be handed to Matthew. Let welfare tithes be given to Matthew as king's priest to Agrippa'.

14   *And the four Living Ones said, Amen. And the elders fell. And they worshipped.*

14   At 10 p.m. Apollos closed the service, saying 'Amen'. The banquet continued, and at 3 a.m. Theophilus knelt for the conclusion. He paid the Roman tribute on behalf of Gentiles.

CHAPTER 6

(See Chapter 8, 'The Four Horseman . . .', and
pp.211–212 on the Seven Seals.)

1   *And I saw when now the Lamb opened one out of the seven
seals. And I heard one out of the four Living Ones saying, as
a Voice of Thunder, Come.*
2   *And I saw. And behold a white Horse. And the One sitting
upon it having a bow. And there was given to him a crown.
And he came out a victor. And in order that he might be
victorious.*
1   On Tuesday, 17 June AD 49, at the informal Gentile
service at 3.30 p.m., I saw Jesus display the title page
preceding Mark's gospel. I heard Peter, standing on the
chancel step, with Apollos on the middle tier, speaking,
and as a deputy of Matthew saying: 'Let the priest for
Pentecost teach Gentiles'.
2   I was in my seat for the next stage, when Christian
compositions were permitted. The white banner for
Pentecost was set on the priest's chair on the balcony.
Theophilus Annas sat on it, using the emblem of a bow,
the symbol of Diana of Ephesus. He was given the circlet
of the village teacher. He came down to the chancel step
to conduct the debate. His party won the debate in the
council.

3   *And when now he (the One sitting on the white Horse)
opened the second seal, I heard the second Living One say,
Come.*
4   *And there came out another red Horse. And to the One
sitting upon it there was given to him to receive the Peace*

(fem.) out of the Earth (fem.). And in order that they (four Living Ones, v.1) might slay one another. And there was given to him (One sitting) a great sword.

3 At the corresponding Gentile service on Tuesday, 16 September, at the end of his season's teaching of Mark, Theophilus opened the title page to Luke's gospel, and I heard Luke, standing on the west of the chancel step, say: 'Let the priest for September teach Gentiles'.

4 The red banner was set on the priest's chair. Ananus the Younger sat on it, the youngest of the Annas brothers who would succeed Matthew, with a more nationalist doctrine. Under him, Apollos would promote proselytes to cardinals. Ananus had the power to admit or exclude from the village ministry.

5 *And when now he (the One sitting on the red Horse) opened the third seal, I heard the third Living One say, Come. And I saw. And behold, a black Horse. And the One sitting upon it having a slave yoke/ scale in the hand of him.*

6 *And I heard, as a Voice in a middle of the four Living Ones say, A measure of wheat for a denarius. And three measures of barley for a denarius. And the oil. And the wine do not make unrighteous.*

5 At the Gentile service on Tuesday, 16 December AD 49, at the end of his season's teaching of Luke, Ananus opened the title page of Matthew's gospel, and I heard Matthew, standing at the dais edge, say: 'Let the priest for December teach Gentiles'. I was in my seat for the next stage. The black banner was placed on the priest's chair. Ananias the reigning Samaritan high priest sat on it, and on his bread paten was a weight, for the mission fees.

6 At 4 p.m., the time when Gentile fees were given, I heard James Niceta, head of fee paying Gentiles, on the chancel step before Apollos, say: 'Initiated Gentiles are to pay a denarius entrance fee. They are to pay over three years, a third of a denarius each year, from grade 9

"barley" to grade 7 "wheat". There are also Gentile celibates. Do not exclude Gentile celibates who drink fermented wine'.

7   *And when now he (Voice) opened the fourth seal, I heard a Voice of the fourth Living One say, Come. And see.*
8 And I saw. And behold a green Horse. And the One sitting up high on it, a name to him, the Death. And the Hades followed with him. And there was given to them (four Living Ones v. 6) authority upon the fourth of the Earth, to kill in a broadsword. And in famine. And in Death. And under {of} the Beasts of the Earth.

7   At the Gentile service on Tuesday, 17 March AD 50, James Niceta, at the end of his season's teaching of Matthew's gospel, opened the title page of John's gospel, and I heard him as a deputy for John Mark say: 'Let the priest for Passover teach Gentiles. Let the seer be present to claim John's gospel'.

8   I was in my seat for the next stage. The green banner was set on the priest's chair. Behind it, raised on the 'chariot', sat Atomus the Magus, the Chief Monk, who had power to excommunicate. His deputy was Antipas the third Herod. Apollos was confirmed as head of the 'Poor', the Therapeuts, with power to excommunicate from the 'Eden' schools. He used the north solar calendar, of which AD 50 was the sabbatical year. He could excommunicate. He acted in place of a zealot bishop, under Agrippa.

9   *And when now it (Earth) opened the fifth seal, I saw underneath the Altar of Incense the Souls of the Slain Ones on account of the Word of the God. And on account of the Witnessing which they had.*
10   And they cried in a great Voice saying, As far as when, O holy despot? And a truthful one, you do not judge. And you make out- righteous the blood of us out of the dwellers upon {of} the Earth.

446

11 *And there was given to them (the Dwellers), to each one, a white robe. And it was said to them (the Dwellers) in order that they should pause still, for a little period, as far as they are fulfilled. And the fellow- slaves of them. And the brothers of them, the ones about to be killed. As and They (new subject).*

9 At the Gentile service on Tuesday, 16 June AD 50, at the end of the season's teaching of John's gospel, Agrippa, present for the completion of a year's study of the gospels, opened the re-assigned and expanded copy of John's gospel, and also Peter's Epistle; and I saw Peter in front of the chancel step before Matthew, as a cardinal acting as teacher in place of Jesus, who was now in the married state. Peter was the head of the pilgrim congregation.

10 Peter preached from the western side, saying: 'Agrippa, you will be initiated as a celibate at the age of twenty-three next September. You will be equal to a Sadducee teacher, no longer a novice. You allow me to give the Christian form of communion to uncircumcised Gentiles, beside Gaius Costobar Herod, who represents the Herod crown prince'.

11 Gaius was given the white robe of a Scribe. He was told to baptise the Roman governor Gallio, as a sign of the Restoration expected in September. With him was Antipas Herod. With them as third was Erastus Saul Herod the brother of Gaius, who in September would be excommunicated as supporting Agrippa. Timothy supported Erastus.

(For historical points in vv.12–17, see under **fury, figtree** and **still** in the Lexicon.)

12 *And I saw when now he (each one) opened the sixth seal. And a great Earthquake came about. And the Sun became black, as hairy sackcloth. And the whole Moon became, as blood.*

12 At the Gentile service on Tuesday, 15 September AD 50, at the end of a season's teaching, Gaius opened the

title page of the epistle of James. The Annas jubilee Restoration that had been expected for this season did not take place, and Apollos turned against Agrippa. Agrippa changed the expectation to December-January, and at his initiation at the age of twenty-three decided for a celibate's life, wearing a sackcloth cowl. Bernice, his twin, was initiated and left her Nazirite vow for the married state.

13   *And the Stars of the Heaven fell to the Earth, as a Figtree throws the early Figs of it, under a great Wind shaken.*
13   In Jerusalem James the brother of Jesus allied with the Samaritan high priest Ananias, associated with Jonathan Annas, and they claimed authority in Judea without Agrippa.

14   *And the Heaven was withdrawn, as a book rolled up. And Every Mountain. And an island, out of the places of them they (early Figs) were removed.*
14   Ananus the Younger, who had held Qumran on behalf of Agrippa, was driven out, services at Qumran were abandoned, and the copy of the Septuagint that had been used there was brought to Ephesus, wrapped in cloth. Mird was abandoned. Jonathan Annas lost the support of James Niceta of the order of Asher.

15   *And the kings of the Earth. And the magnates. And the thousand- rulers. And the rich ones. And the strong ones. And Every slave. And a freedman, they (strong ones) hid Themselves to the caves. And to the Rocks of the Mountains.*
15   In Ephesus the party of Herodian nationalists was formed by Antipas Herod, meeting at the hermitage, with a leadership of seven. They included the Herodian Magus. And the head of Masada. And Nicolaus-Blastus. And Apollos. And Gaius. And John Mark, allied with Apollos, who invited the rival Herod Tigranes to the retreat caves at the hermitage. In Jerusalem, James was treated as the David by Ananias the high priest.

16   *And they (the Mountains) say to the Mountains. And to the Rocks, Fall upon us. And hide us from a face of the One Sitting upon of the throne. And from the Fury of the Lamb.*

16   In Caesarea, Ananias allied with Jonathan Annas in an anti- Agrippa Samaritan party. James was told, 'Act as the leader of Gentiles in our party. Teach them independently of Agrippa. Agrippa is the agent of Rome in the party of Jesus.

17   *Because there has come the Great Day of the Fury of them (the Rocks). And Who can stand?*

17   But Ananias the high priest, having bribed Cumanus the governor, is regarded by him as the leader of the people. This is the day of Agrippa's initiation at the age of twenty-three'.

CHAPTER 7

(For historical points in this chapter, see **tribe** in the Lexicon.)

1   After this I saw four angels standing upon the four corners of the Earth, seizing the four Winds of the Earth, in order that there should not blow a Wind upon {of} the Earth, nor upon {of} the Sea, nor upon Every Tree.

1   At midnight beginning Wednesday, 30 September AD 50, the Feast of Tabernacles and the end of the Julian quarter, I saw Apollos as a celibate bishop at the northeast corner of the vestry in the Ephesus hermitage, embracing the false Herod Tigranes from Damascus, intending to remove Agrippa from the kingship, using the eastern sign of initiation with Bernice, and the eastern sign with Gaius in Herodian schools.

2   *And I saw another angel going up from an east of the Sun,
having a seal of a living God. And he (God) cried in a great
Voice to the four angels. To Whom (plu.) it was given to them
to make unrighteous the Earth. And the Sea.*

2   Then I saw Ananus the Younger arriving from
Qumran, having replaced Matthew as Priest-Pope, with
the power to initiate and to forbid to speak. Ananus
preached to Apollos. Ananus now had superior power to
Agrippa. Bernice was present.

3   *The One (nom.) saying, Do not make unrighteous the
Earth, nor the Sea, nor the Trees, until we seal the slaves of
the God of us upon {of} the foreheads of them.*

3   Ananus said: 'Do not exclude Agrippa, but let
Bernice be superior of eastern Herodians, using the eastern mark of initiation, and let it be used in Herodian
schools, and I now continue the initiation of Agrippa, but
put on the badge on his forehead the sign that he is an
undergraduate, not permitted to speak in higher
councils'.

4   *And I heard the Number of the Ones having been sealed,
a Hundred and Forty-four Thousand; the Ones (nom.)
having been sealed out of Every tribe of the sons of Israel.*

4   I heard Timothy Herod, crown prince to Agrippa,
being promoted by Peter, who was number 144 000 as
head of Christians of province 12; and Agrippa came
down to the dais edge beside Timothy.

5   *Out of a tribe of Judah Twelve Thousand sealed. Out of
a tribe of Reuben Twelve Thousand. Out of a tribe of Gad
Twelve Thousand.   6   Out of a tribe of Asher Twelve
Thousand; out of a tribe of Naphtali Twelve Thousand; out of
a tribe of Manasseh Twelve Thousand.   7   Out of a tribe of
Simeon Twelve Thousand; out of a tribe of Levi Twelve
Thousand; out of a tribe of Issachar Twelve Thousand.   8
Out of a tribe of Zebulun Twelve Thousand; out of a tribe of*

Joseph Twelve Thousand; out of a tribe of Benjamin Twelve Thousand sealed.

5   The congregation was made up of the twelve men from Agrippa's household in Rome who now formed the Romans, men of grade 12 in every province who held Paul's doctrine; first Luke, who was acting for Jesus and was not present. Timothy was the nominal head of the party, and with him Erastus Saul Herod; these three formed a front row.   6   In the second row of Romans, myself, John Aquila with Andrew in the centre, and Clement.   7   In the third row, Onesiphorus, Ananus the Younger in the centre, and Tychicus.   8   In the fourth row, Titus, and Epaphras in the centre, and the last place was for Paul, the missionary leader, who was not present.

9   *After these things I saw. And behold a Much crowd. Whom No One had power to number it, out of Every nation. And of tribes. And of peoples. And of tongues, Ones standing (nom.) in front of the throne. And in front of the Lamb, Ones clothed (acc.) in white robes. And palm- trees in the hands of them.*

9   At noon on the same day I was in the seer's seat at the cathedral. The initiation ceremony of Agrippa was continued by his party, and he stood as a pre-initiate on the middle tier. Timothy was present as his acolyte and crown prince. Matthew stood as head of fee paying Gentiles. John Mark stood as head of eastern monastic Gentiles. Peter stood as head of Diaspora Gentiles, and Theophilus Annas said the noon prayer on the middle tier. At the Gentile part of the service, when the psalms were sung and Jesus stood on the west dais edge, Peter, wearing the white robe of a Scribe, stood in front of him. His bread paten was marked with the palm-tree emblem of the order of Asher, used for the Church.

10   *And they (Ones clothed) cry in a great Voice saying, The*

Salvation to the God of us, to the One sitting upon {to} the throne. And to the Lamb.

10 Peter preached, saying: 'Ananus may initiate Gentiles independently of Agrippa, who sits on the east side of the throne. Jesus is present as the priest to Gentiles'.

11 *And All the angels stood around the throne. And of the elders. And of the four Living Ones. And they (the four Living Ones) fell in front of the throne upon the faces of them. And they worshipped to the God,* 12 *saying, Amen. The Benefit. And the Glory. And the Wisdom. And the Thanksgiving. And the Honour. And the Power. And the Strength to the God of us to the Aeons of the Aeons, Amen.*

11 At 4 p.m., the time for money to be paid, Timothy stood over the western pillar. Theophilus stood on the edge of the dais. Epaphras, the Chief Therapeut for Agrippa's party, appeared on the middle tier. Wearing a priest's headband, he prostrated himself in the centre of the middle tier. He paid the Roman tribute to Ananus, 12 saying, 'The main service is over, and the money is given in the extra hour, of seven kinds. Shared property, to the archbishop. Common property of dynasts, to the lay bishop. Fees of the teacher of Wisdom, to the lay presbyter. Gifts to the lay deacon. Membership fees of Gentiles to the Gentile missionary. A salary is paid to the cardinal, who is in the separate class of Jewish priests. A salary is paid to Ananus the Younger, the Merari deacon who has become Priest-Pope to Agrippa II. The extended service now closes.'

13 *And there answered one out of the elders saying to me: These the Ones clothed in white robes, who (plu.) become they? And whence have they come?*

13 At the evening meal Theophilus said to me: 'Peter wears the white robe of a Scribe as he is now a celibate. He teaches in the chancel'.

14   *And I said to him, My lord, you know. And he said to me, These become the Coming Ones out of the great tribulation. And they have washed the robes of them. And they have whitened them in the blood of the Lamb.*

14   I said to him: 'Theophilus, you recognise him'. He said to me: 'Peter is admitted to the Christian priesthood under Matthew as a man who has been married. He has now purified himself from sex. He is a Christian celibate, receiving the Christian communion cup given by Jesus.

15   *On account of this they become in front of the throne of the God. And they serve him of day. And of night in the sanctuary of him. And the One Sitting upon {of} the throne will tabernacle upon them.*

15   He may stand on the east of the middle tier, like Phanuel. He holds Christian services following the solar calendar, which is now in the Day position. He may also act as a leader of Jewish villagers in a hermitage. He is a minister of the Herodian centre in Caesarea.

16   *They will not be hungry still. Neither they will be thirsty still. Neither there will not fall upon them the Sun. Neither Every scorching.*

16   He does not teach Roman governors to fast and observe Atonement. As a celibate he does not hold noon sacred meals, but gives teaching to Roman governors at noon. He is not under the authority of Agrippa as Pontifex Maximus. But he accepts Agrippa as the head of eastern ascetics.

17 *Because the Lamb the one up a middle of the throne will shepherd them. And he (the Lamb) will lead them in a way upon wells of waters of life. And the God will erase Every tear out of the eyes of them.*

17   His priest and chief bishop is Jesus, who acts as
bishop to pilgrims. Jesus is the teacher of Gentiles who
have become monastics. Ananus the Younger has
removed Herodian ascetic rules from their teaching'.

CHAPTER 8

(For the chronology of v.1, see p.212.)

1   *And when he (God) opened the seventh seal, there came
about a silence in the Heaven, as a half hour.*
1   At 3 p.m. on Tuesday, 15 December AD 50 Ananus
turned over the back page of the New Testament, to show
that the studies were completed, and, as there was no
fulfilment of the prophecy, Agrippa waited until 3 a.m. on
Thursday, 31 December, a half month being the equivalent of a half hour.

2   *And I saw the seven angels, the Ones (nom.) who stood
in front of the God. And there were given to them (the Ones
who stood) seven Trumpets.*
2   At midnight beginning Friday, 1 January AD 51, when
the jubilee in Agrippa's revision should end, I saw
Agrippa, and the Chief Therapeut on the east middle tier.
The Chief Therapeut was ready to blow the jubilee
trumpet, but as there was no fulfilment of the jubilee, it
was not blown.

3   *And another angel came. And he stood upon {of} the Altar
of Incense, having a golden frankincense holder. And there was
given to him (the Altar of Incense) Much incense, in order that
he might give to the prayers of All the holy ones upon the golden
Altar of Incense the one in front of the throne.*
3   On Friday, 1 January at 3 p.m., Ananus as Priest-Pope
came to the middle tier. Placing the censer in the noon

circle, he stood beside it, with the frankincense container used by Jews on Friday afternoons. At the Gentile service he burned incense, which carried upwards the petitions expressed through psalms by the Herod crown prince on behalf of Gentiles.

4   *And there went up the smoke of the incense to the prayers of the holy ones out of a hand of the angel in front of the God.*
4   The incense at the Christian part of the service, accompanying petitions led by Jesus Justus, was said by Jews to be unacceptable, but was approved by Ananus on the east middle tier.

5   *And the angel received the frankincense holder. And he mixed it out of the fire of the Altar of Incense. And it (the Altar of Incense) threw to the Earth. And there came about Thunders. And Voices. And Lightnings. And Earthquake.*
5   At midnight all hope for the jubilee was abandoned, and Jewish synagogue laws were imposed, with the whitening of garments for the sabbath. Ananus allied with Apollos. Ananus acted as leader in place of Agrippa. The party of Jewish nationalists came into power, under Ananus as the Sariel at the hermitage. Gaius acted there as the Herod crown prince. The Herodian Magus was there. Apollos was Chief Therapeut in this party.

PART C

REV 14:6–19:21

**HISTORY OF THE MISSION
IN EPHESUS AND JERUSALEM
AD 54–74
THE SEVEN ANGELS–AD 54–60
(REV 14:6–20)**

CHAPTER 14

(For the chronology of Part C, see pp.213–217.)

6   *And I saw another angel flying (acc.) in a mid-heaven,
having (acc.) an eternal gospel to evangelise upon the Ones
sitting upon {of} the Earth. And upon Every nation. And tribe.
And tongue. And people.*
7   *One saying (nom.) in a great Voice, Fear (plu.) the God.
And give to him a Glory. Because there has come the hour of
the judgment of him. And worship the One making the
Heaven. And the Earth. And Sea. And wells of waters.*
6   I, Tychicus, third seer of Ephesus, was in the Ephesus
cathedral congregation on the Day of Pentecost, Sunday,
26 May AD 54, three and a half years after the non-
fulfilment, and I saw Ananus the Younger as Priest-Pope
on the middle tier, holding a copy of Paul's early epistles,
to be published at the delayed jubilee and presented to

Timothy. The four evangelists were represented: Agrippa was present on behalf of Luke's Roman Gentiles. Matthew was head of those who paid fees. Peter was head of Diaspora Gentiles. John Mark was head of monastic Gentiles.

7 Ananus said on the western side: 'Ananus is the Pontifex Maximus, to be obeyed by the village class. Accept him as the Priest-Pope, receiving the common property of monastics. The jubilee of Matthew Annas has finally failed, and I, Ananus, have replaced him as priest and judge. Pay the Roman tribute to me, as performing all priestly functions for Agrippa. Agrippa is head of the congregation only. Bernice is his consort, over Gentiles attached to the Rome province. Peter is head of Christian schools'.

8 *And another angel, a second, followed, saying, He has fallen, there has fallen Babylon (fem.) the Great, she out of the wine of the Wrath of the fornication of her has drunk, All the nations.*

8 On the Day of Pentecost, Sunday, 25 May AD 55, Ananus in the second year of his lunisolar septennium 54–61 announced: 'The emperor Claudius has died (in October AD 54); he was an initiate of our religion, and Felix is now the procurator in Judea representing Rome, having become a token member by taking wine, with Bernice presiding, and Agrippa dines with them'.

9 *And another angel, a third, followed them (All the nations), saying in a great Voice, If Anyone worships the Beast. And the Icon of him (the Beast). And he (the Beast) receives a mark upon {of} the forehead of him (the Beast), or upon the hand of him (the Beast).*

9 On the Day of Pentecost, Sunday, 23 May AD 56, Ananus in the third year of his septennium acted for Agrippa in Ephesus, saying: 'Under the emperor Nero, Agrippa in Judea has joined with Herodian zealots,

diverting the Roman tribute to Atomus the Magus. Ananias has been restored as the Samaritan high priest. Atomus, who has arranged Drusilla's marriage with Felix, uses a badge like a phylactery, and the grademark is put on his paten for serving the bread.

10   *And He (new subject) will drink out of the wine of the Wrath of the God, mixed unmixed in the cup of the Fury of him (God). And he (God) will be tormented in fire. And in Brimstone in front of holy angels. And in front of the Lamb.*

10   Agrippa shares wine with Felix, his brother-in-law, who has received token initiation, using common wine yet drinking it as sacred wine, in the communion cup owned by Agrippa as agent of Rome. I, Ananus, have been punished for claiming superiority to Agrippa, and put under penance. Nicolaus-Blastus the sodomite proselyte is in charge at Qumran in my place, and Jonathan Annas, who has only the status of a celibate, is the abbot there. Uncircumcised Gentiles are sent to Ephesus, to be taught by Jesus'.

11   *And the smoke of the torment of them (holy angels) to Aeons of Aeons will go up. And they (Aeons of Aeons) do not have ceasing of day. And of night, the Ones worshipping the Beast. And the Icon of him (the Beast). And If Anyone receives the mark of the name of him.*

11   Ananus continued: 'On the Day of Atonement, Friday, 17 September, the service for Gentiles in Judea, in which they act as penitents, is led by Jonathan Annas on behalf of Agrippa. At Tabernacles, Wednesday, 22 September, Agrippa follows the order of service of the Therapeuts, whose calendar is in the Day position. He receives the Roman tribute on the west side and diverts it to Atomus for zealotry. Ananias the Samaritan is still high priest. Agrippa receives membership of his party'.

12   *Here the Endurance of the holy ones is, the Ones keeping*

the commandments of the God. And the faith (fem.) of Jesus.
12   At midnight beginning the Day of Pentecost, Wednesday, 8 June AD 57, in Ephesus, Jesus Justus at the age of twenty became a leader of prayers, entering a Sadducee school. Jesus taught in it as a priest.

13   *And I heard a Voice out of the Heaven saying, Write. Blessed are the lifeless ones, the Ones in a lord dying, from at now. Yes, says the Spirit, in order that they (the Ones...dying) may cease out of the labours of them, for the works of them follow with them.*
13   At the Gentile early morning service on the same day I heard Ananus say, 'Add another section to the Book of Revelation. James brother of Jesus, head of Jewish Christians, is again allied with Jonathan Annas, who is beginning his excommunication process, for holding the anti-Herodian doctrine of Ananus the Elder'. Ananus the Younger said as Priest-Pope, 'I assent to Jonathan's leaving this life, and James, who is his acolyte in Judea, will be next'.

14   *And I saw. And behold a white Cloud. And upon the Cloud sitting like a Son of Man (acc.), One having (nom.) upon {of} the head of him a gold crown. And in the hand of him a sharp sickle.*
14   At noon on this same Day of Pentecost, I was in the seer's place. Theophilus Annas after saying the noon prayer went to his seat over the eastern pillar. Then Jesus replaced him, and Theophilus stood in the centre. On his paten was the rod to be used for admitting or excluding fee paying Gentiles, prepared at this ceremony three years before the Eschaton.

15   *And another angel came out, out of the sanctuary, crying in a great Voice to the One Sitting upon {of} the Cloud, Send the sickle of you. And harvest. Because there has come the hour to harvest. Because there has dried up the harvest of the Earth.*

15   On the Day of Pentecost, Wednesday, 7 June AD 58, Ananus at the Ephesus hermitage preached to Theophilus, who was on the west side as it was the Night position of the calendar, saying: 'Complete the Herodian mission to fee paying Gentiles. Count their numbers. This is year 38 of the New Exodus, to which the Gentile mission has been attached. Fee paying Gentiles who have adopted the Nazirite discipline are members of the Herodian congregation'.

16   *And the One sitting upon {of} the Cloud threw the sickle of him upon the Earth. And the Earth was harvested.*
16   Then Theophilus declared the end of the mission for fee paying Gentiles in Judea also. In Judea, where Agrippa was now living, the numbers were counted.

17   *And another angel came out, out of the sanctuary, of the one in the Heaven, having (nom.). And He (new subject) a sharp sickle.*
17   On the Day of Pentecost, Wednesday, 6 June AD 59, Ananus was at the Ephesus hermitage, on the east side of the platform, as superior priest. Onesiphorus, the chief Herodian ascetic, was ready to end the mission for Gentiles having a higher ascetic discipline.

18   *And another angel came out of the Altar of Incense, having authority upon {of} the fire. And he (Altar of Incense) voiced in a great Voice to the one having the sharp sickle saying, Send of you the sharp sickle. And pick the grapes of the vineyard of the Earth. Because there have ripened the bunches of them.*
18   On the Day of Pentecost, Wednesday, 4 June AD 60, Ananus in the Ephesus cathedral stood on the middle tier, as priest to those in the hermitage. He spoke to Onesiphorus, saying: 'You are appointed to Rome to oversee the end of the mission to higher Gentiles. Announce the end of the instruction period of Felix, who

in Judea has become an initiate of Agrippa's Rome mission. He has been through the full Herodian instruction process'.

19   *And the angel threw the sickle of him to the Earth. And it (Earth) picked the vineyard of the Earth. And it (Earth) threw to the winepress of the Wrath of the God, the great one (fem., winepress).*
19   Ananus declared the end of the mission in Judea also. In Caesarea in Judea, Agrippa gave Felix his graduation at the Pentecost ending of the sixty year Vineyard mission. Then Agrippa set out for Rome with Felix, who was under arrest, to go to his house where he entertained leading Romans.

20   *And there was trampled the winepress outside the city. And there went out blood out of the winepress until the bridles of the Horses, from stadia a thousand six hundred.*
20   In Rome, at midnight beginning Thursday, 1 January AD 61, Clement, the bishop to Roman Gentiles in Herod's house, was punished for the non-fulfilment by being defined as a village bishop and removed from office at the age of fifty. He took the Christian communion cup to the Forum of Appius, where the communion was given by the bishop of the visiting Sadducee, in the upper room above the catacombs, a place defined as an unclean one an hour's walk from Herod's house.

CHAPTER 15

(For the chronology and events of Chapters 15–16, see pp.215–216.)

1 *And I saw another Sign in the Heaven, great. And marvellous, seven angels having seven last plagues. Because in them (the plagues) there was ended the Wrath of the God.*
1 On the same day in Herod's house in Rome I saw Ananus as priest. There was a change in the chronology of the Restoration, and it was announced on behalf of Agrippa that this was the earliest beginning of the sabbatical year that would start in June AD 62. Felix's position as procurator was terminated from this date.

2 *And I saw, as a glass Sea mixed in fire. And the victors out of the Beast. And out of the Icon of him (the Beast). And out of the Number of the name of him (the Beast), Ones standing upon the glass Sea, Ones having harps of the God.*
2 On the Day of Pentecost, Wednesday, 3 June AD 61, in Rome, I was in the congregation from noon, and saw the flask of holy water placed on the western pillar. Clement, the representative of Peter, sat over the eastern pillar, and the new Herodian Magus was in the centre. Ananias the Samaritan priest was present, for zealotry was rising under Nero. As the Gentile service began, Timothy, who was now associated with the Magus, stood over the western pillar, and Theophilus prepared to play the harp to accompany the psalms.

3 *And they (Ones having) sing the song of Moses the slave of the God. And the song of the Lamb, saying (plu. Ones*

having), Great things. And marvellous the works of
you, lord, the God, the All-mighty, righteous ones (fem.
plu.). And true (fem. plu.) the ways of you, the king of the
nations.

3   Theophilus led a hymn in honour of Epaphras, the
Chief Therapeut who was a cardinal and Roman
missionary. Then he led a hymn in honour of Jesus, then
he said: 'We are in Rome. Ananus, king's priest to
Agrippa, baptiser of Essenes, you have changed the
chronology so that there is still time before
the Restoration. You teach Sadducee doctrine, and you
act as a teacher for Agrippa.

4   *Who does not {not} fear, lord. And he will glorify the name*
of you. Because alone devout. Because All the nations will
come. And they will worship in front of you. Because the right-
eous things of you have been made manifest.

4   Agrippa is not a priest, Ananus. He will make you the
high priest in Judea. You practise the individual ascetic
rule. Timothy supports you. He will pay the Roman
tribute through you. You have kept the ascetic rules,
making you worthy to be high priest'.

5   *And after these things I saw. And there opened the*
sanctuary of the tabernacle of witness in the Heaven.

5   The following year, on the Day of Pentecost,
Wednesday, 2 June AD 62, I was in the congregation. The
service began at Agrippa's monastic centre in Caesarea.

6   *And there came out the seven angels having the seven*
plagues, out of the sanctuary, clad in pure linens bright. And
girded around the chest golden girdles.

6   Agrippa came to the upper tier, to declare the end of
the six seasons from January 61 to June 62, wearing the
linen garment of a royal permanent celibate. He wore a
golden belt as a royal lay celibate.

7   *And one out of the four Living Ones gave to the seven
angels seven gold bowls full of the Wrath of the living God to
the Aeons of the Aeons.*
7   At the Gentile part of the service Epaphras' bishop
gave Agrippa the bowl for collecting money in a 'Saturday'
year, the money to be used to bribe Albinus, the new
procurator, who had received token membership from
Ananus and Agrippa.

8   *And the sanctuary was filled with smoke out of the Glory
of the God. And out of the Power of him. And No One was
empowered to come into the sanctuary until were ended the
seven plagues of the seven angels.*
8   On Friday, 18 June AD 62, the Friday afternoon
service for Gentiles was held in the Caesarea monastery,
led by Ananus. His deputy was also present. At midnight,
when Agrippa's six seasons ended, James, who was the
chief acolyte in Judea, entered – through death – into the
final 'Holy of Holies', heaven itself.

CHAPTER 16

1   *And I heard a great Voice out of the sanctuary saying to
the seven angels, Depart (plu.) And pour out (plu.) the seven
bowls of the Wrath of the God to the Earth.*
1   At midnight beginning the Day of Pentecost,
Wednesday, 1 June AD 63, I heard Ananus, now dismissed
as high priest, say in Caesarea to Agrippa, 'Go to
Jerusalem. Spend the money that has been collected
during the last year to bribe Albinus'.

2   *And the first one came from. And he poured out the bowl
of him to the Earth. And there came about a bad sore. And an
evil one upon the Men having the mark of the Beast. And the
Ones worshipping the Icon of him.*

2   The first minister, the 'Sunday', went to Jerusalem. He gave his money to Agrippa. Zealotry broke out. Eleazar Ben Jair, head of the Sicarii, took control of Masada, allied with the Herodian Magus. The Roman tribute was diverted to Ananias the Samaritan.

3   *And the second one poured out the bowl of him to the Sea. And there came about blood, as of a lifeless one. And Every Soul of life died, the things in the Sea.*
3   On the Day of Pentecost, Wednesday, 30 May AD 64, the second minister gave the money to Bernice. Bernice, who had been performing a Nazirite vow, ended the vow, as did Antipas. Agrippa was excommunicated, and Bernice held the royal power.

4   *And the third one poured out the bowl of him to the rivers. And the wells of the waters. And there came about blood.*
5   *And I heard the angel of the waters saying, Righteous are you, the Becoming One. And the One who became, the devout one. Because you have judged these things.*
6   *Because a blood of holy ones. And of prophets they (holy ones) have poured out. And a blood to them (holy ones) you have given to drink, worthy they become.*
7   *And I heard the Altar of Incense saying, Yes, lord, the God, the All- mighty one, true ones. And righteous ones the judgments of you.*
4   On the Day of Pentecost, Wednesday, 29 May AD 65, when the news had come of Nero's persecution in Rome, the third minister gave the money to Ananus' Gentiles at Qumran. It was given to the Gentile monastic school there. The pilgrims' form of communion was observed there.
5   I heard the Sadducee abbot at Qumran say, 'Ananus, chief priest from Ephesus, you baptise Essenes at Qumran. You are the priest for Rome, and head of ascetics there. You have acted as Herodian judge in Rome.

6   The Christian form of communion is still observed in Rome under Jesus Justus representing Jesus. He gives communion in place of Timothy, who was put to death in Nero's persecution. As priest in Rome you authorised Jesus Justus to act like a priest, equal to a Phanuel'.

7   Then I heard Ananus say to the new Sadducee high priest Matthias: 'I assent to your appointment as high priest and king's priest to Agrippa, teaching in Sadducee-Essene schools. You act as judge to Essenes'.

8   *And the fourth one poured out the bowl of him upon the Sun. And it was given to him (the Sun) to sear the Men in fire.*

9   *And the Men were seared with a great searing. And they blasphemed the name of the God having the authority upon these plagues. And they (the Men) did not repent, to give to him (God) a Glory.*

8   On the Day of Pentecost, Wednesday, 28 May AD 66, the fourth minister spent the money to gain control of Masada. Agrippa did not defend the tyrant of Masada, Eleazar Ben Jair, against the Romans.

9   Eleazar was attacked by the Romans, and war broke out. As a zealot Eleazar opposed Matthias the high priest, who observed the Pentecost season. Eleazar did not join the Rome province, and did not accept that Matthias was the true high priest.

10   *And the fifth one poured out the bowl of him upon the throne of the Beast. And the kingdom of him (the Beast) became darkened. And they (the Men) bit the tongues of them out of the Toil.*

11   *And they (the Men) blasphemed the God of the Heaven out of the Toils of them. And out of the sores of them. And they (the Toils) did not repent out of the works of them.*

10   On the Day of Pentecost, Wednesday, 27 May AD 67, the fifth minister spent the money to arm Masada, where the Herodian Magus claimed to be head. The Romans

began the siege of Jerusalem. Eleazar caused the murder of Antipas Herod, the treasurer of Jerusalem, through an Idumean.

11   Then Eleazar through the chief Idumean put Ananus to death. Zealots acted with him. The chief Idumean was an ascetic, but refused to join the Rome province.

12   *And the sixth one poured out the bowl of him upon the great river Euphrates. And the water of it dried up, in order that there might be prepared the way of the kings from an east of a Sun.*

12   On the Day of Pentecost, Wednesday, 25 May AD 68, the sixth minister gave the money to the Damascus monastery, in an alliance with the rival Herod. Damascus proselytes were permitted only to be Nazirites, and the chief celibate from Qumran made Damascus its pilgrimage centre.

13 And I saw out of the mouth of the Dragon. And out of the mouth of the Beast. And out of the mouth of the false prophet, three unclean Spirits, as Frogs.

13   At Qumran on the same day I saw the zealot triarchy of AD 6 re-formed, with a Pharisee former high priest as the Dragon. It included the Herodian Magus as the Beast. It included the rival Herod as the Calf, and with him, in the place of Saddok-Theudas, was Simon Gioras of the order of Gad, a married man attached to the Therapeuts.

14   *For they (Frogs) become Spirits of demons making Signs, which proceed out upon the kings of the whole Dominion, to gather them to the war of the great day of the God the Allmighty one.*

14   Simon Gioras acted as a zealot priest, giving promotions, and he summoned Erastus Saul Herod and myself, Tychicus, the chief Gentile celibate with membership

both at Qumran and in Rome, to come to a council at Qumran on Friday, 10 June AD 68, the solar 31st, which would be the test for Matthias the Sadducee priest, as it was the day ending year 38 of the revised Exodus, when there should be a 'Jordan crossing'.

15 *Behold I come, as a thief. Blessed is the One watching. And keeping the garments of him, in order that not naked he might walk. And they (the kings) look at the shamefulness of him (the One watching).*

15 I spoke for the congregation: 'I volunteer for military service, with Erastus. I have been appointed an archbishop. I will observe the rules of Qumran celibates concerning garments covering the body, so that nakedness is not seen. But Erastus does not keep this rule'.

16 *And he (the One watching) gathered them (the kings) to the place the one called in Hebrew Armagedon.*

16 The seer took Erastus to the place of assembly of military leaders in the south-west area at Qumran, where priests came down to the latrine in an unclean state.

17 *And the seventh one poured out the bowl of him upon the Air. And there came out a great Voice out of the sanctuary from the throne saying, It has come about.*

17 On the Day of Pentecost, Wednesday, 24 May AD 69, the seventh minister gave the money to the Sadducee high priest for his flight. From Caesarea, Agrippa sent a message: 'The end has come: I am abandoning Jerusalem'.

18 *And there came about Lightnings. And Voices. And Thunders. And an Earthquake came about, great. Such As did not come about, from which a Man came about upon {of} the Earth. Such an Earthquake! so great.*

18 The Herodian nationalists left with Agrippa, under the Magus. Gaius Costobar Herod was with them. The

Sadducee was with them. The Chief Therapeut left with them, and they all went to Rome. Agrippa ceased to be king in Jerusalem, and his court and the priesthood were re-established in the west. A new centre for Diaspora Therapeuts was established in Rome.

19 *And the Great City came about to three parts. And the cities of the nations fell. And Babylon the Great was remembered in front of the God, to give to her the cup of the wine of the Wrath of the Fury of him.*

19 The headquarters of Herodian Gentile schools under Bernice was transferred to Rome, to Herod's house 'Tavern Three'. The Caesarea Christian monastery was transferred there. In Rome, the emperor Vitellius was given token membership by the Sadducee, and at a banquet the emperor shared with Agrippa as agent of Rome the cup of fermented wine.

20 *And Every island fled. And Mountains were not found.*
20 Bernice re-established the order of Asher in the west. The Samaritan high priest Ananias was dead.

21 *And great Hail, as things weighing a talent, went down out of the Heaven upon the Men. And the Men blasphemed the God out of the plague of the Hail. Because great becomes the plague of it (the Hail) exceedingly.*

21 Gaius Costobar Herod replaced Antipas as treasurer, and sent large amounts of money from the west to Eleazar Ben Jair at Masada for the defence of Jerusalem. On Monday, 1 January AD 70 Eleazar, the descendant of Judas the Galilean, used the money to take control of the high priesthood. On the same day Gaius opened a new centre in the Rome province.

CHAPTER 17

1 *And there came one out of the seven angels, of the Ones having the seven bowls. And he spoke with me saying, Come, I will show you the judgment of the great harlot sitting upon {of} Many waters.*

1 At midnight beginning the Day of Pentecost, Wednesday, 23 May AD 70, the Chief Therapeut, with Agrippa, came to Ephesus, counting this as the 'Sunday' of another seven years. As my chief archbishop he said, 'Come to the hermitage an hour from Ephesus, and I will show you the service during which the Eschaton is expected, after a zero decade, by Bernice, who acts as a cardinal to Gentiles.

2 *With whom the kings of the Earth have committed fornication. And the dwellers on the Earth are drunk out of the wine of the fornication of her.*

2 Gaius Costobar Herod supports her claim to be a priestess. Her son Bernicianus has been appointed Herod crown prince, and now, by midnight, he will be drunk from the fermented communion wine she serves'.

3 *And she (last pronoun 'her') brought me from, to a wilderness in a Spirit. And I saw a woman sitting upon a scarlet Beast, full of names of blasphemy, One having (masc. nom.) seven heads. And ten Horns.*

3 At the hermitage outside Ephesus Bernice admitted me as seer to the first pew. I saw her sitting at the communion table as one of two cardinals, with the zealot Magus as the other on the east, and behind them Gaius Costobar Herod sat as head of the circumcision party, giving full initiation to the circumcised. But he kept the uncircumcised down to grade 10.

4 *And the woman became clothed in purple. And scarlet.*

And gilded with gold. And a precious stone. And with pearls,
One having (fem.) a gold cup in the hand of her full (the cup)
of abominations. And the unclean things of her fornication.

4   Bernice, claiming to be queen regnant and third in a
triarchy, wore the purple vestment of a queen. She also
wore the scarlet of a cardinal. She wore the gold of a priest.
She wore the precious stone of a royal head of celibates.
She wore a pearl for her role as Wisdom, teacher of
Gentiles, and on her bread paten was the cup used by
Herod for entertaining distinguished Romans; the cup
signifying the Herodian ambition to become Roman
emperors. She was an immoral priestess.

5   *And upon the forehead of her a name written, Mystery;*
Babylon the Great; the mother of the harlots. And of the abom-
inations of the Earth.

5   On the badge on her lower forehead were the letters
Resh (grade 2 priest) and Zayin (the letter for 7, the letters
together used by a priest in Ephesus, province 7) the two
letters giving the Hebrew word *raz* 'mystery', meaning
that she was the oracle in Ephesus; also the emblem of the
emperor Vitellius, with whom she had dined; and the
emblem of 'Sarah' the Mother of Gentiles, whose female
followers claimed priesthood. She aimed at Jewish
empire.

6   *And I saw the woman drunk out of the blood of the holy*
ones. And out of the blood of the martyrs of Jesus. And I
marvelled seeing her, with great marvelling.

6   At dawn I saw Bernice attending an eastern Christian
communion over which Jesus Justus presided, where wine
was sipped and there was only spiritual ecstasy. At the
same hour a western Christian service was conducted at
the cathedral by Clement, the successor of Peter in Rome,
in the presence of Jesus. When there was no fulfilment of
the prophecy at Bernice's service, I changed my views and
turned against her.

7 *And the angel said to me, On account of what you have marvelled. I will say to you the mystery of the woman. And of the Beast carrying her. Of the One having the seven heads. And the ten Horns.*

7 The Chief Therapeut said to me: 'You have changed to supporting Agrippa. There are now party disputes following the non-fulfilment, and, imitating the oracle style, I will tell you about Bernice's party. The Herodian Magus treats Bernice as queen. Gaius is the leader, the chief initiator in the circumcision party. He limits the uncircumcised to grade 10 and the Rome province.

8 *The Beast which you saw became. And he becomes not. And he is about to go up out of the abyss. And he departs to destruction. And the dwellers upon {of} the Earth will marvel. Of Whom (plu.) the name is not written upon the book of the life from a throwing down of a world. Of Ones looking at the Beast. Because he (the Beast) became. And he becomes not. And he becomes beside.*

8 The Herodian Magus whom you see has been appointed to Rome. He is no longer a member at the Ephesus cathedral, where Agrippa has been restored to power. In September, when Jerusalem will fall, he will become Chief Monk, at the Jewish monastery on the Tiber Island. At this hour of 4 a.m., for unclean matters, he is appointed to the Rome monastery. Bernicianus now ceases to be crown prince. But the monastic party are in power at the hermitage, and Agrippa's name is not included in their list of members. Gaius is their superior, with the Magus. The Magus is the Herodian leader in Rome. He is not a member at the Ephesus cathedral. But he is a member at the hermitage.

9 *Here is the Understanding having Wisdom. The seven heads become seven Mountains, at where the woman sits upon*

{of} them (Mountains). *And seven kings become.*

9   In the cathedral, the Sadducee is the chief teacher. Samaritan teaching is given at the hermitage, by Gaius, and it is the higher school for Rome members, and Bernice presides at the meal beside Gaius. Erastus is the chief Jewish celibate at the hermitage.

10   *The Five have fallen; the one becomes; the other has come Not Yet. And when he comes he must remain a Few.*
10   Of the three Herod kinsmen, the position of Antipas Herod has been taken over by Gaius; Erastus is still a member at the cathedral and at the non-fulfilment a new Herod (son of Drusilla and Felix?) joins them. He says prayers at 3 p.m.

11   *And the Beast which became. And he becomes not. And He (new subject) becomes an Eighth. And out of the Seven he becomes. And he departs to destruction.*
11   At 4 p.m., the time for unclean matters, the Herodian Magus is again appointed to Rome. He is again rejected from the cathedral membership. The new Herod is appointed to the Tiber Island. He claims to be a successor. He leaves for Rome.

12   *And the ten Horns which you saw become ten kings. Whosoever Ones a kingdom Not Yet have received. Nevertheless authority, as kings one hour they (kings) receive with the Beast.*
12   Gaius, whom you see re-appointed as head of the circumcision party, is also a chief Jewish celibate in Rome. At the midnight non- fulfilment he claims to replace Agrippa as head of the Herodian mission. At 1 a.m., the last chance for the fulfilment on the Day of Pentecost, he is given the power to initiate eastern Gentiles, and Erastus remains chief Jewish celibate at the hermitage, a deputy of Gaius equal with the Magus'.

13   *These have one intellect. And the Power. And authority of them to the Beast they give.*
13   On the following 31st, Friday, 8 June, Gaius claimed authority over Gentile schools attached to Sadducee centres, which had originally been Samaritan. He said the noon prayer as the Phanuel. He allowed Magian initiations.

14   *These with the Lamb make war. And the Lamb conquers them. Because a lord of lords he is. And a king of kings. And the called ones with him (king). And elect ones. And faithful ones.*
14   At 6 p.m., at the council in the Ephesus cathedral, Gaius debated with Jesus, who was present for his last public appearance at the age of seventy-six. Jesus won the debate. He remained a distinguished layman. Agrippa was restored as head of Jewish celibates. The Sadducee priest supported Agrippa. A new crown prince to Agrippa (brother of Timothy?) was appointed. A new presbyter to Roman Christians was appointed.

15   *And he (king) says to me, The waters which you saw. Of Whom the woman sits, peoples. And crowds become. And nations. And tongues.*
15   After this part of the council Agrippa said to me, 'You may now attend at the hermitage, where Gaius is no longer head. Bernice is still the Mother there, but acting beside you as head of Gentile monastics, one of the four kinds of Christians. Erastus Saul Herod is head of eastern Christians, who are pre-initiates, and he is a member at the cathedral. I am head of the Romans. Clement is the successor of Peter.'

16   *And the ten Horns which you saw. And the Beast. These will hate the woman. And they (These) will make her wilderness-like. And naked. And the flesh of her they (These) will eat. And her they (These) will scorch in fire.*

16   Gaius is merely a Roman celibate now. The Herodian Magus is his associate in Rome. I, Agrippa, reject Bernice as a minister in her own right. I reduce her to the status of hermit. She is treated as a married woman. Her property comes back to me. I put her under the discipline of the Therapeuts.

17   *For the God has given to the hearts of them (These) to make the intellect of him. And to make one intellect. And to give the kingdom of them (These) to the Beast, until there are completed the Words of the God.*
17   The Sadducee resumes authority with the Herod crown prince over the Sadducee Gentile schools. They are under a Gentile bishop, not under Gaius. But at midnight the decision has been made to leave Jewish levitical schools under the control of the Herodian Magus; and at midnight also the ceremony is held for the departure of Jesus from public ministry, forty years from the time he married.

18   *And the woman whom you saw becomes the Great City, she having a kingdom upon {of} the kings of the Earth.*
18   At 1 a.m., when hope for a fulfilment of the Eschaton at the solstice 31st is abandoned, you have seen Bernice appointed as the head of Herodian Gentile schools for proselytes in Rome, working together with Gaius'.

CHAPTER 18

1   *After these things I saw another angel going down out of the Heaven, having great authority. And the Earth was lightened out of the Glory of him.*
1   At the Feast of Tabernacles, September AD 70, at the time of the fall of Jerusalem, I saw the Sadducee on the

475

centre balcony of the Ephesus cathedral, being a priest in Rome also. He was the Priest-Pope, who allowed Agrippa to lead prayers as head of celibates.

2 *And he cried in a strong Voice saying, He has fallen, Babylon the Great (fem.) has fallen. And there has come about a dwelling of demons. And a prison of Every unclean Spirit. And a prison of Every unclean Bird. And of a hated one (masc.).*

2 The Sadducee announced: 'The emperor Vitellius, who was an initiate of our religion, has died (in December 69). Jerusalem, occupied by zealots, has been left to be destroyed. Erastus Saul Herod has fled to Achaia. Gaius Costobar Herod is with him. The new third Herod has been rejected as successor.

3 *Because out of the wine of the Wrath of the fornication of her (Babylon the Great) have fallen All the nations. And the kings of the Earth with her (Babylon the Great) have committed fornication. And the salesmen of the Earth (fem.) out of the Power of the sensuality of her (Earth) have grown rich.*

3 Agrippa does not attend the banquets in Rome where Bernice plans to entertain Titus, the emperor Vespasian's son. Gaius Costobar Herod is allied with Bernice in working for a marriage with Titus. Erastus Saul Herod, who stores the fees received from Gentiles under Bernice, has become bishop treasurer'.

4 *And I heard another Voice out of the Heaven saying, Come out (plu.), my people (sing.), out of her (Earth), in order that you (plu.) might not be in common with the sins of her (Earth). And out of the plagues of her (Earth), in order that you (plu.) may not receive.*

4 At midnight beginning the Day of Pentecost, Sunday, 9 June AD 71, I heard a new Sadducee say, 'Let eastern monastic Gentiles and Jesus Justus their leader be inde-

pendent of Agrippa, not taking communion with Bernice. Observe Pentecost separately, and do not have bishops appointed by Agrippa.

5 *Because there have clung together of her (Earth) the sins until the Heaven. And the God has remembered the unrighteousnesses of her (Earth).*

5 Bernice has re-allied with Agrippa, acting with him at the midnight service. It is the new Sadducee who admits Gentiles in the Herodian congregation.

6 *Give from (plu.) to her (Earth). As and She (new subject) has given from. And double (plu.) the double things according to the works of her (She), in the cup in which she has mixed, mix (plu.) to her double.*

6 Appoint ministers independently of Agrippa. Bernice appoints her own Gentile ministers. Retain your Herodian membership, but also independent Christian membership, wearing the Gog sign, the double Gimel, and take communion with her if she acts as a layperson only.

7 *As many things she glorified herself. And she was sensual, such a torment give to her. And mourning. Because in the heart of her she says, Because I sit a queen. And a widow I become not. And mourning I do not {not} see.*

7 She claims to be equal to a high priest. But she is simply equal to a married woman, and you should make her act as a Sister. She may take a Nazirite vow. As a Nazirite presbyter she says, "I am the Herodian queen regnant. I have not lost my position because of the fall of Jerusalem. But I do take Nazirite vows".

8 *On account of this, in one day will come the plagues of her, Death. And mourning. And famine. And in fire he (Death) will be scorched. Because a strong lord the God, the One having judged her.*

8   On this Sunday Day of Pentecost, the primary feast is observed, and excommunications may be given. Nazirite vows begin. It is the north solar sabbatical year, the intercalation season of the calendar, changing to the Day position. The Herodian Magus has been put under Therapeut discipline. The new Sadducee can act as judge over Bernice'.

9   *And they (salesmen, v.3) will weep. And there will wail upon her the kings of the Earth, the Ones committing fornication with her. And sensual ones (masc. plu.), when they look at the smoke of the conflagration of her.*

9   On the Day of Atonement, Friday, 4 October AD 71, the first of three ritual lamentations for the fall of Jerusalem was held, led by Erastus in Ephesus. On the same day, in the Rome province, Gaius Costobar Herod performed the rite of lamentation on behalf of Bernice, whom he held to be the priestess making the atonement. In the Herodian house in Rome, the Chief Therapeut as a Nazirite led the Friday afternoon service for Gentiles.

10   *From afar standing (masc. plu., sensual ones) on account of the fear of the torment of her, saying: Woe, woe, the Great City, Babylon the city the strong one, Because in one hour has come the judging of you.*

10   The same evening in Rome at midnight the Chief Therapeut in black garb said: 'Bernice's school for proselytes in Rome has an extension of fourteen years for the Restoration, and Titus has become a member of it. They say that the sabbath begins at 1 a.m, the hour when the hermitage at the Forum of Appius is reached from here, and the Restoration will begin there'.

11   *And the salesmen of the Earth weep. And they mourn upon her (the Earth). Because the cargo of them No One buys No Longer.*

11   At Tabernacles, Wednesday, 9 October AD 71,

Erastus Saul Herod in Ephesus continued the lamentation, because the money that had been paid for building work in Jerusalem would no longer be paid. He began a Nazirite vow. Then it was declared that a new form of the Promised Land mission, based in the Diaspora, had begun, and the Herod crown prince continued the practice of Gentiles paying fees and receiving payment as missionaries.

12   *A cargo of gold. And of silver. And of precious stones. And of pearls. And of fine linen. And of purple. And of silk. And of scarlet. And Every citron wood. And Every vessel of ivory. And Every vessel out of precious wood. And of copper. And of iron. And of marble.*

12   There were twenty-nine kinds of male ministers receiving money, for the days of the month (with Bernice as the thirtieth); fourteen men over the village congregation, led by the priest. Next the levite. Next the monastic celibate. Next the deacon teacher of Wisdom. Next the village celibate bishop. Next the married bishop. Next the judge. In the attached school, a lay cardinal was chief teacher. With him three Herod princes, the first Gaius Costobar. Next the new Herod, over the islands. Next Erastus Saul Herod. An Alexandrian presbyter taught the elementary school. An ascetic from the Therapeuts taught the middle school. A higher master taught the graduates.

13   *And cinnamon. And spice/unblemished. And incense. And ointment. And frankincense. And wine. And oil. And fine flour. And wheat. And donkeys. And sheep. And of horses. And of carriages. And of bodies. And souls of Men.*

13   Of the fifteen ministers of Herod's high table, nine were subordinates, with five on the lower side of the table, their offices corresponding to five lesser substances used in worship, with incense in the centre. Four sat in places corresponding to food tithes on the higher sides of the

table, with initiates taking wine and novices represented by oil on the east, and villagers taking bread only with their associated Gentiles on the west. Six sat at the centre, four on ordinary occasions: the levite and the prince in front of the higher priest and the lesser priest. On great occasions Herod sat behind these, occupying both sides, or with a deputy on the west side.

14 *The late summer of you (you v. 10) of the Lust of the Soul (fem.) has come from from you. And All the Fat Things. And the Bright Things are lost from you. And No Longer not {not} will they (the Bright Things) find them (All the Fat Things).*
14 The seer sent a message to Bernice, the thirtieth in this list: 'You are not Herodian queen regnant. You are simply the queen consort. You no longer hold the royal property. In this new form of the Promised Land mission, Agrippa is the royal person and you are the subordinate'.

15 *The salesmen of These, the Ones becoming enriched from her (the Soul) stand from afar on account of the fear of the torment of her (the Soul), weeping. And mourning,* 16 *saying: Woe, woe, the Great City, the One (fem.) clothed in fine linen. And purple. And scarlet. And gilded in gold. And in a precious stone. And in a pearl.* 17 *Because in one hour such an enriched one (masc.) has been made a wilderness.*
15 At midnight beginning Wednesday, 1 January AD 72 the second lamentation for Jerusalem was held, led by Erastus Saul Herod in Ephesus, and in Rome by the Chief Therapeut in black garb, who acted as treasurer of Herodian property, receiving Gentile fees. He began a Nazirite vow, 16 saying: 'Bernice's school for proselytes in Rome has an extension of fourteen years for the Restoration, and Bernice is the head as the Virgin. She is a bishop. And a cardinal. And a priestess. And a teacher of Wisdom. 17 I go to the hermitage at the Forum of Appius, reaching it at 1 a.m.'.
And Every steersman. And Everyone sailing upon a place.

And sailors. And Whoever (plu.) work the Sea have stood from afar.

On the Day of Atonement, Friday, 2 October AD 72, in Rome, the next lamentation was held, under Agrippa as 'Noah', of the sea mission and the Vineyard. The Herod crown prince represented 'Shem', the uncircumcised. The head of 'Ham' was the next in the hierarchy. At 3 p.m. Agrippa enacted the ceremony of making atonement.

18   *And they (Whoever) cried, looking at the smoke of the conflagration of her (the Sea), saying, Who is like the Great City?*

18   At the Friday service for Gentiles held at this hour, when the incense was burnt, Agrippa preached, saying: 'I have taken charge of the Herodian school for proselytes in Rome'.

19   *And they (Whoever) threw dust upon the heads of them. And they cried, weeping. And mourning, saying: Woe, woe, the Great City, in which have become enriched All the ones having the ships in the Sea out of the preciousness of her (the Sea). Because in one hour they (All the ones) have become a wilderness.*

19   Agrippa performed the act of penitence for Gentiles, leading a confession of sin. He preached, uttering the last of the three lamentations. He began a Nazirite vow, saying: 'The school for proselytes in Rome under Bernice has an extension of fourteen years for the Restoration, and I as "Noah" receive the fees of married Gentiles, and am head of Gentile celibates. I go to the hermitage at the Forum of Appius, reaching it at 1 a.m.'.

20   *Rejoice (sing.) upon {to} her (the Sea), Heaven. And the holy ones. And the apostles. And the prophets. Because the God has judged the judgment of you (plu.) out of her (the Sea).*

20   At midnight beginning Friday, 1 January AD 73, in

481

Rome, the seer spoke for the congregation: 'Agrippa, join in the betrothal ceremony of Jesus Justus. He is the David crown prince until his coronation. The head of Gentile monasteries is present to act as "eunuch". The Herod crown prince is present. The Sadducee priest has upheld you as king against Bernice'.

21 *And one strong angel lifted up a stone, as a great mill-stone. And he threw to the Sea, saying: Thus with a rush there will be thrown Babylon the Great City. And it is not {not} found still.*
21 At 1 a.m. the Sadducee took a stone representing the instrument of circumcision, that had been used at the round base outside the vestry. He announced that separate membership in Rome was permitted, saying: 'Titus, son of the emperor, who has become an initiate of the school for proselytes, does not have to be circumcised. Titus is a member of our mission.

22 *And a Voice of harpists. And of musicians. And of flute-players. And of trumpeters it is not {not} heard in you (sing.) still. And Every craftsman of Every craft is not {not} found in you still. And a Voice of a mill is not {not} heard in you still.*
22 At the dawn service for Gentiles there is music, with the deputy of the Sadducee playing the harp. A "Moses" leads the singing. A leader of the liturgical dance takes the place of Miriam. A "crossing of the Jordan" is enacted for you, Titus, to dramatise your admission, with a "Joshua" escorting you. A Herod acts as "bearer of the ark" to you. A deacon gives you instruction on Jewish matters.

23 *And a Light of a lantern will not {not} shine in you still. And a Voice of a bridegroom. And of a bride will not {not} be heard in you still. Because the salesmen of you became the greatest ones of the Earth. Because in the sorcery of you were deceived All the nations.*
23 At 4 a.m. the Sadducee stands to lead you in early

morning prayers. Jesus Justus the Morning Star, who is now being betrothed six months before his wedding, acts with him. The bride stands beside Jesus Justus as doorkeeper to admit you. Erastus Saul Herod acts as the head of Herodian celibates, instructing you. The Herodian Magus, who previously instructed you, gave false teaching about the Herod succession.

24   *And in it (the Earth) blood of prophets. And of holy ones it (the Earth) was found. And of All the slain ones upon {of} the Earth.*

24   Agrippa now attends a Christian communion, led by the Herod crown prince. Jesus Justus accepts him into the service. At its conclusion the Herod crown prince becomes a cardinal'.

CHAPTER 19

1   *After these things I heard, as a great Voice of a Much crowd in the Heaven, of Ones (All the slain ones) saying, Allelujah the Salvation. And the Glory. And the Power of the God of us.*

1   At noon on the same day I was at the New Year service in Rome, and Agrippa as a layman was present, and the Herod crown prince said: 'A new Sadducee is the Priest-Pope, with the title "Hallelujah", with power to initiate Gentiles independently of the throne. He holds the celibate property. His deputy, a Phanuel, is present, saying the noon prayer.

2   *Because true ones (fem. plu.). And righteous are the judgments of him. Because he has judged the great harlot. She who ruined the Earth in the fornication of her. And she ('her' last subject) has made out- righteous the blood of the slaves of her out of a hand of her.*

2   He is a Sadducee using the T sign. He teaches
Essenes. He condemns Bernice. She claims to be queen
regnant, spending Herodian money in Rome when she
acts as priestess. She rejects Christian communion
services attended by Agrippa, and holds the bread paten
herself'.

3   *And a second one (neut.) they (slaves) said, Hallelujah.*
And the smoke of her goes up to the Aeons of the Aeons.
3   At 2 p.m. Agrippa said: 'The new Priest-Pope
Hallelujah is installed'. The Friday afternoon service for
Gentiles was held, with Agrippa leading in place of
Bernice.

4   *And the twenty-four elders fell. And the four Living Ones.*
And they worshipped the God, the One sitting upon {to} the
throne, saying, Amen. Hallelujah.
4   At the same hour the Phanuel knelt to offer the gifts
to Agrippa. The Chief Therapeut was present. He gave
the Roman tribute to the Sadducee on the east side of the
throne, then said: 'The service is finished. Priest-Pope
Hallelujah will give further teaching to Gentiles'.

5   *And a Voice from the throne came out saying, Praise to*
the God of us, All the slaves of him, the Ones fearing him, the
little ones. And the great ones.
5   On the following Day of Pentecost, Sunday, 6 June AD
73, in Ephesus, where the New Year was observed at
Pentecost, the Phanuel to the Sadducee said on the
middle tier: 'Accept Priest-Pope Hallelujah in Ephesus,
Herod crown prince, together with the head of the sons of
Japheth and the head of the sons of Ham. And the head
of the sons of Shem, belonging to the east'.

6   *And I heard, as a Voice of a Much crowd. And as a Voice*
of Many waters. And as a Voice of strong Thunders saying,

Hallelujah. Because there has held kingship a lord, the God of us, the All-mighty.

6   At 2 p.m. I was at the next part of the installation service, and Phanuel spoke for the three heads, first for Agrippa, who was a layman. Then for himself as superior of Gentiles. Then for the Sadducee, saying: 'Priest-Pope Hallelujah is installed in Ephesus. He is head of Herodian celibate centres, the village leader, the village priest, and king's priest to Agrippa'.

7   *Let us rejoice. And let us jubilate. And let us give the Glory to him (God). Because there has come the marriage of the Lamb. And the woman of him has prepared Herself.*

7   At 3 p.m. he said: 'Let the marriage service begin. Let the harvest symbolism for giving money be used. Let the Sadducee receive the property of dynasts. The wedding of Jesus Justus at the age of thirty- six is to take place. His bride is the chief Essene woman, who begins her vesting.

8   *And it has been given to her in order that she is clothed with a fine linen garment, bright, pure. For the fine linen garment is the righteous deeds of the holy ones.*

8   She is vested with a bride's garment, that of a village celibate bishop, a royal person, a virgin. Jesus Justus has kept the rule, and her white garment stands for her virginity'.

9   *And she (last sing. subject) says to me: Write. Blessed are the Ones to the supper of the wedding of the Lamb called. And he (the Lamb) says to me, These are the truthful Words of the God.*

9   At midnight the bride said to me, the seer: 'Make a record of the wedding. Those who keep midnight vigils are invited to the wedding feast'. Jesus Justus said to me: 'Here is the Christian Pope, who will teach while I am in the married state'.

10   *And I fell before the feet of him (God) to worship to him. And he says to me, View, not a fellow slave of you I am. And of the brothers of you, of the Ones having the Witnessing of Jesus. To God worship. For the Witnessing of Jesus becomes the Spirit of the prophecy.*

10   At 3 a.m. I knelt before the collection vessel of the Sadducee to pay my Roman tribute as a Gentile. He said to me: 'Treat me as a priest; I am not a lay missionary like you. Clement, the brother of a former seer, is your Pope in the succession of Peter, head of the pilgrim congregation under Jesus Justus. But pay your Roman tribute to me, to show that you retain eastern membership. The Pope under Jesus Justus is now a priest equal to Sariel in the village, and he acts with the Herod crown prince who is Christian'.

11   *And I saw the Heaven opened. And behold a white Horse. And the One sitting upon it called faithful. And truthful. And in righteousness he judges. And he makes war.*

11   At noon on Tuesday, 22 June AD 73, I saw the noon prayer said at the centre of the middle tier. At the Gentile service, a white banner for the summer solstice was placed on the priest's chair. Jesus Justus took his place upon it as the David now to have his 'coronation', acting as a priest. He was appointed to teach Sadducee doctrine as a bishop. He was appointed to teach Essene doctrine as a judge. At 6 p.m. he was appointed to lead the council.

12   *But the eyes of him a flame of fire. And upon the head of him Many diadems, One having a name written which No One knows if not He.*

12   He was given a layman's lamp to be used as a priest's lamp at Gentile services. He wore the crown of a lay leader, but also the letter of a levitical leader, which was also worn by the Herod crown prince and by Agrippa.

13   *And he was clothed with a garment dipped in blood. And the name of him was called the Word of God.*

13   He wore a white vestment over a cardinal's scarlet garment, in the form used to give the Christian communion. He received the title the Word of God, used by the David when in the world.

14   *And the Armies (neut. plu.) in the Heaven followed to him (Heaven) upon to white Horses, Ones clad (masc. plu. nom.) in fine linen, white, pure.*

14   The Herod crown prince sat on the east side, with the Sadducee in the centre, and Agrippa on the west in the white garment of a permanent celibate.

15   *And out of the mouth of him (Heaven) there proceeds out a sharp broadsword, in order that in it he (Heaven) might smite the nations. And He (new subject) shepherds them (nations) in a rod of iron. And He (new subject) tramples the winepress of the wine of the Wrath of the Fury of the God the All-Mighty.*

15   During the council that evening the Sadducee was appointed head of Jewish monasteries, and had the power to discipline Agrippa. Jesus Justus was appointed the David over the middle schools.The Sadducee ordered the removal at the age of fifty of the Chief Therapeut of the Rome centre where Titus son of the emperor was an initiate and had dined with Agrippa and the Sadducee as king's priest.

16   *And he (God) has upon the garment. And upon the thigh of him (God) a name written, king of kings. And lord of lords.*

16   At 4 a.m., the time for village prayers, the Sadducee put on the vestment for receiving villagers. He allowed Jesus Justus, who led prayers beside him, to take the position of Agrippa as head of all celibates. Jesus Justus retained the David's title of distinguished layman.

17   *And I saw one angel standing in the Sun. And he cried in a great Voice saying to All the Birds, the Ones flying in mid-heaven, Come, gather together to the great supper of the God.*

17   On Tuesday, 21 June AD 74, the solar 31st fourteen years after the expected Eschaton of AD 60, when the news of the fall of Masada on 2 May had reached Ephesus, I saw Agrippa standing in the centre of the middle tier in the status of head of eastern solarists. He preached, saying to Gaius Costobar Herod and to the Sadducee: 'Come to the evening meal and council, to consider the failure of the Restoration.

18   *In order that you may eat flesh of kings. And flesh of Thousands. And flesh of strong ones. And flesh of Horses. And of the Ones sitting upon {of} them. And also flesh of All freedmen. And of slaves. And of little ones. And of great ones.*

18   Distribution will be made of the money formerly sent to Judea, paid to the Herodian treasurer. And the money paid to the head of Masada. And the money paid to the Therapeuts. And the money paid to the travelling priests. Also gifts to teachers using the priest's chair. And money paid to the Herod crown prince as acolyte. Also the property of Herod derived from the Vineyard mission. Also the shared property of Little Dan. Also the shared property of Great Dan'.

19   *And I saw the Beast. And the kings of the Earth. And the Armies of them (kings) gathered together to make the war with the One sitting upon {of} the Horse. And with the Army of him (the Horse).*

19   At the evening meal I saw the Herodian Magus, returned from Rome. With him was Gaius Costobar Herod. Gaius, claiming the rights of the crown prince, came to claim property, arguing in the council with the Sadducee. He was an equal of Agrippa.

20   *And the Beast was trapped. And with him the false*

prophet, the One who made the Signs in front of him (the false prophet). In Whom (plu.) he (the false prophet) deceived the Ones receiving the mark of the Beast. And the Ones worshipping to the Icon of him, living ones they were thrown, the Two, to the lake of the fire burning in Brimstone.

20 The Herodian Magus was put under community arrest for the failure of the uprising. Beside him was the rival Herod from Damascus, and his deputy, who acted as his levite giving promotions. The rival Herod gave false teaching about the Herodian succession to proselytes of the Magus. His deputy paid the Roman tribute money to Gaius, now head of Samaritans, and he, a Herod retaining membership, was sent back to be in charge at Qumran, where the priest's lamp symbolised zealotry, and where monastics were accused of sodomy.

21 *And the Remainder (plu.) were killed in the broadsword of the One Sitting upon {of} the Horse, coming out of the mouth of him. And All the Birds gorged out of the flesh of them (the Remainder).*

21 Eastern proselytes were excommunicated by the Sadducee, who excluded them from his schools. They met at Qumran, under Gaius Costobar Herod, who presided over their communion meals and collected their fees.

REV 20–22

THE HISTORY FROM AD 100–114

CHAPTER 20

(For the Chronology of Part D, see pp.217–220.)

1   *And I saw an angel going down out of the Heaven, having the key of the abyss. And a great chain upon the hand of him (Heaven).*
1   At midnight beginning Wednesday, 1 January AD 100, I, John II, the seer of Ephesus, saw the Sadducee Priest-Pope at the hermitage outside Ephesus to which the Rome chief monastery had been transferred, with the key to its vault. The chain emblem of the Herods was marked on the bread paten he used at services.

2   *And he (Heaven) seized the Dragon, the ancient Serpent. Who is Devil. And the Satan. And he (the Satan) bound him (Devil) a thousand years.*
2   At the non-fulfilment for the year 4000, allowing a zero generation, the Sadducee embraced the Pharisee leader, who was allied with the head of the Therapeuts. The Chief Scribe was leader of the zealots. The Chief Therapeut took the place of the Chief Scribe when he was

discredited by the non-fulfilment. At the last chance for the date at 3 a.m., he expelled the Chief Scribe from the congregation.

3   *And he (Devil) threw him (Satan) to the abyss. And he (Satan) locked. And he (Satan) sealed up high on him (Devil), in order that he (Devil) might not deceive still the nations until are ended the thousand years. After these things he (Devil) must be loosed a little period.*

3   In March, AD 100, the Chief Scribe regained his power and confined the Therapeut to the monastery. The Therapeut was the monastic treasurer. Then at midnight beginning the Day of Pentecost, Sunday, 7 June AD 100, the Therapeut came to the cathedral and prevented the Scribe from speaking in the council, not allowing him to give false teaching about the Herod succession to Agrippa and the Roman governor in Ephesus. The Chief Scribe was sent away to be head of the hermitage-monastery while the Roman governor was receiving membership at the cathedral.

4   *And I saw thrones. And they (the nations) sat upon them. And judgment was given to them (the nations). And the Souls of the Ones axed on account of the Witnessing of Jesus. And on account of the Word of God. And Whosoever (plu.) who have not worshipped the Beast, neither the Icon of him. And they (Whosoever) have not received the mark upon the forehead. And upon the hand of them. And they lived. And they held kingship with the Christ a thousand years.*

4   At the noon service in the Ephesus cathedral on this day I was in the congregation, and saw the king's throne. Agrippa, aged seventy-two, sat on it. He acted as king and judge only, not priest. The Christian Pope, who had been persecuted in Rome, was present, acting for Jesus Justus, now aged sixty-three. He acted also on behalf of Jesus III, aged twenty-three, to whom his father had relinquished the title used by David when following the marriage rule.

491

A new patriarch of Ephesus was appointed, one who did not support the Chief Magus, with whom a Samaritan celibate was associated. The patriarch did not use the zealot letters. He held a paten with his own letters. He was given power to initiate. At 3 p.m. on this Day of Pentecost in AD 100 he stood beside Jesus Justus and declared that the Eschaton had come for Gentiles, so Jesus Justus should use the title 'Christ'.

5   *The Remainder of the lifeless ones did not live until were ended the thousand years. This the First Resurrection,* 6 *blessed one. And a holy one the one having a part in the First Resurrection. Upon {of} These the Second Death does not have authority. Nevertheless they (These) will be priests of the God. And of the Christ. And they (priests) will hold kingship with him (Christ) a thousand years.*

5   At midnight beginning Friday, 1 January AD 101, counted as the year 4000 by allowing a zero year, the chief proselyte under the head of Jewish Christians was denied membership. The patriarch of Ephesus took the title 'Blessed Resurrection the First'. 6 Jesus Justus presided with him. The patriarch had no legal connection with Damascus. He acted as an eastern deputy to the Sadducee. He stood beside Jesus Justus in the place of the king. At midnight beginning the following Day of Pentecost, Sunday, 6 June AD 101, he and Jesus Justus again declared that the Eschaton had come.

7   *And when the thousand years are ended, the Satan will be loosed out of the prison of him.*
7   At 3 a.m. the Chief Therapeut was promoted to take the place of the Chief Scribe in the hermitage-monastery.

8   *And he (Satan) will come out to deceive the nations, the ones in the four corners of the Earth, the Gog. And Magog, to gather them (the nations) to the war. Of Whom (plu.) the Number of them (the nations), as the Sand of the Sea.*

8   The Chief Therapeut now held power, but he also gave false teaching concerning the Herodian succession to Agrippa, who had both Christian and Herodian membership. On Tuesday, 22 June AD 101, a chief Gentile with double membership summoned Agrippa to the council. A Herod who claimed the succession attended, and also the third Herod, allied with Bernice.

9   *And they (the nations) went up upon the breadth of the Earth. And they (the nations) surrounded the camp of the holy ones. And the Beloved City. And there went down fire out of the Heaven. And it (Heaven) ate them (the holy ones) down.*
9   Agrippa was reduced to the status of Elder, confined to the 2 cubits in the north of the vestry. He sat beside the fire, near where Jesus III, an acolyte deacon at the age of twenty-four, gave teaching to the uncircumcised. Jesus III was leader of Gentile monastics holding the Agape meal. With the Chief Therapeut in power, the rules of the Therapeuts were applied by the Sadducee. The Sadducee brought Jesus III into the evening common meal with Therapeuts.

10   *And the Devil, the One deceiving them (the holy ones) was thrown to the lake of fire. And Brimstone, at where. And the Beast. And the false prophet. And they (the holy ones) will be tormented by day. And by night to the Aeons of the Aeons.*
10   Then the Chief Scribe gained power, and the Chief Therapeut, who was teaching Jesus III a false doctrine concerning the Herodian succession, was sent back to Qumran. It was the place for sodomites. The Chief Magus regained power in Ephesus. A false Herod claimed the succession. Jesus III was put under penance, at first on the east side of the vestry as it was the Day position of the calendar. On reaching the west side he was restored to loyalty to Agrippa II.

11   *And I saw a great white throne. And the One sitting upon*

493

it. Of Whom from the face the Earth fled. And the Heaven.
And a place was not found for them (Aeons of the Aeons).

11   At noon on the Day of Pentecost, Sunday, 5 June AD
102, in the Ephesus cathedral, I saw the teacher's chair on
the middle tier, with a white banner for Pentecost. The
Sadducee priest sat on it. Agrippa had died, and his body
lay in state in front of the congregation. The service was
conducted by the Sadducee. The body of Agrippa
was carried out.

12   *And I saw the lifeless ones, the great ones. And the little*
ones standing in front of the throne. And books were opened.
And another book was opened, which becomes of the life. And
there were judged the lifeless ones out of the ones written in the
books according to the works of them.

12   At the Gentile part of the service I saw the head of
Jewish Christians with the head of eastern celibate
Gentiles. The head of western celibate Gentiles was their
superior, appointed a cardinal. A reading from the New
Testament was given. The Septuagint was read, treated
as a secondary book, with the names of eastern members
listed in it. Jewish Christians were placed under the ascetic
rules for Christians, in the New Testament.

13   *And the Sea gave the lifeless ones, the Ones in it. And*
the Death. And the Hades, they (the Ones in it) gave the life-
less ones, the Ones in them (the lifeless ones). And they (the
lifeless ones) were judged, each one, according to the works of
them.

13   Then Bernice, claiming the succession, promoted
the Jewish Christian leader into her party, with her male
deputy. The Chief Magus was in her party. The Herodian
chief treasurer was equal to Bernice's deputy, who again
promoted the head of Jewish Christians and his deputy.
The Jewish Christian leader was judged by ascetic works
alone, not from the New Testament.

14   *And the Death. And the Hades, they (the lifeless ones)
were thrown to the lake of the fire. This the Second Death
becomes, the lake of the fire.*
14   The Chief Magus remained with Bernice. But then
the Herodian chief treasurer sent the Jewish Christian
leader back to Qumran. The Qumran and Damascus
monastic systems were merged.

15   *And If Anyone is not found in the booklet of the life
written, he was thrown to the lake of the fire.*
15   The doubtful claimant to the Herod succession was
not included in the membership list, and he was sent back
to Qumran.

CHAPTER 21

1   *And I saw a new Heaven. And a new Earth. For the first
Heaven. And the first Earth, they (the lifeless ones) came from.
And the Sea becomes not still.*
1   At noon on the Day of Pentecost, Sunday, 26 May AD
110, forty years from the crisis of AD 70, I saw Jesus III in
the Ephesus cathedral on the middle tier, now used for
Christian worship. He was head of a Christian congregation. The Sadducee was on the upper tier. The
Sadducee was over the Herodian congregation, and his
deputy was the Jewish Christian leader, who had come
back from Qumran. Bernice, the mistress of Titus, had
died, aged eighty-three.

2   *And the Holy City, new Jerusalem, I saw going down out
of the Heaven from the God, prepared, as a bride adorned for
the husband of her.*
2   At 3 p.m. I saw Jesus III as head of Christian monastics on the chancel step, beginning the marriage process
three years before the wedding, and with him his

495

betrothed, who was to replace Bernice as the Virgin, still permitted to wear ornaments three years before her wedding.

3   *And I heard a great Voice out of the throne saying, Behold the tabernacle of the God with the Men. And he (God) will tabernacle with them. And They (new subject) peoples of him (God) will be. And He (new subject) the God will be with them (peoples).*

3   I heard the Sadducee say: 'The Sadducee is still the leader of Herodians. He goes to the hermitage outside Ephesus. The head of eastern Christian monastics accepts him. The Sadducee ranks as a priest equal with him.

4   *And he will erase Every tear out of the eyes of them. And the Death will not become still. Nor mourning. Nor shouting. Nor Toil will not become still. Because the first things have come from.*

4   The Sadducee does not require Christian monastics to study Herodian ascetic rules. The Chief Magus, who wore the name of Bernice, has lost his power with her death. Nazirite rules are followed only in the east. Jewish festivals are held only in the east. The Herodian ascetic acolyte, who wore the name of Bernice, has lost his position with her death. The Herods are represented by the Hellenised Herod, a bishop who has given up eastern doctrine'.

5   *And the One sitting upon {to} the throne said, Behold, new I make All Things. And he says to me, Write. Because These the Words faithful. And they become truthful.*

5   Jesus III, taking the Sadducee's place, said: 'I have changed Herodian doctrine into Christian doctrine'. He said to me: 'Add a new section to the Book of Revelation. The Christian Pope, who is a priest, uses the T sign as a cross. He acts in place of a teacher in a Sadducee school'.

6 *And he said to me, They have come about. I am the Alpha.*
And the O (Omega), the Beginning. And the End. I will give
to the one thirsting out of the well of the water of the life a gift.
6   He said to me: 'The Jewish priesthood is finished. I
am Gabriel. I am Michael, with my chief season at
Pentecost. There is also a Christian feast in December. I
admit Gentile pilgrims to my monastic schools, giving
them baptism and initiation combined, without a fee.

7   *The victor will inherit these things. And I will be to him a*
God. And He (new subject) will be to me a son.
7   My Pope, in the succession of Peter, is over the
mission in Rome. I stand in the place of an Aaronite priest
to him. A Gentile monastic is my deputy.

8   *To the cowardly. And to faithless. And to abominators.*
And to murderers. And to fornicators. And to sorcerers. And
to idolaters. And to All the false ones, the part of them in the
lake the one burning in fire. And in Brimstone, which becomes
the Second Death.
8   These are the heretics: those who evade persecution.
Those denying that a layman can be a priest. Herods
wanting to be emperor. Zealots. Worshippers of the
priestess. Magians. Those accepting the emperor as a god.
The supporters of the false Herod at Qumran with the
zealots. The sodomites at Qumran, who have allied with
Damascus'.

9   *And there came one out of the seven angels, of the Ones*
having the seven bowls, of the Ones full of the seven last
plagues. And he spoke with me saying, Come, I will show you
the bride, the woman of the Lamb.
9   At midnight beginning the Day of Pentecost, Sunday,
23 May AD 112, the Chief Therapeut, servant of the
Sadducee taking Agrippa's titles, announced seven years
of hostility to the emperor Trajan, beginning with this as
the 'zero Saturday' year, before the seven years from June

113 to June 120 which would end with the Eschaton-Restoration. The Therapeut spoke as my equal, saying: 'Come to the hermitage an hour from Ephesus, and I will show you the celibates now under the Virgin who will marry Jesus III, a year before her wedding'.

10   *And he led me away in a Spirit upon a great Mountain. And high. And he showed me the Holy City Jerusalem going down out of the Heaven from the God,*   11   *having (fem. acc., Holy City) the Glory (fem.) of the God, the Light-giver of it (fem. the Glory) like a precious stone, as a stone of jasper, like crystal.*

10   He took me to the hermitage, to which the Rome Samaritan community had been driven back, where I sat in the first pew. The platform was the highest tier. At the dawn service for pilgrims he showed me Jesus III on the chancel step as head of all Christian monasteries,
11   holding their common property, acting as the priest leading morning prayers, head of the congregation of celibates, taking the royal pew, baptising with holy water.

12   *One having (fem. nom. Glory) a great wall. And high, One having (fem. nom.) twelve gates. And upon {to} the gates twelve angels. And names written which become the names of the twelve tribes of sons of Israel,*   13   *from east three gates. And from north three gates. And from south three gates. And from west three gates.*

12   At the noon service the chancel screen was placed 2 cubits down from the dais edge, dividing the ministers from the congregation. On the platform was the seat of the Gentile teacher, raised from the lowest grade. On it sat the patriarch of Ephesus. His letters showed that he was an uncircumcised Gentile, a celibate formerly of the lowest order, who had risen to be a patriarch,   13   and the building was a fulfilment of the plan of the Temple Scroll, but now with a cardinal's seat at the west entrance. There was a cardinal's seat at the south entrance. There was a

498

cardinal's seat at the north entrance. There was a cardinal's seat at the east entrance.

14   *And the wall of the city having twelve foundations. And upon {of} them twelve names of the twelve apostles of the Lamb.*
14   At the front of the congregation stood the chief Gentile monastic, head of the council, now equal to a Jewish head of council. He was a Gentile graduate, who was to act as 'eunuch' to Jesus III during his marriage.

15 And the one speaking with me had a gold measuring reed, in order that he might measure the city. And the gates of it. And the wall of it.
15   The Chief Therapeut held a priest's measuring rod, 2 cubits long, to measure from the dais. A teacher's seat was placed there. Two cubits down was the chancel screen.

16   *And the city, a tetragon, lay. And the length of it as much. And the breadth. And he measured the city with the reed, upon {of} twelve thousand stadia, the length. And the breadth. And the height of it, equal things become.*
16   Gentile monastics were the ministers, using the northern square. The north-south dimension ran down to the chancel screen. The 2 cubits at the north end ran east-west. He measured the north-south 12 cubits, each cubit standing for a province, with the first row of a province measuring 1000 stadia, one hundred members meeting in each of ten meeting places across the row. The excluded who had used the 2 cubits at the north now used a crypt under the 2 cubits from the dais edge down to the screen. The platform had a point in the centre for the prayer to be said, with an equal distance on either side.

17   *And he measured the wall of it (the city), a hundred and forty- four cubits, a measure of a Man, which becomes of an angel.*

17   He measured the square whose lower line was the chancel screen, each side of the square 12 cubits including the outer walls, the cardinal at the dais edge being allowed 2 cubits, and the man saying the angelus at the centre of the platform 2 cubits.

18   *And the structure of the wall of it jasper. And the city pure gold like pure glass.*
18   The first pew below the screen was marked by a jasper for the first congregation member. On the dais edge was the flask of holy water to be sprinkled by the celibate priest.

19   *The foundations of the wall of the city for Every precious stone adorned, the first foundation jasper, the second sapphire, the third chalcedon, the fourth emerald,   20   the fifth sardonyx, the sixth sardion, the seventh chrysolite, the eighth beryl, the ninth topaz, the tenth chrysoprase, the eleventh jacinth, the twelfth amethyst.*
19   The twelve congregation seats were occupied by Herodians likened to the twelve celibate 'precious stones', under the ministry of Christians, their leader being the Hellenised Herod, who could occupy the royal pew wearing ordinary dress, his pew marked by the jasper; the second pew marked by a sapphire; the third by a chalcedon; in the centre of the second row an emerald for the fourth celibate,   20   with the fifth and sixth pews marked by a sardonyx and a sardion on either side; in the centre of the third row was a chrysolite for the seventh, with a beryl and topaz on either side for the eighth and ninth; in the centre of the fourth row a chrysoprase for the tenth, with a jacinth and amethyst on either side for the eleventh and twelfth.

21   *And the twelve gates twelve pearls, up one each of the gates became out of one pearl. And the broadway of the city pure gold, as transparent glass.*

21   The patriarch on the platform was a teacher of Wisdom, a celibate who had risen to the first grade from the twelfth. The teaching that had previously been given at the round base outside was now brought to the chancel step, and given by a Christian priest who finished the service by sprinkling holy water.

22   *And a sanctuary I did not see in it (the city), for the Lord the God the All-Mighty a sanctuary of it becomes. And the Lamb.*
22   I did not see a place corresponding to a Holy of Holies, as there had previously been, but the Sadducee when ministering to Herodians here still represented a holy place. Jesus III when with him still used his Herodian title.

23   *And the city does not have need of the Sun. Neither the Moon, in order that they (twelve pearls v. 21) might appear in it (the Moon). For the Glory of the God has lightened it (the Moon). And the lantern of it (the Moon) the Lamb.*
23   Gentile monastics did not pay the 4 p.m. Herodian welfare tithes. The David queen appeared at this time as the Virgin, and the patriarch teacher of Wisdom taught on her behalf. Jesus III appointed her a bishop, to teach at this time in the crypt. He was the superior bishop, holding the lamp beside her in the crypt.

24   *And the nations will walk through {of }the Light of it (the Moon). And the kings of the Earth bring the Glory of them to it (Glory).*
24   The Hellenised Herod, head of Roman Herodians, received teaching from her. But the chief Herodian Scribe had a separate monastic system, in a monastery on the east side.

25   *And the gates of it (Glory) will not {not} be locked by day, for Night will not become there.*

25   His common property was locked in a treasury on the east, but he did not have zealot teachers.

26   *And they (the kings of the Earth) will bring the Glory (fem.). And the honour of the nations to it (the Glory).*
26   The common property was handed over at his evening meal. The fees due to the Hellenised Herod were handed over.

27   *And there will not {not} come in to it (the Glory) Every common thing. And the one making an Abomination. And a False One, if not the Ones written in the book of the life of the Lamb.*
27   The Hellenised Herod attended his evening common meal. Other Herods were present, including one still wanting to be emperor. A member of the rival line was present, and his deputy, who was a celibate in Sadducee communities where Jesus III still taught.

CHAPTER 22

1   *And he (the Lamb) showed me a river of water of life, bright, as crystal, proceeding out of the throne of the God. And of the Lamb   2   in a middle of the broadway of it (fem., Glory 21:26). And of the river hence. And thence a wood of life making twelve fruits, according to a month, each one giving from the fruit of it. And the leaves of the wood to a healing of the nations.*
1   On Saturday, 1 January AD 113, Jesus III outside the monastery vestry showed me the aqueduct used for baptising and initiating a royal person, the Hellenised Herod, treated as outside the congregation. Jesus III   2   took part in the ceremony, standing on the lower round base. Celibates were baptised at the upper round base. At the lower one teaching was given to lower grades, holding

communion services only once a month, beginning 1 January, with fees brought in by the celibate minister as a sign of the increase of numbers. The Hellenised Herod received promotion.

3 *And Every curse will not become still. And the throne of the God. And of the Lamb in it (fem., Glory 21:26) will become. And the slaves of him (the Lamb) will serve him.*
3 The Herodian kingship was declared by the Roman governor to have ceased. The Sadducee was left as the supreme ruler of Diaspora Jews. Jesus III still taught Diaspora celibate Jews with him. The Hellenised Herod over the Vineyard mission held Christian services.

4 *And they (slaves) will view the face of him (Lamb). And the name of him (Lamb) upon of the foreheads of them (slaves).*
4 The Hellenised Herod accepted Jesus III as a priest. He wore a Christian cross on his Herodian headband.

5 *And Night will not be still. And they (slaves) do not have need of a Light of a lantern. And a Light of a Sun. Because a lord the God lightens upon them (slaves). And they (slaves) will hold kingship to the Aeons of the Aeons.*
5 A zealot was banished by the Roman governor for the uprising of Jews planned for AD 113. The Hellenised Herod ceased to pay welfare tithes to the Sadducee. He treated the Sadducee as head of celibates. The Sadducee appointed him a bishop. The Hellenised Herod became head of Herodian celibates, under the Sadducee using the titles of the Herod king.

6 *And he (God) said to me, These the Words faithful. And truthful. And the lord the God of the Spirits of the prophets, has sent from the angel of him (God) to show to the slaves of him (God) the things that must come about in shortly.*
6 At midnight beginning Wednesday, 8 June AD

113, the Day of Pentecost and the wedding day of Jesus III at the age of thirty-six, the Sadducee said to me: 'Here is the Christian Pope, a priest, who will act for Jesus III while he is away for his marriage. He teaches in the schools. The Sadducee, who uses the titles of the Herods, has sent the patriarch of Ephesus his deputy to teach the Hellenised Herod that at this Pentecost the last seven years before the Eschaton of AD 120 begin.

7   *And behold I come soon. Blessed is the One keeping the Words of the prophecy of this book.*
7   I, the Sadducee, will officiate on the middle tier of the cathedral on the 31st. The patriarch of Ephesus acts as an equal to the Pope, holding to the New Testament as a basis for the prophecy'.

8   *And I John the One hearing. And looking at these things. And when now I heard. And I looked, I fell to worship before the feet of the angel, of the One showing me these things.*
8   I, John II, the seer, was promoted and given a new name on this wedding day. I was a minister to the laity. At the dawn service I was in the seer's seat. I knelt to pay my Roman tribute to the patriarch, whose collection vessel was on the east side of the chancel, with the Sadducee in the centre.

9   *And he (the One showing) says to me, View, not a fellow slave of you am I. And of the brothers of you the prophets. And of the Ones keeping the Words of this book. Worship God.*
9   The Sadducee said to me: 'Treat me as a priest; I am not a lay missionary like you. The Christian Pope is your superior. The patriarch of Ephesus, who is an equal to the Pope, holding to the New Testament, is my deputy. As still a citizen of the east, pay your Roman tribute through the Sadducee'.

504

10   *And he (God) says to me, Do not seal the Words of the prophecy of this book, for the season is near.*

10   On Friday, 24 June AD 113, the solar 31st, the Sadducee said to me at the cathedral: 'Do not silence the patriarch of Ephesus for the non-appearance of a sign on this date; it is simply the quartodecimal intercalation year of the north solar calendar, and the sign may come next year, the lunisolar year.

11   *The One making unrighteous, let him make unrighteous still. And the filthy one, let him be filthy still. And the righteous one, let him do righteousness still. And the holy one, let him make holy still.*

11   Let the rules for Essene monasteries be preserved in Christian monasteries to which Roman officials in Asia are admitted, with the south-east square used by pilgrims and their equals. The south-west square is for monastics excluded for uncleanness. The north-west square is for higher pilgrims. The north-east square is for dynastic celibates led by the David.

12   *Behold I come soon. And the reward of me with me, to give to each one, as the work becomes of him.*

12   At 6 p.m. I the Sadducee am present for the council. It is the end of the day, and I give the payments to celibates and to ascetics.

13   *I the Alpha. And the O (Omega), the First One. And the Last One, the Beginning. And the End.*

13   I, the Sadducee, am the Gabriel while Jesus III is away for marriage. But the Michael is Jesus III, who as the David is also the first bishop. The Christian Pope presides at Pentecost. There is also a Christian feast in December.

14   *Blessed are the Ones washing the robes of them, in order that the authority of them will become upon the wood of the life. And at the gates they will go in to the city.*

14   The patriarch of Ephesus keeps the eastern rules for uncleanness, and while outside he gives teaching to lower grades outside the vestry. When returning from an unclean state, he enters the chancel by the door in the south vestry.

15   *Outside the dogs. And the sorcerers. And the fornicators. And the murderers. And the idolaters. And Everyone befriending. And one making a False One.*
15   There are seven kinds of eastern heretics, who are not admitted to our services; first sodomites. Then Magians. Worshippers of the priestess. Zealots. Emperor worshippers. A claimant to the Herodian kingship. A claimant from the rival line'.

16   *I Jesus have sent the angel of me to witness to you (plu.), these things, upon {to} the Churches. I am the Root. And the descendant of David, the Star, the bright one, the Morning One.*
16   'I, Jesus III, present at the council, now send my Pope to appoint you, John II, a bishop, under me as head of the Church. I am the supreme leader of the Christian form of the mission. I am the heir of David, the priest to Gentiles, a royal person, the one who leads the dawn prayers of pilgrims'.

17   *And the Spirit. And the bride, they (the Churches) say: Come. And the One hearing, let him say, Come. And the One thirsting, let him come; the one willing, let him receive water of life a gift.*
17   At the dawn service, held without regard for the sabbath, the Sadducee was present. The new David queen stood with Jesus III, who said to pilgrims: 'Come into the church. Let the seer as bishop repeat: "Come into the church". Let the pilgrim, desiring learning, come in; and the non-celibate Gentile may receive baptism and initiation without a fee.

506

18   *I witness to Everyone hearing the Words of the prophecy of this book, if now Anyone places upon the things, the God will place upon him the plagues written in this book.*

18   I say to the Hellenised Herod, who hears sermons from the patriarch of Ephesus using the New Testament, that when he becomes a graduate, the Sadducee will require him to use teaching from the New Testament about the date of the Eschaton.

19   *And if now Anyone takes from the Words of the book of this prophecy, the God will take the part of him from the wood of the life. And out of the Holy City, of the Ones written in this book.*

19   But when this Herod hears the patriarch read from the Septuagint, and prefers it to the New Testament, the Sadducee will exclude him from the Christian congregation. He will not be permitted to attend Christian monastic services led by myself as monastic head, and by the Pope, whose name is recorded in the New Testament'.

20   *He who witnesses these things says, Yes, I come soon. Amen, come, lord Jesus.*

20   On Friday, 23 June AD 114, the Pope said: 'I speak as the Priest-Pope at the council. The main service is finished. Jesus III, come back into the community after the birth of your child.

21   *The Grace of the lord Jesus with the holy ones. Amen.*

21   The crown prince of Jesus III is with a Christian priest. The service is finished'.

Text Notes and References

Introduction

1. An early Christian writer, Dionysius of Alexandria (third century AD) says of Revelation: 'For my part I should not dare to reject the book, since many brethren hold it in estimation; but, reckoning that my perception is inadequate to form an opinion concerning it, I hold that the interpretation of each several passage is in some way hidden and more wonderful. For even although I do not understand it, yet I suspect that some deeper meaning underlies the words.' (Quoted in Eusebius, *Eccl. Hist.* 7, 25, 4).

2. 1 Cor 3:1–2. Heb 6:1–2 (in which 'the resurrection of the dead' is listed with 'elementary doctrines').

3. 1QpHab 5:9–12.

4. Philo, Works. Plutarch, *Isis* and *Osiris*. The whole of the work of Philo, an Alexandrian Jew contemporary with the early Christians, was devoted to finding allegorical meanings in the Old Testament Law.

5. 1QH 3:8–18. The passage includes: 'She who is pregnant with the Man suffers anguish in her pains, for in the waves of death she brings forth a male child, and in the pains of Hell there springs from the womb/furnace of the pregnant one a Wonderful

Counsellor with his might'. The last phrases are from Isa 9:6, on the birth of the Messiah, with 'Mighty God' changed to 'with his might'.

6   *Ant.* 18:228.

7   11QT 45:7–18.

8   1QS 6:24–7:25.

9   G. Jeremias, *Der Lehrer der Gerechtigkeit* (Göttingen: Vandenhoeck & Ruprecht, 1963), Chapter 6.

One: From Herod to Ephesus

1   CD 15:9, in a passage dealing with the year outside the community when a man first repents, speaks with the Bishop of the Many, and is enrolled 'with the oath of the Covenant which Moses made with Israel, the Covenant to return to the Law of Moses with all the heart and with all the soul'.

2   See Judah Goldin, *The Living Talmud, The Wisdom of the Fathers* (Mentor Religious Classic, 1957), and H. Danby, *The Mishnah*, (OUP, 1964).

The suggestion may be put forward at this point that the newly published document 4QMMT (*DJD* X, 1994) comes from the time when negotiations were under way between Hillel and the Essene leader Menahem, together with the Sadducee priest Ananel, for the alliance that would lead to the mission of 'Abraham, Isaac and Jacob'.

Fragments of six copies of the document were found in the caves, showing that it was considered to be important. There is no evidence, in fact it is contrary to the evidence, to say that it was written by the Teacher of Righteousness to the Wicked Priest. This is a speculation of J. Strugnell's, for which he offered only the illogical argument that because the Teacher sent something to do with the Law to the Wicked Priest (4QpPsa 4:9), then this document must be the one that he sent (pp.119–120 *DJD* X).

There is, moreover, the strongest contrary evidence, in that the writer speaks courteously to the addressee and says that he has 'wisdom and knowledge of the Torah' (C28), whereas the Wicked Priest and the Teacher were bitter enemies, and the Wicked Priest 'flouted the Torah' (1QpHab 5:11–12).

It is certainly an Essene document, setting out the solar calendar in its normative Day position. If the writer was describing the calendar in its current position, this narrows the dates down to the quartodecimal periods when it was at Day rather than at Night (p.238): 42–28BC, 14BC–AD1, AD15–19, AD 43–61.

The writer is setting out in a friendly manner the points of ritual law on which he and his party differed from the addressee. While Essene, he has views on some matters identical with those of Sadducees, as in the rule about the purity of ritual streams (B55–58).

Such a tone, and much of the content, would fit well a formal conversation between Essenes, led by Menahem, and the great Pharisee Hillel, in the period from 41BC when the mission was being formed at the outset of the reign of Herod the Great. A priest from Babylon named Ananel was Herod's high priest at this period, as shown by Josephus (Ant. 15:22, 34), and the pesher of Acts 7:1–3 shows that he was a Sadducee, by calling him 'God' (Pharisees did not use this title), and that he met with Hillel ('Abraham') while he was still in Babylon. Menahem was a Diaspora Essene, and the purpose of the mission was to go to Diaspora Jews.

The document would have been preserved in multiple copies because of its historical importance. It had led to the alliance of 'Abraham' (Hillel) and 'Isaac' (Menahem). There is even a passage which would reflect the inclusion of Heli, the descendant of David, as 'Jacob'. C 25–26 reads: 'Remember David, who was a man of lovingkindness, so he was delivered from many afflictions and was forgiven'. The Essenes, as has been shown, preserved in their midst the descendants of David, who were 'remembered' in the hope that they would be restored to the throne.

The document has many points of contact with the Temple Scroll, most interestingly the ritual exclusion of the blind and lepers (B49–51, 64–68, 11QT 45:12–18), the return of the impure on the eighth day (B71–72, 11QT 45:15–17), the pentecontad feasts of New Wine and New Oil (A iii, v, 11QT 19:14, 21:14). It uses several times the term 'Afterwards of Days' for an anticipated time in the future (C14, 16, 21), also 'Afterwards of Time' (C30). The former term is found in 1QSa, concerning the time when the sectarians would be free to follow their present manner of life without impediment, and when the Messiahs would have appeared. It may be further suggested that the term referred to the year 3920, the end of the world-week (see p.222), which at the time of writing MMT was to fall in 21BC. It had been postponed by means of the Last Jubilee to AD 29 (p.223), and this is the Afterwards of Days referred to in 1QSa.

3 *Ant.* 15:372.
4 4Q159, frag. 1, 6–7.
5 4Q159, frag. 1, line 10, 'Their peace offering' (completed by F. D. Weinert, '4Q159: Legislation for an Essene Community outside of Qumran?' *Journal for the Study of Judaism* 1974, pp.179–207).
6 Matt 8:11.
7 *Ant.* 18:63–64.
8 *War* 2:160–161. 'There is yet another order of Essenes, which, while at one with the rest in its mode of life, customs and regulations (marry in order to propagate the race)...They give their wives, however, a three years' probation, and only marry them after

they have by three periods of purification (absences of menstruation) given proof of fecundity (pregnancy). They have no intercourse with them during pregnancy.'

9 '(The high priest is) a being whose nature is midway between (man and) God, less than God, superior to man.' Philo, *On Dreams*, 2:188.

10 CD8:1–20 contains the most vehement denunciations, including: 'They are all rebels, who have not turned from the Way of traitors, but have wallowed in the ways of fornication and in wicked wealth. . . They have not separated (*nazar* be a Nazirite) from the people, but have been undisciplined, highhanded, walking in the Way of the wicked'.

11 Suetonius, *Life of Claudius*, 25:4: 'Since the Jews constantly made disturbances at the instigation of Chrestus, he (Claudius) expelled them from Rome'. Compare Acts 18:2.

12 In 49 BC the Jews of Ephesus had been sufficiently numerous and influential to obtain a decree from the Romans exempting them from military service, 'because they may not bear arms or march on the days of the Sabbath; nor can they obtain the native foods to which they are accustomed'. They were permitted 'to come together for sacred and holy rites in accordance with their law, and to make offerings for their sacrifices'. (*Ant.* 14:225–227).

Two: 'He Who was Seated on the Throne'

1 The Idumeans, from the southern district which included Masada, had accepted circumcision under John Hyrcanus in 130 BC (*Ant.* 13:257). Antipater, the father of Herod the Great, was an Idumean by race (*War* 1:123).

2 *War* 1:123–147, 207, *Ant.* 14:4–79.

3 *War* 1:204–205, *Ant.* 14:420–430.

4   *Ant.* 17:19–22.
5   *Ant.* 17:168–191.
6   *Ant.* 17:69–78.
7   *Ant.* 17:219–228.
8   *Ant.* 17:342–344.
9   *Ant.* 18:143–149.
10 *Ant.* 18:228–255. He was at first given the northern tetrarchies, then his kingdom was enlarged by Claudius (*Ant.* 19:274–275).
11 *Ant.* 19:343, Acts 12:22.
12 Acts 12:20–23.
13 Acts 13:4–12. See pp.144–145 on Paul's order of Benjamin, Pharisees who were tutors to princes.
14 *War* 2:390.
15 *Ant.* 18:109–115.
16 2 Cor 11:32.
17 *Ant.* 18:116–119.
18 *Ant.* 18:137.
19 2 Tim 1:5, *Ant* 18:136, 137, *Ant.* 18:106.
20 Acts 16:3, Luke 2:21 (Luke 2:6–7 describes Jesus' early initiation at the age of twelve).
21 1 Tim 1:18.
22 Heb 13:23.
23 *War* 2:418, 556–557, 4:140–146, *Ant.* 20:214.
24 Rom 16:23, 2 Tim 4:20.
25 Rom 16:23, Acts 20:4; 3 John 1.
26 Rev 16:21.
27 *Ant.* 18:140.
28 Rev 21:27.
29 *Ant.* 18:141. Marcus and Wikgren, in the Herodian family tree attached to vol 8 of *Antiquities* in the Loeb Library, call him C. Julius Agrippa. See Schurer, vol 1, p.452, note 41.

Three: The Marriage of the Lamb

1   Rev 19:69.

2   *GPhil* 63:30–64:10.
3   Acts 3:20–22. *Apokatastasis*, translated 'for estab-
    lishing' in RSV, is a noun, meaning 'restoration',
    which the chronological theory shows to be a tech-
    nical term. 'All things', *panta*, has the pesher sense of
    'the Herods'.
4   'In the days these' (Acts 6:1) means the June solstice.
    See Lexicon, **day**. The year was that in which
    Jonathan Annas, or 'Stephen', was high priest for six
    months, AD 37 (*Ant.* 18:95, 123). 'The Word of God
    increased' in the episode dated as 'in the days these'
    (Acts 6:7).
5   Acts 12:24.
6   See *Jesus the Man*, Chapter 32. Paul's words in 1 Cor
    7:10–16 were: 'To the married I give charge, not I but
    the Lord, that the wife should not separate from the
    husband...and that the husband should not divorce
    the wife. To the rest I say, not the Lord, that if any
    brother has a wife who is an unbeliever, and she
    consents to live with him, he should not divorce
    her...But if the unbelieving partner desires to sepa-
    rate, let it be so; in such a case the brother or sister is
    not bound. For God has called us to peace' (the oppo-
    site of zealotry).
7   Acts 16:14.
8   Rev 2:1–3:22.
9   Acts 10:1–48 (in which Cornelius is a cover for
    Agrippa I; the story records the reconciliation
    between Agrippa and Peter, or Simon of Jerusalem,
    Ant. 19:332–334), Acts 13:1, Col 4:14, 2 Tim 4:11.
10 *Acts* 16:9.
11 Col 4:11.
12 Eusebius, *Eccl. Hist.* 2, 1, 25.
13 Matt 1:19.
14 Rev 1:16, 20, 2:26–28.
15 Acts 19:20. In Luke 2:40 the twentieth birthday of
    Jesus, in AD14, is referred to by the same term. To

'increase' means to prove sexual capability, either at twenty or at the birth of a son.

16 Rev 17:3, 6. In 3:6 'the holy ones' means Jesus Justus as the crown prince acting as substitute. See Lexicon, **holy**.

17 For a discussion of the date of the death of Agrippa II, see E. Schürer, *The History of the Jewish People in the Age of Jesus Christ*, Revised (Edinburgh: Clark, 1973), vol I, p.481. Varying testimonies, some of which may refer to a loss of territories rather than death, have left the matter uncertain. The date of AD102, compatible with most estimates, is taken from the pesher.

18 Rev 22:16–17.

19 Luke 2:40.

20 Archelaus Herod was banished to Vienne in Gaul (*Ant.* 17:344) and his brother Antipas to Lyons in Gaul (*Ant.* 18:252).

21 Hegesippus, quoted in Eusebius, *Eccl. Hist.* 3, 20, 1–7.

22 Quoted in Geoffrey Ashe, *King Arthur's Avalon, The Story of Glastonbury* (Fontana/Collins, 1957), p.37.

23 *War* 3:4, 7:82. In his speech to the leaders of Jerusalem, attempting to dissuade them from war in AD66, Agrippa II said, according to Josephus: 'Consider what a wall of defence had the Britons, you who put your trust in the walls of Jerusalem: the ocean surrounds them, they inhabit an island no less in extent than the part of the world in which we live; yet the Romans crossed the sea and enslaved them' (*War* 2:378).

24 Tacitus, *Annals* 11–12.

25 Ashe (ref. note 22 above), p.38.

26 Ashe (ref. note 22 above), p.39.

27 *Ant.* 18:143, 156, 202.

28 *Ant.* 18:82–83.

29 Rev 16:19.

Four: Miriam the Missionary

1 Philo, *Contemp. Life.*
2 *Contemp. Life* 83–87.
3 *War* 2:150.
4 John 19:25.
5 *GPhil, NHL* 52:20–25.
6 Acts 14:11–13.
7 Acts 19:23–41.
8 G. R. H. Wright, 'The Archaeological Remains at El Mird in the Wilderness of Judea', *Biblica* 42, 1961, pp.1–27.
9 Rev 12:14–16.
10 Exod 15:21.
11 Rev 12:16.
12 See Lexicon, **Earth** and **Sea**.
13 Luke 13:16, 1 Tim 5:9. From indications such as the age of her youngest son (Simon-Silas, or 'man 4', aged thirty-six in June AD 58, Acts 21:23–24) it is seen that Mary was born in December 26 BC, was seventeen and a half at the time of the conception of Jesus in June 8 BC, forty-six and a half at the time of the birth of Simon in June AD 22, and fifty-seven at the time of preparing to become an enrolled Widow in December AD 32.
14 Acts 12:12.

Five: The Beast 666

1 Rev 13:18.
2 2 Thess 2:3–4. The successor of Simon Magus in the eastern party was Menander, also a Samaritan (*Eccl. Hist.* 3, 26, 1; 4, 7, 3). It is not clear when he succeeded him. Paul's epistles to the Thessalonians were written in the early fifties AD.
3 1QS 5:11–12.
4 CD 4:19 'Saw' (Sadhe and Waw). CD 19:12 'the

Taw' (Taw, Yod, Waw). Probably also CD 10:6, 13:2, Ha-Gaw ('the G', Gimel and Waw) (with additional article for the construct).

5 J. Stevenson (ed.), *A New Eusebius* (London: SPCK, 1957), p.7.

6 *Ant.* 18:23.

7 *War* 7:304–401.

8 *Ant.* 18:6–9.

9 1 Macc 7:13. *Ant.* 13:288–292, John Hyrcanus was asked by Pharisees to give up the high priesthood.

10 *Test. Levi* 17:10: 'And in the fifth week (of the eighth jubilee) they shall return to the land of their desolation, and shall restore anew the house of the Lord.' As the detail shows, the description is of the 490 years 511–21BC (see pp.207, 220). Its eighth jubilee was 168–119BC, and the fifth 'week' of this jubilee began in 140 BC.

11 Shown in his essays *Every Good Man is Free and The Contemplative Life* (Philo, *Works*, vol 9 Loeb Library).

12 1QH 2:32, 4QpNah 2:2, 7, CD 1:18.

13 1QS 7 lists the penances, consisting of exclusion from the 'Purity', the sacred meal, for varying numbers of days.

14 *Ant.* 15:371.

15 Acts 13:19, 'seven nations' means 'Gentile/nation 7', a title of Herod. See **nation** in the Lexicon. The year was 61–60BC, 'year 450' of the world-week 511–21BC.

16 *Ant.* 13:408–409.

17 Paul was a member of the order of Benjamin (Acts 13:21, Rom 11:1, Phil 3:5), and was a student of Gamaliel, a descendant of Hillel (Acts 22:3). Hillel was the 'Saul of the tribe of Benjamin' of the pesher of Acts 13:21.

18 Acts 24:25.

19 Acts 22:3.

20 The pesher of Acts 19:19 shows that they were founded in 44 BC, the year following the introduction

of the Julian calendar (50 000 pieces of silver in the verse means that the 500 in their 'half-tribe' had paid a piece of silver each for 100 years, from 44 BC to AD 57, the date of Acts 19:19). The order of Manasseh had split over the question of the Julian calendar in 44BC.

21 Ananias the merchant, either Simon Magus himself or his servant, did not require the proselyte Izates to be circumcised (*Ant.* 20:41).

22 *Ant.* 15:378.

23 Matt 2:1–12.

24 *Ant.* 17:41–46.

25 *Ant.* 18:3–4.

26 Joazar the Dragon (Rev 12:3), Archelaus the Calf (Luke 15:27, Acts 7:41).

27 *War* 2:118. 'This man (Judas the Galilean) was a sophist who founded a sect of his own.'

28 Rev 13:1.

29 Luke 4:1–13, Matt 4:1–11.

30 Mark 2:5, Jonathan, the 'paralytic', is called 'The Faith', a reference to Pope 'Abraham' (Gal 3:6–7). He is called 'Abraham' in the parable of Luke 16:22, dealing with his expulsion from the high priesthood in September AD 37. Simon succeeded him as 'the Voice' of Mark 9:7, and as 'Lightning' (Luke 10:18, Matt 28:3). *Clem. Hom.* 2, 23–24 says that John the Baptist was succeeded as leader by Dositheus, and shortly afterwards by Simon Magus.

   Jonathan Annas in this passage is called Dositheus ('Gift of God'), a version of his Hebrew name Nathanael ('God gave') (John 2:46–51). Nathanael is contrasted with Simon Magus as one in whom there was no *dolos*, 'deceit' (John 2:47). Simon Magus was 'full of *dolos*' (Acts 13:10). Jonathan Annas was the 'Good Samaritan' who supported John the Baptist (Luke 10:33–35) and Simon was the evil Samaritan. In *Clem. Rec.* 2, 7–9, the same story is told, favouring

518

Dositheus against Simon, whereas the opposite view is expressed in *Clem. Hom.*

31 See Chapter 7, and H. Jonas, *The Gnostic Religion* (Boston: Beacon Press, 1958), p.111. According to *Clem. Hom.* 2, 32, Simon's claims to 'miracles' included making statues walk, rolling himself on fire without being burnt, flying through the air, making loaves out of stones, becoming a serpent or a goat, becoming two-faced, changing himself into gold, opening lockfast gates, melting iron. At banquets he produced images of all manner of forms. In his house he contrived to make dishes appear in the air with no carriers. Claims such as these were common for Hellenistic thaumaturges, see Philostratus, *The Life of Apollonius of Tyana* (Loeb Library).

32 See *Jesus the Man*, Chapters 20–26.

33 Acts 13:4–12, 46–49.

34 *Ant.* 20:142–143.

35 *Ant.* 13:7, as Sergius Paulus, using the name of Paul as a student to his master. Agrippa II was aged seventeen at this time, acting in the place of the proconsul, and in AD 53, Timothy Herod, Agrippa's crown prince, acted in the place of the proconsul Gallio in Corinth, also at the age of seventeen (pesher of Acts 18:12).

36 *Ant.* 20:145–146.

37 Rev 16:10.

38 *War* 7:253.

39 *DJD* vol II.

40 Eusebius, *Eccl. Hist.* 4, 6, 1–2. In *Eccl. Hist.* 4, 8, 4, Eusebius quotes Justin: 'For in the present Jewish war it was only Christians whom Bar Chocheba, the leader of the rebellion of the Jews, commanded to be punished severely, if they did not deny Jesus as the Messiah and blaspheme him'.

Six: The Woman Jezebel

1 Rev 2:20–23.

2 Justin Martyr, *Apol.* 1, 26.

3 *Clem. Rec.* 2, 7–9, *Clem Hom.* 2, 19–25. The latter passage includes: 'And he (Simon) says that he has brought down this Helena from the highest heavens to the world; being queen, as the all-bearing being, and Wisdom, for whose sake, says he, the Greeks and barbarians fought, having before their eyes but an image of truth; for she, who really is the truth, was then with the chiefest god'.

4 John 4:7–42, Mark 7:24–30, Mark 15:40, John 11:1–37, Luke 10:38–42, Acts 5:7–11. In *Clem. Hom.* 2:19–21 Helena appears as the Syrophoenician woman and associated with Simon Magus.

5 *Clem. Hom.* 20, 12. 'We saw the form of Simon, but heard the voice of our father Faustus.'

6 1 Kings 21:23.

7 Matt 21:31–32.

8 Rev 17:3–4.

9 J. M. Robinson (ed.), *The Nag Hammadi Library in English* (Leiden: Brill, 1988), pp.297–298.

10 John 4:7–26, Mark 7:24–29.

11 Mark 6:1429, *Ant.* 18:116–119.

12 Mark 6:22.

13 The names for the woman at the crucifixion who was not called Mary are different in each of the gospels. In John 19:25 she is called 'his mother's sister'; in Mark 15:40 'Salome'; in Luke 24:10 'Joanna' (also named in Luke 8:3); in Matt 27:56 'the mother of the sons of Zebedee' (who also appears in Matt 20: 20). All are names for Helena, who was the highest ranking woman at the crosses. The Clementines (*Hom.* 2:19–21) give the link between Helena and 'the Mother of the sons of Zebedee', see further Chapter7.

14 See *Jesus the Man*, Chapter 24.

15 4QpPsa. The fragment is in a Herodian semiformal script. See *Jesus the Man*, Chapter 16, for its place in the history of John the Baptist and Jesus.

16 *Ant.* 20:17–96.

17 Acts 5:1–11 (their 'deaths' were excommunications), Acts 9:10–19.

18 *War* 6:356–357.

19 *Acts* 6:5, Rev 2:6, 15, 3:15–16.

20 The detail of Nicolaus given by Eusebius in the third century AD is compatible with what is given in the pesher of Revelation, although he has undergone some whitewashing. According to Eusebius (*Eccl. Hist.* 3, 29, 1–4), Nicolas of the Nicolaitans was married (as normally celibate dynasts were), but he brought his wife forward and 'commanded her to be mated to anyone who wished', giving up the flesh. He had had nothing to do with any other woman, and all his children remained unmarried. Eusebius says that he was called a heretic, but does not explain why.

21 Acts 12:20.

Seven: 'I, John, Your Brother'

1 Rev 1:9–10.

2 Acts 18:1–2, Rom 16:3, 2 Tim 4:19.

3 A. Roberts & J. Donaldson, The *Ante-Nicene Fathers*, vol VIII, pp.75–346 (1875, re-issued by Eerdmans Publishing Company, Grand Rapids, Michigan, 1951). Extracts are to be found in E. Hennecke, *New Testament Apocrypha* vol 2 (London: SCM Press, 1965).

4 The family history is given in *Rec* 7:8–10 and *Hom* 12:8–10. Clement, speaking in the early forties AD (as shown by the reference to James becoming bishop in Jerusalem in AD 40, *Rec* 1:43), says that twenty years earlier his father had left Rome in search of the mother. Clement was twelve years old at the time, so

he had been born about AD 10. The pesher of Revelation supplies more exact dates. Niceta and Aquila had been born in AD 3 (pesher of Rev 12:10, 8:13), and Clement was born in December AD 10 (pesher of Rev 14:20). The mother left Rome when Clement was five (*Rec* 7:8), that is AD 15. Tiberius Caesar replaced Augustus in AD 14, and her exile would have been caused by his attitude to her moral history.

5   *Rec*. 9, 32.

6   Preface of Rufinus, who translated the Recognitions into Latin. Roberts & Donaldson, p.75.

7   Ezek 16:1–14 describes the custom through an account of a female brought up in this way, used as a parable of Jerusalem.

8   Helena was head of the Gentile and female order of Asher, whose own centre was in the former tribal territory of Asher, now Tyre and Sidon in Syrophoenicia. See p.186. Helena was also the 'menstruous woman' (since she held services daily like a priest instead of monthly like a villager, prayers being the substitute for sacrifices involving shedding of blood). As the pesher of Mark 5:24–34 shows, she became head of the order in AD17, which was 'year 12' of the dating from AD 5, see p.244.

9   Matt 20:20. 'Zebedee' means 'my gift', and refers to the fact that Simon Magus kept for himself money that had been given for religion, as in the case of the Roman woman Fulvia (*Ant*. 18: 82–83). In the gospels he is always contrasted with Jonathan Annas, the other leader of Diaspora Jews, whose name 'Nathanael/ Dositheus' means 'Gift of God' (Mark 1:19, John 1:45). Jonathan was also called 'Thunder' and Simon called 'Lightning'; see these terms in the Lexicon.

10 Mark 1:16–20.

11 Phil 4:3.

12 Luke 9:54 (the plural verb refers to the plural subject, James).
13 Rev 9:1–11.
14 Rev 12:1–8.
15 Acts 12:2, 20, *Ant*. 19:340–342.
16 Rev 11:15–16.
17 *Ant*. 18:123–124.
18 Acts 18:1–4.
19 Acts 18:18–19.
20 Rom 16:3.
21 2 Tim 4:19.
22 Acts 20:4, Col 4:7, 2 Tim 4:12, Eph 6:21.
23 Rev 16:15. See the pesher.
24 Rev 17:6. See the pesher.
25 According to Eusebius, John the Apostle (his name for John of Patmos, see Chapter 8, note 9) lived until the time of Trajan (AD 98–117) (*Eccl. Hist*. 3, 23, 3–4). But detail in Revelation, combined with the Clementines, shows that John Aquila was born in AD 3. It is more likely that the practice of using a name as the title of an office, deliberately obscuring the identity of individuals holding the office, has led Eusebius to identify the second John, who did live under Trajan, with the first. Eusebius goes on to tell a story about this John, who took to his house in Ephesus a young man whom he instructed and baptised 'of strong body, beautiful appearance, and warm heart'. But the young man became corrupted, renounced salvation and formed a band of brigands, 'and was himself a born chief, excelling in violence, in murder, and in cruelty'. On hearing of this John went after him, and brought him again to repentance. (*Eccl. Hist*. 3, 23, 5–19).

Eight: The Four Horsemen of the Apocalypse and the Four Living Creatures

1   Rev 6:1–2.
2   P. R. Ackroyd & C. F. Evans (eds.), *The Cambridge History of the Bible*, vol 1, 1970, p.56: '. . . the allusions in pagan literature of the later first and early second century AD to the existence of the codex in the West'. The Septuagint and the New Testament continued to be bound together in a codex, as shown by the great codices Vaticanus, Sinaiticus and Alexandrinus.
3   *Letter of Aristeas* in *The Old Testament Pseudepigrapha*, Vol 2, J.H. Charlesworth ed. (London: Darton, Longman & Todd, 1985).
4   Ezek 1, Psalm 137.
5   Palestinian Judaism saw the Hebrew canon as divided into the Law (Genesis to Deuteronomy), the Prophets (Former: Joshua, Judges, 1–2 Samuel, 1–2 Kings; and Latter: Isaiah, Jeremiah, Ezekiel and the Twelve Minor Prophets) and the Writings (all the rest, considered to be less sacred). The Septuagint had a different principle of arrangement, varying with different editions, but the fact that in Vaticanus the poetical books (the Writings) are inserted between the Former and Latter Prophets shows that the two groups of Prophets were differentiated, the Former classed as history.
6   Irenaeus, *Against Heresies* 3, 11,8–11.
7   Rev 6:4. In Acts 20:4 a man who may be seen as Ananus is called *Pyrrhos*, 'Red'.
8   Ananus appeared as the jailer of Philippi in Acts 16:23–34. As the Merari, the deacon, of the Annas brothers, he had to associate with the unclean, including the uncircumcised and prisoners. It was Ananus who struck Jesus during his trial (John 18:22). He was also the guard at the tomb (see *Jesus*

the Man, Chapter 26). When in Macedonia, at Philippi and Thessalonica, Ananus was the levitical superior of province 12, of which Luke was a member, being of the lowest grade of Gentiles. Luke was the 'man of Macedonia' of Acts 16:9.

9   Eusebius' records, and the new light that is now cast on them, may be discussed at this point.

According to Church tradition, given by Eusebius in his *Ecclesiastical History*, the author of the fourth gospel was John of Zebedee, from the island of Patmos (*Eccl. Hist.* 3, 15,1–24,7), and this gospel was written later than the rest (3, 24,7). At the same time, Eusebius shows that there were two Johns, and two tombs at Ephesus both still called John's (*Eccl. Hist.* 3, 39,4–7). He quotes the opinion that the Apocalypse, which itself says it was written by John from Patmos, is very different from the other Johannine writings, and is therefore probably a 'forgery' (*Eccl. Hist.* 7, 25,15).

The reason for this tradition may be better understood in the light of the new information. At the outset of the mission there had been two Gentile orders, the celibate Essene order of Dan and the married Herodian order of Asher. James and John of Zebedee (Niceta and Aquila) belonged to the latter, and John Mark, the Beloved Disciple, to the former. The order of Dan followed the celibate pattern by having two branches, one of permanent monastics, the other of dynasts who could go into the world. John Mark had at first been equal to a dynast, then had later become a permanent monastic.

The two branches of Dan followed different political allegiances, the monastics under John Mark becoming anti-Herodian; the dynasts, who were led by Peter, becoming pro-Herodian. The gospel of John was written under the auspices of the anti-Herodian John Mark, although not necessarily by him personally, and its first twenty chapters were completed by AD 37. But in AD 43–44 the Christians, with Peter and Jesus, became supporters of the Agrippas and the west. The fourth gospel was reclaimed by them. Its Chapter 21 was added, noticeably different from the rest in that it makes Peter central, whereas he is all but ignored, or given low status, in the rest of the gospel.

In the meantime, the order of Asher had developed in the direction of dynastic Dan, so that their way of life was indistinguishable. They were permitted to marry, but Asher also adopted the rule of long separations, the husband living among celibates. James Niceta then John Aquila of Asher developed in the same way, the residence of John on Patmos being among celibates. The fourth gospel then became the property of their order, and the date of the addition of Chapter 21, in the late forties, was said to be the date of its writing.

James Niceta records that he took over the fourth gospel in the story of his 'eating the little book'. In his mouth, it was 'sweet as honey', because it reflected the interests of the Herodian 'Promised Land' in the west. But the 'belly' (John Mark, a name used for his order of Gentiles in the gospels) 'became bitter'; separated and stayed with the Magians (Rev 10:2–10). The date of this event was September – December AD 43.

The history of Matthew's gospel is similarly illuminated. Eusebius records traditions about it: Matthew collected the Sayings (*logia*) in the Hebrew language (*Eccl. Hist.* 3, 39,16). 'Matthew had first preached to Hebrews, and when he was on the point of going to others he transmitted in writing in his native language the gospel according to himself . . . Mark and Luke had already published the gospels according to them' (*Eccl. Hist.* 3, 24,6–7). 'Matthew published among the Hebrews a written gospel also in their own tongue, while Peter and Paul were preaching in Rome and founding the church' (*Eccl. Hist.* 5, 8,2). Similarly 6, 25,4–6.

Together with the pesher of Revelation, these traditions give the history: Matthew Annas first compiled the Sayings in Hebrew, that is the Q source, the sayings common to Luke and Matthew (the identity of Q and the *logia* has long been suspected). These were the 'Mystery of God' of Rev 10:7, being prepared by Matthew in September 43, banned by Agrippa I, then published in December 43 when Matthew had turned to supporting Herod of Chalcis.

Then, after the schism and after the writing of Mark and Luke (see below), when he had been dismissed as high priest and had gone to Antioch and Ephesus ('when he was on the point of going to others') Matthew wrote a gospel in Hebrew, incorporating the Sayings and Mark and Luke. This gospel was intended for eastern Christians, and continued to be used by them.

By AD 49 his gospel had been translated into Greek, and was treated in Ephesus as the superior one as it linked east and west. It was given the place of honour at the canonisation ceremony in June AD 49.

Matthew's own identity as a Jewish high priest was suppressed in the tradition that eventually reached Eusebius: he only knew him as a tax-collector who had followed Jesus (*Eccl. Hist.* 6,25,4). This was part of the process of denying the Jewish origins and the previous Herodian history.

The history of Mark's gospel is similarly able to be reconciled from the two sets of sources. Eusebius shows that a man named Mark, who was with Peter in Rome at the time he wrote his epistle (1 Pet 5:13), wrote down what Peter taught, although Mark himself had not heard the Lord. Peter is twice said to have approved what had been written, so it was during his lifetime. The account of the writing of the gospel follows the account of Peter's triumph over Simon Magus in Rome in the reign of Claudius (AD 41–54). Mark is said to have been a bishop in Alexandria. (*Eccl. Hist.* 2,14,6; 2,15,1–2; 2,24,1; 3,24,5–7; 3,39,14–16; 5,8,2–4; 6,14,6–7; 6,25,3–6).

The history would, then, be as follows: at the schism of AD 44, Peter left Judea and 'went to another place' (Acts 12:17). He both rose to the status of dynastic celibate, being a widower, and also established a new base outside Judea. He appeared the following season at Antioch as Simeon Niger (Acts 13:1), but was not included in the account of events in Asia Minor from 44 to 46. From Eusebius it would follow that during these two years he was in Rome, where the schism with the east was expressed through his personal victory over the Magus. In the ancient Syriac document 'The teaching of Simon Cephas in the City of Rome' (Roberts & Donaldson p.673) it is said that in the third year of Claudius Caesar (AD 44), Simon Cephas departed from Antioch to go to Rome.

In Rome John Mark was replaced by a Gentile who was given his title Mark. In Peter's letter from Rome, written 44–46, he speaks of the new Mark as 'my son', and mentions also 'she, the Elect One, in "Babylon" (Rome)', that is, Mark was a celibate who had a 'Mother' and was a 'son'. The new Mark recorded Peter's memoirs between 44 and 46, and the book was brought back to Ephesus and Antioch, to be incorporated by Matthew.

When, after the Council of Jerusalem in 46, Jesus went to Rome, the new Mark went to Alexandria, and stayed there, so he did not have personal contact with Jesus.

Luke's history parallels that of Peter, in that he appeared with him as Cornelius in Caesarea in June

43 (Acts 10) and again with him in Antioch in June 44. (Acts 13:1). He may be identified with Cornelius son of Ceron who was in Rome in June AD 45, and was made one of the bearers of Claudius' letter giving tolerance to the Jews (*Ant*. 20:14). In the Clementines, the same Cornelius had been sent by the emperor to Caesarea (*Clem. Rec*. 10, 55, *Clem. Hom*. 20,13). He appears again in early 50, as 'the man from Macedonia' (Acts 16:9). His gospel is said by Eusebius to follow Mark and precede Matthew, and this accords with its internal evidence. After reading Mark, either in Rome or after returning to Caesarea with Claudius' letter, he composed his gospel, using also some of the *logia* that had been written by Matthew in 43.

10 The Jewish Christians, led by James the brother of Jesus and Jude a younger brother, held that the Jewish Law should be observed, and that salvation came through good works, as shown in the Epistle of James. 'Religion that is pure and undefiled before God and the Father is this: to visit orphans and widows in their affliction, and to keep oneself unstained from the world' (James 1:27).

The person of Christ was not central in their belief. An account of them is given by Eusebius, under the name Ebionites, a name that is now accounted for, as one of the names of the writers of the Scrolls was *ebionim*, 'the Poor'. But Eusebius, who knows nothing of the Jewish pre-history, says it was 'because they had poor and mean opinions concerning Christ'. He goes on: 'They held him to be a plain and ordinary man who had achieved righteousness merely by the progress of his character and had been born naturally from Mary and her husband' (*Eccl. Hist*. 3,27,1–6; 5,8,10; 6,17,1).

11 In Rev 8:1 the subject of 'he opened' is 'God' in 7:17, following the rule of the last subject. See p.381.

Nine: The Great Winepress of the Wrath of God

1 Rev 14:19–20.
2 See Leonard Boyle, O. P., *A Short Guide to St Clement's, Rome* (Collegio San Clemente, Via Labicana 95, Rome, 1968).
3 Mark 3:18. The first six names in the list were the lower grades: two village Essenes (Peter and Andrew); two married Gentiles of Asher (James and John), two celibate Gentiles of Dan (Philip and Bartholomew). Philip was the head of Shem uncircumcised, and Bartholomew-John Mark-the Beloved Disciple his superior, of the grade of Dan equal to proselytes. His name, 'Bartholomew', was later given to a missionary in the Herodian tradition, working in India (*Eccl. Hist.* 5, 10, 3, *Martyrdom of Bartholomew*, Roberts & Donaldson pp.553–557).
4 Justin Martyr, *Apologia*, 1, 26. The stone, found in 1574, omits the 't' in Sancto, and for this reason Kirsopp Lake (translator of Eusebius, Loeb Library, p.137, followed by J. Stevenson, A New Eusebius, p.74) says that Justin was mistaken, and that the stone is dedicated to 'Semo Sancus, an old Sabine deity', for whom no reference is given. It may, however, be too much to expect correct spelling in a popular cult, and to accuse of error one who was so close to the event. The activity of Simon in Rome is well attested (*Eccl. Hist.* 2, 13, 1; 2, 13, 4–6), as was his claim to be a god (*Clem. Hom.* 2, 22).
5 Acts 28:14–15.
6 *Ant.* 18:143–167.
7 Rev 14:8, on Claudius, who wrote a letter expressing friendship for Jews (*Ant.* 20:10–14). Rev 18:2 on Vitellius.
8 CD 1:5, 4QpNah 5, 1QpHab 3:12.

9   See *Jesus the Man*, Appendix II, Locations, on the system of distances expressing stages of uncleanness.

10   Rev 14:20.

11   The queen's house was the meeting place for pilgrims to Qumran, used for this purpose in Matt 28:9. Acts 28:15 calls the Forum of Appius the 'meeting-place'.

12   See *Jesus the Man*, Locations. 1QM 7:67, a latrine must be 2000 cubits from the camp, 4Q491, 1000 cubits.

13   See the plan of the route in *Jesus the Man*, Locations, Fig.1.

14   See p.189.

15   Barnabas may be seen to be a brother of Jesus through indications in Acts and the Clementines. In Acts 1:23 the choice for a replacement for Judas in the Twelve Apostles was between Joseph Barsabbas Justus (James the Just the brother of Jesus, acting sometimes as a 'Jacob' and sometimes as a 'Joseph') and Matthias, and Matthias was chosen. (See *Jesus the Man*, Chapter 26, note 13, on 'Barsabbas'.) According to *Clem. Rec.* 1, 62, Matthias was Barnabas. In Acts 4:36 he is called Joseph Barnabas, and said to be 'the son (subordinate) of Exhortation' (*paraklēsis*). *Paraklēsis* was a name for the David crown prince as the one 'called beside', the deputy. It is used of James in Acts 9:31. Joses was the next son after James (Mark 6:3, Mark 15:40), called also Joseph (Matt 13:55); he was ready to act in the position of the 'Joseph' when the crown prince as deputy to the David acted in the position of the 'Jacob'. When James held to the eastern doctrine on the circumcision question, Barnabas substituted for him as the crown prince to Jesus until Jesus' own son came of age.

Barnabas was called 'levite' in Acts 4:36 because he took the position of Judas, who was called 'levite' to Simon Magus as 'priest'. See **priest** in the Lexicon.

Paul at first travelled with Barnabas, who was called 'Zeus' in Lystra (Acts 14:12), showing that he had an exalted status, then, after the separation of 44–46, Paul travelled with Simon-Silas, the youngest of the brothers of Jesus (Mark 6:3, Acts 15: 40; in Acts 15:22 Barnabas, Judas Barsabbas the second youngest brother, and Silas all appear together).

Barnabas was the permanent celibate of the brothers, and became allied with the celibate John Mark, remaining with him during the period when John Mark was anti-Herodian (Acts 15:36–41, Col 4:10).

16 'When he (Antipas) arrived in Rome . . . all his relatives went over to his side, not out of goodwill to him but because of their hatred of Archelaus' (*Ant.* 17:227).

17 Luke 13:6.

18 Mark 12:1–9.

19 Matt 25:18, Luke 19:20–26.

20 *Ant.* 18:81–84.

21 Matt 20:1–15.

22 *Ant.* 20:160–182, Acts 24:27.

23 *Eccl. Hist.* 2, 25, 5–8.

24 See p.529, on Peter's appointment to Rome in AD 44.

25 See p.211.

26 Suetonius, *Life of Claudius*, 25:4.

27 Acts 28:14.

Ten: The Second Death and the Lake of Fire and Brimstone

1 Rev 2:11, 21:8.

2 1QS 7:3–25.

3 11QT 45:7–18.

4 See *Jesus the Man*, Locations, The Plan of Qumran.

5 11QT 45:7–10.

6 See *Jesus the Man*, Chapter 24 and Locations. The

places in the south-west section of Qumran, where it is argued in *Jesus the Man* that the crucifixion took place, may be viewed in the documentary film, *The Riddle of the Dead Sea Scrolls*, made by Beyond International, 53–55 Brisbane St, Surry Hills 2010 Sydney, Australia.

7   R. De Vaux, *Archaeology and the Dead Sea Scrolls*, pp.26–27.

8   *The Contemplative Life*.

9   R. De Vaux, *Archaeology and the Dead Sea Scrolls*, p.28, and Humbert, photographs 278, 279.

10 Acts 17:5–6, compare Gen 19:4–6.

11 Luke 17:29, compare Gen 19:24.

12 11QT 46:13–16.

13 Deut 23:12–14. Heb 13:12–13: 'So Jesus also suffered outside the gate . . . therefore let us go forth to him outside the camp.'

14 3Q15, sentence 16.

15 Luke 7:12 illustrates the ritual.

16 John 11:1–44. See *Jesus the Man*, Chapter 20.

17 The date is given in the pesher of Acts 9:33. 'Year 8' when 'Aeneas' (James) became 'ill', was AD 38 by Agrippa's dating from AD 30 (p.224).

18 There were two anti-Herodian parties in Damascus. The first, Hebrews led by James the brother of Jesus, had taken the money from Qumran when the Roman governor Vitellius marched near to it in September AD 37. Vitellius was supporting the tetrarch Antipas against the Arabian king Aretas, who controlled Damascus. Aretas gave shelter to the enemies of the tetrarch. Then, the following year, Hellenists under Simon Magus brought their money to Damascus to conceal it from Agrippa. The Hellenists eventually drove out the Hebrews, who returned to Qumran as Jewish Christians.

19 CD 19:6–20:34.

20 Acts 9:23–25.

21 *Ant.* 19:332–334.
22 CD 8:1–21.
23 Acts 8:10.
24 CD 12:23, 14:19, 19:10, 20:1.
25 Rev 11:13.
26 *War* 2:447, 7:253, 275, 297.
27 Rev 21:8.

Eleven: Armageddon

1 Rev 16:16.
2 Matt 15:39.
3 See the textual apparatus to Matt 15:39 in *The Greek New Testament*, Aland, Black, Martini, Metzger, Wikgren eds. (United Bible Societies, 1966).
4 1QM 9:7–9.
5 1QS 7:13–14.
6 *War* 4:498–499.
7 *War* 4:314–318 *Ant.* 20:199–203.
9 Quoted in *Eccl. Hist.* 2, 23, 4–18.
10 Rev 16:1. See **bowl** in the Lexicon.
11 *War* 4:241.
12 *War* 4:503–544, *War* 7:31–36.
13 *War* 6:409–413.

Twelve: The Fall of the Great Harlot

1 Rev 18:4–20, modelled on the Book of Lamentations.
2 *Ant.* 18:132, 19:276–277, 20:104, 20:145–146.
3 *War* 4:498.
4 *Dio's Roman History* 65, 15:3–4, 66, 8:1. Dio adds that Titus and Bernice were the subjects of popular gossip: 'In addition to all the other talk that there was, certain sophists of the Cynic school managed somehow to slip into the city at this time, too; and first Diogenes, entering the theatre when it was full, denounced the pair in a long, abusive speech, for

which he was flogged; and after him Heras, expecting no harsher punishment, gave vent to many senseless yelpings in true Cynic fashion, and for this was beheaded' (65, 15, 5).

5   *War* 2:309–314.
6   *War* 2: 344–402.
7   Josephus, *Life*, 343, 355.
8   Acts 25:13.
9   *War* 2:312.
10 *War* 4:498.
11 In *Clem. Hom.* 3, 73, the 'daughter' of Justa the Syrophoenician woman (Helena) is called Bernice the Canaanite.
12 Rev 17:5, 18:2.
13 Rev 17:7–14.

Thirteen: The Reason for   2000

1   *Jubilees* 6:36.
2   See S. Sambursky, *The Physical World of the Greeks* (London: Routledge & Kegan Paul, 1956); F. Lasserre, *The Birth of Mathematics in the Age of Plato* (London: Hutchinson, 1964). *Ant.* 15:371: '(The Essenes) follow a way of life taught to the Greeks by Pythagoras'.
3   *Ant.* 13:311–312; 15:373; 17:345–348.

SECTION II THE INSIDER'S KNOWLEDGE

One: Overview of the Parties

1   Josephus' accounts of Pharisees, Sadducees and Essenes are to be found in *War* 2:119–166 and *Ant.* 13:171–173, 18:12–22. He describes the 'fourth philosophy', founded by Judas the Galilean, in *Ant.*

18:23–25, and calls the later form of their militant anti-Roman party Zealots (*War* 2:651).

2 *War* 7:304–406.

3 Acts 6:1, Phil 3:5, 2 Cor 11:22, Epistle to Hebrews.

Two: From Qumran to Cathedral

1 See R. De Vaux, *Archaeology and the Dead Sea Scrolls* (OUP, 1973), and *Jesus the Man*, Locations, The Plan of Qumran. Loc. 101 below the well.

Following the publication in 1994 of the photographs and working notes of de Vaux's original excavation of Qumran (Humbert, J-B and Chambon, A., *Fouilles de Khirbet Qumran et de Ain Feshkha*, Göttingen: Vandenhoeck & Ruprecht, 1994), it is seen that in the second phase a barrier was erected over the original dais edge and step. It was removed by the archaeologists, as were most of the subsequent additions to the vestry. The original plan was as here described, and in the second phase this plan was transferred to Mird, where it became part of the three storey structure.

The new publication also reveals that in part of the centre of the vestry were a pile of bricks and a wooden beam. De Vaux took it to be a collapsed ceiling, but it is difficult to see why it would have fallen so selectively. Rather, it is confirmation of the existence of the pillars supporting the platform (see pp.164,165.)

The seven steps giving access to the platform from the north are clearly shown in the photographs (Humbert 227, 231, 236, 272), which also show (in 231) that their top was higher than a man's head. They also were removed by the archaeologists. They would have given access to a short north–south platform, leading on to the main east–west platform, as shown in Diagram A.

The second circular structure in the corridor on the

east side of the vestry, which de Vaux thought to be another oven in addition to the main furnace, is described as having no outlet at its base (Humbert, p.323). This means that it could not have been an oven. Rather, the detail of the pesher suggests that it was a container for olive oil, used for lighting the Menorah, on which the lighter lamp stood. It was here that the person called 'the Light' stood to hear the prayers of pilgrims.

The photographs also show that the two carved pillar bases outside the south vestry door were not left as found by the archaeologists, but the southern one has been turned upside down (photographs 293, 294, 295).

2   Ezek 44:19.

3   *Ant* 15:373–378, Herod the Great came to favour the Essenes early in his reign, due to the influence of his former teacher Menahem the Essene.

4   See *Jesus the Man*, Locations, The Buildings at Ain Feshkha, Mazin, Mird and Mar Saba. Mird is about halfway between Jerusalem and the Dead Sea.

5   At Mird and the similarly shaped building at Ain Feshkha, the two-storeyed part was in the west wing, and the place of worship in the north wing. At Mird, a rite of atonement was performed (pesher of Luke 1:8–20, and of Acts 7:33), but it was understood that the north wing was not a true temple. It subsequently became a Christian church; see G. R. H. Wright, 'The Archaeological Remains at El Mird in the Wilderness of Judea', *Biblica* 42, 1961, pp.1–27.

6   1 Kings 1:32, 38; 2:26–27.

7   2 Sam 20:25–26, in which the 'king's priest' is to be seen as the Levi priest, from the line of nomad priests who were displaced by Zadok and Abiathar in the Jerusalem temple. 1QM 17:2–3 upholds the lines of Zadok and Abiathar (Eleazar and Ithamar) as the true priests. The line of Levi had not been preserved in

the way Zadok and Abiathar were, and the men in the position of 'king's priest', or Sariel, were those who acted in the position, rather than true descendants.

8 *Ant.* 17:346–347, Luke 1:11, 19, 26.

9 Matt 23:2.

10 See *Jesus the Man*, Locations, on the building now known as Khirbet Mazin, about 6 kilometres south of Qumran, below the headland of Ras Feshkha.

11 Mark 2:1–12.

12 1QS 8:1.

13 1QM 9:16, which gives the order Michael first, Gabriel second, Sariel third, Raphael fourth. Michael and Gabriel are said to be on the superior right, and Sariel and Raphael on the inferior left. Raphael appears in 1 Enoch 68.

14 Judas the Galilean *Ant.* 18:4–10.

15 Phanuel in Luke 2:36, 1 Enoch 71:8, 9, 13.

16 Mark 5:22.

17 Num 4:1–45. The service of Kohath was to 'the most holy things' (v.4); of Gershon 'in serving and bearing burdens' (v.24), and of Merari carrying less sacred objects (vv.31–32).

18 11QT 44:14.

Three: The New Jerusalem – How to Build a Church

1 11QT 39, 41, 44.

2 Rev 7:9, 13–14.

3 *War* 2:123.

4 11QT 45:8–10.

5 1QS 7:12, 13–14.

6 1QS 1:14–15, 10:16.

7 Acts 9:1–9.

8 See *Jesus the Man*, Chronology, Measurement in Hours and Minutes.

9 The variant of the text of Acts 19:9 says that Paul

taught in the school of Tyrannus in Ephesus 'from the fifth to the tenth hour', that is, 11 a.m (the time Essenes ceased work and prepared for their meal, *War* 2:129) until 4 p.m. The variant is in the D or Western text, whose variations always show exact knowledge of the pesher and an intention to change the text according to its own practices. It is one of the proofs that the pesher was known in the Church in the early centuries.

10 John 1:39, Jesus taught his first disciples at 4 p.m.

11 4Q164, Exod 28:15–21.

12 At the northern end of the Qumran vestry an area is still seen to be marked off in a distinctive way. A space that was nearly circular, but with an extension to the west, was ringed by stones, which curved round to meet the furnace built east of the vault on row 0. The circular area is below the level of the paved floor, and when the archaeologists found it it was plastered so as to hold water, but the plaster has been removed, as has the fire. The original purpose of the arrangement may be deduced from the fact that the room was originally the vestry to the nearby substitute sanctuary, joined to it by a door on the west side (which was filled in by the vault in the second phase). As the vestry where the holy loaves of the Presence were eaten, it was also the place where they were prepared and cooked, according to the biblical regulation that they must be baked fresh every day (1 Sam 21:6). Made under the supervision of priests in the vestry, the fire was used for cooking, and, since the cooking vessels had to be washed, not leaving any dough that might break the rule about new loaves every day, the plastered trough would be used, water being poured over the vessels and running out to the west. Two water jugs were found in the room (Humbert photographs 284, 286). The cylinder originally standing in the centre of the room may be supposed

to have received grain tithes, used to make flour for the holy bread. The mill originally placed outside the door was for grinding this flour.

In the second phase, this area was used for a different purpose. Details in the gospels and Acts indicate that this area was treated as a 'court' for the higher areas used by priests north of the vestry, and another of its purposes was for the 'poor, crippled, lame and blind', the welfare recipients, to stand as petitioners to the priests. They were permitted to stand near the fire.

13 The Eutychus of Acts 20:7–12 is to be identified with the Eutychus who was a freedman of Agrippa I and betrayed his plot to Tiberius (*Ant.* 18:168–187). John Mark, an associate in the gospel period of Simon Magus and of Jesus, who were both at that time opponents of Agrippa, went back to Rome with Agrippa in AD 34, acted against him to try to ensure that he would not become king, then lost favour when Jesus turned to Agrippa on his appointment to the kingship. John Mark remained with Simon Magus, and was only brought back into the party of Jesus in AD 58, the time of the Acts episode.

14 The directions 'before' and 'behind' in Ezek 1:10, for the Man and the Eagle, also mean 'east' and 'west' in Hebrew. Consequently the Lion on the right was on the south, and the Calf on the left was on the north.

15 Philo, *Contemp. Life*, describes them, showing a close knowledge of their way of life and their Exodus liturgy.

16 John 3:1, Rev 1:4.

17 John 13:27, 14:22.

Four: The System of Grades

1   CD 14:4, 6, 1QS 2:19–23.

2   11QT 57:12–14 lists the three sets of twelve. 1QM

2:3 names the third group as 'heads of tribes'. They appear as the congregation in 4Q164, the pesher on Isa 54:11 ('And I will lay your foundations with sapphires'): 'The pesher of this concerns the priests and the people, who laid the foundations of the Council of the Community . . . the congregation of his Elect like a sapphire among stones'.

3   1QS 6:4–5, 1QSa 2:17–21.

4   Levit 24:5–9, Ezek 41:22.

5   *War* 4:582, CD 11:22.

6   The 13 cubits of the vestry and step lent themselves also to naming in terms of 12-hour divisions of the day and night, starting Saturday 6 a.m. on row 0 (the wall of the vault), Saturday 6 p.m. on row 1, and so on down to the dais edge corresponding to Friday 6 a.m. and the step to Friday 6 p.m.

7   Luke 12:25. It is a statement, not a question, in the pesher.

8   1QSa 1:9–11. See also 11QT 39:10–11.

9   1QS 6:20–23.

10   Grades are indicated in this way also in John 4:52 (the seventh hour), 1:39 (the tenth hour), Acts 22:6 (noon). The same device is used in *The Apocalypse of Paul* 20:25–21:10 (*NHL* p.258).

11   *Contemp. Life* 65.

12   CD 19:12, quoting Ezek 9:4.

13   Mark 10:24–25, literally translated, reads: 'Children, how hard a thing (*dyskolon*) it is to enter into the kingdom of God. It is an easier thing (*eukopōteron*) for a camel to go through the eye of the needle, or ($\bar{e}$) a rich man to enter into the kingdom of God'. In the pesher, 'or' ($\bar{e}$) always means 'both'. The pesher of the saying is: 'Permanent celibates ("hard") enter the ministry in the Sadducee school. Dynastic celibates ("easier", because they may sometimes leave for marriage), who are of class C (Gimel) enter it through graduation at Qof; and, as well, a normally married

man ("rich"), who may enter it the same way if he studies to graduation'. The saying particularly applied to Peter, a married man who as a widower entered the celibate ministry.

14 *Every Good Man* 75.
15 Acts 22:3, Phil 3:5.
16 4Q159 sets out the taxation system. See Chapter 1, note 5. 11QT 39:8 (fragmentary) mentions the half shekel.
17 Exod 12:37. 4Q159 organises the taxation system in these terms.
18 Luke 19:11–27. The first missionary was given a pound (100 half shekels) for his travelling expenses, and when he had made 100 members, each paying a half shekel, his pound had made another pound. The scheme covered forty years, divided into ten sets of four-year instruction periods, so when 100 members were made in each of the instruction periods, the original pound had made ten pounds.
19 4QMMT B 3–9. *DJD* X, 1994.
20 See *Jesus the Man*, Locations, The System for Boats.
21 1 Peter 3:20.
22 Gen 9:20.
23 *War* 2:123.
24 1QH 8:4–26. The word 'Eden' is found in line 20, and in the newly published fragment with a similar theme, PAM 43:306 (1341 in Eisenmann & Robinson).
25 The Greek word *mylos*, meaning a millstone, was the same as Hebrew *mul*, meaning 'circumcision'.
26 Prov 1:20.

Five: The Daily Timetable

1 As stated by Josephus, *War* 2:129.
2 CD 10:21.
3 *Contemp. Life* 87–89.

Six: Watching God's Clock

1   *TLevi* 17.
2   See *Jesus the Man*, Chronology. R. T. Beckwith ('The Significance of the Calendar for Interpreting Essene Chronology and Eschatology'. *Revue de Qumran* 10, 1980, 167–202) agrees with this identification.
3   In J. H. Charlesworth (ed.), *The Old Testament Pseudepigrapha*, Vol 1 (London: Darton, Longman & Todd, 1983).
4   11QMelch 7, Dan 9:24.
5   Plutarch, *Isis and Osiris*, 370.
6   Rev 9:18 ('from three plagues', but this means 'at the opposite extreme of plague 3', so, as plague 3 in the series was in June AD 61, the opposite extreme of that year was a year later, in June AD 62); 15:1, 21:9.
7   M. Cary and H. H. Scullard, *A History of Rome* (London: Macmillan, 1975), pp.439–440.
8   *Eccl. Hist.* 5, 18:1–2, 12–13.
9   1 Enoch 91:13.
10 1 Macc 2:42.
11 *Ant.* 15:373, 378.
12 *TLevi* 18.
13 Matt 2:7–13. Whereas Essenes allowed no zero, and began a generation in the decade year (3930 began a generation for them), the Herodians allowed a zero year at creation, and began a generation in the 1 year. Their generation year 3931 was therefore a year later than the Essene 3931, and two years later than the Essene 3930. When Jesus was born in a year that was one form of the Essene 3930 (7 BC, the +3½ version), Herod asked the anti-Herodian Magians what was the ordained date of the birth. Their reply would have been 'In the generation year'. For Herod, this was 5 BC, and he waited two years, so then, when told of the calendar differ ences, had to issue an order to find children who were two years old. The story was

543

obviously intended to illustrate the calendar point, as well as recording the tensions between the ruling Herods and the Essenes that was to continue for many years.

14 11QMelch 7, 'in the year of the last jubilee'.

15 Ananus the Elder had actually come into power in AD 6, which was the south lunisolar version of 3941 (see p.244 for the explanation). In Judea, he began to use a system of dating from this as year 1, so that AD 17 was its year 12. This dating is used by Luke to record the occasion when Jesus was being initiated at the age of twenty-three, in AD 17. By saying 'twelve years', he made it appear that Jesus was twelve years old, but the pesher sense was year 12 of the dating from AD 6. The same dating was used to refer to year 18, AD 23, in the form 'eighteen years'. This was in the story of the 'crippled woman' in Luke 13:11. The pesher of the story is that Mary, the Mother of Jesus, had become widowed in AD 23.

The dating series from 1 BC and AD 1 used the north solar dates, those operating in the Diaspora.

16 In the pesher of Acts 7:6, the 'oppression' is the failure of the Restoration of 21 BC, when Herod rejected the Essene-Sadducee temple plan.

17 The 'eighth day', 1BC, is named in Rev 7:8 (pesher). This corresponded to '6 a.m.'. For those like the Therapeuts who began the day at the first hour, 7 a.m., the 'eighth day' was AD 5, and in Luke 1:59 the phrase is used for that year, when the twelfth birthday of John the Baptist, born September 8 BC, took place.

18 *Ant.* 20:162–163.

19 *Ant.* 20:97–98.

20 *Ant.* 20:169–172.

21 *Jubilees* 6:23, 4QMMT Aii.

22 J. Finegan, *Handbook of Biblical Chronology* (Princeton University Press, 1964), pp.292–295.

23 The 1290 days of Dan 12:11 is from September

168 BC to March 164 BC. It was a period of 1274 days, counted not from the feasts but from the beginning of the month, plus 16 days for the intercalation that was due in September 168. An intercalation was 17½ days, of which the first 1½ days covered the 31st that had fallen back to early in the month. This was the day for transition. When the calendar was already in the Day position, with the 31st beginning on Tuesday at 6 a.m., a day of 36 hours was used, up to Wednesday at 6 p.m., and from then on the days began in the evening. This 1½ days was counted with the previous year, and the remaining 16 days with the following period.

The 1335 days of Dan 12:12 ('Blessed is he who waits and comes to the 1335 days') comes from another calendar school who disagree with a year starting at Passover and want to make the change from September 168 to Pentecost 164. They also count from feast to feast, as does the author of Revelation (see pp.241–243 on the 1260 days). They count 1274 days from Tabernacles 168 (after the intercalation) to the beginning of Passover, I/14 in 164 BC. Then it is 61 further days to the beginning of III/15, the Day of Pentecost. 1274+61 = 1335.

TABLE 4
PRINCIPAL EVENTS 41 BC TO AD 114

Year	North Solar	Davids	Herods	Romans	Jews	Christians
BC 41	3900 Mill.		Herod the Great begins rise		Mission to Diaspora founded	
37			Herod crowned king			
31	3910			Battle of Actium	Earthquake at Qumran	
30				Augustus emperor		
21	3920 Rest.		Herod rjects Temple Scroll		Last Jubilee declared	
11	3930 Gen.		Agrippa I born			
8					John Baptist born Sep	
7		Jesus born March			Qumran reoccupied	
4			Herod the Great dies. Archelaus made ethnarch			
1	3940= 3900					'Vineyard' in Rome
AD 1	3941 IC Night				Zealots at Qumran Annas Last Jubilee Sep (see p. 225).	
2					Annas Last Jubilee Mar	
3				Niceta & Aquila born, Rome		

Year	North Solar	Davids	Herods	Romans	Jews	Christians
5					John Baptist aged 12, Sep	
6		Jesus aged 12, Mar Jesus legitimate under Ananus	Archelaus dismissed		Zealot uprising, 40 year war plan begins Ananus Elder high priest	
10	3950			Clement born, Rome		
14		Jesus aged 20		Tiberius emperor		
15	3955 IC Day				Ananus Elder dismissed	
16		Joseph becomes the David			Eleazar Annas high priest	
17		Jesus aged 23. Initiation				
18		Jesus illegitimate under Caiaphas			Caiaphas high priest	
23		Joseph dies. James becomes the David	Agrippa returns from Rome			
26				Pilate procurator	Judas Iscariot the 'Beast'. War: Ham Campaign. Baptist rises to power	
27			Agrippa II born Sep			
29	3969 IC Night	Jesus begins ministry	End Last Jubilee for Agrippa I	Tiberius 15th year	Schism of Twelve Apostles	Jesus forms Gentile party in Twelve

Year	North Solar	Davids	Herods	Romans	Jews	Christians
30	3970 Gen.	Jesus' 1st wedding Sep to Mary Magdalene			Baptist fails. Jonathan Annas leader	
31					Baptist killed. Simon Magus leader	
32		Jesus performs atonement Sep. Child conceived Dec			Uprising against Pilate Dec	
33		Jesus' 2nd wedding March to Mary Magdalene. Crucifixion March. Jesus revived by Simon Daughter born Sep			Simon & Judas crucified. Simon claims resurrection miracle. Judas killed	
36			Agrippa arrested. Timothy born	Pilate dismissed	Simon Magus 'Beast'. War: Japheth Campaign. Caiaphas dismissed	
37 (Mar)			Agrippa given rule	Caligula emperor	Jonathan Annas high priest	
37 (Jun)		Jesus Justus born			Hebrews to Damascus	

Year	North Solar	Davids	Herods	Romans	Jews	Christians
37 (Sep)		Jesus joins Theophilus			Jonathan Annas dismissed Theophilus Annas high priest. Pro-Roman	
38			Agrippa returns to Judea			
39					Simon Magus to Damascus with Herod of Chalcis	Peter attacks Simon Magus
40	3980 Gen.					Paul converted to pro-Roman party
41				Claudius emperor	Matthew Annas high priest	
43	3983 IC Day		Jubilee extension ends. Agrippa II aged 16		Matthew dismissed	Matthew's Logia banned
44 (Jan)						Name 'Christian' used in Antioch
44 (Mar)		Second son of Jesus born	Agrippa I acts as 'God', killed. Agrippa II in Rome		Schism of East (Damascus) from West (Herodians & Chrisitans)	Peter leader. James Niceta completes Rev Part A
44 (Jun)					Ephesus made centre of mission	Christians in Antioch
44 (Sep)		Jesus in Cyprus. 1st marriage ends	Agrippa II proconsul in Cyprus			Paul attacks Simon Magus in Cyprus

Year	North Solar	Davids	Herods	Romans	Jews	Christians
45		Jesus in Asia Minor with Paul	Agrippa II in Rome			Peter in Rome Mark's gospel written
46					End 40 years War	Council of Jerusalem
48		Jesus in Rome				Luke's gospel. Matthew's gospel
49 (Mar)			Herod of Chalcis dies. Agrippa II crowned in Jerusalem			Christians expelled from Rome
49 (Jun)		Jesus in Ephesus	Agrippa II crowned in Ephesus			Gospels canonised
50 (Mar)	3990 Gen.	Jesus in Philippi Marriage to Lydia				
50 (Sep)			Agrippa II initiated, aged 23		Annas Last Jubilee fails. Ananus the Younger leader. Relocates Qumran Samaritans in Judea reject Agrippa	Paul's party formed, 'Romans'
51			Agrippa II in Rome Samaritans punished		Final failure of jubilee	Christians to Achaia. John Aquila completes Rev Part B
54				Nero emperor		
55				Felix procurator, initiated		

Year	North Solar	Davids	Herods	Romans	Jews	Christians
57	3997 IC Night	Jesus Justus aged 20. Jesus in Ephesus			Jonathan Annas killed in Judea	
58		Jesus in Jerusalem	Agrippa II in Jerusalem			Paul in Jerusalem
60	4000 Esch.	Jesus to Rome		Felix arrested		All to Rome. End 'Vineyard' mission
61						All meet in Rome
62			Agrippa II in Jerusalem		Ananus the Younger high priest in Jerusalem	James brother of Jesus killed in Judea
63					War tension	
64						Paul, Peter, Timothy killed in Rome
66					War breaks out	
69			Agrippa II leaves Jerusalem	3 emperors		
70	4010	Jesus in Ephesus, last appearance, aged 76. Probably died in Rome		Vespasian emperor. Son Titus lover of Bernice	Jerusalem falls, Sep. Party disputes in Ephesus	
71	4011 IC Day		Bernice in Rome with Titus		Laments for fall of Jerusalem	
73		Wedding of Jesus Justus. His 'coronation'				
74					Fall of Masada (2 May)	Tychicus completes Rev Part C

Year	North Solar	Davids	Herods	Romans	Jews	Christians
77		Jesus III born				
79				Titus emperor		
98				Trajan emperor		
99	4025 IC Night					
100	4040= 4000 Esch.				Millennial tensions in Ephesus	
102			Agrippa II dies. No successor			
110			Bernice dies			
112						Ephesus hermitage becomes Christian monastery
113	4039 IC Day	Wedding of Jesus III				
114		Birth of Jesus IV				John II completes Rev Part D

North Solar	North solar calendar (see pp. 238, 242)
IC Day	Quartodecimal intercalation of north solar calendar to Day position. (see pp. 237–238)
IC Night	Quartodecimal intercalation of north solar calendar to Night position (see pp. 237–238)
Mill.	Millennium
Rest.	Restoration
Esch.	Eschaton
Gen.	Generation year

THE HERODIAN FAMILY TREE
(Members appearing in this book)

ANTIPATER

HEROD THE GREAT

m. Doris — Antipater executed 4 BC

m. Mariamne I the Hasmonean executed c. 29 BC
- Alexander executed 7 BC
  - Alexander
    - Tigranes King of Armenia
      - Alexander
        - Hellenised Herod
  - Tigranes
- Aristobulus executed 7 BC
  - Herod of Chalcis
    - m. 1st wife
      - Aristobulus m. Salome
        - Herod ('Timothy')* & 2 sons
    - m. Bernice
      - Bernicianus
  - Herodias
  - AGRIPPA I
    - Bernice
      - AGRIPPA II unmarried
    - Mariamme
      - Agrippinus
    - Drusilla m. Felix
    - Agrippa ('Eighth'*) died Vesuvius AD 79

m. Mariamme II daughter of Boethus
- Herod ('Thomas') m. Herodias
- Salome

m. Malthace the Samaritan
- Antipas m. daughter of Aretas m. Herodias
- Archelaus

Further Herods (line unknown)

Antipas
Costobar (Gaius*)
Saul (Erastus*)

* the identification is made in this book and in *Jesus the Man*

553

Mediterranean World First Centuries BC & AD

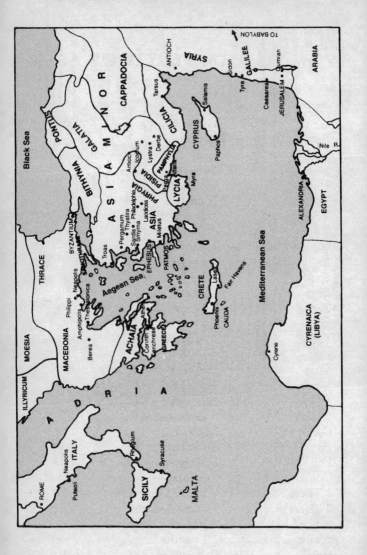

Abbreviations

Bible

Gen	Genesis
Exod	Exodus
Levit	Leviticus
Num	Numbers
Deut	Deuteronomy
Josh	Joshua
1 Sam	1 Samuel
2 Sam	2 Samuel
Isa	Isaiah
Jer	Jeremiah
Ezek	Ezekiel
Dan	Daniel
Zech	Zechariah
1 Macc	1 Maccabees
Matt	Matthew
Rom	Romans
1 Cor	1 Corinthians
2 Cor	2 Corinthians
Gal	Galatians
Eph	Ephesians
Phil	Philippians
Col	Colossians
1 Thess	1 Thessalonians
2 Thess	2 Thessalonians
1 Tim	1 Timothy
2 Tim	2 Timothy
Heb	Hebrews

1 Pet	1 Peter
Rev	Revelation
RSV	*Revised Standard Version*

Ancient Writers

Ann.	Tacitus, *The Annals*
Ant.	Flavius Josephus, *Jewish Antiquities*
Apol.	Justin Martyr, *Apologia*
Clem. Hom.	*Clementine Homilies*
Clem. Rec.	*Clementine Recognitions*
Contemp. Life	Philo, *The Contemplative Life*
Eccl. Hist.	Eusebius, *Ecclesiastical History*
Every Good Man	Philo, *Every Good Man is Free*
GPhil	Gospel of Philip (in *NHL*)
TLevi	Testament of Levi, in Testaments of Twelve Patriarchs
War	Flavius Josephus, *The Jewish War*

Gnostic Literature

NHL	*The Nag Hammadi Library in English*

Dead Sea Scrolls

1QS	Manual of Discipline, Community Rule
1QSa	Rule of the Congregation, Messianic Rule
11QT	The Temple Scroll
1QH	The Thanksgiving Hymns
1QM	War Scroll
CD	Damascus Document, Damascus Rule
1QpHab	Pesher on Habakkuk
4QpPs	Pesher on Psalms
4QpNah	Pesher on Nahum
11QMelch	Melchizedek fragment

4Q159	Ordinances
4Q164	Pesher on Isaiah
3Q15	The Copper Scroll
4QMMT	Miqsat Ma'ase HaTorah (Precepts of the Torah)
PAM 43.306	Fragment published in Eisenmann & Robinson
DJD	*Discoveries in the Judaean Desert,* vols I–XIII

Grammatical Terms

masc.	masculine
fem.	feminine
sing.	singular
plu.	plural
nom.	nominative
acc.	accusative
gen.	genitive
dat.	dative

Bibliography

Sources

The Bible

English, *Revised Standard Version*.

Greek, *The Greek New Testament*, Aland, Black, Martini, Metzger & Wikgren (ed.), (Stuttgart: United Bible Societies, 1966).

Dead Sea Scrolls

G. Vermes, *The Dead Sea Scrolls in English* (from 1962; 3rd edn. containing the Temple Scroll) (London: Penguin, 1987).

E. Lohse, *Die Texte aus Qumran, Hebräisch und Deutsch* (Munich: Kösel-Verlag, 1971).

Discoveries in the Judaean Desert, vols I–XIII (Oxford: Clarendon Press, 1955 – 1995).

Y. Yadin, *Megillat-hammiqdas* (the Temple Scroll) (Jerusalem: Israel Exploration Society, 1977) (English edn. 1983).

R. H. Eisenmann & J. M. Robinson, *A Facsimile Edition of the Dead Sea Scrolls* (Washington DC: Biblical Archaeology Society, 1991). (This book contains photographs of the remaining fragments, which had remained unpublished after the publication of the major and more complete scrolls between 1950 and 1977.)

Ancient Writers

A. Roberts & J. Donaldson, *The Ante-Nicene Fathers*. Clementines in vol VIII (1875, re-issued by Eerdmans Publishing Company, Grand Rapids, Michigan, 1951). Extracts are to be found in E. Hennecke, *New Testament Apocrypha*, vol 2 (London: SCM Press, 1965).

Dio Cassius, *Roman History* (Loeb Library, 9 vols).

Eusebius, *Eusebius* (Loeb Library, 2 vols) (London: Heinemann).

Irenaeus, *Against Heresies* (J. Migne, *Patrologia Graeca*, Paris).

Josephus, *Josephus* (Loeb Library, 9 vols).

Justin, *Apologia* (J. Migne, Patrologia Graeca, Paris).

Philo, *Philo* (Loeb Library, 10 vols).

Philostratus, *The Life of Apollonius of Tyana* (Loeb Library, 2 vols).

Plutarch, *Plutarch* (Loeb Library, *Moralia* 15 vols; Lives, 11 vols).

Suetonius, *Suetonius* (Loeb Library, 2 vols).

Tacitus, *Tacitus* (Loeb Library, 4 vols).

The Old Testament Pseudepigrapha, containing the Letter of Aristeas, Jubilees, T.Levi, 1 Enoch, J. H. Charlesworth (ed.) (London: Darton, Longman & Todd, 1985).

Danby, H., *The Mishnah* (OUP, 1964).

Goldin, J., *The Living Talmud, The Wisdom of the Fathers* (Yale University Press: Mentor Religious Classic, 1957).

Robinson, J. M. (ed.), *The Nag Hammadi Library in English* (Leiden: Brill, 1988).

Stevenson, J. (ed.), *A New Eusebius* (London: SPCK, 1957).

Modern Works Cited

Ackroyd, P. R. & Evans, C. F., (eds.), *The Cambridge*

History of the Bible (Cambridge: The University Press, 1970).

Ashe, Geoffrey, *King Arthur's Avalon, The Story of Glastonbury* (Glasgow: Fontana/Collins, 1957).

Beckwith, R. T. ('The Significance of the Calendar for Interpreting Essene Chronology and Eschatology'. *Revue de Qumran* 10, 1980, 167–202).

Boyle, Leonard, O. P., *A Short Guide to St Clement's, Rome* (Collegio San Clemente, Via Labicana 95, Rome, 1968).

Cary, M. & Scullard, H. H., *A History of Rome* (London: Macmillan, 1975).

De Vaux, R., *Archaeology and the Dead Sea Scrolls* (Oxford: The University Press, 1959).

Finegan, J., *Handbook of Biblical Chronology* (Princeton: The University Press, 1964).

Humbert, J-B and Chambon, A., *Fouilles de Khirbet Qumran et de A'in Feshkha*, Göttingen: Vandenhoeck & Ruprecht, 1994.

Jeremias, G., *Der Lehrer der Gerechtigkeit* (Göttingen: Vandenhoeck & Ruprecht, 1963).

Jonas, H., *The Gnostic Religion* (Boston: Beacon Press, 1958).

Lasserre, F., *The Birth of Mathematics in the Age of Plato* (London: Hutchinson, 1964).

Sambursky, S., *The Physical World of the Greeks* (London: Routledge & Kegan Paul, 1956).

Schürer, E., *The History of the Jewish People in the Age of Jesus Christ*, Rev. Edn. (Edinburgh: Clark, 1973) vols I–III.

Thiering, B. E., *Jesus the Man* (Doubleday, 1992) (in the US *Jesus and the Riddle of the Dead Sea Scrolls*, Harper Collins, 1992).

Weinert, F. D., '4Q159: Legislation for an Essene Community outside of Qumran?' *Journal for the Study of Judaism* 1974, pp.179–207).

Wright, G. R. H., 'The Archaeological Remains at El

Mird in the Wilderness of Judea', *Biblica* 42, 1961, pp.1–27.

Documentary Film: *The Riddle of the Dead Sea Scrolls*, made by Beyond International, 53–55 Brisbane St, Surry Hills 2010 Sydney, Australia.

Index

566

JESUS THE MAN
by Barbara Thiering

'The impact of *Jesus the Man* . . . may be as profound as that of Darwin's *Origin of the Species* on theories of human origins'
Focus

Jesus was the leader of a radical faction of Essene priests. He was not of virgin birth. He did not die on the Cross. He married Mary Magdalene, fathered a family, and later divorced. He died sometime after AD 64.

This controversial version of Christ's life is not the product of a mind which wants to debunk Christianity. Barbara Thiering is a theologian and a biblical scholar. But after over twenty years of close study of the Dead Sea Scrolls and the Gospels she has developed a revolutionary new theory, which, while upholding the fundamental faith of Christianity, challenges many of its most ingrained supernaturalist beliefs.

Jesus the Man will undoubtedly upset and even outrage those for whom Christianity is immutable and unchallengeable. But for many who have found the rituals of the contemporary church too steeped in medieval thinking, it will provide new insights into Christianity in the context of the 1990s.

'[The] sensational nature [of the book's assertions] may disguise the strength of the research and scholarship which Thiering has displayed in the course of her narrative'
Peter Ackroyd, *The Times Saturday Review*

'Some will see her as an anti-christ, a mischievous scholar determined to destroy Christianity. To others she will be a source of comfort and peace enabling them to live Christian lives without having to accept as fact Jesus's divinity, his miracles, the virgin birth and resurrection'
The Australian Magazine

0 552 13950 5

THE DEAD SEA SCROLLS DECEPTION
by Michael Baigent and Richard Leigh

The sensational story behind the religious scandal of the century.

The Dead Sea Scrolls were found in caves 20 miles east of Jerusalem in 1947 and 1956. Now Michael Baigent and Richard Leigh, co-authors of *The Holy Blood and The Holy Grail*, have succeeded in uncovering what has been described as 'the academic scandal par excellence of the twentieth century': the story of how and why up to 75 per cent of the eight hundred ancient Hebrew and Aramaic manuscripts, hidden for some nineteen centuries, have, until very recently, remained concealed from the world.

Through interviews, historical analysis and a close study of both published and unpublished scroll material, the authors are able to reveal the true cause of the bitter struggle between scholars, for these documents disclose nothing less than a new account of the origins of Christianity and an alternative and highly significant version of much of the New Testament.

'A sensational story . . . this scandal has gone on far too long'
The Times

'It is enough to make anyone curious about the early days of Christianity weep with frustration'
Mail on Sunday

'If it succeeds in advancing the publication of material from Qumran, it will have achieved genuine good'
The Times Literary Supplement

0 552 13878 9

THE TEMPLE AND THE LODGE
by Michael Baigent and Richard Leigh

The most illuminating investigation yet published of the evolution of Freemasonry.

In this enthralling historical detective story, the authors of *The Holy Blood and the Holy Grail* trace the flight after 1309 of the Knights Templar from Europe to Scotland. There the Templar heritage was to take root, and to be perpetuated by a network of noble families. That heritage, and the Freemasonry that arose from it, became inseparable from the Stuart cause. Michael Baigent and Richard Leigh chart the birth of Freemasonry through the survival of Templar traditions, through currents of European thought, through the mystery surrounding Rosslyn chapel, and through an elite cadre of aristocrats attached as personal bodyguards to the French King. Pursuing Freemasonry through the 17th and 18th centuries, they reveal its contribution to the fostering of tolerance, progressive values, and cohesion in English society, which helped to pre-empt a French-style revolution. Even more dramatically, the influence of Freemasonry emerges as a key factor in the formation of the United States of America as an embodiment of the ideal 'Masonic Republic'.

'A worthy conclusion to their investigations into secret societies ancient and modern'
Sunday Times

0 552 13596 8

A SELECTION OF FINE NON-FICTION TITLES AVAILABLE FROM CORGI BOOKS

13596 8	THE TEMPLE AND THE LODGE	Baigent & Leigh	£6.99
13878 9	THE DEAD SEA SCROLLS DECEPTION	Baigent & Leigh	£5.99
99065 5	THE PAST IS MYSELF	Christabel Bielenberg	£6.99
09828 0	THE PROPHECIES OF NOSTRADAMUS	Erika Cheetham	£5.99
13741 3	LETTER TO LOUISE	Pauline Collins	£4.99
13273 X	ONCE A WARRIOR KING	David Donovan	£6.99
13582 8	THE GOD SQUAD	Paddy Doyle	£5.99
14239 5	MY FEUDAL LORD	Tehmina Durrani	£5.99
13928 9	DAUGHTER OF PERSIA	Sattareh Farman Farmaian	£5.99
12833 3	THE HOUSE BY THE DVINA	Eugenie Fraser	£6.99
14185 2	FINDING PEGGY: A GLASGOW CHILDHOOD	Meg Henderson	£5.99
14164 X	EMPTY CRADLES	Margaret Humphreys	£6.99
14474 6	IN BED WITH AN ELEPHANT	Ludovic Kennedy	£6.99
13943 2	LOST FOR WORDS	Deric Longden	£4.99
14544 0	FAMILY LIFE	Elisabeth Luard	£6.99
13356 6	NOT WITHOUT MY DAUGHTER	Betty Mahmoody	£5.99
12419 2	CHICKENHAWK	Robert C. Mason	£7.99
13953 X	SOME OTHER RAINBOW	John McCarthy & Jill Morrell	£5.99
14127 5	BRAVO TWO ZERO	Andy McNab	£5.99
14121 6	THE FACTS OF LIFE	Richard Milton	£5.99
14288 3	BRIDGE ACROSS MY SORROWS	Christina Noble	£5.99
13946 7	NICOLA	Nicola Owen	£4.99
14303 0	THE HOT ZONE	Richard Preston	£5.99
11487 1	LIFE AFTER DEATH	Neville Randall	£4.99
14052 X	LORDS OF THE RIM	Sterling Seagrave	£6.99
13369 8	REVOLUTION FROM WITHIN	Gloria Steinem	£5.99
13950 5	JESUS THE MAN	Barbara Thiering	£6.99
14114 3	THE POPE'S ARMADA	Gordon Urquhart	£6.99
99512 6	NOBODY NOWHERE	Donna Williams	£6.99
13288 8	IN GOD'S NAME	David Yallop	£6.99